Nietzsche as a Scholar of Antiquity

Bloomsbury Studies in Philosophy

Bloomsbury Studies in Philosophy presents cutting-edge scholarship in all the major areas of research and study. The wholly original arguments, perspectives and research findings in titles in this series make it an important and stimulating resource for students and academics from a range of disciplines across the humanities and social sciences.

Some other titles in the series:

Nietzsche as a Scholar of Antiquity

Edited by Anthony K. Jensen and Helmut Heit

Bloomsbury Studies in Philosophy

Bloomsbury Academic
An imprint of Bloomsbury Publishing Plc

B L O O M S B U R Y
LONDON • NEW DELHI • NEW YORK • SYDNEY

Bloomsbury Academic
An imprint of Bloomsbury Publishing Plc

50 Bedford Square
London
WC1B 3DP
UK

1385 Broadway
New York
NY 10018
USA

www.bloomsbury.com

**BLOOMSBURY and the Diana logo are trademarks of
Bloomsbury Publishing Plc**

First published 2014
Paperback edition first published 2015

British Library Cataloguing-in-Publication Data
A catalogue record for this book is available from the British Library.

ISBN: HB: 978-1-4725-1152-2
PB: 978-1-4742-4201-1
ePDF: 978-1-4725-1333-5
ePUB: 978-1-4725-1408-0

Library of Congress Cataloging-in-Publication Data
Nietzsche as a scholar of antiquity/edited by Anthony K. Jensen and Helmut Heit.
pages cm. – (Bloomsbury studies in philosophy)
Includes bibliographical references and index.
ISBN 978-1-4725-1152-2 (hardback) – ISBN 978-1-4725-1408-0 (epub) – ISBN 978-1-4725-1333-5 (epdf)
1. Nietzsche, Friedrich Wilhelm, 1844-1900. 2. Philology–Greece. 3. Greece–Civilization. I. Jensen,
Anthony K., 1978- editor of compilation.
B3317.N4495 2014
193–dc23
2013031550

Series: Bloomsbury Studies in Continental Philosophy

Typeset by Fakenham Prepress Solutions, Fakenham, Norfolk NR21 8NN

"Actually I'd much rather have been a Basel Professor than God."
Letter to Jacob Burckhardt, January 6, 1889

"There are of course also Philologica by me; but that need not concern either of us anymore."
Letter to Georg Brandes, April 10, 1888

Anthony Jensen dedicates this volume to the memory of Robert Rethy and Steven K. Strange

Helmut Heit dedicates this volume to Joachim Müller-Warden

Contents

Acknowledgments

The conference out of which this volume grew was generously supported by the Volkswagen Foundation. Special thanks are due to the Technische Universität Berlin for hosting and administering the event, and to the members of the Berliner Nietzsche Colloquium, especially to Lisa Heller.

The production of this volume has been supported by the Volkswagen Foundation, the Alexander von Humboldt Foundation, and by Providence College's Philosophy Department and its Committee on Aid to Faculty Research. The editors are deeply grateful for their support.

We would like to thank the reviewers and editorial staff at Continuum-Bloomsbury, especially Rachel Eisenhauer, Colleen Coalter, Nick Fawcett, Kim Storry, Kim Muranyi and Camilla Erskine.

To Walter de Gruyter Press, especially Tiziana Ziesing, we express our gratitude for permission to reproduce the chapters by Jonathan Barnes ("Nietzsche and Diogenes Laertius." In: *Nietzsche-Studien* 15 (1986), 16–40), and Glenn Most and Thomas Fries. ("Die Quellen von Nietzsches Rhetorik Vorlesung." In: Tilman Borsche, et al. [eds], 1994, *Centauren-Geburten: Wissenschaft, Kunst, und Philosophie beim jungen Nietzsche*. Berlin [De Gruyter], 17–46). We would also like to thank the editorial team of Tilman Borsche for allowing us to translate and reproduce the Most and Fries chapter.

Special thanks are owed to Henry Albert, Laura Fatuzzo, Phillip Roth, and Ian Thomas Fleishman for their painstaking efforts at multi-lingual and multi-discipline translation; our gratitude, too, goes to Kelly Hudgins for her diligent assistance with formatting and editing, and to Axel Pichler for editorial advice, checking proofs, and compiling our index.

Abbreviations

BAB   *Historisch-kritische Gesamtausgabe: Briefe*, 4 vols., edited by Joachim Mette, et al. (Munich, 1933–43)

BAW   *Historisch-kritische Gesamtausgabe: Werke*, 5 vols., edited by Joachim Mette, et al. (Munich, 1933–43)

GA   *Friedrich Nietzsche, Werke (Großoktav-Ausgabe)*, 19 vols., edited by the Nietzsche-archive (Leipzig, 1894–1913)

KGB   *Kritische Gesamtausgabe: Briefwechsel*, edited by Giorgio Colli and Mazzino Montinari (Berlin, 1975ff.)

KGW   *Kritische Gesamtausgabe: Werke*, edited by Giorgio Colli and Mazzino Montinari (Berlin, 1967ff.)

KSA   *Sämtliche Werke: Kritische Studienausgabe*, 15 vols., edited by Giorgio Colli and Mazzino Montinari (Berlin, 1988)

KSB   *Sämtliche Briefe: Kritische Studienausgabe*, 8 vols., edited by Giorgio Colli and Mazzino Montinari (Berlin, 1986)

Where specific published works of Nietzsche are cited, the following abbreviations are used:

AOM   *Vermischte Meinungen und Sprüche* (in *Menschliches Allzumenschliches II*): frequently translated as *Assorted Opinions and Maxims*

BGE   *Jenseits von Gut und Böse*; translated as *Beyond Good and Evil*

BT   *Die Geburt der Tragödie*; translated as *The Birth of Tragedy*

CW   *Der Fall Wagner*; translated as *The Case of Wagner*

D   *Morgenröthe*; frequently translated as *Daybreak* or *Dawn*

DS   *David Strauss* (*Unzeitgemäße Betrachtungen* I)

GM   *Zur Genealogie der Moral*; frequently translated as *On the Genealogy of Morals* or *On the Genealogy of Morality*

GS   *Die fröhliche Wissenschaft*; frequently translated as *The Gay Science* or *The Joyful Wisdom*

HH   *Menschliches, Allzumenschliches*; translated as *Human, All Too Human*

HL   *Vom Nutzen und Nachteil der Historie für das Leben* (*Unzeitgemäße Betrachtungen* II); frequently translated as *On the Use and Disadvantage of History for Life*

IM   *Idyllen aus Messina*; translated as *Idylls from Messina*

RWB   *Richard Wagner in Bayreuth* (*Unzeitgemäße Betrachtungen* IV)

SE   *Schopenhauer als Erzieher* (*Unzeitgemäße Betrachtungen* III); translated as *Schopenhauer as Educator*

TI   *Götzen-Dämmerung*; translated as *Twilight of the Idols*; references to this work also include an abbreviated section name

UM   *Unzeitgemäße Betrachtungen*; frequently translated as *Untimely Meditations*

WS   *Der Wanderer und sein Schatten* (in *Menschliches, Allzumenschliches* II); translated as *The Wanderer and His Shadow*

Z   *Also sprach Zarathustra* (part IV originally published privately); translated as *Thus Spoke Zarathustra*; references to this work also include an abbreviated section name

Abbreviations for other frequently cited private publications, authorized manuscripts, and well-known collections of Nietzsche's unpublished writings and notes:

A   *Der Antichrist*; frequently translated as *The Antichrist*

DD   *Dionysos-Dithyramben*; translated as *Dionysian Dithyrambs*

DW   "Die dionysische Weltanschauung"; translated as "The Dionysian Worldview"

EH   *Ecce homo*; references to this work also include an abbreviated section name

FEI   "Über die Zukunft unserer Bildungsanstalten"; translated as "On the Future of Our Educational Institutions"

GST   "Der griechische Staat"; translated as "The Greek State"

HC   "Homer's Wettkampf"; translated as "Homer's Contest"

HCP   "Homer und die klassische Philologie"; translated as "Homer and Classical Philology"

NCW   *Nietzsche contra Wagner*

PPP   "Die vorplatonischen Philosophen"; translated as "The Pre-Platonic Philosophers"

PTAG   "Die Philosophie im tragischen Zeitalter der Griechen"; translated as "Philosophy in the Tragic Age of the Greeks"

SGT   "Sokrates und die griechische Tragödie"; translated as "Socrates and Greek
        Tragedy"

TL   "Über Wahrheit und Lüge im aussermoralischen Sinne"; frequently
        translated as "On Truth and Lies in an Extra-moral Sense"

WPH   "Wir Philologen"; translated as "We Philologists" or "We Classicists"

Citations to Nietzsche's personal unpublished notebooks correspond to the classification system of the Goethe-Schiller Archiv in Weimar by Hans Joachim Mette.
Digital versions of the notebooks can be found at Walter de Gruyter's "Nietzsche
Online" (http://www.degruyter.com/view/db/nietzsche) and the Nietzsche Source
(http://www.nietzschesource.org/).

Notes on Contributors

Babette Babich is Professor of Philosophy at Fordham University and Executive Editor of *New Nietzsche Studies*. The author of more than one hundred articles and chapters, among her principal works are *Nietzsche's Philosophy of Science: Reflecting Science on the Ground of Art and Life* (1994); *Words in Blood, Like Flowers: Philosophy and Poetry, Music and Eros in Hölderlin, Nietzsche, and Heidegger* (2006); *La fin de la pensée? Philosophie analytique contre philosophie continentale* (2012); and *The Hallelujah Effect: Philosophical Reflections on Music, Performance Practice and Technology* (2013).

Jonathan Barnes has been Professor at Oxford, Geneva, and the Sorbonne. He is the author of *The Presocratic Philosophers* (1979); *The Toils of Scepticism* (1990); *Aristotle: A Very Short Introduction* (2001), and *Truth, etc.: Six Lectures on Ancient Logic* (2007); and editor of the two-volume *Complete Works of Aristotle* (1984). A portion of his collected papers has been published in two recent volumes: *Essays in Ancient Philosophy* (2011–12).

Douglas Burnham is Professor of Philosophy at Staffordshire University. He is the author of *Kant's Philosophies of Judgment* (2004) and, with Harvey Young, a guide to Kant's *Critique of Pure Reason* (2008). With respect to Nietzsche, he has authored an analysis of *Beyond Good and Evil* (2007) and has co-authored commentaries with Martin Jesinghausen on *The Birth of Tragedy* (2010), *Thus Spoke Zarathustra* (2010), and *Beyond Good and Evil* (2006). His *Nietzsche Dictionary* will appear with Bloomsbury-Continuum.

Hubert Cancik is Emeritus Professor in the Institute of Philosophy and History at the University of Basel and board member of the Humanistic Society of Berlin-Brandenburg. He is co-editor of the *New Pauly Encyclopedia*, and is author, among numerous books and papers on Greek culture and its European reception, *Nietzsches Antike: Vorlesung* (1995) and, with Hildegard Cancik-Lindemaier, *Philolog und Kultfigur: Friedrich Nietzsche und seine Antike in Deutschland* (1999).

Hildegard Cancik-Lindemaier is an independent classical philologist and historian of Roman and the Christian religion. Her collected papers have recently been published as *Von Atheismus bis Zensur. Römische Lektüren in kulturwissenschaftlicher Absicht* (2006). With respect to Nietzsche, she is co-author with Hubert Cancik of *Philolog und Kultfigur: Friedrich Nietzsche und seine Antike in Deutschland* (1999) and many articles.

Thomas Fries is titular Professor of New German Literary Studies at the University of Zurich. Besides having written numerous articles, he is the author of *Dialog der Aufklärung: Shaftesbury, Rousseau, Solger* (1993), and editor (with Peter Hughes and Tan Wälchli) of *Schreibprozesse: Zur Genealogie des Schreibens* (2007).

Helmut Heit is Dilthey Fellow at the Technische Universität Berlin and the Director of the Berliner Nietzsche Colloquium. His major publications include *Der Ursprungsmythos der Vernunft. Zur philosophiehistorischen Genealogie des griechischen Wunders* (2007) and *Grundwissen Philosophie: Frühgriechische Philosophie* (2011), as well as several collected volumes, e.g. on Nietzsche's philosophy of science (2012).

Anthony K. Jensen is Associate Professor of Philosophy at Providence College and Associate Editor of the *Journal of Nietzsche Studies*. He is the author of *Nietzsche's Philosophy of History* (2013) and of several papers on Late Modern European philosophy.

Joachim Latacz is Emeritus Professor at the University of Basel and Director of the Swiss National Research Project on Homer. He has published more than three hundred papers on Homer, Greek Lyric Poetry, Attic Tragedy, and the history of philology. Among his principal books are *Homer: Der erste Dichter des Abendlands* (1985), *Achilleus: Wandlungen eines europäischen Heldenbildes* (1995), and *Troia und Homer: Der Weg zur Lösung eines alten Rätsels* (2001).

Matthew Meyer is Assistant Professor of Philosophy at the University of Scranton. His *Reading Nietzsche through the Ancients: An Analysis of Becoming, Perspectivism, and the Principle of Non-Contradiction* will appear with Walter de Gruyter Press.

Glenn W. Most is Professor of Ancient Greek at the Scuola Normale Superiore in Pisa and teaches at the University of Chicago in the Committee on Social Thought, and in the Departments of Classics and Comparative Literature. The author of more than two hundred articles, chapters, and translations, among his principal recent works are *Doubting Thomas* (2005); as editor, *Hesiod*, 2 vols. (2007); as editor (with Anthony Grafton and Salvatore Settis), *The Classical Tradition* (2013); and a multiple-volume collection of Early Greek Fragments forthcoming with the *Loeb Classical Library*.

James I. Porter is Professor of Classics and Comparative Literature at the University of California at Irvine. He is the author of *Nietzsche and the Philology of the Future* (2000); *The Invention of Dionysus: An Essay on the Birth of Tragedy* (2000); and *Origins of Aesthetic Thought in Ancient Greece* (2010).

Carlotta Santini is a doctoral candidate in philosophy jointly at the Università del Salento and Université Paris IV Sorbonne. For Adelphi Verlag, she is preparing Nietzsche's lectures on the *Geschichte der griechischen Literatur* and on the Greek lyric poets.

Vivetta Vivarelli is Professore Ordinario at the Università degli Studi di Firenze. Working at the intersection of philosophy, philology, and literary studies, and on figures like Nietzsche, Lichtenberg, Hölderlin, Rilke, and Trakl, she is the author of *Nietzsche und die Masken des freien Geistes* (1998) and *Nietzsche e gli Ebrei* (2011).

Alexey Zhavoronkov is a Konrad Adenauer Fellow at the Humboldt Universität in Berlin. He has published in Russian and in German on Homer, Hesiod, and philological methodology, and is presently Associate Editor of the critical Russian edition of Nietzsche's works.

Introduction

"Mr. N by no means presents himself as a scholarly researcher" (Ulrich von Wilamowitz-Moellendorff). "It is mere nonsense, of which nothing can be made: anybody who has written such a thing is dead as a scholar" (Herman Usener). "Nietzsche's opinion is not only highly uncertain and more frail than a spider's web, but also palpably false" (Hermann Diels). "The history of philology has no place for Nietzsche: he did not make enough positive contributions" (Karl Reinhardt).

"As many young scholars as I have seen developing under my supervision in the last 39 years, I have never known a young man, never tried to advance the career of anyone within my discipline, who so early and so young was as mature as this Nietzsche. [...] He is the object of admiration and the leader (without wanting to be) of the entire philological world of Leipzig, who can hardly await the time when they will hear him as their docent. You will say that I am describing a kind of 'phenomenon'; well, he is that" (Friedrich Ritschl). "Your investigations on the sources of Diogenes are certainly of the highest value; and the conclusion, which had already been recommended to me in your earlier essay—that Diocles had been the main source—has now been further confirmed" (Eduard Zeller). "Friedrich Wilhelm Nietzsche [...] has made splendid achievements" (Conrad Bursian). *The Birth of Tragedy* is "a work of profound imaginative insight, which left the scholarship of a generation toiling in the rear" (F. M. Cornford).

Here, in essence, stands the ambivalent status of Nietzsche as a scholar of antiquity. On the one hand we have exuberant praise of his insight and potential, and on the other, equally exuberant revulsion at his dilettantism and failure to have actualized that potential. For their divergence, what they all have in common is that their judgment is not of a philosopher, but of a young scholar. It is this Nietzsche whom we wish to consider here: Nietzsche, the scholar of antiquity, whom no one doubts was brilliant, but about whose scholarly reputation deep ambivalence remains.

Indeed, before Friedrich Nietzsche became one of the preeminent philosophers of the nineteenth century, before the thunder of *Zarathustra* and the *Antichrist*, before the *Overman* and the *Eternal Recurrence*, he was a professional scholar of antiquity. As a philology student at Bonn (1864–5) and then Leipzig (1865–9), he studied under the distinguished classicists Otto Jahn and Friedrich Ritschl. On the merit of his philological publications concerning the text of the poet Theognis and that of the biographer Diogenes Laertius he was famously granted a doctorate from the University of Leipzig without examination and at age 24 was appointed *Extraordinarius* professor of philology at Basel University in the spring of 1869. He was promoted to *Ordinarius* Professor just a year later. He lectured for a decade with mixed success at both the university and the local Pädagogium on themes ranging from early Greek philosophy, the Platonic Dialogue, and Aristotle's *Rhetoric*, to Greek music drama, religious institutions, lyric poetry, Latin grammar, literary history, Aeschylus, Homer, and Hesiod. And while his lecture notes and correspondence fill out many thick volumes, his published philological corpus amounts to eight articles—half in Latin and half in German—and eight short reviews dating from 1867 to 1873. He requested, and was rejected, to transfer to the philosophy department in January, 1871. Having taken a year-long curative leave from the university in 1876, he resigned due to poor health in May 1879.

Although there has been no shortage of voices praising or denouncing Nietzsche, few researchers of Nietzsche and fewer classicists have taken the time to understand him on his own terms as a scholar of antiquity. Nietzsche's articles have gathered little but dust over the past century. His copious volumes of lecture notes were left out of the *Kritische Studienausgabe* entirely, and some did not even merit inclusion in the allegedly comprehensive *Kritische Gesamtausgabe*. And while of course there have been collections published on Nietzsche's scholarly activity before, even these only scrape the surface of Nietzsche's activity.

The main reason for this neglect, said briefly, is that his work is widely considered "immature" by philosophers and "non-classical" by classicists. Philosophically minded Nietzsche scholarship, on the one hand, values his philological work mainly as a preparatory stage for his more mature thought. Such presentations are intrinsically interesting for those who wish to understand the origins and development of Nietzsche's most famous mature theories. But by measuring Nietzsche's scholarship in the light of his later philosophy, these scholars persistently overlook the value of his early ancient studies in-themselves. Nietzsche's lectures on Greek religion, his reflections on lyric poetry, and his insights about the function of rhythm were intended to inform and convince his readers and students about those subjects, not to reveal immature traces of future genius. Unlike those approaches, our primary aim is to show not how Nietzsche's earlier works on antiquity help us to understand Nietzsche, but how they may improve our understanding of antiquity.

Classical scholars, on the other hand, have consistently overlooked the value of Nietzsche's scholarly efforts insofar as they, too, tended to value him through the lens of his later philosophical works. And a fair part of that philosophical work involves criticizing, and indeed mocking, academics generally and scholars of antiquity particularly. Nietzsche's scholarly resumé is marred insofar as he was unfairly disdainful towards the views of his colleagues; insofar as his work stands unsupported by the critical apparati of rigorous academic scholarship; and insofar as his interpretations are said to be "Nietzschean" rather than "scholarly." These judgments, which have persisted among philologists from the time of Hermann Usener and Ulrich von Wilamowitz-Moellendorff, may to some extent be an accurate condemnation of *The Birth of Tragedy*. But they are plainly false with respect to Nietzsche's scholarly articles, professional reviews, and philological lectures, each of which reveals their author to be a remarkably careful and insightful scholar. Our collection will hopefully go some way towards dispelling the long-held image of Nietzsche as a scholarly dilettante.

Even if we consider the work strictly on its own merits, the question as to how we might assess Nietzsche as a scholar remains. Should we count up the number of articles and the impact rating of the journals in which he published? Nietzsche would probably have earned tenure but not a professorship in today's university. Should we consider the scope of influence of his theory of tragedy? If so, then his name would rank above Winckelmann and Mommsen. Should we measure Nietzsche's work against some standard of universally accepted interpretation? Nietzsche admittedly fails here, as few would accept his theories without qualification; but then again, so do Wolf and Schliemann. Should we judge whether Nietzsche successfully applied the accepted methods and produced work in keeping with his scholarly climate? Such would be to ignore Nietzsche's criticisms of those same methods and climates, criticisms which did, in fact, make a major contribution to the transformation of classical studies today.

There is, one may argue, no single universal measure by which to assess Nietzsche's value as a scholar of antiquity. So, to address the question of value without forcing it into one standard or another, the editors of this volume held a workshop at the Technical University in Berlin in November 2011. Gathering experts in both Nietzsche-studies and philology, we sought to critically examine Nietzsche's positions on Ancient themes themselves in order to let the experts decide what Nietzsche's value has been and will continue to be. Covered were topics ranging from Nietzsche's knowledge and use of philology, his lectures on Greek literature, his contribution to Homeric studies, the interpretive contours of his work on early Greek philosophers, and his appreciation of Ancient science. The workshop participants—Babette Babich, Joachim Latacz, Matthew Meyer, Glenn Most, Carlotta Santini, Alexey Zhavoronkov, and ourselves—have published revised versions of our papers here. We are joined by the new research of our colleagues Douglas Burnham, Hubert Cancik and Hildegard Cancik-Lindemaier, James I. Porter, and Vivetta Vivarelli. To round out this selection, we have been given generous permission from Walter de Gruyter Press to publish a new translation of "Die Quellen von Nietzsches Rhetorik-Vorlesung" by Glenn Most and Thomas Fries, as well as the seminal "Nietzsche and Diogenes Laertius" by Jonathan Barnes.

We believe that such an interdisciplinary and international dialogue will be of significant benefit to both Nietzsche studies, in uncovering what has been so long neglected, and classical studies, in reexamining the reputation of one of its own greatest prodigies. The hope is that, having weighed these 13 papers on their own terms, the reader will form their own opinion on Nietzsche's value as a scholar of antiquity.

The two opening chapters can be read as complementary approaches to the question of how we consider Nietzsche as a scholar. Both are convinced of his importance for classical studies, though for quite different reasons. Joachim Latacz shows how Nietzsche's meteoric rise in the field must be contextualized within the social, political, and academic conditions of classical studies in the nineteenth century. Drawing especially on Nietzsche's 1871 publication "Certamen Homeri et Hesiodi," Latacz situates Nietzsche's achievement as an ingenious but not unassailable contribution to meat-and-potatoes classical scholarship.

James I. Porter also esteems Nietzsche's scholarship highly; but it is on account of his iconoclasm, his critique of then current methods and ideals, and his undermining of what had long been uncritically accepted under the name philology that Porter locates Nietzsche's value. Porter turns to Nietzsche's notebooks and lectures—especially to his fascinating but unheralded lectures on Aeschylus' *Choephori*, his work on metrics, and his "Encyclopedia of Classical Philology"—to reconstruct the radicalism of his thinking, and points to overlooked connections between Nietzsche and J. G. Droysen's *History of Hellenism*.

The co authored piece by Glenn W. Most and Thomas Fries forms a thematic unit with Douglas Burnham's chapter as well. Both papers are concerned with the process by which Nietzsche produced aspects of his work—two unique glimpses into the artist's studio, as it were. But, as before, Nietzsche can present two different faces to the philological and philosophical sides of his thinking. Most's and Fries' examination of how Nietzsche constructed his Basel lectures on rhetoric reveals Nietzsche *in situ* as a workaday philologist, critically examining sources, parsing the arguments of earlier scholars, and arranging a welter of historical material for the sake of his students. Most and Fries are able to show that the specific ways Nietzsche drew on his sources were in fact grounded in what he himself understood about the ancient tendencies of borrowing, epitomizing, etc.

What Douglas Burnham reveals, by contrast, is a portrait of a genius who has already done the philological leg work, and who proceeds from there to intuit the wider scope of antiquity. That scope, as is well known, was only fully explicated in Nietzsche's first book, *The Birth of Tragedy*. But never before have the various stages, the twisting developments that led to Nietzsche's eventual pronouncement about the duality of the Dionysian and Apollonian, been elucidated. Burnham particularly emphasizes the significance of Apollo and of Apollonian cheerfulness as a conscious necessity of illusion. His chapter makes a substantial contribution to the question of how the philological Nietzsche became the philosophical Nietzsche.

The three papers arranged in the cluster "Scholarly Achievement" each investigate Nietzsche's earliest publications and their impact on the field. Anthony K. Jensen elucidates Nietzsche's innovations with respect to manuscript analysis and critico-linguistic philology in his Schulpforta valediction and first article, on Theognis of Megara. He shows how Nietzsche attempted to reconstruct the authentic text of Theognis out of a maze of corruptions, emendations, and editorial falsifications. Nietzsche's article was relatively well received by colleagues in the field, and retains a certain currency today.

A reprint of Jonathan Barnes' paper on Nietzsche's source criticism of Diogenes Laertius' *Lives of the Philosophers* will remind readers of the painstaking and meticulous nature of Nietzsche's research. Despite his status as the "night watchman" of our knowledge of antiquity, Nietzsche demonstrates that large portions of Diogenes' biographies are taken over—often entirely and often uncritically—from other sources, especially from Diocles of Magnesia. Nietzsche identified a major problem in philology, and offered solutions that to this day still receive some support.

On the "Homer Question," which seemingly left little room for innovation in Nietzsche's day, Alexey Zhavoronkov is able to prove that Nietzsche's insights still carry weight for a wide swathe of scholars. Even though relatively few contemporary Homer scholars cite Nietzsche as an authority, his particular variant on the "single-author" mode of interpretation receives frequent echoes throughout European and

Anglophone Homer studies. Nietzsche's focus on the non-literary background of the Homeric poems connects him with the strong movement of oral poetry studies.

Turning to Nietzsche's massive collection of notes for his lecture series *On the History of Greek Literature*, Carlotta Santini's contribution is one of three papers that address Nietzsche's fascinating ideas about Greek literature, language, and culture. Santini reconstructs Nietzsche's lectures from the perspective of a singular question: what does it mean for our historical reconstruction of Greek literature that it grew out of an oral—and what's more, a mostly illiterate—culture? The twentieth century's preoccupation with orality in history and literature is prefigured in Nietzsche's consideration of literacy as a somewhat unwelcomed cultural byproduct.

Vivetta Vivarelli's paper also investigates Greek literary culture, but this time from the perspective of Nietzsche's focus on the receiver rather than the producer of literary affect: namely, the audience. Especially in his "On Greek Music Drama," Nietzsche incorporated his developing philosophical theory of linguistic affectivity into his scholarly discoveries about Greek music drama, poetry, tragedy, and rhythmic versification. He was able to illuminate the holistic dynamic of affectation between authors and audience, and thereby discern the wide gap between early Greek high culture and what became "learned" Western culture.

That relationship between what counts as proper philosophy and what counts as affective poetry is also considered by Matthew Meyer, through the lens of Nietzsche's *Birth of Tragedy*. Nietzsche understood Plato's noted quarrel between poetry and philosophy not simply as two means of expressing ideas, but as the changing of a cultural epoch. The scholarly-philosophical turn inculcated by Plato meant not only the end of that kind of literary activity indicated by Santini and Vivarelli—it meant the death of the entire "tragic age" that gave rise to it. This insight bears on Nietzsche's own vision of learned scholarship, and by implicit extension, on our conception of Nietzsche as a scholar.

The last group of papers proves how wide Nietzsche's interests were: covering core questions about philosophy, science, and religion. Helmut Heit examines Nietzsche's engagement with early Greek philosophy in his lectures on the pre-Platonic philosophers and in "Philosophy in the Tragic Age of Greece." A comparison with contemporary studies like those of Eduard Zeller or Friedrich Ueberweg indicates timely as well as untimely features. Nietzsche's genealogy of Greek philosophy, Heit argues, is particularly original due to his focus on the personality of philosophers, his revision of the order between archaic and classic Greece, and his uncovering of artistic and metaphysical aspects within the alleged rise from myth to reason.

Babette Babich focuses on the gap between early Greek and later Hellenic culture, too; but through the lens of Nietzsche's attention to the phenomena of Greek science. Babich's question is Nietzsche's: given that the early Greeks already possessed the theoretical, mathematical, and technical prerequisites to develop what we today call "science," why didn't they do so? While there is, of course, no simple answer, to even address the problem—as Nietzsche was the first to do—requires a similarly wide range of investigations into the nature of truth, value, and life itself.

Hubert Cancik and Hildegard Cancik-Lindemaier exemplify our volume's goal to read Nietzsche's early work carefully and in a contextualized way. Drawing from two sets of notes recorded in a single notebook, the Canciks are able to show the fascinating interconnection between Nietzsche's Basel lectures on early Greek religion and his thoughts about the shortcomings of his contemporary philology, which were to have been published as the fourth *Untimely Meditation,* called "We Philologists." Doing so allows the Canciks to trace the substantial development in Nietzsche's thinking about early culture, religion, and civil society immediately after his publication of *The Birth of Tragedy.*

Taken individually, the reader will, we hope, find that Nietzsche almost always has something insightful to say on each of these topics, a fresh and penetrating insight that contributes genuinely to the enduring and interdisciplinary conversation about Greek antiquity. Taking this book as a collection, and in its intrinsic interdisciplinarity and international tenor, our hope is that the reader will have a more exact and more comprehensive portrait of Nietzsche's activities as a scholar of antiquity.

Anthony K. Jensen and Helmut Heit
Providence / Berlin, Fall 2013

Part One

Nietzsche's Place in Philology

On Nietzsche's Philological Beginnings

Joachim Latacz

"Übrigens, lieber Freund, bitte ich dich aufrichtig, deine Augen fest
auf eine einmal einzuschlagende akademische Carrière zu richten ..."

Nietzsche to Rohde, 1868

Within academic circles the question still lives on how it could come about that Friedrich Nietzsche, as a 24-year-old student from Leipzig, without a doctorate, much less a habilitation, was appointed Professor Extraordinarius of Classical Philology at Basel University in February 1869. Since I happened to be the seventh successor of Nietzsche on the chair for Greek Philology in Basel, I have been confronted with the issue for 21 years—from 1981 until my retirement in 2002. Therefore I gratefully accept the opportunity to answer this question, to a hopefully somewhat satisfying extent, which apparently continues to gnaw on the self-confidence of many students and also colleagues.

To clarify at the start: there was neither ignorance nor fraud involved in Nietzsche's appointment. At the time, it was both justified and reasonable, as I will establish in the following. Therefore let us go for a moment to the "low-lying areas of philology"—to speak with the later Nietzsche—those areas which—as Nietzsche also emphasized in his later work—were one way or another the *preconditions* for his later intellectual flight. In *Gay Science*, 102, it says, under the heading "A Word for the Philologists": "That there are books so precious and royal, that good use has been made of whole races of scholars, when through their labor these books are preserved purely and intelligibly – to assure this belief is the purpose of *philology*" (KSA 3, 458f.). So we may hope that Nietzsche will gaily accompany us on the way hereafter.

First, a brief sketch of biographical circumstances: The dates and facts are of course known. They shall nevertheless be brought to mind, to ensure that the *young* Nietzsche and indeed the young Nietzsche as a *philologist* will be at the center of my presentation.

Year	Age	Location
*1844, Oct. 15		Röcken near Leipzig
1850–1858	6–13	Private school and Dom-Gymnasium in Naumburg/Saale
1858, Oct.	14	Schulpforta near Naumburg/Saale
1864, Oct.	20	University of Bonn
1865, Oct.	21	University of Leipzig
1869, Feb. 10	24	Call for the University of Basel
Summer Term 1869	24	Basel University, extraordinary Professor
1870, Mar.	25	Basel University, ordinary Professor
1870, Mar.–Aug.	25	German-French War (corpsman)
1879, June 14	34	Retirement (pension: 3000 CHF p.a.)

After childhood at the parsonage of the village Röcken (between Naumburg and Merseburg near Halle/Saale) and having enjoyed private tutoring and thereafter attendance at the cathedral school in Naumburg, the 14-year-old Nietzsche received a free-of-charge place at the then elite boarding gymnasium Schulpforta near Naumburg in October 1858. In September 1864, at the age of 19, he completed his high school education. (Two years earlier, Ulrich v. Wilamowitz-Moellendorff joined Schulpforta; so the 17-year-old Nietzsche and the 14-year-old Wilamowitz were indeed acquainted.) Only one month after graduation from Schulpforta, Nietzsche enrolled for theology and philosophy at the University of Bonn for the 1864/65 winter term, but as soon as the following spring term, 1865, he changed his studies to philology—which then meant *Classical* philology. When his revered teacher Friedrich Ritschl, after the well-known 1865 *Bonner Gelehrtenstreit* [Scholar's Fight at Bonn] with Otto Jahn, went to the University of Leipzig, Nietzsche followed him for the 1865/66 winter term. From October 1865 until February 1969, i.e. nearly nine semesters, Nietzsche stayed in Leipzig. On February 10, 1869, the 24-year-old received an offer of appointment at Basel, which he immediately accepted. Just three and a half months later, on the 28th of May, Nietzsche gave his inaugural lecture in Basel on "Homer and Classical Philology" (BAW 5, 283–305). A year later he was made a full professor. So much for the chronological frame.

How was such a speedy career possible? The answer will be given in the form of three partial elaborations and an outlook: (1) The social *preconditions* for acquiring a high philological competence at a young age at Nietzsche's time, (2) the *attitude* of the young Nietzsche towards philology, (3) Nietzsche's philological *achievements* from Schulpforta until Basel (exemplarily exhibited through the "Certamen Homeri et Hesiodi"), and (4) outlook: The *impact* of Nietzsche's youthful achievements on Classical Philology in his time, and until the present.

1. The social preconditions of higher education

Nietzsche's attitude towards philology as a youth must be viewed in light of the ordinary course of education in middle- and high-class German-speaking societies. Children in families of teachers, pastors, physicians, attorneys etc.—naturally mostly boys—were already made familiar with literature and art at a preschool age. They were indeed to be trained for similar professions and lives as their fathers. At the time that Nietzsche grew up—a time without modern media!—*literature, history*, and *music* stood at the forefront. Literature mostly meant the classics, thus Shakespeare, Lessing, Goethe, Schiller, Kleist, but also Jean Paul, Rousseau etc., and additionally the philosophy of the Enlightenment and German Idealism. History meant *national* history—beginning with Germanic heroic legends—and, on the other hand, *antiquity*. Stories and discussions on matters and topics from these areas belonged to a domestic preschool education. Antiquity formed the basis for poetry and philosophy. It was omnipresent in Nietzsche's childhood and teenage years.

Four years prior to Nietzsche's birth Gustav Schwab's *Schönste Sagen des klassischen Alterthums* was published in three volumes. These might well have had a place on the bookshelves of every middle-class house. One can imagine the acquaintance with books of this sort in the description of the 22-years-older Heinrich Schliemann, also the son of a pastor. In his autobiographical account of his childhood, he writes:

> Although my father was neither a philologist nor an archaeologist, he had a passionate interest in the history of antiquity; with warm enthusiasm [!] he often told me about the tragic decline of Herculaneum and Pompeii [...] He often told me admiringly about the deeds of the Homeric heroes and the Trojan War, too [...] (Schliemann 1892, 4)

The nostalgic and romantic, and at times involuntarily comical tone of these reminiscences should not delude anyone. This was only common during the period, which they were recalling, namely: Romanticism. Admittedly, Schliemann is known to have mythified his childhood, but we possess enough autobiographical material by intellectuals who grew up during the mid-nineteenth century to be able to achieve a general sense of the atmosphere at the time. In those days, education, education and again education was at the center of the *aspiring bourgeoisie*. It is not for nothing that we speak of "Bildungsbürgertum." In the process, antiquity played the main role. The foundations for the later development of young people were thus laid here.

Those foundations were fostered and strengthened further in school. The gymnasium in those years quite naturally was that of the classical type. In the last third of the eighteenth century the Second Humanism or Neo-Humanism had begun to flourish, which among other things meant a revival in the fascination with antiquity not only for the sciences. At the end of the century Christian Gottlob Heyne in Göttingen and his student Friedrich August Wolf in Halle had freed philology from the bonds of theology and established it as a proper discipline (cf. Latacz 2002). In 1787 Wolf had instituted the first *"Philologisches Seminar"* in Halle. Greek and Latin teachers, who were educated here and in similar seminars, brought the movement as "Gymnasialprofessoren" into the then rather ailing landscape of secondary education, too. That landscape, on the other hand, was already quite well prepared for this tempest, fortunately: In 1809/10 Heyne's student Wilhelm v. Humboldt and his friend Friedrich Schleiermacher had replaced the old Fürstenschulen and Latin-schools with the "humanistic" Gymnasium through the Prussian university- and school-reforms. They were chosen to implement Humboldt's "core formula in the history of education of the 19th century" (Landfester 1988, 208). In the original, this formula read: "The true end of man [...] is the highest and most proportional formation of his powers into a whole" (Humboldt [1792] 1960–81, 64)—and as ideal objects for this formation were briefly destined the "products of the Greek minds," because, per Humboldt, "only the character of the nation of the Greeks [...] comes closest to that human character, which in every situation, without regard to individual differences, can exist and should be existent" (Humboldt [1793] 1960–81, 9; cf. Landfester 1988, 36–43, for a concise analysis). Afterwards Friedrich August Wolf gave this formula, which in his opinion was too narrowly aesthetic and emotional, a realistic, *pragmatic* determination of aims. In the lecture "Encyclopaedia philologica" (Pfeiffer 1982, 217), which he repeated 18 times and later published, Wolf described "classical scholarship"[1] as *the knowledge of antiquity in all its forms of appearance* (language, literature, art, science, religion, customs, etc.), and that knowledge was reconstructed from all available types of sources (texts, artworks, and everyday phenomena such as inscriptions, coins, etc.). Therewith he defined philology—for this is what he meant by "classical scholarship"—as a *historical* science, which must always view and understand its objects of inquiry as far as possible in their original historical context. This *universal* requirement—based on a historical foundation and connected to the demands for methodological rigor in the acquisition and connection of particular phenomena—became, thanks to the reforms of 1810, the basis for classes in gymnasia for nearly one hundred years.

Soon the gymnasia were flooded with new grammars of Greek and Latin, dictionaries, volumes on stylistics, editions, commentaries, etc. Manfred Landfester has illustrated how this new cultural beginning affected everyday school life on the grounds of diverse documents from the actual school practice, especially time tables (Landfester 1988): Latin and Greek classes held primacy, even before German, with a remarkable number of lessons per week by today's standards: Latin up to 16 lessons, Greek up to 12 or 14. In elite gymnasia, such as Nietzsche's Schulpforta, not only the extent but also the intensity of teaching was even considerably higher. Nietzsche's diary entries from August 9 and 18, 1859 provide us with what he calls an "image of the quite ordinary life in Pforta":

> Get up at 5 a.m., then—after the morning wash, the common prayer and a quick breakfast—class starts at 6 a.m. with two repetition-periods, lunch at 12 p.m., afterwards recreational time in the school yard, at 2 p.m. again class, reading and writing classes, after a short break, at 5 p.m., another two repetition-periods until 7 p.m. Then dinner and some spare time in the yard until 8:30 p.m., the evening prayer after and bedtime at 9 p.m. (BAW 1, 119f., 123, 131)

So the pupils are "in motion," so to speak, from five in the morning until nine in the evening.[2] Basically we have here a miniature version of the Republic of Letters of the Alexandrian *Mouseion*. Since pupils were taught Latin from the fifth grade on, i.e. at the age of ten, it is not surprising that the best students of higher grades could almost write better in Latin than in German, and could often enough speak[3] the language better too (in his graduation diploma, Nietzsche is also credited with good skills in *speaking* Latin),[4] and accordingly they generally were more familiar with classical mythology, history, and literature by the time of high-school graduation than many contemporary students of our discipline by the time of their final university exams. This training persisted into most students' later professional lives as a sort of conditioned routine, though it nevertheless formed a quite useful basis for communicating within the leading elite. The best students, however (and Friedrich Nietzsche belonged among them),[5] students who were enchanted by the topics offered and who sought to penetrate into their depths with an inherited and then cultivated thirst for knowledge, almost always inevitably developed into experts of antiquity at an early age.

2. The young Nietzsche's attitude towards philology

Nietzsche's early *attitude* towards philology needs to be understood in front of this roughly sketched background. For with a person of such character and talents, his attitude is no exception to the contemporary societal context, but rather a consequence. Some comments by Nietzsche and others on this matter:

(1) Already in September 1863, thus almost a year before graduation from Schulpforta, he writes to his mother: "One now lives a lot in the future and is making plans for the time at university; I am even starting to adapt my studies to it," and for his upcoming nineteenth birthday two weeks later, Nietzsche requests "only scholarly works," i.e. philological ones (to Elisabeth Nietzsche, September 25, 1863; KSB 1, 257).[6] By "studies" he undoubtedly means his Pforta valediction, which dealt with the early Greek poet Theognis of Megara, in Latin of course: "De Theognide Megarensi" (BAW 3, 21–64; completed September 7, 1864).

(2) Shortly before transferring to Bonn in 1864, Nietzsche writes in retrospect about Schulpforta in one of his characteristic self-assurances under the typical title "My Life":

[After the] transition from the Naumburg Gymnasium to Pforta, which falls on my fourteenth year, [...] my affinity for *classical* studies grew increasingly; with the most pleasant memories I think of the first impressions of Sophocles, of Aeschylus, of Plato, chiefly of my favorite piece of poetry, the *Symposium*, then of the Greek poets. I still stand in this striving, to further deepen my knowledge. (BAW 3, 66, 68)

(3) Five years later in Leipzig, with his intended graduation in sight, he writes another "My Life"-retrospective:

Some external contingencies were lacking; otherwise I would at the time [at the beginning of the Pforta time] have dared to become a musician, because it was to music that I felt the strongest drive from my ninth year on [...]. Only in the last part of my Pforta time, in full self-awareness, I abandoned all artistic plans for my life;

the resulting gap was thereafter filled with *philology*. For I demanded a counter-balance against these till then varying and unsettled inclinations, for a science, which could be promoted with a *cool sobriety, with logical coldness, with uniform labor*, without having one's heart be immediately touched by the results. All this I believed at that time to find in philology. The preconditions for this field are literally put in the hands of a Pforta student. Sometimes specifically philological tasks are set in this institution, e.g. critical commentaries on specific Sophoclean or Aeschylean choruses. It is furthermore a specific merit of Schulpforta, to the advantage of a *future philologist*, that an intense and wide-ranging reading of Greek and Roman authors is common habit amongst students, too. The luckiest thing, however, was that I encountered excellent *philological teachers*, through whom I developed my judgment on their science. If I would have happened to have teachers at that time, like the ones sometimes found at gymnasia, *petty frog-blooded micrologists* [Mikrologen], *who know of science nothing but bookish dust: I would have tossed the thought of ever belonging to a science, to which such poor wretches belong, far afield*. But like this, such philologists as Steinhart, Keil, Corssen, Peter lived before my eyes, men with a free view and a fresh drive, who sometimes even gave me their closer penchants. That is how it came about that in the last years at Pforta, I already dealt independently with two *philological* works. (BAW 5, 253f.—he is referring to the "Ermanarich" and the "Theognis"; my emphasis)

(4) So far we have seen a few of Nietzsche's own testimonies. From them we can infer not only sympathy for philology, but also a strong will and intention to definitely take on a *philological* career—hence, neither the theological one naturally desired by his mother, nor the philosophical one often suggested in Nietzsche-literature. Without a doubt Nietzsche read philosophical works already in Schulpforta—Schopenhauer,[7] Hegel, Kant and others (that was *de rigueur*)—but neither in contemporaneous letters nor in later retrospectives does there appear such a decisive devotion, such a clear identification with philosophy, as it does with philology. Nevertheless, one should pay close attention: Already back then, Nietzsche distinguished between philology as technicistic dust-devourer's work and philology as an encompassing field of the humanities. As of yet he does not express these alternatives with his later pointedness and maturity—most likely is not yet able to do so—but it is already implied in the strongly negative tone of rejection: the "petty frog-blooded micrologists, who know of science nothing but bookish dust" on the one hand, and the philologists "with a free view and a fresh drive" on the other, the latter of which he wishes to "serve."[8]

(5) And these "men with a free view and a fresh drive" had for their part already found an intellectual kin in the young man. On September 7, 1864, the above-mentioned Steinhart writes in a letter of recommendation to the Bonn philosophy professor Carl Schaarschmidt: "Nietzsche is of a deep, ruminative nature, gushy about philosophy, namely Platonic philosophy, about which he has already been rather well introduced. He is still oscillating between theology and philology; however, the latter will probably win."[9] One should notice the phrase "gushy about philosophy." Already the adjective "gushy" ["schwärmerisch"] accurately reveals the contrast between philosophy and philology in Nietzsche's early decisions. Having Nietzsche's own

retrospective on Schulpforta in mind, we recall: "I demanded [...] for a science, which could be promoted with a *cool sobriety, with logical coldness, with uniform labor* [...]. All this I believed to find in philology" (BAW 5, 253).

(6) So it is absolutely logical that Nietzsche writes about his final decision in 1869:

> After I gratefully said farewell to a strict but beneficial teacher after a six years-stay at Schulpforta, I went to Bonn. Here my studies were for a while directed at the *philological* side of gospel critique and the *basic research* of the New Testament [neutestamentliche *Quellenforschung*]. Beyond this theological foray, I was an auditor in the *philological and archaeological* seminars. [So there is no mentioning of philosophy.—JL] I admired the personality of Friedrich Ritschl from afar. That is why I thought it quite natural to leave Bonn at the same time he did and to choose Leipzig as my new academic home. (BAW 5, 255)

(7) So the decision is reached: in the fall term of 1865 Nietzsche begins determined studies in Classical Philology in Leipzig with a distinct emphasis on Greek. Just one year later, he becomes co-founder of the "Philologischer Verein zu Leipzig" and Ritschl's favorite student. He pursues his studies with such success (soon producing papers ready for publication) and such certainty for the career future that he can write to his friend Erwin Rohde three years after, in May 1868, the words recorded in my prelusion: "By the way, dear friend, I am asking you sincerely, to firmly set your eyes on an academic carrière, which is to be pursued someday..." (to Rohde, May 3 or 4, 1868; KSB 2, 275). I have omitted how it continues. It reads—doggedly, but also with a clearly perceivable connotation of self-irony (one could almost say with a suggestion of fatalistic self-denial), which already points to the future:

> [...] a fearful self-examination is not at place (here): we simply *need* to, because we *cannot* otherwise, because we do not have a more appropriate career for our lives in front of us, because we have obstructed the way to more useful [!] positions, because we have no other means to make our constellation of vigor and view useful for our fellow human beings, than by precisely the indicated path. (To Rohde, May 3 or 4, 1868; KSB 2, 275)

A few lines further:

> [...] as future university-knights we must do a lot ὥσθε γνωρίζεσθαι ["to become known"], thus bring up our names into journals from time to time, setting Anekdota into the world from Paris etc. After 1½ – 2 years we will habilitate in Berlin or somewhere and survive the time of "distilled hopelessness," the time as lecturers [das Privatdozententhum], σὺν ἐρχομένῳ ["marching together," "in lockstep"] [...]. At any rate we will both meet this academic career without exaggerated hopes. But I think it is possible, that in the position of professor first of all a decent amount of leisure for own studies, second a useful sphere of influence, and lastly a passably independent political and social situation can be acquired and maintained. The latter, which I hinted at, we will have to our advantage before any public carrière, be it as lawyers or as schoolmasters. (To Rohde, May 3 or 4, 1868; KSB 2, 275f.)

So a love for philosophy is surely not at the forefront, but rather the wish for a secure middle-class existence with some reputation (indeed, a primarily philological one). The strategic, business-like manner with which Nietzsche plans the steps for this goal is remarkable for a 23-year-old.[10] In plain words, Nietzsche wanted to become professor of Classical Philology. Not even a year later, he would be one. His aim seemed achieved. Yet we will see why this aim would very soon afterwards become a heavy burden. Before that, however, a glance at Nietzsche's *philological achievements*, which had made the unforeseen early attainment of his aim possible.

3. Nietzsche's philological works from age 16 to 28 (Schulpforta to Basel)

Year	Age	Location / Selection of his works
1858, Oct.	14	**Schulpforta**
1861, Jul.	16	"De rebus gestis Mithridatis Regis"
1862	16	"Fatum und Geschichte"; "Willensfreiheit und Fatum" (for the students league 'Germania', with Wilhelm Pinder and Gustav Krug)
1862, Oct.	17	"Prooemium Livi historiarum explicatur"
1862, Nov.	18	"Primi Ajacis stasimi interpretatio cum brevi praefatione"
1863, May/June	18	Translations and Commentary to "Callinus, Tyrtaeus, Mimnermus, Sappho, Anacreon"
1863, Oct.	18	"Gestaltung der Sage vom Ostgotenkönig Ermanarich bis in das 12te Jahrhundert"
1864, Apr./May	19	"Primum Oedipodis regis carmen choricum"
1864, Jul.	19	"De Theognide Megarensi" (Valediktionsarbeit [school-leaving exam])
1864, Oct.	20	**Bonn**
1865, Oct.	21	**Leipzig**
1866, Jan. 18	21	"Die letzte Redaktion der Theognideae" Lecture at the *Philologischer Verein* (PhV)
1866, Jun. 1	21	"Über die litteraturhistorischen Quellen des Suidas" (PhV)
1867, Jan.	22	"Die Pinakes der aristelischen Schriften" (PhV)
1867, Jul.	22	"Der Sängerkrieg auf Euböa" (PhV)
1867	22	"Zur Geschichte der Theognidischen Spruchsammlung" in: *Rheinisches Museum* (RhM) NF 22, 161–200
1868, Apr. 25	23	"G. F. Schoemanns Theogonie des Hesiod" in: *Literarisches Centralblatt für Deutschland* (LC)
1868, Oct. 31	24	"Valentin Roses Anacreon" (LC)
1868	24	"De Laertii Diogenis fontibus I" (RhM NF 23, 269–96)
1868	24	"Beiträge zur Kritik der griechischen Lyriker. I: der Danaë Klage" (RhM NF 23, 480–9)
1868, Nov. 6	24	"Über die Varronischen Satiren und den Cyniker Menippus" (PhV)
1868, Nov. 21	24	"R. Nietzsches 'Quaestiones Eudocianae'" (LC)

Year	Age	Location / Selection of his works
1869, Jan. 30	24	"Chr. Zieglers Theognis-Edition" (LC) "J. Bernays 'Heraklitische Briefe'" (LC) "P. Marquards Edition der Fragmente der 'Harmonie' des Aristoxenos" (LC)
1869, Feb. 10	24	**Call from Basel**
1869, Apr. 03	24	"E. Rohdes 'Lucian's Schrift: *Loukios ē ónos' [etc.]*" (LC)
1869	24	"De Laertii Diogenis fontibus II" (RhM, NF 24, 296–358)

Already in his years at Schulpforta Nietzsche had created at least nine philological works, of which five are in Latin. He starts with themes from Roman history and literature (Mithridates, Livy); then come themes exclusively concerned with Greek literature, except for the Ermanarich piece:[11] two on Greek tragedy (Sophocles' *Ajax* and *Oedipus the King*), two from early Greek poetry (from Callinus to Anacreon, and eventually the work on Theognis). Notably, there are *no* works on philosophy.

In Leipzig he then works out around twenty papers, some drafted for presentation in the "Philologischer Verein," some prepared for publication. The first of the latter was for the *Rheinisches Museum für Philologie* of 1867, composed at the age of 22; the last of this group appeared in the *Rheinisches Museum für Philologie* of 1871 when he was 26 years old (this publication of the "Certamen Homeri et Hesiodi" was of course already prepared in Leipzig, thus will be counted among the Leipzig works). The thematic range is extraordinarily broad for such a young man. It covers the early Greek poets, from Theognis to the "Certamen"—thus from the sixth century BC to the second century AD—and even up to the empress and writer Eudokía in the fifth century AD. Here we again see the same picture as from the works in Schulpforta: from the twenty works only one (at least half of it) is devoted to a theme from Roman literature, namely the one on Varro's "Saturae" from 1868; the other nineteen are on *Greek* poets and prose authors. And here too not a single work on philosophy is found. What sounds like studies on Aristotle or Heraclitus is *source research* [Quellenstudien], and the works on Diogenes Laertius also have the disclosure of the sources for this third-century history of philosophy as their principal aim. So here too it is not a prospective philosopher speaking, but a philologist. And this philologist speaks in exclusively philological terms: Nietzsche practices ordinary philology in the old ways and according to the state of the art: in terms of its conventional diction, with its meticulous detail-analysis of texts, its examination of traditions, and with exemplary method.

To reveal this with *all* of his works is of course not possible. Accordingly, Nietzsche's procedure, his argumentative acuity and, foremost, his resultant ways of problem-solving (which have often been acknowledged as secured even today), will be revealed by means of one especially fruitful example: his work on the "Certamen Homeri et Hesiodi." That we will have to descend then deeply down to the last philological detail and therefore frustrate and bore some "philosophical" readers who lack philological training is inevitable. Whoever can nevertheless convince himself to stay with the matter will notice how profound, encompassing, and detailed the scholarly and methodological basis on which Nietzsche erected his later buildings of thought really is.

3.1 The "Certamen Homeri et Hesiodi"[12]

First, in brief, the facts: During the early period of the Roman Empire, in the context of a renewed flourishing return to the great classical Greek past, a development of extensive biographical literature took place. Especially popular were biographies of poets, so called βίοι, i.e. vitae. Homer-vitae made up the majority of these. Nine of these have come down to us. All of them were composed during the Roman Empire, separated from the life and times of the creator of the *Iliad* by 800 to 1,700 years (like the *Suda*). Seven of these nine texts are by anonymous authors, the remaining two from a companion on literature (Proclus) and from the massive tenth-century encyclopedia, *The Suda*, respectively (Latacz 2011, 13ff.). All are compilations from various earlier writings, indeed some are probably at least partly the result of a subterranean stream of oral tradition attributable to the "collective memory": the richer the respective source-material was, the more random the subsequent compilations. Their core consisted of a reporting string of numerous conflicting opinions by "Homer-experts" and anonymous remarks along the lines of "some say ... whereas others say." This core was furthermore enriched with the respective author's own ideas, inventions, and misunderstandings. In his large volume on the history of Greek literature from 1971, Albin Lesky speaks of the "hopeless state of ancient biography" (Lesky 1971, 778). The common formula of these vitae consists in, at most, six thematic points: (1) parentage, (2) place of birth, (3) name-giving, (4) (possibly) profession and travels, (5) death, (6) and maybe a catalogue of works. The value of insights from these "βίοι" is equal to nothing. In the words of Geoffrey Kirk: "Antiquity knew nothing definite about the life and personality of Homer" (Kirk 1985, 1).[13]

One of the longer texts in this pseudo-biographical type is the "Certamen" (Contest). The extent of it is roughly eight pages. It was recovered from a mixed codex of various essays on different themes in the *Laurentiana* (the Laurentianus 56, written in the fourteenth century) in Florence by Henricus Stephanus. The first thing to note is that the manuscript does not have an *author's name*; Stephanus edited it in 1573 as Ὁμήρου καὶ Ἡσιόδου ἀγών. *Homeri et Hesiodi certamen. Nunc primum luce donatum. Matronis et aliorum parodiae. Genavae anno MDLXXIII.*

The edition was reprinted repeatedly in volumes throughout the nineteenth century (e.g. in A. Westermann's 1845 Βιογράφοι); the underlying manuscript was then no longer known, though. Westermann believed, for example, that a lost early *Codex Parisinus* served as its source. But in 1863 Valentin Rose rediscovered the original manuscript in Florence, and his reports thereon in 1863/64 created a minor sensation. Rose's rediscovery must have incited Nietzsche to give a paper on "Der Sängerkrieg auf Euboea" in the Leipzig "Philologischer Verein" in July 1867. It has been suspected that Nietzsche modeled the title of his paper after Wagner's opera "Tannhäuser und der Sängerkrieg auf Wartburg", which premièred at Dresden in 1845 (Vogt 1962, 105). This is indeed possible; however, it is not substantial for determining Nietzsche's intention, namely to evidence the authorship of the till-then-anonymous Greek text.

In his lecture, Nietzsche pays special attention to the text's tripartite structure.[14] Of its 18 sections (following Wilamowitz's division of 1916 here), only eight (6–13) deal with the sort of "contest of Homer with Hesiod" ("Certamen") after which Stephanus had named the entire text. Before and after this contest (Greek ἀγών), sections 1–5 and 14–18, respectively, contain the usual information of that six-point formula. Hence, the title is inaccurate. Nietzsche will later discover that this is due to Stephanus' delight in abbreviations. The more accurate and justified title of the transmissing manuscript of the fourteenth century is: *On Homer and Hesiod and their Ancestry and Competition.* This agrees much better with the content, and in that tripartite structure the text really forms a—though incongruous—whole:

Part I (sections 1–5): [pseudo-] biography (place of birth, ancestry, name, priority; transition to the actual "Certamen")

Part II (sections 6–13): "Certamen"

Part III (sections 14–18): the fate of the two protagonists after the "Certamen," their deaths.

In section 3, which treats Homer's parentage and presents a variety of fantastical genealogies, the anonymous composer (better "compiler") discloses triumphantly that he had heard "the godliest αὐτοκράτωρ [i.e. emperor] Hadrian" had come to learn a definitive answer to the question of Homer's lineage from the Delphic oracle: namely, that Homer was the son of Telemachus and Nestor's daughter, Epicaste.[15] Hadrian ruled from AD 117–138, so the text was composed in or after this time.

In the beginning of section 5 the compiler passes over to the actual "agōn":

But some say both [Homer and Hesiod] lived during the *same* time and actually met at Aulis in Boeotia. Because Ganyktor, son of Amphidamas the king of Euboea, offering enormous awards, had at this time summoned the most illustrious men not only in the disciplines of 'strength' and 'speed', but also in the area of 'wisdom' ('sophía') to the burial ceremony of his father, who had just died, both had sailed from Aulis to Chalcis.

This tale is spun from Hesiod's *Erga kai Hemerai* ("Works and Days"), wherein Hesiod humorously remarks at one point that he had gone to sea only *once* in his life, to travel from Aulis to Chalcis (a passage which is today spanned by a little bridge about 213 feet wide), where he had won a tripod in a hymn-agōn.[16] One notices the fiction immediately, since Hesiod does not mention one word about an "agōn" in "sophia," let alone an "agōn" with *Homer*.

The author continues: the referees were respected people from Chalcis chaired by the deceased's brother, *Pan-edes* (Nietzsche *en passant* correctly translated the name to "All-Know" [All-Weiß]). Then Hesiod stepped into the middle and *queried* Homer— and Homer *answered*. This distribution of roles will then remain like this almost throughout the entire "agōn" (note that we do not have a competition here exactly, but rather a sort of viva). That examination begins in section 6: question and answer appropriate for two epic poets, i.e. in hexameters. There are three "courses" or "rounds."

At first Hesiod asks what the best would be for mortals and what people desire the most. After Homer answers this to Hesiod's annoyance, Hesiod challenges him in the second round with a seemingly unsolvable riddle, an ἄπορον ("aporia"), and, after Homer solved this elegantly too, he moves on to a new sort of question, which Martin West has called a "party game" (West 1967, 440): Hesiod presents a completely absurd hexameter and Homer offhandedly turns it into something comprehensible, thus spontaneously improvising (σχεδιάζειν in §14: this term is crucial for the intention of the whole): "So they feasted now all day long without having anything," and Homer complemented this paradox to a meaningful: "[...] in their own homes: it was given to them by the prince of men Agamemnon."

After Homer brilliantly solved 14 such paradoxes, Hesiod turns to more radical means: How many Achaeans came with the Atrides to Ilios? Homer solves this "adynaton" impressively, too, with the help of a complicated calculation. Hesiod becomes envious and, in the third round, asks *ethical* questions, seven in total; the final one reads: "To fortune now—what do people consider it?" Homer replies: "To die after having suffered the least, and having been happy the most instead." Then the *Héllēnes*, so the text continues, cannot take it any longer and demand victory for Homer. But the referee "All-Know" demands both to recite that passage from their works, over and above, which each of them considers most beautiful. Thereupon Hesiod recites a praise of field-work from his *Erga*. Homer, however, offers a shining depiction of the fighting from the thirteenth book of the *Iliad*, in which he speaks of manliness, courage, and the glory of arms. Again the Hellenes demand victory for Homer. But Pan-edes, the "All-Know," declares victory instead for Hesiod, since it is just to honor the representative of field-work and peace rather than the representative of war and slaughter. Hence the "agōn," i.e. the actual "certamen," is concluded. In the paragraphs following, a depiction is given of how each agonist died—Hesiod shamefully and disgracefully, Homer highly honored by all the Greeks. One could say much about the paradoxical awarding of the prize, but that has to be omitted here.

After Nietzsche presents this text in a (for a 22-year-old student) remarkably precise, clear, and systematic form, he comes to his actual task: the *source-analysis*. Regardless of the many content-questions the text poses, Nietzsche indeed focuses narrowly only on the analysis of its sources, as he did with his works on Theognis and Diogenes Laertius. This analysis he did using traditional measures, as they were appropriate for contemporary philologists. Nietzsche is conducting pure text-philology—we must keep this in mind. Yet in this way, he does make a wholly new and impactful discovery: He takes a till-then often-overlooked source reference in §14 more carefully into focus for the first time. There the imperial-age compiler speaks of the murder of Hesiod by two young men in Lokris, who then decide to flee to Crete in a fishing vessel, only to be struck by Zeus' lightning along the way and drown in the sea. In the following it says: "ὡς φησιν Ἀλκιδάμας ἐν Μουσείωι" ["as Alcidamas says in the *Mouseion*"] ("Certamen" §14). Nietzsche combines this with another observation: the first question Hesiod addresses to Homer in the "Certamen" *itself* reads: What is the best (ἄριστον) for men? And Homer answers:

ἀρχὴν μὲν μὴ φῦναι ἐπιχθονίοισιν ἄριστον,
φύντα δ' ὅπως ὤκιστα πύλας Ἀΐδαο περῆσαι.

To not be born is the best for earth-dweller; having been born, however, to step through Hades' gate as soon as possible. ("Certamen," §7)

Here Nietzsche remembers having read these two verses somewhere else before: in Stobaeus, the fifth-century composer of a four-volume collection of excerpts intended for the improvement of his son's knowledge of literature and philosophy. In Volume 4, chapter 52.22, Stobaeus quotes the *exact same two verses verbatim* under the heading Περὶ τοῦ θανάτου ["On Death"]—however with additional information: Ἐκ τοῦ Ἀλκιδάμαντος Μουσείου ["From the Mouseion of Alcidamas"]. Nobody before Nietzsche had brought this in connection with the "Certamen." Now Nietzsche has two corresponding source references—one at the *end* of the imperial text, the other with Stobaeus, but in reference to the *central* part of the imperial text, i.e. to the *actual* "agōn." Nietzsche concludes that the imperial compiler's main source at least had to be the *Mouseion* by the rhetorician Alkidamas, who is, from being mentioned and cited numerously, among others in Plato and Aristotle (Nietzsche lists the material), known as the pupil of the sophist Gorgias, and by whom *one* text has survived: "On the Authors of Written Speeches or on Sophists." So much for the 1867 lecture as it concerns us here. (We can disregard further conclusions Nietzsche draws in the lecture; he later rejected them.)

The paper was offered in July 1867, in Nietzsche's fourth semester, and must have been received enthusiastically; for Nietzsche followed up the theme during the next months. During his sixth semester, on November 9, 1868, he suggests a book-collaboration to Rohde in Bonn, which was to contain also a text by him on the "Certamen."[17] It never came to fruition. However, just a month later, on December 9, 1868, he tells Rohde that he is planning on newly editing "the short text περὶ Ὁμήρου καὶ Ἡσιόδου καὶ γένους καὶ ἀγῶνος αὐτῶν" (so by now he knows the original title), which is to include a thesis on "questions on the transmission of Homer" (to Rohde, December 9, 1868; KSB 2, 349). By now he has also received (from Leiden) the handwritten transcription of the time by Stephanus from the Florentine *Codex Laurentianus*. So he is very much working towards an *edition* of the text. His philological precision is then also revealed by the fact that he wants also to have a *collation* of the text in the Stephanus edition and the handwritten original codex from Florence. Several attempts fail, but he does not give up. Lastly, Rohde, who is in Italy at the time, sends him the collation from Florence on September 24, 1869 (KSB 2, 49). Now, in his second semester at Basel, Nietzsche can conclude the planned critical edition. It is eventually published in 1871 as the first issue of the *Acta Societatis Philologae Lipsiensis*, edited by Ritschl.

Whoever goes through this edition—mostly composed in Leipzig but concluded in Basel—thoroughly, will encounter a highly professional and acute 26-year-old editor. Nietzsche corrects Stephanus at various points, elucidates hard-to-read or unreadable passages, rearranges, makes conjectures, etc. The editing of a text is regarded as the supreme discipline within Classical Philology. It requires not only outstanding paleographic, linguistic, stylistic, and even (as we have here) metric understanding, but also profound knowledge of the environment of the author, his diction, his sources and his use of them, not to mention of the historical development of the literary genus

16   *Nietzsche as a Scholar of Antiquity*

πάντες ἐπὶ τὸν αἰγιαλὸν ἔδραμον καὶ τὸ cῶμα γνωρίcαντες
ἐκεῖνο μὲν πενθήcαντες ἔθαψαν, τοὺς δὲ φονεῖc ἀνεζήτουν. οἱ
δὲ φοβηθέντες τὴν τῶν πολιτῶν ὀργὴν, καταcπάcαντες ἁλιευ- 230
τικὸν cκάφος διέπλευcαν εἰc Κρήτην· οὓc κατὰ μέcον τὸν πλοῦν
ὁ Ζεὺc κεραυνώcαc κατεπόντωcεν, ὥc φηcιν Ἀλκιδάμαc ἐν
Μουcείῳ. Ἐρατοcθένηc δέ φηcιν ἐν Ἡcιόδῳ Κτίμενον καὶ Ἄντι-
φον τοὺc Γανύκτοροc ἐπὶ τῇ προειρημένῃ αἰτίᾳ ἀνελόντας cφα-
γιαcθῆναι θεοῖc τοῖc ξενίοιc ὑπ' Εὐρυκλέουc τοῦ μάντεωc. τὴν 235
μέντοι παρθένον, τὴν ἀδελφὴν τῶν προειρημένων, μετὰ τὴν
φθορὰν ἑαυτὴν ἀναρτῆcαι, φθαρῆναι δ' ὑπό τινος ξένου cυνόδου
τοῦ Ἡcιόδου, Δημώδους ὄνομα, ὃν καὶ αὐτὸν ἀναιρεθῆναι ὑπὸ
τῶν αὐτῶν φηcιν. ὕcτερον δ' Ὀρχομένιοι κατὰ χρηcμὸν μετε-
νέγκαντες αὐτὸν παρ' αὑτοῖc ἔθαψαν καὶ ἐπέγραψαν ἐπὶ τῷ 240
τάφῳ·

> Ἄcκρη μὲν πατρὶc πολυλήιος, ἀλλὰ θανόντος
> ὀcτέα πληξίππων γῆ Μινυῶν κατέχει
> Ἡcιόδου, τοῦ πλεῖcτον ἐν ἀνθρώποιc κλέος ἐcτίν
> ἀνδρῶν κρινομένων ἐν βαcάνῳ cοφίης.   245

καὶ περὶ μὲν Ἡcιόδου τοcαῦτα. ὁ δ' Ὅμηρος ἀποτυχὼν τῆc
νίκηc περιερχόμενος ἔλεγε τὰ ποιήματα, πρῶτον μὲν τὴν Θηβαῖδα,
ἔπη Ζ, ἧc ἡ ἀρχή·

232 Ἀλκιδάμαc ἐν Μουcείῳ] Goettlingius temere coniecit aut Καλλίμα-
χοc ἐν Μουcείῳ aut Ἀλκιδάμαc ἐν Μεccηνιακῷ. Heffterus in Diariis antiqu.
a. 1839 p. 860 nihil mutandum esse dicit: quem Osannus sequitur. Cf.
Bergkius in Anal. Alexandr. part. I p. 26 et Val. Roseus Aristot. pseu-
depigr. p. 508   233 ἐν Ἡcιόδῳ] F ἐν ἐνηπόδῳ, S ἐνηπόδῳ, Barnesius
ἐν Ἀνδραπόδῳ: cf. Bernhardyus Eratosth. p. 241. Ἡcιόδῳ Goettlingius
et Bergkius Anal. Alex. I p. 26   232 in F fol. 18ᵃ κεραυνώcαc vocabulo
incipit   234 Γανύκτοροc] S γαννύκτοροc | ἀνελόντας] sic ego cum F:
vulgo ἀνελθόντας   235 θεοῖc] restitui: quod F praebet. S θ μοῖc, S
θεcμοῖc et sic omnes editiones | τοῖc] addidit Bernhardyus: om. FSE
237 φθορὰν] sic ego cum F: vulgo φωράν   239 αὐτῶν] sic FSE:
Bernhardyi coniectura ἀcτῶν, quam Westermannus recepit, prorsus est
reicienda   242 Ἄcκρη] S Aᵉcηρη, rubr. ἄcκρη   243 Μινυῶν] Barnesius
ex Pausania IX, 38: FSE μινυάc, Tzetzes ex eodem fonte (Westerm.
p. 49) μινύηc vel μινύος vel tale aliquid; apud eundem in codd. V P M
πληξίππου. Fortasse igitur communi fonti πληξίππου γῆ Μινυάc lectio
vindicanda est   245 βαcάνῳ] Tzetzes βαcάνοιc, ubi Westermannus p. 49
mavult βαcάνῳ   248 ἔπη Ζ] sic G. Hermannus p. 286. F ἔπη Ζ̆. Wel-
ckerus ep. Cycl. p. 204 auctorem voluisse βιβλία Ζ censuit. [Cf. Opusc.
phil. I p. 82 sq. F. R.]

2*

Figure 1.1 From Nietzsche's "Certamen" edition, 1871. Facsimile of Nietzsche's personal
copy. (With kind permission of the Herzogin Anna Amalia Bibliothek, Weimar; call
number C4527)

of which the author is part, and much more. Nietzsche fulfills all these preconditions remarkably, as a sample from his edition proves.

We see a critical apparatus below the text, in the kind of form one can only wish for in editions today: Nietzsche does not only note the original manuscript (F for "Florentinus"), the manual transcription by Stephanus (S) and finally the printed "editio princeps" by Stephanus (E, for "Editio"), but also includes the corrections and conjectures by earlier scholars—often even noting down the place where they are made. He further notes his own corrections and conjectures, and, even as a 26-year-old, is not afraid to rebuke preceding opinions of established scholars: "Goettling *inconsiderately* [*temere*] conjectured either 'Callimachus in the Mouseion' or 'Alkidamas in [his speech] Messeniakós'" (so to line 232); or: "the conjecture by Bernhardy 'ἀστῶν,' which Westermann has adopted, must be discarded completely [*prorsus est reicienda*]"; so to line 239 (Bernhardy, professor in Halle, was a distinguished 71-year-old great authority in the field at that time, especially with his "Grundriss der griechischen Litteratur" of 1836, 5th edn. 1875). Best of all: Nietzsche was right!

We could list several more advantages of this edition. Two years later in the *Rheinisches Museum* (1873) Nietzsche judges his work self-confidently, but quite correctly: "In the new edition [...] I did not only aim at presenting the *henceforth decisive* critical apparatus, but also at the same time the *history* of the text" [my emphasis]. And he succeeded at that.

At this point I briefly return to the initial question of this contribution: "How was Nietzsche's early appointment to Basel at the age of 24 possible?" I think we see now what an outstanding philological mind had been formed there in Leipzig. In his letter of recommendation Ritschl wrote to Adolph Kiessling, at the time Latin professor in Basel, who had requested his resignation in Basel due to his appointment to the Johanneum in Hamburg and had asked Ritschl to recommend a successor, on December 9, 1868:

> [...] never before had I known a young man, who *so* early, at *such* a young age was *so* mature as Nietzsche. He wrote his *Museum*-essays in the second and third year of his academic triennium! [...] So I predict that he will one day be at the forefront of German philology [...]

At about the same time, also the Basel Greek Professor Wilhelm Vischer-Bilfinger, simultaneously Director of Education at the time, requested names of candidates for Kiessling's succession from the very same Ritschl. Ritschl simply includes that letter to Kiessling he just had finished in his answer to Vischer, and requests of him to forward it to Kiessling subsequently. Vischer then copied the passage on Nietzsche by hand and used it in the following for his recommendations to the administration at Basel.[18] Vischer also inquired for recommendations from Ritschl's successor in Bonn, Hermann Usener, who on December 19, 1868 wrote: "Among the youngest generation F. Nietzsche stands out, whose works in the Rhein. Museum (vol. 22 and 23) astonish through their juvenile freshness and penetrating view" (Stroux 1925, 33f.). Let these remarks on the process of Nietzsche's appointment suffice to show that Basel indeed made a fortunate choice.

A few closing words on the *conclusion* of Nietzsche's "Certamen-research" before we come to the impact of Nietzsche in philology: In two essays in the *Rheinisches Museum* of 1870 and 1873 Nietzsche wrote what he had earlier called in a letter to Rohde the "subsequent elaborations on questions of the transmission of Homer." In the first of these essays he presents with most precise arguments his *discovery* from the "Sängerkrieg auf Euboea" lecture of that time: the main source is Alkidamas.[19] In the second essay, however, two highly consequential thoughts are added: First, that Alkidamas' authorship of the "Certamen" comes as a result from Alkidamas' *general theory of rhetoric*, as we know it from his text "On Sophists": a pupil of Gorgias, Alkidamas always admired his teacher whenever he shouted to the public "Προβάλλετε" ("throw it to me!", i.e. a topic), whereupon Gorgias would improvise freely but cleverly on that topic. As a student of such a speech-improviser, Alkidamas' preference for improvised "free" speech over the memorized recitation of the written is only logical. (From today's point of view, one should add that Alkidamas, and probably also Gorgias, must almost inevitably have placed themselves in the tradition of *Homer* in this respect, who in the *Odyssey* depicts himself as the character of the Phaeacian singer Demodocus, who was able the same way to sing about a topic upon receiving a shouted challenge [*Odyssey* 8, 487–98]; this would then explain the role of Homer as a master-improviser with Alkidamas.) Nietzsche's second new thought is related to the *title* of Alkidamas' work, in which the "Certamen" stood among other things: "*Museion*" (literally "place of the muses"). Calling on different parallels, Nietzsche explains the title as "school-" or "text-book," namely of rhetoric. Most likely this is also correct: the *museum* as a place of gathering and teaching, just as later on the μουσεῖον of Alexandria.[20]

The final touch is added by the fact that Nietzsche's thesis on Alkidamas was verified by two papyrus discoveries after his death. The 1891 discovery and publication of a third-century-BC papyrus from Egypt bears clear reference to the "Certamen": The editor Mahaffy ends his edition with the following words:

> The text here recovered proves to demonstration that the Contest was not an invention of Hadrian's age, but existed in much the same form four hundred years earlier. Its occurrence among the Fayyum papyri, where classical fragments are not very numerous, points to a widespread popularity. *So far, then, the theory of Nietzsche has received the most brilliant confirmation.* (Mahaffy 1891; my emphasis)

This first papyrus discovery then proved that the "Agōn" ran with very similar wording in the third century BC as with our imperial compiler. Thus the compiler must have drawn his "Certamen" from at least one *Hellenistic* source. In 1925 a second papyrus came to light;[21] here the editor concludes:

> The first to discuss the relation of the *Certamen* to its source was F. Nietzsche, who advanced the theory that the *Certamen* was compiled in the age of Hadrian by a writer whose source was the Μουσεῖον of the rhetorician Alkidamas, the pupil of Gorgias and rival of Isocrates [... Now] we are warranted in asserting that Alkidiamas wrote an account, entitled Περὶ Ὁμήρου, which was the immediate

source of the end of the *Certamen. So much is now fact, no longer theory.* (Winter 1925)

With this, Nietzsche's discovery was finally secured.

4. The impact of Nietzsche's youthful achievements on Classical Philology

In conclusion, I offer a few words on the impact of the philological works from young Nietzsche's work on Classical Philology. I start with a claim raised by the long-term editor of the "*Gnomon,*" Ernst Vogt, in his meritorious essay from 1962, "Nietzsche und der Wettkampf Homers." It reads:

> [...] an insurmountable suspicion relentlessly accompanies also, and especially, his most brilliant insights and dazzling formulations. On the other hand, philology [...] gladly refers to Nietzsche as one of her great representatives, which she, with a sort of naive pride [...], regards as one of her own. (Vogt 1962, 103)

Subsequently Vogt says that between the figure of Nietzsche and philology as a scientific discipline, two irreconcilable worlds meet. And this

> shall not hide the fact that Nietzsche had believed in the possibility of bringing his gradually forming thoughts and understandings to bear in the realm of professional philology for years—as was to be proven soon, a complete misapprehension of the actual situation. (Vogt 1962, 103)

I do not want to join this view. First, on the supposed "insurmountable suspicion," this view does not hold in this way. Let us stay with the example of the "Certamen." During Nietzsche's *own* time his relating research was only sporadically disputed; and Nietzsche refuted the few criticisms in the *Rheinisches Museum* of 1873 with patient philological meticulousness. Since then, both his method and his conclusions on the whole have been recognized. For one example: In his still-useful work "Geschichte der classischen Philologie in Deutschland von den Anfängen bis zur Gegenwart," the expert philologist and archeologist Conrad Bursian claims: "In research on the sources used by Diogenes for the compilation of his work, a young philologist, [...] Friedrich Wilhelm Nietzsche, has made splendid achievements" (Bursian 1883, 929). He then adds in a note that the same scholar had produced "remarkable studies," i.e. the 1870 and 1873 "Florentine tract on Homer and Hesiod, their ancestry and competition." Bursian not only claims this, but within the same sentence expressly regrets (with the word "sadly") that Nietzsche had to cease his university service at Basel in 1879 due to health reasons. Such praise, in an encompassing manual on the history of the discipline from a respected scholar, was weighty.

Basically, only *one* classical philologist of rank expressed himself unfavorably concerning Nietzsche's work on the "Certamen": Ulrich von Wilamowitz-Moellendorff. In his great "Die Ilias und Homer" (1916) he tried to portray the "Certamen" itself as an "old book of folk tales" and, as was to be expected, did not overlook the opportunity of kicking afterwards against the already 16-years-dead Nietzsche—with the special but just therefore revealing insidiousness of not even mentioning Nietzsche by name. He claims that the Alkidamas discovery (by Nietzsche) is a "windy hypothesis," and: "it is not worth wasting more words on such a figment" (Wilamowitz-Moellendorff 1916, 401). How objective we should take this judgment to be must be weighed against the fact that in his own "Certamen" edition (also published in 1916) Wilamowitz adopted at least four of Nietzsche's conjectures, and here *with* the addition of mentioning him by name. These and further acuities of Nietzsche live on, even in the most recent "Certamen"-edition by Martin West (2003).

And as for the words "not permitted" by Wilamowitz: other scholars *did* "waste" them on Nietzsche's philological "figments." Indeed, since the debate on the "Certamen," with all its twists and turns, reaches into the present day, references to Nietzsche are in no way rare. Research on oral poetry and the question of improvisation has grown greatly, and hence we find in the *"Reallexikon für Antike und Christentum,"* for example, a reference to Nietzsche's discovery (p. 1246) and in the entry on "Alcidamas d' Élée" in the *"Dictionnaire des Philosophes antiques"* of 1989, where the entire history of research is summarized: "M.L. West 1967 [...] a confirmé [...] la thèse de Nietzsche, à la suite de E. Vogt 1959" (Goulet 1989, 105f.). And Johan Schloemann (today an editor of the *Süddeutsche Zeitung*), in his dissertation on improvisation-theory, claims, "this compiled text is rightly viewed as going back to Alkidamas *since Nietzsche*" (Schloemann 2001, 150). The appreciation of Nietzsche as a professional philologist has thus remained until today (cf. Latacz 2011, 17f.).

So much for Nietzsche's impact on particular areas of Classical Philology, in which his status is secure. We turn at last to address a much more important question: How did Nietzsche, as a philologist, affect Classical Philology *tout court*? Did *The Birth of Tragedy* really cause a complete rejection of Nietzsche in the discipline, as is usually claimed? I can only see the opposite. Wilamowitz is certainly not the *whole* of Classical Philology. In my Basel university speech of 1998, I did point out that, as long as Wilamowitz was alive (†1931), Nietzsche was ostracized from the field—not seldom with a sense of embarrassment—but that he afterwards (and not only incidentally after the tremors of the First World War) caused more and more thoughtfulness and eventually even enthusiasm with Wilamowitz's own *pupils* (cf. Latacz 1998). People were sick and tired of the idolization of Wilamowitz's micrological research; one no longer wanted to be the kind of "philological youth of Germany" invoked by Wilamowitz in his thunderbolt against Nietzsche in 1872, "which should learn by an asceticism of self-denying labor, to everywhere only seek the truth" (Wilamowitz-Moellendorff 1969 [1872], 55). Thus does Wilamowitz's student Max Pohlenz write the outrageous sentence, clearly directed against Wilamowitz's "house maid"-definition (following Stefan George) of Greek tragedy: "In contrast, Nietzsche's indication of the *Dionysian* trait of Hellenism leads us to the character of tragedy. Because tragedy is *in essence, not incidentally*, connected to the cult of Dionysus and Dionysian ecstasy" (Pohlenz 1930, 8; my emphasis). And with another Wilamowitz student of the highest scholarly rank, Karl Reinhardt, Nietzsche becomes almost the exemplar of a *new* study of Hellenism, which wants to transcend the positivism of textual criticism, source study, etc. to a new "humanistic self-determination" which wants to penetrate to the depths. Philology, according to Reinhardt in a lecture of 1942, became "toilsome" around 1900, like an "over-organized, idly running machine"—asceticism, performance of duties, enduring heroism. Reinhardt claims that Nietzsche ended this. He was the first to diagnose the rigor mortis of Classical Philology. And he ultimately got everything started, breathing a new life that now finds its way into Hellenistic studies.[22] At this point we might remind ourselves of young Nietzsche's distinction between "petty frog-blooded micrologists, who know of science nothing but bookish dust," on the one hand—and the "philologist [...] with a free view and a fresh drive" on the other (BAW 5, 254).

The rediscovery of Nietzsche continued after Reinhardt, the details of which I address elsewhere.[23] Today, anyway, Classical Philology cannot be said to have forgotten Nietzsche, although the field no longer speaks of him in the high tone of the time of Stefan George, as Reinhardt does. She has turned into a science, which unites within herself methodological strictness, detailed exactness, and systematics on the one side, and, on the other, lively empathy with the *essence* of the classical works and an attempt to enliven one's life thereby. Wilamowitz and Nietzsche are united in this.[24] This was only possible because Nietzsche was *not* able to follow the planned path in Basel. He could *not* become a "frog-blooded micrologist" in Basel any more after the publication of *The Birth of Tragedy*, even if he had wanted to. For that book brought him existential disappointment. In a draft for a letter to the publisher Engelmann, Nietzsche claims to seek "to explain Greek tragedy in a totally new way," in that he "for the time being [!] wants to refrain from any philological approach on the question and only wants to focus on the aesthetic problem" (to Engelmann, April 20, 1871; KSB 3, 193f.). He apparently wanted to provide the *philological* foundations, which he knew remarkably well, only afterwards.[25] But it seemed more urgent to him back then—being under the pressure to justify himself professionally—to quickly publish a larger work which would cause a sensation (i.e. "in a completely new manner").[26] He believed also in achieving this through an entirely new *form* of presentation. Nietzsche let a new kind of mythical-vitalistic manner of speech take the place of the common scientific diction. But no one could understand this; it was all too fast. As far as one did not take the book seriously from the start, one felt overwhelmed, probably also besieged, downright disavowed. The 23-year-old Wilamowitz, with his almost brutal Junker-style attack,[27] was not even decisive for this fact; he was not actually taken seriously either.[28] It was far worse that a man like Ritschl, whom Nietzsche admired so much, proved to be so much disconcerted.[29] And the experts generally—they cloaked themselves in silence.[30] At this point Nietzsche's old suspicion of not actually belonging in academic philology was all but certain. In *Zarathustra* it says "Of Scholars":

> And when I lived *with* them, I did live *above* them. Thus they bore me ill will. They did not want to hear someone walking above their heads; and so they put wood and earth and dirt between me and their heads. Thus they deafened the sounds of my steps: and I have hitherto been heard least by the most learned. (Z scholars; KSA 4, 162)

The break had to happen. And so Basel became the place where Nietzsche experienced his crucial turn. The city had appointed a great philologist, and saw a great philologist fail. But from this failure emerged a great thinker; a thinker who thought deeply about philology. Thus Basel in the end did become a fortunate case in philology.

Translated by Philip Roth

Notes

1   Wolf's student August Boeckh became the most important representative of this current; see Pfeiffer 1982, 222.
2   Even Sundays were no great exception, save for that there were no classes and the pupils only had to get up at 6 a.m. "Working hours" were, however, also required then, and these were only interrupted by prayers and morning church attendance. See BAW 1, 125f.
3   As an example, Landfester quotes from the biography of the then quite famous Leipzig classicist Gottfried Hermann. He indeed had a "freely creative" and "complete" command of Latin; however, of German only a "clear, simple and pithy" one. Landfester 1988, 97. Landfester is relying on Koechly 1874, 15.
4   "Latin. He has an excellent skillfulness in translating the classics and his written expression is also correct, clear and in good Latin, so that he, although the oral examination brought less opportune results, can nevertheless receive the grade '*excellent*'. He also shows quite good skills in *speaking* Latin" KGB I/4, 261; my emphasis. Nietzsche's diploma is stored at the Goethe- and Schiller-Archive in Weimar.
5   Nietzsche was almost always at the top of his class. See letter to Franziska and Elisabeth Nietzsche, September 25, 1862; KGB I/4, 207f.
6   Here he wishes for Lachman 1851, Dronke 1861, and also for Schubert's composition "Grand Duo à quatre mains."
7   That he especially adored him is sufficiently known; these readings were nevertheless more a hobby. They never caused him to turn away from philology.
8   Nietzsche's "discontent with philology" (which indeed is a discontent with the *wrong philology of his time*) reveals itself repeatedly and emphatically during his time as a student at university and will literally become a trauma after the "scandal" over *GT*. Nietzsche cannot free himself from traditional philology, but neither can he establish the "new and correct" philology he has in mind. Cf. now the more extensive Schwinge 2011, 246.
9   Quoted according to Hoppe and Schlechta 1938–42, I, 409. Montinari's projected fourth KGB volume of "letters on Nietzsche (with life documents and occasional notes from Nietzsche's manuscripts)" was a project sadly abandoned in 1993. See KGB I/1, v; KGB I/4, vi.
10   Nietzsche will later underline his "cleverness" more often; for example, in his application for the professorship of philosophy in Basel 1871, when he requests a change of chairs and recommends Erwin Rohde as his successor: "one should say about me, that I had the cleverest ideas to the benefit of friendship." To Rohde, February 8, 1871; KSB 3, 183.
11   Ermanarich was a Germanic (Gothic) king (4th century). He plays a part also in *Beowulf*.
12   In the following I gratefully acknowledge the work of Ernst Vogt (1959; 1962), as well as his contribution to my *Zweihundert Jahre Homer-Forschung, Rückblick*

und Ausblick (1991). Vogt's earlier studies are now more than half a century old, though they still have not been acknowledged properly by philosophers or philologists working towards an understanding of Nietzsche's intellectual development. An exception is Cancik [1995] 2000, 1–25. See also the hints in Latacz 2011, 1–25.

13 Differentiating, but not negating the "definite" is Latacz 2011, 18f.

14 "Der Sängerkrieg auf Euboea: Vortrag von Friedrich Nietzsche." Found at BAW 3, 230–44. This work is not included in the KGW. The first specific mentioning of the planned lecture appears in spring 1868 under the heading "Themata meiner nächsten Arbeiten." BAW 4, 123. Preliminary work on the planned "text with collation and commentary" as well as on the later "Certamen"-essays developed in the winter of 1868/1869. See BAW 4, 133–62, BAW 5, 168–71, 190–202, 212–17, 220–33. See also Karl Schlechta's "Nachbericht" in his 1940, 439f. Already at *that* time Nietzsche gained the crucial insights for his understanding of the "Certamen." See BAW 5, 170f., at right.

15 Nietzsche accurately corrected the name to "*Poly*caste" to reflect the name of Nestor's daughter per *Odyssey* 3. 464f.

16 Hesiod, Ἔργα καὶ ἡμέραι, 646–60.

17 "[W]e will make a book together called *Beiträge zur griechischen Litteraturgeschichte* in which we will collect a couple of longer essays (e.g. the ones by me on Democritus' authorship, on the Homeric-Hesiodic ἀγών, on the Cynic Menippus) and also include some miscellanea. What do you think of that?" To Rohde, November 9, 1868; KSB 2, 342.

18 See Stroux 1925, 29ff. The dates of some letters are not always accurate with Stroux; however, the time of December 1868/January 1869 is relevant here.

19 Thus, Nietzsche had already concluded that "the entire story in the ἀγών was from Alcidamas' Museion." BAW 5, 170f.

20 And like the periodical "Rheinisches Museum," in which Nietzsche presents these insights—a nice little punchline, most likely not even noticed by Nietzsche.

21 For a discussion of this papyrus, see West 1967, 434–8.

22 Thus Reinhardt certifies the late success of Nietzsche's life-long effort for a "new" philology. Reinhardt's appraisal, and even admiration, of Nietzsche is contextualized in Latacz 1995, 50–3; see also Schwinge 2011, 287.

23 I have called some points to mind in Latacz 1998, 29–31. On Nietzsche's impact (and on the Nietzsche cult) in and outside of Classical Studies, see Cancik 1995, 381–402.

24 Laid out extensively by Hölscher 1995, esp. 85.

25 See my 1998, 16–21. The concrete evidence developed on those pages (even for the development of the only seemingly external aspects "title of the book" and "title-page-vignette" on the side) has apparently not made it into Nietzsche-research as of yet. Barbara von Reibnitz has repeatedly pointed out that Nietzsche already in his preliminary work on the final book "named references to other authors [...] or marked them as quotations – also here with *significant exceptions* from *scientific* works of predecessors": Reibnitz 1992, 38; my emphasis. Reibnitz's example is Müller 1857, as a text Nietzsche demonstrably used permanently. One would have to first consult the extensive list of scholarly literature which Nietzsche checked-out from libraries, especially the Basel University Library, prior to The Birth of Tragedy. Cf. Reibnitz 1992, 353–7. If one considers the noted draft of a letter to the publisher Engelmann, it becomes obvious that Nietzsche purposely suppressed his sources in the *secondary literature of contemporary Classical Philology* (a practice familiar

to him from the preparation of his lectures in his first Basel years): "I wish that the text may be treated as a *belles-lettres brochure* [...] for this regard I favor a *German* typeface [he means the "Fraktur."—JL] and namely a *big* German type, a big octavo format, with no more than 28–32 lines and above all—pretty paper." To Engelmann, April 20, 1871; KSB 3, 194; only the italics are *my* emphasis. Something "completely new" (as he says to Engelmann), as it is symbolized in the "Prometheus bursting his chains" of the title-page vignette, was not allowed to have predecessors, of course (cf. Reinhardt 1942, 435). Research may forgive Nietzsche's "cleverness," of which he was himself so proud (see above), but it should not ignore it.

26 In a long letter from January 1871 to Vischer-Bilfinger, Nietzsche applied for the vacant philosophy chair in Basel. It is therefore understandable strategically that he emphasizes his "philosophical tendencies" as a central interest in all of his works so far. "As long as I studied philology, I never grew tired of remaining closely attached to philosophy; indeed my main concerns were always with the philosophical questions." To Vischer-Bilfinger, January, 1871; KSB 3, 176. This, however, is not reconcilable with the facts, as revealed in the "certificate of proficiency" contained in the letter: "I will soon be able to publicly show myself as sufficiently fit for the position as a philosophy teacher: my printed works on Laert. Diog. are to be asserted for my philosophic-historic ambitions [!] at any rate." To Vischer-Bilfinger, January, 1871; KSB 3, 177. We showed above that just these works on Diogenes Laertius are purely philological source criticism. And as for "publicly showing himself as sufficiently fit" (he is referring to *The Birth of Tragedy*) a sentence from a letter to Rohde gives the enlightening commentary: "I also have to reveal and legitimate myself as somewhat philosophical in addition; a small work on the 'Origin and Aim of Tragedy' has been finished for that, except for a few strokes of the brush." To Rohde, March 29, 1871; KSB 3, 189. So BT is foremost revealed as a piece of career writing, with a philological core and "philosophical" "brushstrokes." Cancik's carefully assessing judgment points in the same direction; see Cancik 2000, esp. 20f., 15, and 33. That the book would later—aside from its cult-book status outside of the discipline—contribute to a principal turn in the self-understanding of the field was not seriously entertained by its author (though he did maintain that hope). In his later "Attempt at Self-Criticism" (1886), Nietzsche calls the book "impossible," "badly written, cumbersome, embarrassing, raging and confused with images sentimental, here and there even sugared unto femininity, unsteady in its tempo, without a will to logical cleanliness, very convinced and therefore presumptuous of proof" (BT Attempt 3; KSA 1, 14; Landfester 1994, 100. See also Cancik 2000, 50: "That is all very true" ("all" seems to me to be exaggerated. This is the typical angry self-chastisement after finding out a mistake too late. Beyond that, it is a 42-year-old speaking about the book of a 27-year-old in this "self-criticism"!—a book, which he obviously did not really understand himself anymore: an often-encountered circumstance; an objective, rational judgment can only be acquired from outside).

27 Wilamowitz-Moellendorff 1969 [1872]. Wilamowitz later described it as "desperately naive" and "boyish." Wilamowitz-Moellendorff 1929, 129f.

28 Ernst Vogt rightly emphasized that Wilamowitz in retrospect "greatly overestimated the immediate impact of his polemic"; the text contributed only "*not insignificantly* to the condemnation of Nietzsche in the field." Vogt 1962, 111n. 36; my emphasis.

29 Nietzsche writes to Ritschl: "Most revered Mr. Privy Counselor, you will not hold my amazement against me, that I have not received a single word from you on my

recently published book, and hopefully also not my openness, with which I express my amazement to you." To Ritschl, January 30, 1872; KSB 3, 281. Ritschl allegedly may never have encountered anything more hopeful in his life for classical research than this book—and so on. Ritschl notes on this occasion in his journal: "Fabulous l[etter] from N[ietzsche] (= megalomania)." Cf. Vogt 1962, 111n. 34. Nietzsche also admitted to Rohde how saddened he was by the Basel-students' boycott of his classes in the winter term of 1872/73 as a response to the "scandal." Cf. to Rohde, November, 1872; KSB 4, 85.

30   "Our dear colleagues are quite silent on the subject of my book: they don't even utter a sound." To Rohde, May 12, 1872; KSB 3, 323. Nietzsche's letter continues: "half and half people even think of me as mad." From a later letter, one learns that Hermann Usener (who had also recommended Nietzsche for Basel at the time, see above) was publicly spreading the opinion that Nietzsche was "dead as a scholar" due to his book on tragedy. To Rohde, October 25, 1872; KSB 4, 70f.; Cf. Cancik 1995, 384, esp. n. 12 and Schwinge 2011, 269ff. for further material.

Works cited

Bursian, Conrad (1883): *Geschichte der classischen Philologie in Deutschland von den Anfängen bis zur Gegenwart*. Munich (Oldenbourg).

Cancik, Hubert (1995): "Der Einfluss Friedrich Nietzsches auf Klassische Philologen in Deutschland bis 1945. Philologen am Nietzsche-Archiv (I)." In H. Flashar (ed.): *Altertumswissenschaft in den 20er Jahren. Neue Fragen und Impulse*. Stuttgart (Steiner), 381–402.

—([1995] 2000): *Nietzsches Antike*. Stuttgart (Metzler), 2nd edn.

Dronke, Gustav (1861): *Die religiösen und sittlichen Vorstellungen des Aeschylos und Sophokles*. Leipzig (Teubner).

Goulet, Richard (ed.) (1989): *Dictionnaire des Philosophes Antiques*. Paris (Edn. du Centre national de la recherche scientifique). Vol. I.

Hölscher, Uvo (1995): "Strömungen der deutschen Gräzistik in den zwanziger Jahren." In H. Flashar (ed.): *Altertumswissenschaft in den 20er Jahren. Neue Fragen und Impulse*. Stuttgart (Steiner), 65–85.

Hoppe, Wilhelm and Karl Schlechta (1939–42): *Friedrich Nietzsche. Werke und Briefe. Historisch-Kritische Gesamtausgabe. Briefe bis 1877*. Munich (Beck).

Humboldt, Wilhelm von ([1792] 1960–81): "Wie weit darf sich die Sorgfalt des Staats um das Wohl seiner Bürger erstrecken?" In A. Flitner and K. Giel (eds): *Werke in fünf Bänden*. Darmstadt (Cotta), Vol. I.

—([1793] 1960–81): "Über das Studium des Alterthums, und des griechischen insbesondere", In A. Flitner and K. Giel (eds): *Werke in fünf Bänden*. Darmstadt (Cotta), Vol. II.

Kirk, Geoffrey Stephen (1985): *The Iliad: A Commentary*. Cambridge (Cambridge University Press). Vol. I: Books 1–4.

Koechly, Hermann (1874): *Gottfried Hermann*. Heidelberg (C. Winter).

Lachmann, Karl (1851): *Nibelungen*. Berlin (G. Reimer).

Landfester, Manfred (1988): *Humanismus und Gesellschaft im 19. Jahrhundert. Untersuchungen zur politischen und gesellschaftlichen Bedeutung der humanistischen Bildung in Deutschland*. Darmstadt (Wissenschaftliche Buchgesellschaft).

Latacz, Joachim (1995): "Reflexionen Klassischer Philologen auf die Altertumswissenschaft der Jahre 1900–30." In H. Flashar (ed.): *Altertumswissenschaft in den 20er Jahren. Neue Fragen und Impulse*. Stuttgart (Steiner), 41–64.

—(1998): "Fruchtbares Ärgernis: Nietzsches 'Geburt der Tragödie' und die gräzistische Tragödienforschung." In *Basler Universitätsreden* 94. Basel (Schwabe).

—(2002): "Philologie. Moderne Philologie (ab 1800)." In H. Cancik and H. Schneider (eds): *Der Neue Pauly. Enzyklopädie der Antike*. Stuttgart (Metzler). Vol. 15/2, col. 255–78.

—(2011): "Zu Homers Person." In A. Rengakos and B. Zimmerman (eds): *Homer-Handbuch. Leben – Werk – Wirkung*. Stuttgart (Metzler), 1–25.

Lesky, Albin (1971): *Geschichte der griechischen Literatur*. Bern and Munich (Francke). 3rd edn.

Mahaffy, John Pentland (1891): "Papyrus No. XXV." In his *The Flinders Petrie Papyri*. Dublin (Academy House). Vol. 1.

Müller, Karl Otfried (1857): *Geschichte der griechischen Literatur*. Breslau (J. Max). 2nd edn.

Pfeiffer, Rudolf (1982): *Die Klassische Philologie von Petrarca bis Mommsen*. Munich (Beck).

Reibnitz, Barbara v. (1992): *Ein Kommentar zu Friedrich Nietzsche, 'Die Geburt der Tragödie aus dem Geiste der Musik' (chpt. 1–12)*. Stuttgart and Weimar (Metzler).

Reinhardt, Karl (1942): "Die Klassische Philologie und das Klassische." In his *Von Werken und Formen. Vorträge und Aufsätze*. Godesberg (Küpper), 419–57.

Schlechta, Karl (1940): "Nachbericht." In BAW. Vol. 5, 427–42.

Schliemann, Heinrich (1892): *Selbstbiographie: Bis zu seinem Tode vervollständigt*. Sophie Schliemann (ed.). Leipzig (Brockhaus).

Schloemann, Johan (2001): *Freie Rede: Rhetorik im demokratischen Athen zwischen Schriftlichkeit und Improvisation*. Berlin (dissertation).

Schwinge, Ernst-Richard (2011): "Zwischen Philologie und Philosophie: Zu Nietzsches Frühzeit." In his *Uralte Gegenwart: Studien zu Antikerezeptionen in Deutschland*. Freiburg (Rombach), 241–90.

Stroux, Johannes (1925): *Nietzsches Professur in Basel*. Jena (Fromannn).

Vogt, Ernst (1959): "Die Schrift vom Wettkampf Homers und Hesiods." In *Rheinisches Museum für Philologie*. Vol. 102, 193–221.

—(1962): "Nietzsche und der Wettkampf Homers." In *Antike und Abendland*. Vol. 11, 102–13.

—(1991): "Homer – ein großer Schatten?" In Joachim Latacz (ed.): *Zweihundert Jahre Homer-Forschung, Rückblick und Ausblick*. Stuttgart and Leipzig (Teubner), 365–77.

West, Martin L. (1967): "The Contest of Homer and Hesiod." In *The Classical Quarterly*. Vol. 17, 433–50.

—(ed. and trans.) (2003): *Homeric Hymns – Homeric Apocrypha – Lives of Homer*. Cambridge, MA and London (Harvard University Press).

Wilamowitz-Moellendorff, Ulrich von (1919): *Die Ilias und Homer*. Berlin (Weidmann).

—(1929): *Erinnerungen*. Leipzig (Weidmann). 2nd edn.

—(1969 [1872]): "Zukunftsphilologie! eine Erwidrung auf Friedrich Nietzsches, ord. Professors der classischen Philologie zu Basel, 'Geburt der Tragödie.'" In Karl Gründer (ed.): *Der Streit um Nietzsches 'Geburt der Tragödie'. Die Schriften von E. Rohde, R. Wagner, U. v. Wilamowitz-Möllendorff*. Hildesheim (G. Olms).

Winter, John G. (1925), "A New Fragment on the Life of Homer [The Papyrus Michigan Inv. 2754]." In *Transactions of the American Philological Association*. Vol. 56, 120–9.

Nietzsche's Radical Philology

James I. Porter

Nietzsche is known, and in some quarters despised, for having overthrown Classical Philology. What is less widely known is that he did so not by standing outside of philology but only from within, by radicalizing its internal assumptions. This is as true of the work that is thought to mark his break with traditional philology, *The Birth of Tragedy out of the Spirit of Music* (1872), as it is of the classical scholarship that he produced prior to and after this risky book, which seemed at the time, and continues to seem, to seal his fate as a philologist.[1] And while the record of Nietzsche's philological accomplishments is slim, it is less so than one might suspect given the sheer ambition and range of his efforts as a classical scholar.

What potential Nietzsche might have realized had he persisted as a scholar is anyone's guess, but he at least deserves to be remembered in the history of philology as the gifted and promising classicist that he was—surely as one of the more promising and least realized classicists of all time. His record of publications testifies to this alone.[2] His notebooks back up the claim still further, for they are a mine of projects imagined but never carried out. A history of classical scholarship that awarded points to classicists on the basis of imagination—as it were, an *imaginary* history of classical scholarship—would have to rank Nietzsche among the stars in its galaxy. As it happens, you will look nearly in vain for mentions of his name in the definitive histories of the field, even though several of his findings have made their way, often namelessly, into the main stream of classical scholarship. Thus, to Nietzsche must be accorded a final, paradoxical honor: that of being the least remembered—or most repressed—scholar in the history of classics. But let us return to the record we have. Because I have discussed elsewhere aspects of Nietzsche's career as a philologist and its aftermath, I wish to dwell a bit more closely here on the philology that he conducted in his notes rather than in his published works (which in any case are few in number).

While Nietzsche's published writings from his earliest period are frequently astonishing, they are for the most part tame in comparison with his notebooks, which reflect the true abandon of Nietzsche's thought and his classroom performances. Indeed, it is arguable that Nietzsche's most radical philology was performed in the classroom and in his notebooks. Nevertheless, to give an idea of the kinds of topics Nietzsche's lectures touched on, consider those contained in the critical edition under the general supervision of Colli-Montinari. These four volumes (to date), presenting notes to lecture courses, represent the entire span of Nietzsche's teaching career.[3] Their range is impressive, but only partially indicative of the full range of Nietzsche's research interests, his vast learning, or his teaching:[4] The notes run the full gamut of classical studies, but they also vary greatly in quality, from continuous narrative in fair copy to chaotic and disorderly fragments that rival the ancient fragments in their degree of difficulty. They invariably shed light on Nietzsche's evolving larger vistas onto classical antiquity. At times they afford a precious glimpse of the ways in which he tested out his ideas in the classroom on live audiences.

1. Nietzsche in the classroom

A case in point is a lecture on Aeschylus' *Choephori* taught successively on seven occasions: four times between 1869 and 1872, once in 1874, and then twice in a single academic year (1877–8).[5] Nietzsche's notes start off with a short preamble that concludes with a general outline in seven parts. As with other lectures (e.g. those on rhythm and meter), Nietzsche's original, core lectures are the most organized and articulated of the lot, while later accretions lose sight of these initial contours. In the present case, the numeration of the outline is followed for 30 pages, but then the order breaks down with "Zusätze" (supplements) assigned by the editor (Bornmann) to "1872/1874" (KGW II/2, 30-2). The sequence resumes, or rather backtracks, with "Trilogie" (Ibid., 32–4), then with a relatively shorter section, "<Zu den Choephoren>" (Ibid., 34–44), which embraces several subheadings ("<Zu den Choephoren>" "Die Choephoren. Betrachtungen über den Künstlerischen Stil des Aischylos," "Ueber die Choephoren des Äschylus. mit der größten Theaterwirkung"), and finally gives over to "<Kommentar zu den Choephoren> [1869–74]" (Ibid., 45–104), a (generally) lemmatic, sequential, and wide-ranging commentary on the play. From this somewhat typical example one gets a rough sense of what Nietzsche's lectures must for the most part have been like: general scholarly and philological discussion of overarching issues, obeying a crisply delineated, methodical order (here guided, interestingly, by the order of topics typically listed in Alexandrian *argumenta* but absent from the codices of this play; Nietzsche's method thus represents something of a speculative recreation of, and inquiry into, Hellenistic philology and its habits of reading[6]), with a brief interlude on aesthetic questions of Nietzsche's own making, was followed by a blow-by-blow commentary in the best tradition of modern textual philology. And if Nietzsche's notes are any indication, he will have diverged from his magisterial lecturing in the grand German style in only one respect: he got beyond the prologue of the drama, and indeed covered the whole of the play! The question is, of course, what kind of indication Nietzsche's lecture notes (or rather, notebooks) can be said to represent, and how closely these mapped onto his actual practice.

The *Choephori* lecture notes are typical of Nietzsche's lecture notebooks in one further respect. As he drifts away from his outline, his thoughts become more ambitious and less tidy. The digression on aesthetic questions mentioned above is a case in point. It is in these moments that another side of Nietzsche reveals itself, less the teacher than the writer, or perhaps just the dreamer. At one point in the middle of this segment on "Wirkung" ("impact"), a list of topics in staccato form appears suddenly and vertically on the page: "Die Gliederung der Tragödie. / Die Tetralogie / Die Bedeutung des Chors. / Religion des Aeschylus. / Die Rollenverteilung. / Das Theater. / Leben des Aeschylus" ("The Articulation of Tragedy. / The Tetralogy / The Meaning of the Chorus. / Religion of Aeschylus. / The Allotment of Roles. / The Theater. / Life of Aeschylus") (KGW II/2, 38). All pretense to coherence with the previous game-plan is gone here. And if we seem to be in the midst of a new outline, we are—only now it seems that we are reading the table of contents of a book in the making, as the next entry further suggests: "Einleitung: Versuch, den äschyleischen Kunststil, im Vergleich mit Soph. u. Eurip. nachzuweisen" ("Introduction: Attempt to demonstrate the Aeschylean style of art in comparison with Soph[ocles] and Eurip[ides]").

What appeared over the past few pages as section headings to a particularly fascinating interlude now have the feel of competing book titles that Nietzsche is trying on for size, as much for their look as for anything else ("Betrachtungen über den Künstlerischen Stil des Aischylos" ["Reflections on the Artistic Style of Aeschylus"], KGW II/2, 35; "Ueber die Choephoren des Äschylus" ["On the *Choephori* of Aeschylus"], KGW II/2, 36). This casting about, too, is typical of Nietzsche's notebooks.[7] The experimental titles may also include attempts to visualize the very name of Aeschylus, whose orthography wanders here and there, albeit in a way that is typical for German scholarship of the period. And then, suddenly, we remember that we are (perhaps) somewhere between 1869 and 1872, at a time when Nietzsche was brewing the broth that would eventually turn out as *The Birth of Tragedy*, and would simultaneously seal his fate as a classical scholar. In this interlude Nietzsche is plainly exploring the sensibilities of Aeschylus the artist and contrasting them in his mind with those of the two other great tragedians. He is groping after something like an Aeschylean "uncanny," a dramaturgy of gloom and terror—one that is manifestly unclassical (all this is in line, at least superficially, with *The Birth of Tragedy*).[8] Compare the following note:

On the *Choephori* of Aeschylus.

with the greatest theatrical effect.

1. The artistic problem of the middle position [in the trilogy]. Naïveté of its solution. No agony of conscience. Nothing Hamlet-like.
2. The figures and images. No individuals, only types, generic scenes.
3. Sequence of the scenes. The *uncanny* [is] firmly maintained, the gloomy, frightening tomb, the black dirge procession, nighttime, presentiment of death and revenge, dreams, φοβεῖται δέ τις, pointlessly so, intrigue. The drama is chthonic ὦ Ἑρμῆ χθ⟨όνιε⟩. The scenes rigorously symmetrical. The drama lacks perspective. Scene after scene is treated in the same way. *All the scenes are equally close and detailed.* [...] Orestes goes mad, the eery [unheimliche] large cloth as background. The cloth perhaps illuminated with *torches*.[9]

(The Soph[oclean] *Electra* is entirely matutinal) [...] (KGW II/2, 36)

Nietzsche's lectures from the time are filled with such intensely compressed moments, which make one want to go back over the rest to look for the clues to their existence in even the least promising stretches of text. And, as a rule, Nietzsche's career can be traced through the shape of his lecture notes. The notes begin in sober philological fashion, but then modulate quickly into envisioned publications, while becoming more imaginative and in places fantastical. The publications that result, by contrast, tend to emulate the tone of the initial classroom lectures: they may turn on provocative theses, but they are comparatively restrained and in their form utterly conventional. It is no wonder that the majority of Nietzsche's ideas never saw the light of day. His ideas went well beyond the generic constraints of the contemporary research format. His notebooks, the lecture notebooks included, were the place where he toyed with new imaginary possibilities. They show his mind at work as he is playing with, and not only within, the limits of accepted scholarly practice. To judge Nietzsche by his published scholarship alone would be to gain an impoverished impression of his mind at the time. But the reverse is true as well: the radical elements of his publications, which exist but are subdued, emerge clearly only against the background of his notebook experimentations. The question, put simply, is whether notebooks contain lecture notes or notes of another kind (for instance, diaries of a creative mind). The answer may be anything but simple.

A further problem not answered by the notes is how they were actually used in the classroom. For the reasons just mentioned, it might be hazardous to try to deduce too much about Nietzsche's teaching style from his notebooks. On the other hand, it would be wrong to deny any connection. Nietzsche frequently prefaces his lectures with large, imaginative invitations to his hearers. His notes sometimes pursue these perspectives (as in the case of the *Choephori*). It is hard to believe that Nietzsche denied himself or his students the pleasures of the intellectual chase in the classroom. But there is more. Nietzsche's flights of imagination are for the most part not into the Empyrean heights of the Classics. He was in ways a counter-classical thinker, or rather, and more simply, a counter-thinker, a lover of heterodoxy. He despised the mechanized assumptions of the professional scholar, and he aspired to a different kind of philology, what he called, long before Wilamowitz flung the epithet at him as an insult, a "philology of the future."[10] Without tracing out the contours of that outsize project here we can note that one of its elements, indeed one of the techniques at Nietzsche's disposal and used for opening up vistas onto the as yet invisible future or possible futures, was to scandalize his audience, to unsettle their expectations and in this way to bring them to think more critically about what they knew and the way they were supposed to know it—in a word, about their disciplinary formation. This is the devilish side of Nietzsche that occasionally makes itself heard in the *Nachlass* and in correspondence from the time, but that is everywhere to be felt once you scratch beneath the surface of his writings.

Thus, he could proudly write to Erwin Rohde, his closest friend and confidant, that in the spring of 1869 in his first semester at Basel he was "infecting" his pupils with "philosophy" (he was teaching Plato's *Phaedo* at the time). The same conspiratorial glee is evident in another letter, this time from June 7, 1871, where he discloses, "I am now giving my lecture, *Einleitung und Encyclopädie* [his "Introduction to

Classical Philology"], to the amazement of my audience, who can scarcely recognize themselves in the picture of the ideal philologist that I am sketching" (KSB 3, 197). Nietzsche clearly enjoyed shocking his students out of their complacency, whether by stretching the customary boundaries of philology to include philosophy (his habitual instinct), or by warning his students, in the same lecture series, that in order to be complete classicists what they first had to be was completely "modern"; that in order to understand antiquity they first had to acquaint themselves with the "great thinkers" of modern culture ("wahrhaft mit den modernen Größen verbunden"), by consuming heavy doses of Winckelmann, Lessing, Schiller, Goethe, and Kant (KGW II/3, 368), and in this way develop their receptive and aesthetic faculties (their "Schönheitstrieb," Ibid., 345); that they had, in other words, to cultivate anachronism, to become thoroughly familiar with a characteristically modern notion of "das Klassische" before being able to detect it in the ancients (classicism [Klassicität] is "the philosophical precondition of classical philology," Ibid.). Only so, only once they had learned to "feel the differences" between past and present (that is, had developed a sufficiently modern and sentimental "nostalgia" for the classical past), could they embark on the project of imaginative investment and immersion ("Hineinleben") in the ancient world (ibid., 368; cf. 345: "What a difficult task to prepare someone for the enjoyment, viz., the sentimental enjoyment, of antiquity!"). How anyone was supposed to do all of that without stumbling into a painful performative contradiction is unclear.[11] But what is clear is that these paradoxes were the daily bread of Nietzsche's thinking, which must have found its way into his teaching on more than one occasion.

The *Choephori* lectures again help establish this point and allow us to extrapolate some of what Nietzsche's procedure in the "Encyclopädie" course must have been like. In a short passage from these earlier notes Nietzsche actually scripts in his theatrical cues, in what appears to be an introductory segment to a lecture. The passage is worth citing *in toto*, so rare, informative, and unusual a glimpse into Nietzsche's teaching style in the classroom, whether real or imagined by himself, does it provide:[12]

> No one among us has seen the *Oresteia*; no one has heard it: an elaborate and backbreaking *guesswork* is required to understand things that would have been simple and easy [to follow] at the performance. Here goes one attempt to view things as they were in their *actuality*: I will tell you what I saw there. Naturally, much of this will be sheer fantasy. But we need to experience an *effect*; once we have that we can form an opinion about the artist. I want to sit in the theater not as an ancient but as a modern: my observations may well be pedantic; but at first I have to wonder at everything so as to comprehend it all afterward.
>
> I have a certain impression of the *Choephori* and this is what I want to describe. But what does it matter to us, you will say, what my impression is? Why don't I appeal to yours? Or to the work?—An impression is something rare. To attain it one has to add so much—which not everyone is able and willing to do.
>
> One shouldn't talk about poems, as Socrates says in the *Protagoras*. But I want to investigate for once what this *impulse* [*Trieb*; viz., to discuss poetry, especially Greek poetry] *is really worth*. Through one example [sc., the *Choephori*].

Result: you students will be proved right in the particulars [if you follow the standard approach and don't follow my approach]: but on the whole, it [sc., the standard approach] is an act of insolence. How little there is to know at the point where knowledge first starts to be of value! That cannot possibly be the goal of a science! Critique of conjectural criticism. (KGW II/2, 34–5)[13]

The lecture not only gives us a glimpse of Nietzsche's lecture style, it also shows a total coherence between his proposed "philology of the future" and whatever he wanted to put into practice.[14] However else we may describe it, Nietzsche's philology of the future is a self-doubting practice; it puts to the test the certainties of philological tradition and exacerbates, even plays upon, its inbred tradition of uncertainty. Historically, philology was first and foremost a Pyrrhonian exercise that lived on first and second-order doubts (doubts, and then doubts about doubts) concerning the authenticity of texts and of transmission and the validity of readings—so much so that philology can be called, without exaggeration, a crisis in "krisis" (to which Nietzsche responds with his "critique of criticism").

2. On rhythm and meter (1870–1)

The lectures and notebooks on rhythm and meter (1870–1) are founded on such a critique. The premise and conclusion of these rarely analyzed notes on the rhythm of the Greek language is the incommensurability of ancient and modern sensibilities to time. What the notebooks on rhythm purport to give is "a history of sensations," and especially of the sense of time. This history Nietzsche finds to be irrecuperable inasmuch as the modern sensibility to dynamic rhythm, based on accentual measures and the rhythmical ictus (*intensio vocis*), is constitutionally unfit to grasp the products of the ancient sense of time, which he argues are quantitative and proportional in their architectonics (and thus totally lacking the ictus as a marker of rhythm). Once again, Nietzsche is exploring the paradoxes of Classical Philology, and so his theory is as much a meta-critical one as it is a positive (albeit skeptical) contribution to the history of an ancient field. At stake in the background to the essays are theoretical reflections on temporality, history, and sensation, as well as the relation between force and force's limits. These inquiries flow directly into *The Birth of Tragedy*, into Nietzsche's general conceptions of historiographical and recuperative writing (evident most prominently in a text like the famous second essay of *Untimely Meditations*, "On the Uses and Disadvantages of History"), and eventually into the late doctrine of "the will to power." But they do so in unexpected ways.[15]

It was Nietzsche's original intention to include in *The Birth of Tragedy* a section devoted to rhythm (NF 1870, 6[18]; KSA 7, 136, under "*Griechische Heiterkeit*"; NF 1870/71, 7[176]–[178]; KSA 7, 209); in its place we find a few stray comments on rhythm (mainly in connection with Apollo), but also implicitly a wholesale and covert adaptation of Nietzsche's thesis from the lecture notes, which profoundly throws into doubt any straightforward reading of the later work (for instance, any reading which wishes to view the Dionysian as a valorized physiological or metaphysical condition, and not as an allegory for a dubious idealism retrojected from the present onto antiquity). This is hardly the only instance in which Nietzsche's early notes undermine the narrative premises of *The Birth of Tragedy*. To take up one example in this connection, a problem raised explicitly by the notes and *sub rosa* in *The Birth of Tragedy* is that of periodization, namely the historical characterization of Greek Dionysian rhythms. Although Nietzsche gives no absolute dates for the *incipit* of the Dionysian rhythms in the notes, he does date them in a relative way, and this is revealing. In the first notebook, he associates them with early cultic practices (KGW II/2, 112–13). In the final notebook, the same rhythms, notable for their exploitation of rhythmic changes and "dissonances in time-measures" (KGW II/2, 329), are more closely dated. They appear to be a later, and in any case post-quantitative, development in musical sensibility:

> The nature of ancient music must be reconstructed: the mimetic dance, ἁρμονία [viz., musical scales], ῥυθμός. Essential differences in so-called melody, in rhythm, and also in dancing, for the moderns. *Originally* (in citharodic music), *the note functions as a measure of time.* The nature of the *scales* needs to be discovered (acutest feeling for proportions of height [viz., tonal intervals][16]). Why could the Greeks deploy the quarter-tones? Harmony was not drawn into the realm of the symbolic for them. Establishment of the classical (antiken) symbolics. *The Dionysian innovations in tonality (Tonart), in rhythm (ἀλογία?).* (KGW II/2, 322; all emphasis, with the exception of "scales," is my own)

Dionysianism an "innovation" (Neuerung)? The chronology is elusive, or better yet, symbolic. Presumably, the cults mentioned earlier are archaic and post-Homeric, and yet the aesthetic system that the Dionysian "innovations" act against is patently quantitative and classical. For the same reason, the Dionysian innovations, said to be "in tonality," are likely to be just *of* tonality, as contrasted with the essentially temporal character of the classical note and its corresponding scales (Tonleitern), which, due to their peculiar restrictions, are not "tonal" in the modern or relatively more modern and "Dionysian" sense of the word. The Dionysian phenomenon emerges against the backdrop of the classical order of things, as its corruption.

That it does represent this very change, or its incipient moment, is corroborated by a passage from *The Birth of Tragedy* where Nietzsche comes at the problem once again. The correspondence, unexpected as it is, is astonishing. There, Nietzsche is concerned to underscore the innovative character of the Dionysian reveries, wherein one is reminded that "pain begets joy, that ecstasy may wring sounds of agony from us":

> The song and pantomime of such dually-minded revelers was something new and unheard-of in the Homeric-Greek world; and the Dionysian *music* in particular excited awe and terror. If music, as it would seem, had been known *previously* as an Apollonian art, it was so, strictly speaking, only as the wave beat of rhythm, whose formative power was developed for the representation of Apollonian states. The music of Apollo was Doric architectonics in tones, *but in tones that were merely suggestive*, such as those of the cithara. The very element which forms *the essence of Dionysian music* (and hence of music in general) is carefully excluded as

un-Apollonian—namely the emotional power of the *tone*, the uniform flow of the *melody*, and the utterly incomparable world of *harmony*. (BT 2; KSA 1, 33; trans. Kaufmann; all italics added, except for the first)

The parallels between the two accounts of change are remarkably close. Again, the innovations appear to take place in a post-Homeric but still-archaic Greek world, yet the aesthetic regime that is overturned is the Apollonian, classical, and (quite plainly) quantitative system of rhythmic proportions. And again, it is tonality, or vocality, that paves the way to change.[17] Stately proportions yield to dynamic, "pathological" movements. Temporally defined rhythm yields to "music" in a new and unheard-of sense of the word, connected now with melodic and harmonic structures. That sense is a thoroughly familiar one, at least to Nietzsche's contemporary world.[18]

From a musicological perspective, Dionysianism plainly appears to be a *post-classical* phenomenon, if not in historical time, then surely in tendency. Can Dionysianism possibly be associated with the decline of classical sensibilities, that is to say, with the advent of the *modern* sensibility, whether as its prelude or its harbinger? The notebooks on rhythm and *The Birth of Tragedy* itself suggest that it can. The progression described in both is towards music in a thoroughly and unmistakably modern sense. It captures the moment when "the other symbolic powers suddenly press forward impetuously, particularly those of music, *in rhythm, dynamics, and harmony*" ("Sodann wachsen die anderen symbolischen Kräfte, die der Musik, in Rhythmik, Dynamik und Harmonie, plötzlich ungestüm"; BT 2; KSA 1, 34; italics added; trans. Kaufmann, adapted). And these last, being the principal ingredients of the modern sensibility to time, are for Nietzsche thoroughly out of place in any account of Greek quantitative rhythmics, which represents the classical sense of time. Nietzsche knows very well the difference between "Greek music as compared with the infinitely richer music known and familiar to us" (BT 17; KSA 1, 110), which is to say, "the utterly incomparable world of harmony" (BT 2; KSA 1, 33). Hence, "the more we have resorted to modern music in order to understand [Greek] metrics, the further we *have estranged* ourselves from the reality of metrics in antiquity" (to Ritschl, December 30, 1870, KSB 3, 173; cf. KGW II/3, 399). Nietzsche's account of Dionysian music in *The Birth of Tragedy* is an anachronism, and self-advertisingly so. Surely the hope expressed in that work for a return *ad fontes* and to a musical spirit that could be reclaimed today as "ours" is overshadowed by the very sorts of impossibility that Nietzsche is demonstrating in his lectures on rhythm at the very moment he is composing his first book. Similar points are made in the "Encyclopedia of Philology," which contains further parallels to and further dramatic reversals of the narrative surface of *The Birth of Tragedy*, and to which we may now turn.

3. The "Encyclopedia of Philology" (1871/1873–4[?])

Although announced for the winter semester of 1873/4, official records confirming that the second lecture actually took place are lacking. What we have is a letter from November 7, 1873 to Gersdorff in which Nietzsche somewhat mysteriously writes,

"I'm reading my lectures on Plato and forgoing the other one [ich wälze das andere ab], which likewise has found takers [a sensitive point after the debacle of *The Birth of Tragedy*], in favor of my eyes," which were already starting to fail him. When we turn to Janz for a second opinion, we find that his results are both equivocal and inconsistent. In one summary table,[19] he concludes on the basis of Nietzsche's testimony, and in the confirming light of a letter from Gersdorff from May 29, 1874, that the second lecture never took place: "nicht abgehalten (trotz Teilnehmern)." In another table (KGW II/3, 203), he writes, "SS 1871; evtl. [possibly] WS 73/74." The editors of KGW II/3 follow the latter formulation, without comment (KGW II/3, 339). It is doubtful, in view of the letter to Gersdorff alone, that Nietzsche would have revised the lectures in 1873/4 even in the unlikely event that he repeated them. I take it that the notebook we have represents the original lecture, with annotations dating from the same semester.

Be that as it may, the "Encyclopedia of Classical Philology" (EkP) is a treasure-trove of learning and of what today appears to be Nietzschean heterodoxy. In fact, most of what Nietzsche presents is either a reproduction or an extrapolation of contemporary philology. He has merely seized on its own internal heterodoxies—its inner quirks, illogicalities, inconcinnities, circularities, and the like—and made these painfully manifest. One further example will help to bring the point home, and this will preoccupy us in the remainder of the present chapter.

In two intercalated pages from the "Encyclopedia" notes, Nietzsche details the genesis and transformations of the Greek gods from the archaic age down into the Hellenistic period and a little beyond. The text, which has never before been translated into English, deserves to be quoted in full and then commented upon in some detail. The text is printed as a numbered footnote in KGW II/3 (414–16, n. 37), but this represents a grossly misleading editorial decision. The manuscript of the lectures in fact contains no numbered notes and no footnotes. In question are rather annotations written onto the blank sides of a notebook (not marginally, "auf dem Rand," as the editors of GA state; see GA 19, 410–11). Just what the status of these annotations is meant to be and when they were added is unclear: they may be afterthoughts, clarifications in gloss-like form, cues for oral delivery, or genuine intercalations written after the fact. In the minority of cases they have a kind of footnoting function, which is to say, that of providing bibliographical references (but such references can appear in the "body" of the text as well). To judge from the handwriting and the ink, it appears that the annotations are probably contemporary with the lecture notes, but a more experienced eye than mine would be needed to confirm this. The editorial apparatus of KGW, thin as it is, gives no indication that any of this is a problem. It obviously is. But the problem will make little difference to us in what follows, in which I will treat the annotations as integral elements of Nietzsche's lecture text and as supplementing or spelling out rather than changing its internal logic.

The second of the two addenda is remarkable in another respect. By far the longest and most complex addition to the lectures (it is a tightly structured lecture in miniature), it miraculously takes up the two interleaved sides and then a little under a third of a third side which were left free as Nietzsche entered his running text into the notebook. The third side begins after the end of the table with five items in it. How Nietzsche managed to calculate this intercalation and fit in advance, with no signs of cramming or compression, is immensely puzzling! Unlike all other addenda to the text, which as I stated earlier probably stems from the time of the lecture's delivery, this one is in an untidy hand, as if written in haste or out of excitement. Nonetheless it is relatively free of corrections, even more so than many of the other pages of the lecture notes, as though it were copied out whole from another set of pages in draft and inserted into the blank pages of the notebook. Whatever the explanation, these two-and-a-third ms. pages contain one of the more fascinating bits of ratiocination and narrative in Nietzsche's philological notebooks. They also happen to be seminal in content.

Let's start with some of the larger contours of this narrative and then work our way into the finer details. The overall pattern charted out by Nietzsche is a familiar one from a nineteenth-century perspective, being largely (and surprisingly) Hegelian, as a quick comparison with Hegel's *Lectures on Aesthetics* would confirm, the logic, language and structure of which Nietzsche takes over wholesale. Myths pass through three stages of ideation: "it is the way from the sublime to the beautiful and then to the symbolic," which is to say, to allegory (KGW II/3, 415n. 37). The picture, so viewed, is one of decline. At the same time, the process brings with it, in the age of Greek tragedy, the evolution of justice into an abstract ethical ideal as well as a waning belief in myth and a rehabilitation of previous, darker superstitions ("the blinding daemonic force of ruin, a residue of the belief in Titanic divinity," ibid.). The eclipsing of the classical moment and the gradual assertion of the postclassical in the Hellenistic age is likewise familiar territory and an inherited trope. The same cliché governs the narrative pattern of *The Birth of Tragedy*. What the lecture on mythology adds to our picture of Nietzsche is an idea of just how well informed he was in this inherited cliché. Indeed, one of the very great surprises of the lecture, and one that I myself previously overlooked in my own earlier treatment of this same material, is the degree to which Nietzsche's picture of antiquity was informed by J. G. Droysen, the great Prussian historian of the Hellenistic age (1808–84), who taught first at Kiel and later at Jena and Berlin. Droysen was not merely the great historian of the Hellenistic era. He was also the first to make it into a discrete and fully characterized historical entity (he dubbed it "Hellenismus," or "Hellenism") and to insert it into modern consciousness with his monumental work in three volumes, *Geschichte des Hellenismus* (1836–43). Droysen's concept swept the field: it had no competitors and it towered above all others, even though it would take a good half-century or more before the Hellenistic era finally came to gain a modicum of respect as a valid research field in classics (without ever fully displacing the classical era).[20] It only stands to reason that Nietzsche would have known about Droysen. In point of fact, Droysen's impress is to be felt both here in the lectures on "The Encyclopedia of Philology" and in *The Birth of Tragedy*, though his presence in Nietzsche has, to my knowledge, gone undetected in the literature until now.[21] A brief account of "Hellenism" as Droysen understands this will be essential.[22]

4. J. G. Droysen's *Geschichte des Hellenismus* (1836–43)

Droysen's underlying conception is both Hegelian and Christianizing. Mapping Hellenism onto a concept of universal history that was inherited from Herder and others, Droysen sees in Hellenism a paradoxical self-overcoming of pagan antiquity. Classical Greece prepared the ground for Alexander, who unified the disparate Greek tribes, drowning as they were in their own particularism, into a universal imperial power (Macht) under one umbrella language, culture, and political system, very much an ancient Napoleon. Henceforth Greece was "raised above the confines of the local and familiar (der Heimatlichkeit) into a universal power encompassing the world" (Droysen [1836–43] 1998, III, 20).[23] A fusion of East and West occurred, albeit under the auspices of the Greek West; syncretism in religion paralleled the blending together of cultures and races; and a new era was heralded: "The name of Alexander signals the end of one world epoch, and the beginning of a new one" (Ibid., I, 1). This new world, a "neue Zeit," was not merely "the modern age of pagan antiquity" (ibid., III, xvii; III, xxii). It was the dawn of the *modern* world, the current *Neuzeit*.[24] Droysen's last point about the modernity of postclassical antiquity would prove influential, from Nietzsche to the Greek historian Eduard Meyer in 1895 (the Hellenistic era "was in essence completely modern")[25] to Heidegger in 1942/3 ("[what] we call the modern age [...] is founded on the event of the Romanizing of Greece," which is to say, the move beyond the "classical" era of Greece),[26] but the analogy was basic to modern philology from the very start. F. A. Wolf (1759–1824), for example, recognized in the Hellenistic scholars the modern philologist's, and his own, next of kin. And the same analogy is already found in Wolf's teacher, C. G. Heyne 1785 [1763], in his own study of the age of the Ptolemies.[27]

Usually understood as having "invented," historiographically, the decidedly unclassical and much spurned Hellenistic period,[28] Droysen was in fact rewriting the mission of the classical ideal. The age of Alexander was a continuation by other means of the Athenian revolution, which had launched Hellenism: "thoughts of the new [sic., modern] age (der neuen Zeit) spread everywhere, radiating out [from Athens] irresistibly; democracy, enlightenment, the doctrine of critique all begin to dominate Hellenic life," much like the French Revolution, but by the same token eating away at the foundations of traditional life (Ibid., I, 9). Polis-based citizenship gave over to cosmopolitanism and a blending of races (Völkermischung). Religious beliefs weakened, and then found a higher, more abstract and univer-salizing realization. As with races, so with divinities: "nothing had greater effect in this connection than that curious appearance of the blending of divinities (Göttermischung), of theocrasy, in which all the peoples of the Hellenistic era had a share in the next few centuries" (Ibid., I, 443; cf. I, 444–5). Political structures went the same way, converging now in a single sovereign, a Hellenized barbarian. The result was inevitable:

> If destroying paganism was the highest task of the ancient world, just so did Greek culture [or: "Greek antiquity"] (Griechentum) first dig the ground out from under its own feet, the very ground in which it took root, in order next, having colonized

the barbarians through the actions of enlightening, fermenting, and undermining, to bring about the very same thing over there. (Ibid., III, 18)

Hellenism is the spirit of Greece serving a new global mission.

One consequence of Droysen's rehabilitation of Hellenism is that the concept became a chiffre for a historical process, encompassing both Greekness *and* its "Aufhebung" (destruction *and* sublimation), and pointing straight to the Christian and Prussian present (Ibid., III, 424). In Droysen's wake, scholars even now are disputing the word *Hellenism*, uncertain as to its meaning, its coherence, and its reach in space and time.[29] No less significantly, Droysen's vision of Hellenism as a "mirror of the present,"[30] his projection of the (Prussian) present onto the antique past, helped to codify and legitimize a tendency that was in evidence before him but which now became more or less explicit. It may be that the past can be understood in no other way. The extent of this identification can, however, be unconscious, or simply disavowed.

5. Nietzsche and Droysen: The logic of anachronism

Taking stock, we can see several points of intersection with Nietzsche's account. Though Nietzsche does not avail himself of the term "Hellenismus" either in the "Encyclopedia" lecture or in *The Birth of Tragedy* as he does elsewhere. In every other respect Droysen's complex picture of Greece is exactly what he has in mind. The trend from early multiplicity to later unification is reflected in both accounts, above all in politics and in theology. The political and religious mood captured by both is identical, as are the causal connections they draw: dashed from the proud achievements of the fifth century, a defeated, bowed Greece declined—literally plummeted—into a higher unity driven by a higher, virtual transcendental need, or rather a need *for* a transcendental unity.

It was the work of the Hellenistic centuries to bring about a higher and truer unification of the elements [of religion], and to develop the feeling of finiteness and impotence, the need for repentance and consolation, the power of the deepest humility and exaltation to the point of discovering a sense of freedom in God and of being God's children. These were the centuries of the world and the heart made godless, of the deepest sense of loss and desolation, and of the ever-louder call for salvation. (Ibid., I, 444–5)

For Droysen, this passage into "Hellenism" and away from the classical is a transition into the modern world. It is, accordingly, fraught with ambivalence. To begin with, the idea of the classical has problems of its own, being a utopian projection of modern aspirations and therefore a betrayal of the ancient historical realities (more on this below). On the other hand, the Hellenistic age, the age of Alexander, being a maturation of earlier tendencies and their consolidation on a higher level—marked by greater conceptual and organizational abstraction—are both a sign of progress rather than one of decline (despite what the contemporary models of classical history said), and an approximation to the contemporary present, never an unambivalent prospect. For despite everything, from Humboldt to Nietzsche and beyond, there was only one prospect that was worse than the loss of an ideal antiquity: that of its *all-too-proximate recovery*, its too-immediate identification with the anxiety-ridden present-day. Progress brought with it the simultaneous specter of decline: to affirm an analogy between the two modernities was to risk reaffirming current modernity's own decrepitude (Verfall; Ibid., III, xvii). An ameliorating factor for Droysen would have been that Christianity is the natural outgrowth of the modernizing tendencies of antiquity. In fact, Christianity seems to be nothing less than the natural *fruit* of classical antiquity, its hidden "telos." Such a view was a controlling narrative in any number of accounts of antiquity from the Enlightenment era onward, of which Foucault's *History of Sexuality* merely represents the latest expression.[31]

Nietzsche's account shares all of these traits, while adding others, as we shall see. He would have been readily drawn to Droysen's account for one obvious reason: Droysen's *Geschichte des Hellenismus* was in fact an antidote to the exclusive adoration of the high classical fifth-century Greece. Droysen did not disguise his disdain for the classical ideal. About his own study, he ruefully wrote,

> I have to be prepared to be scolded for my views by the philologists too—I mean by the true enthusiasts, by those who never tire of decking out classical antiquity, conceived as a lost paradise of all that was most beautiful and noble, with the most charming images of the imagination, with utopic ideals of presumptive marvel. Already quite a few of these were annoyed with me on prior occasions if I failed to join Demosthenes blindly and patriotically in his hatreds, or if I saw more of the rogue in Aristophanes than the preacher of virtue. Far be it from me to belittle the splendor of classical antiquity! But here, as so often, what Lichtenberg has to say about the millipede is apt, namely that it has only fourteen feet. (Ibid., III, xiii = "Privatvorrede" [= Foreword to the 1st edn.])[32]

Later on in the same work, Droysen takes up a firm position against the classical ideal erected in the name of pedagogy and without regard for historical accuracy:

> The artistic splendor of ancient Greece is rightly an object of marvel. But the aesthetic and even pedagogical standpoint has driven the study of antiquity (die Altertumswissenschaft) from its historical ground. One is accustomed to see the classical era only in the sun-lit clarity of its most idealized perspectives, rather than conceiving it in its objective realities. The nobility of the Sophoclean hero and the beauty of perfected divinities are made into the prototypes for the kinds of people one imagines to have populated ancient Greece. Everything that is most noble and beautiful is projected and grafted onto (übertragt man) this "golden age of the human race"; every predicate of true and false veneration is lavished on it. Doubt and sober inspection are discouraged as a profanation and are confronted with a kind of moral indignation: anything that distracts from doting on the charming trickery of one's own imagination is spurned. [...] So utopic and unhistorical is one's view of ancient [sc., classical] Greece [...] that one is completely unable to grasp its connection with Hellenism. (Ibid., III, 414–15)

Droysen was right, but only partly so. Nietzsche would heartily agree with Droysen's attack on the liberal humanism of German classicism, but he would also turn Droysen somewhat on his head. Classicism in Nietzsche's view turns out to be not a product of the modern mind, but an inheritance of the Alexandrian age, which looked back to classical Athens with a self-blinding nostalgia, as the following notebook entry from 1869–70, written in Nietzsche's own characteristically vituperative style, makes abundantly clear:

> The "Hellenic" since Winckelmann: an intense superficialization [or "flattening," Verflachung]. Then [came] the Christian-German conceit that one was completely beyond it [sc., antiquity in its classical form]. The age of Heraclitus, Empedocles, etc. was unknown. One had the image of [Greece as seen through] Roman-universal Hellenism, Alexandrianism. Beauty and superficiality (Flachheit) in league, indeed necessary! Scandalous theory! Judaea! (NF 1869/70, 3[76]; KSA 7, 81)

Nietzsche's notebook entry, which predates his "Encyclopedia" lectures by a couple of years, indicates how thoroughly he has imbibed Droysen's concept of Hellenism, but also how he was learning to adapt it to his own purposes.

There are palpable differences between their two outlooks. Where Droysen appears to take classicism as an import from contemporary modernity ("übertragt man"), Nietzsche follows through with Droysen's logical identification of the two modernities, ancient (Hellenism) and modern (post-Goethe, et al.), and acknowledges what Droysen also surely knows but does not dwell on, namely that classicism was very much a product of ancient Alexandrianism: it was very much an "image of [Greece as seen through] Roman-universal Hellenism, Alexandrianism." Where Droysen strategically validates the Hellenistic era so as to displace the classical ideal, Nietzsche normally goes the other way, validating (at least to all appearances) the preclassical era, the age of the pre-Socratics and the lyric poets, of Heraclitus, Pindar, and Aeschylus, to the same effect—that is, in order to demystify and demythologize, and to rehistoricize, the image of "the classical" (to reconceive it "in its objective realities"). But in the current lecture on mythology, Nietzsche pursues a different course altogether. Here, he gives no sign that an earlier redemptive element is to be found in Greek culture. Instead, the pattern he draws moves forward and down its inexorable course of unification, consolidation, abstraction, intensified and deepened spirituality (mysteries and cults), but also decline. What is more, and this *is* typical of all of Nietzsche's narratives of antiquity, the actual seeds of these tendencies are already detectable in the earliest phases of Greek culture. Theocrasy is deeply rooted in Greek religion: "all individual gods were merely so many transitory manifestations of the One, of the divine power that permeates Nature [...]. The accommodation and blending together of cults is as old as history" (KGW II/2, 414–15). And, significantly, all of the divine transformations outlined in the lecture take place under the aegis of Dionysus and Dionysianism. Everything begins there ("In the Dionysian myths all gods were mortal," Ibid., 414), and the chain culminates there as well: "With Alexander, this impulse sets in once again: it is characterized by an expansion in the worship of Dionysus" (Ibid., 416–17). Finally, to crown everything, Dionysus turns out to be a harbinger of Christ, who is merely most recent transformation of the Greek God, his final cultic identity: "Thus, not only is the general dissolution of paganism favorable to Christianity; one can also see countless approximations and pavings of the way [sc., leading to Christianity]" (Ibid., 417–18). (Cf. also NF 1870, 6[14]; KSA 7, 134: "Alexandrianism of knowledge, the movement towards India. Wild outbreak of the Dionysian." Alexander literally drove Greece towards India, and it is from the East that Dionysus originates, as we are reminded in BT 1; KSA 1, 29.[33])

The focus on Dionysus here should come as no surprise given the timing of the lecture, which in its first delivery coincided with the composition of *The Birth of Tragedy*. What is surprising, however, is the role that is being awarded to the god of ecstatic self-dissolution and intoxicating self-oblivion. Until, that is, one recognizes how Dionysus even in *The Birth of Tragedy* is consistent with the traits that this divinity enjoys in Droysen's *Geschichte* and in Nietzsche's contemporary lecture. In *The Birth of Tragedy*, Dionysus is associated with "a longing anticipation of a metaphysical world" (BT 10; KSA 1, 74) and a Beyond ("Jenseits", 7; KSA 1, 57). "The eternal phenomenon of Dionysian art [...] gives expression to the will in its omnipotence, as it were, behind the *principium individuationis*, the eternal life beyond all phenomena and despite annihilation" (16; KSA 1, 108). The language may be Schopenhauerian and Kantian, but we should not be misled by this. At the close of section 12, we read how after Socrates "put to flight the powerful god," Dionysus "sought refuge in the depths of the sea, namely the mystical flood of a secret cult which gradually covered the earth" (KSA 1, 88). The "secret cult" named here is none other than Christianity itself. Nietzsche can scarcely be endorsing this prospect. And parallels in other notes confirm that this direction is precisely what he is envisioning:

> The development of logic unleashed this [sc., "the impulse to truth and wisdom," which had been "reconciled" and thus quenched in the tragic worldview] and forced the creation of the *mystical* worldview. The great institutions decline, the states and religions, etc. [...]. Absolute music and absolute mysticism develop in tandem. As Greek enlightenment becomes increasingly universal, the old gods take on a *ghostly* character. (NF 1870/71, 5[110]; KSA 7, 123)

Two entries later we read: "*Continuation of the Birth*" (NF 5[112]; KSA 1, 123). Similarly, "With the [rise of the] oriental-Christian movement, *the old Dionysianism* inundated the world, and all the work of Hellenism seemed in vain. A *deeper* worldview, an inartistic one, established itself" (NF 5[94]; KSA 7, 184; emphasis added). Here, Nietzsche is using Droysen's term *Hellenism* to designate the failed essence of Greekness rather than the historical period of Alexander and his Ptolemaic successors. If the picture is one of modernity gone awry, as it assuredly is (*Alexandrianism* and *modernity* are used synonymously in *The Birth of Tragedy*), then it is also decidedly a despairing portrait of historical processes. Nor would Nietzsche veer from this portrait. In one of his last works, the *Antichrist*, we read how "Christianity [was] the formula for outbidding all the subterranean cults, those of Osiris, of the Great Mother, of Mithras for example—*and* for summing them up" (A 58; KSA 6, 247). (A contemporary note adds to the list "Dionysus"; NF 1887/88, 11[295]; *KSA* 13, 116.) A few sentences earlier in the same passage from *Antichrist*, Nietzsche plainly makes the identification we have been tracing: "[Epicurus] opposed the subterranean cults, the whole of *latent Christianity*" (Ibid.; emphasis added).

Wilamowitz likewise found the implications of *The Birth of Tragedy* too "vaguely pessimistic" for his tastes.[34] He would attempt to vitiate Nietzsche's vision of the secret Dionysian mysteries for being anachronistic and romanticizing: they smacked too much of the later, degenerative developments of the Hellenistic age and beyond, with "all their nonsense about mystical vapors, their crude syncretism," not to mention their affinity with the glazed visions of "Creuzer" and "Schopenhauer."[35] This, of course, does nothing to diminish the force of Nietzsche's critique, insofar as the present is directly continuous with the postclassical past. In other words, Nietzsche has put his finger on a neuralgic issue of classicism. Wilamowitz's point, moreover, is obliquely acknowledged already in *The Birth of Tragedy*. Above, we saw how Nietzsche applied the epithet "degenerate" to the underground mysteries of Dionysus. Soon after he adds: "the Dionysian worldview [...] lives on in the mysteries and, in its strangest metamorphoses and debasements, does not cease to attract serious natures. Will it not some day rise once again out of its mystic depths [...]?" (BT 17; KSA 1, 110–11). Exponents of Nietzsche's Dionysianism overlook these ironies at their peril.

While the correspondences with the lecture notes are obvious, we should not be deluded by this last false promise, which is characteristic of *The Birth of Tragedy* as a whole. And while Nietzsche does not avail himself of the term *Hellenism* in that work, he does use its synonym frequently in the later chapters (BT 17–23): *Alexandrian*. A brief consideration of its meaning is in order.

With "Alexandrianism" in *The Birth of Tragedy* Nietzsche pursues Droysen's logical identification of the two modernities, ancient (Hellenism) and modern, only he does so by radically completing that logic and collapsing the two entities into one, or rather into a single historical continuum: "Alexandrian culture" *just is* modernity, and it is "our" modernity ("our Alexandrian culture"; BT 18; KSA 1, 116). It extends forward to Rome in antiquity and then to "the reawakening of Alexandrian-Roman antiquity in the fifteenth century" with Renaissance classicism (BT 23; KSA 1, 148). And it continues without rupture into contemporary modernity (hence, "opera is based on the same principles as our Alexandrian culture"; BT 19; KSA 1, 123). Nor is this the end of Nietzsche's deformation of Droysen's logic, or rather his perfection of the inner logic of Droysen's Hellenism. Alexandrianism is backdated by Nietzsche to the first appearance of Socrates and of Socratism in Greek culture. Attached to features like "blissfulness" or "cheerfulness" (Heiterkeit—"Alexandrian cheerfulness," BT 17; KSA 1, 115; 19; KSA 1, 125–8), rationality, theory, bookishness, un-Dionysian spirit, the "Alexandrian man" (BT 18; KSA 1, 120) is "the Socratic man" (BT 20; KSA 1, 132), or rather a hyphenated creature: "Socratic-Alexandrian" (cf. BT 18; KSA 1, 116), thoroughly modern, no longer ancient, no longer even truly *Greek*, but merely an aberration and abomination of Greekness.

Grafting his own logic of modernity onto Droysen's, Nietzsche produces an uncomfortable paradox that undoes the foundations of contemporary philology, which is premised on the assumption that as a modern science it takes as its object a distinctly knowable "antiquity." He is right to stress that *if* modernity begins with the decline of the classical ideal, then it most surely antedates Hellenism in Droysen's narrow sense of the term: Alexandrianism so conceived does begin with the historic life of Socrates and the age of Euripides. But if so, if *Socratism-Alexandrianism* signifies the onset of this decline, then Nietzsche also knows that this decline was never real but only ever imaginary, and that Greece was trapped in a myth of decline from its first beginnings.[36] In that case, it begins to look as if Alexandrianism is the inescapable condition of antiquity, and that Greece was always, so to speak, on the verge of becoming modern. With the very boundaries of historical periods at stake here, both for Droysen and for Nietzsche, at issue is the most fundamental boundary of all: where and how to draw the line between antiquity and modernity. Another way of approaching the problem is to trace not the decline of antiquity in some pristine form (be it archaic or classical), but its imposition, by asking the question: When does Greece (or antiquity) become recognizably a modern myth, whether in the form of a classical ideal or as its Romanticizing (anti-classical) Dionysian alternatives? Either way, the logic of the two modernities reveals the more troubling question of the temporal logic of historical understanding, the role of history and—or rather *as*—cultural myth ("for it is the fate of every myth to creep by degrees into the narrow limits of some alleged historical reality," and "without myth every culture loses the healthy natural power of its creativity: only a horizon defined by myths completes and unifies a whole cultural movement," BT 10; KSA 1, 74; BT 23; KSA 1, 145), and the place of anachronism in all of this.

Where for Droysen the role of anachronism was merely suggested by analogy between the two modernities (and this had been the operational premise of German philology since its first generation, for instance in F. A. Wolf), in Nietzsche's case the anachronism is fully foregrounded. Hence the absurd-sounding injunctions in the "Encyclopedia" lectures that his pupils should study Winckelmann, Lessing, Schiller, Goethe, and Kant, cultivate anachronism, in other words become fully *modern* in order to be able to approach antiquity with any degree of familiarity: the point was simply that to approach antiquity *in its modernity* one first had to adopt a modern view of antiquity. And hence, too, his unabashed claim to his lecture students in the *Choephori* seminar that "I want to sit in the theater not as an ancient but as a modern" (KGW II/2, 34). And the same holds for his contemporary studies, contained in his notebooks, in conjectural criticism, his reflections on philological method, and even his more general reflections on natural science, on which both of these were based: "materialism"—Nietzsche's subject here, but it could be any natural posit—"is an idea that facilitates natural science, all of whose results still contain truth for us, albeit no absolute truth. It is after all *our* world, in the production of which we are always actively involved" ("The Preplatonic Philosophers," KGW II/4, 339–40; emphasis added).

These are examples of what might be called *methodological* anachronism. Their logic is further palpable in the narrative logic of rebirth and the structures of desire—the longing for a recovered lost antiquity—that govern the teleologies of *The Birth of Tragedy*, as in the following from the end of section 19, where Nietzsche is announcing, triumphantly, the purported goal of his project, once again in terms of Droysen's analysis. Gazing back on the distant shoals of time, we, as it were, pass through the chief epochs of the Hellenic genius, analogically in *reverse* order, and seem now, for instance, to be passing backward from the Alexandrian age to the period of tragedy. At the same time we have the feeling that the birth of a tragic age simply means *a return to itself of the German spirit, a blessed self-rediscovery.* (KSA 1, 128; second emphasis added)

The last words are significantly double-edged, for instead of pointing to a hopeful resolution of a "Dionysian" union of German and Hellenic spirits, they signal, rather, a more disastrous conclusion—namely, the anachronistic and (in Droysen's terms) "unhistorical" imposition of German values on an unsuspecting Hellenic mythical substrate, a tyranny of Germany over Greece, in other words. The same note of danger is sounded in another later passage:

Yet we were comforted by indications that nevertheless in some inaccessible abyss the German spirit still rests and dreams, undestroyed, in glorious health, profundity and Dionysian strength, like a knight sunk in slumber; and from this abyss the Dionysian song rises to our ears to let us know that *this German knight is still dreaming his primordial Dionysian myth in blissfully serious visions.* Let no one believe that the German spirit has forever lost its *mythical* home when it can still understand so plainly the voices of the birds that tell of that home. Some day it will find itself awake in all the morning freshness following a tremendous sleep: then it will slay dragons, destroy vicious dwarfs, wake Brünnhilde—and even Wotan's spear will not be able to stop this course! (BT 24; KSA 1, 154; emphasis added)

One is reminded of the warnings from *Beyond Good and Evil* about the seductions of metaphysics:

To translate man back into nature; to become master over the many vain and overly enthusiastic interpretations and connotations that have so far been scrawled and painted over that eternal basic text of *homo natura*; to see to it that man henceforth stands before man as even today, hardened in the discipline of science, he stands before the *rest* of nature, with intrepid Oedipus eyes and sealed Odysseus ears, deaf to the siren songs of old metaphysical bird catchers who have been piping at him all too long, "you are more, you are higher, you are of a different origin!"—that may be a strange and insane task, but it is a *task*—who would deny that? (BGE 230; KSA 5, 169; trans. Kaufmann)

The myth, the dream, of returning to natural origins with the hope that of regaining one's destined and "higher origin" is a metaphysical trap—this was the lesson of *The Birth of Tragedy* too. Alas, the seductions of Greek metaphysics and of the myth of Greece itself have proved for the most part too powerful and alluring, and Nietzsche's myth of a return, not to antiquity but to the offspring of modernity, the antiquity born of modern illusions, has continued to win believers rather than critical audiences.

A final warning comes from the startling admission in the "Encyclopedia" lecture that "The divine world of beauty *produces* [or "engenders," (erzeugt)] the chthonic divinities [viz., the "horrible" world of "Hades, Persephone, Demeter, Hermes, Hecate, and the Erinyes" and "then Dionysus"] as its own supplement [Ergänzung]" (KGW

II/3, 415n. 37). Here we find that the dark chthonic divinities have been invented (created as an aesthetic product) by the brighter Olympian world, that the mysteries and a realm beyond ("*Jenseits*"), not to mention ecstatic orgies (initially absent from the scene)—in short, the Dionysian godhead—was invented out of an Apollonian framework. While at first sight this appears to invert the narrative of *The Birth of Tragedy*, a closer reading in fact bears it out: Dionysus is the aesthetic creation of Apollo, of appearances, of classicism, of Winckelmannian and Goethian aesthetics, and of modern German fantasies about ancient Greece. The entire Romantic conceit of Dionysianism is nothing more than this fantastic construction (or myth) of the modern German mind, and Nietzsche is openly advertising the fact.[37] Of course, *both* the Apollonian and the Dionysian are at bottom anachronistic touches in Nietzsche's portrait of antiquity, whereby Apollo is (say) the illusion of undisturbed immediacy, and Dionysus is the disguised trace that a modern presence has touched the ancient scene. But with this point reached, what Nietzsche leaves us with is the prospect of a Greece *untouched* by anachronistic visitation, unattended by the modernizing conceptions of either divinity—of an antiquity unadorned by either Apollo or Dionysus, and equivalent in ways to "the eternal basic text of *homo natura*." And that may prove to be the most lonely and intolerable prospect of all.

Notes

1   For details, Porter 2000c; Porter 2000b. For recent scholarship on Nietzsche's philology, see Cancik 2000; Müller 2005; Benne 2005.
2   On the Laertiana, see the reprint of Barnes 1986 in this volume.
3   The new critical edition is replacing the versions of the notes published in earlier editions, which are less authoritative and often incomplete.
4   Not represented in the modern editions of his notes are the courses he gave on an impressive range of topics, primarily in Greek literature (e.g. on Homer's *Iliad* books 9, 12, 13 (part), 18, Hesiod's *Works and Days*, Aeschylus' *Eumenides* and *Prometheus*, Sophocles' *Oedipus Rex* and *Electra*, Euripides' *Alcestis*, *Medea*, and *Bacchae*, Thucydides, Plato's *Apology*, *Gorgias*, *Protagoras*, *Symposium*, *Statesman*, and *Phaedo*, Xenophon, Isocrates, Demosthenes, Lucian, Plutarch, Platonic and Socratic "Lives," the "Life" of Sophocles, Cicero's *Academica*, Quintilian, and so on. (See Janz 1974 for details). Presumably, these notebooks have been lost.
5   KGW II/2, 1–104. The title in KGW is given as "Prolegomena zu den Choephoren des Aeschylus." Presumably, this stems from Nietzsche's notebook (here, as elsewhere, my experience of the archived materials is limited to a few cases, and this is not one of them); the title is in any case quasi-confirmed by the opening sentence of the notebook. Yet the course title in the official Basel record for 1869 (as given by Janz 1974) reads "Vorl. Aeschylos *Choephoren*," while the Pädagogium (WS 1870) reads "Literarhistorische Übersicht zum griechischen Drama an Beispielen: Aeschylos *Agamemnon* und *Choephoren*; Sophokles *Elektra*; Euripides *Bacchen* und *Medea*." The 1874 SS version taught at the university may have been a seminar or lecture (no distinction is made in the record); the courses from 1877/78 (WS) and 1878 (SS) bear the same title as the 1869 lecture course, but are now announced

as being in "seminar" form. How the same set of notes could serve these diverse contexts is anything but clear, which takes us some way towards understanding why Nietzsche's lecture notes are as chaotic as they often are, as the editors also observe (KGW II/1, vii), but no closer to understanding the genesis of these materials.

6   "Für uns muß das Ziel sein, den Standpunkt der Alexandriner wieder zu gewinnen" ("For us the goal has to be reconstructing the vantage-point of the Alexandrians." KGW II/2, 29)—this, in line with his revival of Wolfian philology, as announced in his inaugural lecture on Homer (1869) and visibly put to work elsewhere. Nietzsche will break with this procedure in a few pages, however (see below).

7   Cf. KGW II/3, 323 and 331, where in the midst of a contemplated book entitled "Rhythmische Untersuchungen von Friedrich Nietzsche" we find a number of alternative plans and titles sketched out. This obsession with titles and outlines continued throughout his life, and the subject would be worth a study of its own.

8   "Das *Unheimliche,*" KGW II/2, 36; emphasis in original. Cf. KGW II/2, 38 (on Aeschylus' "life" and "style"): "overall tone (Gesamtcolorit): uncanny"; also Ibid., 35; and cf. BT 9–10 on the deeper and darker metaphysical attractions that lurk in the background of Aeschylean drama, "the astounding depth of [...] terror" (it is Titanic, anti-Olympian, and literally chthonic: Tartarean), that not even Aeschylus' interpretation of Greek myth can fully "exhaust" (BT 9; KSA 1, 68). A closer reading of BT would want to query the supposed "anti-classicism" of Nietzsche in this work and elsewhere, for starters by querying its premise—namely, its simplification of the phenomenon of "classicism" itself. On the idea of the classical, see Porter 2006b.

9   Note Nietzsche's attempt to visualize the scenography of the play, almost like a stage director.

10   Letter of June 2, 1868 to Paul Deussen, where the phrase is used with reference to Jacob Bernays, "the most brilliant representative of a philology of the future [einer Philologie der Zukunft] (i.e. the next generation after Ritschl, Haupt, Lehrs, Bergk, Mommsen, etc.)" (KSB 2, 284). The allusion must surely be to Bernays' view of Greek tragic catharsis (Bernays [1857] 1970), not to the person, whom Nietzsche grew to despise around this same time (Ibid., 287; 322). Looking at Bernays' work, one can see why Nietzsche would have embraced it, as he did in his *Birth of Tragedy,* and as Bernays later complained (see to Rohde, December 7, 1872; KSB 4, 97). See Porter 2000b, 15 for a translation of the relevant portion of this letter; and Porter 2014 for an analysis of Bernays' essay (with a partial translation, its most proto-Nietzschean section).

11   Cf. NF 14[26], 1871/72; KSA 7, 385): "*Die Grundlagen der neuen Bildung.*[:] Nicht historisch, sondern hineinleben" ("*The foundations of the new pedagogy.*[:] [Approach antiquity] not historically, but rather [by] immersing oneself [in it]").

12   There are, to be sure, reports by his former students (see Gutzwiller 1951 and Gilman [ed.] 1981), but these, produced retrospectively and usually after his psychic collapse, must be used with care.

13   The brackets represent my best guess as to Nietzsche's meaning. The alternatives ("[if you do follow my approach] ... [my approach]") seem less likely given the sequel ("How little there is to know [...]!," etc.), but are equally plausible when taken independently of the sequel.

14   Note how Nietzsche has contravened his own declared purpose, which was to reconstruct tragedy from the Alexandrians' perspective (see n. 6 above). But the approximation of tragedy's first audience is written into the problem of textual criticism from the start. Cf. ibid., 30, where the aim of conjectural criticism,

Nietzsche writes, is "to *establish* what is *corrupt*, unintelligible, ungrammatical, unmetrical, illogical, unaesthetic," and to "*cure the damage.*" All this necessarily entails a "subjective element": "to see the possibilities is a matter of an imagination that is soaked in the language and usages of the poet, in his intuitions."

15 For a fuller elaboration, see ch. 2 of Porter 2000b ("Being on Time").

16 I.e. "Tonhöhe" (differences in pitch and in relative position on a scale), viz., "die Höhenverhältnisse der Töne," conceived as (vertical/spatial) "Raumdifferenzen" (KGW II/2, 321), and ultimately as (horizontal, linear) intervals of time in sound ("Zeiträume"). Many of these observations spill over into a later, puzzling writing on time-atoms, on which see Porter 2000a.

17 See KGW II/3, 11 ("Einleitung in die Tragödie des Sophocles" [SS 1870]) for the contrast between the "lawful architectonic character of music" ("Apollonian") versus "the pure musicality, indeed the pathological quality, of the tone" or "note" ("Dionysian").

18 Cf. also KGW II/2, 157–9 with n. 16 (lecture notes on "The Greek Lyric Poets"), here the section on the Greek dithyrambists. What this latter historical account establishes is that any innovations that bring the dithyramb into the realm of "alogia" ("irrationality") in the ecstatic sense can only refer to the *degenerate* phase (the New Music; "Neuerer Dithyramb") of the dithyramb (KGW II/2, 159, n. 16; similarly, BT 17; KSA 1, 111–12). And it is only in this phase that Dionysianism becomes recognizably palpable.

19 Janz 1974, 199.

20 An irony is that Wilamowitz did much to bolster the prestige of "Hellenism," but remained deeply ambivalent all his life about his allegiances to the classical ideal— and about "Hellenism" (see Porter 2000b, 269–71; 383n. 184). Droysen's Hellenism created a symptomatic stress point within the field (one of many, to be sure).

21 The following is meant to compensate for this massive oversight in Porter 2000b and in Porter 2000c.

22 Droysen is not explicitly named in any of Nietzsche's writings from the time, but his traces are everywhere visible in his accounts of Droysen's signature term and self-coined concept, "Hellenismus," as in "Man hatte das Bild des römisch-universellen Hellenismus, den Alexandrinismus" (NF1869, 3[76]; KSA 7, 81 ("Hellenismus" is an "updating" of "das Hellenische," which is associated with the classicism of Winckelmann in the same note); "Alexander, die vergröbernde Copie und Abbreviatur der griechischen Geschichte, erfindet nun den Allerwelts-Hellenen und den sogenannten 'Hellenismus'" ("Homers Wettkampf" [1872]; KSA 1, 792); "Alexandrinismus der Erkenntniß, Zug nach Indien. Wildes Hervorbrechen des Dionysischen" (NF 6[14] "4," 1870; KSA 7, 134), this last predicting the intrusion of the Dionysian in the "modern" (post-classical) phase, as will be discussed momentarily. It is hard to know whether Nietzsche came by Droysen on his own (he was a household name in Classics) or by Wagner, who was intensively reading Droysen in 1869–70 (see Foster 2010, 285–9).

23 Page references to Droysen's work are to the 1998 edition. Unfortunately no translation of Droysen exists in English, though it is much needed.

24 Droysen repeatedly points to analogies between this era and his contemporary world. Cf. Droysen 1998 [1836–43] III, xx; III, 416–17; Droysen 1893–4, II, 70; Koselleck 1985, 3–5; 231–66.

25 Meyer 1924 [1895], I, 89; cf. ibid., I, 140–2.

26 Heidegger 1992, 43. Heidegger's use of *Romanization* is idiosyncratic: it allows him

to tarnish "the metaphysics of Nietzsche, whom we like to consider the modern rediscoverer of ancient Greece" as founded on seeing "the Greek 'world' exclusively in a Roman way, i.e. in a way at once modern and un-Greek" (Ibid.).

27 Heyne [1763] 1785; cf. Ibid., 117.

28 Cf. Droysen 1998 [1836–43]: III, xiii–xxii; III, 413–15; see Kassel 1987.

29 See Gehrke's *Nachwort*, Droysen 1998 [1836–43] III, 473; Bichler 1983; Momigliano 1994: 147.

30 Droysen 1833: 472; cited by Bravo 1988, 349. The full analogy reads: "The identical Enlightenment, the identical striving for culture (Bildung), the identical traffic between peoples resulting in the dwindling of spatial distances and of ethnic particularities and the beginning of a world literature (Weltliteratur), is reason enough to view that age in the mirror of the present."

31 See Porter 2000b, 220–1, 275; Porter 2005; Porter 2006a; Porter 2012. Long 2001, 33–4 makes an identical observation in passing.

32 "I can't deny the fact that my mistrust of the taste of our times has risen to a quite possibly reprehensible height. Day after day I see how people come by the name of genius—in the same way, that is, as certain insects [lit., the woodlouse] come by the name of millipede, not because they have that number of feet, but because most people don't wish to count up to fourteen. The result is that I no longer believe anyone without putting him to the test" ("Ich kann nicht leugnen, mein Mißtrauen gegen den Geschmack unserer Zeit ist bei mir vielleicht zu einer tadelnswürdigen Höhe gestiegen. Täglich zu sehen wie Leute zum Namen Genie kommen, wie die Keller-Esel zum Namen Tausendfuß, nicht weil sie so viele Füße haben, sondern weil die meisten nicht bis auf 14 zählen wollen, hat gemacht, daß ich keinem mehr ohne Prüfung glaube"). G. C. Lichtenberg, *Sudelbuch* F 962 (Lichtenberg 1902 [1776–80], III, 297).

33 In the mention there of "the dances of St. John and St. Vitus" (Ibid.) we find another buried thread in Nietzsche's allusions to the Christian overtones of the Dionysian. Cf. NF 1869, 1[34]; KSA 1, 19; NF 1870/71 7[13]; KSA 1, 139: "The Gospel of John [was] born out of a Greek atmosphere, from the soil of the Dionysian; its influence on Christianity, in contrast to Judaism." Cf. NF 1870/71, 7[166] and [174]; KSA 1, 203 and 207, etc.

34 In Gründer 1969, 134; cf. ibid., 32, 35–6.

35 Ibid., 42; cf. ibid., 41. Wilamowitz is right about these parallels; there is nothing original in the conceit. See Creuzer 1973 [1836–43 (1st edn., 1810–12)], IV, 664–9; Lange 1866, 20.

36 See Porter 2000b, 155–6; 209–24; 229–49; 284–5; Porter 2000c.

37 See Porter 2000c.

Works cited

Barnes, Jonathan (1986): "Nietzsche and Diogenes Laertius." In *Nietzsche-Studien*. Vol. 15, 16–40.

Benne, Christian (2005): *Nietzsche und die historisch-kritische Philologie*. Berlin and New York (Walter de Gruyter).

Bernays, Jacob ([1857] 1970): *Grundzüge der verlorenen Abhandlung des Aristoteles über Wirkung der Tragödie*. Hildesheim and New York (G. Olms).

Bichler, Reinhold (1983): *"Hellenismus": Geschichte und Problematik eines Epochenbegriffs.* Darmstadt (Wissenschaftliche Buchgesellschaft).

Bravo, Benedetto (1988 [1968]): *Philologie, histoire, philosophie de l'histoire: Étude sur J.G. Droysen, historien de l'antiquité.* Hildesheim and New York (G. Olms).

Cancik, Hubert (2000 [1995]): *Nietzsches Antike: Vorlesung.* 2nd edn. Stuttgart (Metzler).

Creuzer, Georg Friedrich (1973 [1836–43]): *Symbolik und Mythologie der alten Völker.* Rpt. of 3rd edn. 6 vols. New York (G. Olms).

Droysen, Johann Gustav (1833): "Rev. of P[ieter] O[tto] van der Chys [Chijs] (1828): *Commentarius geographicus in Arrianum de expeditione Alexandri Lugduni Batvorum.* Leiden (J. C. Cyfveer)." In *Jahrbücher für wissenschaftliche Kritik.* Vol. 59–60, 471–80.

—(1893–4): *Kleine Schriften zur alten Geschichte.* In Ernst Hübner (ed.): 2 vols. Leipzig (Veit & Comp).

—(1998 [1836–43]): *Geschichte des Hellenismus.* In Erich Bayer (ed.): 3 vols. Darmstadt (Primus Verlag).

Foster, Daniel H. (2010): *Wagner's Ring Cycle and the Greeks.* Cambridge (Cambridge University Press).

Gründer, Karlfried (1969): *Der Streit um Nietzsches Geburt der Tragödie.* Hildesheim (G. Olms).

Gutzwiller, Hans (1951): "Friedrich Nietzsches Lehrtätigkeit am Basler Pädagogium 1869–76." In *Basler Zeitschrift für Geschichte und Altertumskunde.* Vol. 50, 148–224.

Heidegger, Martin (1992): *Parmenides.* In André Schuwer and Richard Rojcewicz (trans). Bloomington (Indiana University Press).

Heyne, Christian Gottlob ([1763] 1785): "Disputantur nonnula de genio saeculi Ptolemaeorum." In *Opvscvla academica collecta et animadversionibvs locvpletata.* 6 vols. Göttingen (I. C. Dietrich), Vol. I, 76–134.

Janz, Curt Paul (1974): "Friedrich Nietzsches Akademische Lehrtätigkeit in Basel 1869–79." In *Nietzsche-Studien.* Vol. 3, 192–203.

Kassel, Rudolf (1987): *Die Abgrenzung des Hellenismus in der griechischen Literaturgeschichte.* Berlin and New York (Walter de Gruyter).

Koselleck, Reinhart (1985): *Futures Past: On the Semantics of Historical Time.* In Keith Tribe (trans.). Cambridge, MA (MIT Press).

Lange, Friedrich Albert (1866): *Geschichte des Materialismus und Kritik seiner Bedeutung in der Gegenwart.* Iserlohn (Verlag von J. Baedeker).

Lichtenberg, Georg Christoph (1902): *Georg Christoph Lichtenbergs Aphorismen: Nach den Handschriften.* In Albert Leitzmann (trans.). 5 vols. Berlin (B. Behr).

Long, Anthony A. (2001): "Ancient Philosophy's Hardest Question: What to Make of Oneself?" *Representations.* Vol. 74 (1), 19–36.

Meyer, Eduard (1924): *Kleine Schriften.* 2 vols. Halle (M. Niemeyer).

Momigliano, Arnaldo (1994 [1970]): "J. G. Droysen between Greeks and Jews." In G. W. Bowersock and T. J. Cornell (eds): *A.D. Momigliano: Studies on Modern Scholarship.* Berkeley (University of California Press), 147–61.

Müller, Enrico (2005): *Die Griechen im Denken Nietzsches.* Berlin and New York (Walter de Gruyter).

Porter, James I. (2000a): "Untimely Meditations: Nietzsche's *Zeitatomistik* in Context." In *Journal of Nietzsche Studies.* Vol. 20, 58–81.

—(2000b): *Nietzsche and the Philology of the Future.* Stanford (Stanford University Press).

—(2000c): *The Invention of Dionysus: An Essay on "The Birth of Tragedy."* Stanford (Stanford University Press).

—(2005): "Foucault's Ascetic Ancients." In *Phoenix.* Vol. 59 (2), 121–32.

—(2006a): "Foucault's Antiquity." In Charles Martindale and Richard Thomas (eds): *Classics and the Uses of Reception*. London (Blackwell), 168–79.

—(ed.) (2006b): *Classical Pasts: The Classical Traditions of Greece and Rome*. Princeton (Princeton University Press).

—(2012): "Discipline and Punish: Some Corrections to Boyle." In *Foucault Studies*. Vol. 14, 179–95.

—(2014): "Jacob Bernays and the Catharsis of Modernity." In Joshua Billings and Miriam Leonard (eds): *Tragedy and Modernity*. Oxford (Oxford University Press).

Welcker, Friedrich Gottlieb (1857–63). *Griechische Götterlehre*. 3 vols. Göttingen (Dieterich).

Part Two

Scholarly Processes

The Sources of Nietzsche's Lectures on Rhetoric*

Glenn W. Most and Thomas Fries

1

Rhetoric constitutes an important emphasis in Nietzsche's academic teaching in Basel from 1869 to 1879. Nietzsche advertised a total of nine courses on classical rhetoric,[1] both on the history of eloquentia and on specific authors (Aristotle, Cicero, Quintilian); however, two of these courses never took place and in other cases it is uncertain whether the intended courses ever came to fruition. Nonetheless, manuscripts exist for four of Nietzsche's lectures as well as a handwritten translation of Aristotle's *Rhetoric*.[2] The notes to these lectures have been published in KGW II, Vols. 2–5; but the critical apparatus is still missing. For this reason, it seems logical first to provide an overview of the context surrounding these lectures on rhetoric (thereby affording an impression of Nietzsche's working method) and briefly to evaluate the existing editions.

Here we will focus on the Rhetoric-lecture from the winter term of 1872/73, keeping in mind the larger context of Nietzsche's engagement with rhetoric. The concentration on these notes is justified both by their chronological precedence and also by the fact that here Nietzsche deals with rhetoric both systematically—notably, with a clear reference to philosophy of language—and historically to the degree that one must understand this lecture course as a *foundational text* for the study of rhetoric.

The lectures were delivered in the winter term of 1872/73 (questions of dating will be addressed later). The two other courses planned for this semester fell

* The following text is a shortened version of a lecture given in Königstein on February 13, 1992. The different components of the lecture are reproduced here in an abbreviated and considerably simplified (with regard to Nietzsche's citational practice) form. [Editors' note: This paper was originally published as Most, Glenn W. and Fries, Thomas, "Die Quellen von Nietzsches Rhetorik Vorlesung." In: Tilman Borsche, et al. (eds), *Centauren-Geburten: Wissenschaft, Kunst, und Philosophie beim jungen Nietzsche*. Berlin (Walter de Gruyter), 17–46. We are grateful to the authors, editors, and publishers for their permission to translate and reproduce this piece.]

through due to a lack of interest, and even in this course, Nietzsche only had two students: a student of German literature and a law student, but no classical philologists. Nietzsche interpreted this fiasco as a conscious boycott resulting from the massive rejection of *The Birth of Tragedy* in philological circles in the year 1872.[3] One of the two participants was Louis (Ludwig) Kelterborn,[4] who had already been Nietzsche's student at the Pädagogium in Basel and who remained close to Nietzsche during the entirety of his time in the city. In the summer of 1875 he gifted Nietzsche his transcript of Jacob Burckhardt's lecture course on Greek cultural history (cf. KSB 5, 58), which Nietzsche used intensively.[5] Louis Kelterborn also attentively transcribed the lectures on rhetoric. In 1901 he sent his memories of Nietzsche to the Nietzsche Archive, and thirty years later they were published in the third volume of the Beck edition of Nietzsche's correspondence (BAB 3, 379–99; cf. Gutzwiller 1951, 203–6). In his report, Kelterborn specifies the precise semester as well as the chapter headings of the lectures on rhetoric. This makes it conclusively possible to date the course to the winter term of 1872/73, as is also confirmed by other indications.[6] Kelterborn describes Nietzsche's lecturing style and mentions both the professor's script as well as his own transcript:

> I again had the privilege of experiencing his teaching at the university while attending a weekly three-hour lecture course on Greek and Roman rhetoric in the winter term of 1872–73. As a citizen of Basel I am still struck by a feeling of shame to think that this course, given by such an important member of the faculty, only had two students then, and, moreover, one a student of German literature and the other [Kelterborn] of law. And this was the only one of his announced courses that was actually held. No wonder that our esteemed professor, whose health was already precarious, soon requested that we attend the later lectures at his home. And thus we gathered for this course three times each week in his cozily elegant abode at an evening hour, listening to him in the lamplight and writing down the phrases that he dictated from a notebook bound in soft red leather. Here he would often pause during the lecture, whether for his own reflection or in order to give us a moment to consider the material. He also had the kindness of offering us beer—Culmbacher—as a refreshment and he was wont to drink his own out of a silver cup. From the scope of the manuscript I copied down—84 quarto pages—one can get a sense of the rich content of this lecture course, and even more from the following headings of the individual subsections. (BAB 3, 386f.)[7]

Of course, it would be quite illuminating to have Kelterborn's complete transcript in order to come to a fuller picture of Nietzsche's lectures—he had a known tendency to expand and garnish the material in an impromptu fashion—and in order to see how he employed his script. Unfortunately, we have not yet been able to locate this document, which Kelterborn himself clearly kept with care.[8]

Nietzsche's own transcript is found in the quarto notebook P II 12a of his Nachlass, along with the lecture course from 1874/75 on Aristotle's *Rhetoric* (written from the back to front of the notebook) and some fragments on readings and writings in the penultimate group of the posthumous fragments of 1874 (NF 1874, 37 [2–5];

KSA 7, 828–30). The script goes to page 101; but since Nietzsche only wrote on the odd pages—a frequent habit of his, in order to leave space for later additions and revisions—the text only comprises around fifty pages. The easily legible manuscript contains—in contrast to others—almost no corrections, ruling out a more extensive revision. Nietzsche's annotations, which appear in the *Großoktavausgabe*, are partly additions on the even pages, partly integrated passages; however, some additions on the even pages have been inserted into the text of the lectures without identification. For unknown reasons, some of Nietzsche's bibliographic allusions and citations have been omitted.[9]

The printing of the lectures undertaken by Otto Crusius in the second *Philologica* volume of the *Großoktavausgabe* of 1912 (GA XVIII, 237–68) has additional flaws but has remained the most important source of quotation to this day.[10] It comprises only the first seven paragraphs—up to page 37 of the script, or a good third of the lecture. Crusius, who alluded to Blass and Volkmann as "guides" for Nietzsche, justifies this abridgement in the following manner: "From §7 onwards, the account becomes sketchier and less coherent; what has been printed here might therefore serve as an example" (GA XVIII, 333). Other than an unemended reprint of the Crusius version in the fifth volume of the Musarion edition (MusA V, 287–319) and an allusion by Walter Jens (Jens 1967, 13), there was no discussion of Nietzsche's lectures on rhetoric, as far as we can tell, for quite some time—until, in 1971, almost exactly a hundred years after the Basel lecture course, Philippe Lacoue-Labarthe and Jean-Luc Nancy translated the Crusius version into French and complemented it with extensive commentary as well as further texts written by Nietzsche on language and rhetoric (Nancy and Lacoue Labarthe 1971, 99–142).[11] They also put their documentation into context with the bilingual edition from two years previous of the so-called "Philosopher's Book" (from the posthumous fragments of 1872–5) with the essay "On Truth and Lies in an Extra-moral Sense" (Marietti 1969). Lacoue-Labarthe and Nancy were the first to recognize, although without elaborating on it, the "collage" character of Nietzsche's lecture script and referred to Volkmann, Spengel, Blass and Gerber as (potential) sources for Nietzsche, although they could only give isolated and in part inaccurate indications.[12] We presume that—rather than satisfying themselves with Crusius' vague allusion—they followed Nietzsche's own indications in coming to these authors but did not have time for a more precise collation. Despite this insight into the collage-character of the lecture, they sold the entire parcel as "Friedrich Nietzsche: Rhetoric and Language" to great interest, amplifying with this weighty name the movement of rhetorical Deconstruction that had been causing such sensation since the 1970s. As is well known, this led quickly to an intensive engagement with the lectures and related texts.

A more exact clarification of the source texts was lacking for some time after Lacoue-Labarthe and Nancy; it was only with careful studies by Anthonie Meijers (Meijers 1988, 369–90) and Martin Stingelin (Stingelin 1988, 336–49) on the subject of Gustav Gerber (and including the essay "On Truth and Lies in an Extra-moral Sense") that the entire scope of the problem was revealed, leading to an impressive concordance to which we are also, of course, indebted (Meijers and Stingelin 1988, 350–68). It is, however, best not even to speak of the so-called "first complete publication" of the lecture notes on rhetoric that appeared in 1989 with Oxford University Press (Gilman, et al. 1989).[13]

Nietzsche's other courses on rhetoric seem to be of little interest to scholars. Otto Crusius dated the second still-extant lecture course on the "History of Greek Eloquence" (GA XVIII, 199–236 [also incomplete]) to the winter term of 1872 and 1873, which cannot be true for aforementioned reasons. But then when did it take place? Certainly not before 1874, as Nietzsche revised his shorter "outline" from 1872 and 1873 with the second volume of Blass' *Attic Eloquence* on Isocrates and Isaeus (Blass 1874), which first appeared in 1874 (before that Nietzsche used Westermann 1833–5]). On the other hand, the script must have been written before the winter term 1875/76, since it is found in the same notebook filled from back to front (P II 13^c) as the third part of the lectures on the history of Greek literature (GA XVIII, 129–98) and is actually located *before* this lecture. This legitimizes the assumption that this text was intended for the lecture course titled "Presentation of Classical Rhetoric" planned for the summer term of 1874, although it is uncertain whether the course ever in fact took place. This course is an extension of the appendix to the lectures on rhetoric, but it is generally limited to the history of eloquentia, thus constituting a kind of genre history of public speaking. The method of "collage" is clearly the same. (We will return to this focus on the relationship of rhetoric to literary history in the fourth part of our essay.)

Concerning the larger social context surrounding the lecture, it is also important to ask to what extent rhetoric was taught at all in German-speaking universities, and in Basel in particular, around the time of 1870. A cursory examination shows that rhetoric is hardly the front-runner among lecture topics offered—which is scarcely surprising considering the general stature of rhetoric in the nineteenth century—but that there are nevertheless a surprisingly large number of rhetoric lectures, both in classical and in German philology. In Basel, German scholar Wilhelm Wackernagel, who died in 1869, held a regular lecture on poetics, rhetoric, and stylistics, which was also published after his death (Wackernagel [1873] 2003); moreover, Nietzsche's less renowned colleague Jacob Mähly also taught courses on rhetoric.[14] The titles of contemporary university courses reveal a recognizable tendency to integrate rhetoric qua theory into poetics or aesthetics but to integrate rhetoric qua practice into the study of "stylistics"—a field made more significant by the necessity of training teachers at the university. In short, with rhetoric Nietzsche had chosen a well-established and practical subject for his lectures.

Nietzsche clearly saw it as his duty to remain abreast of the current state of scholarship. This is evident when we scrutinize his sources in detail.[15] These can be classed into two groups: a *classical philological tradition* (Westermann 1833–5; Spengel 1842; 1862, 604–46; 1863, 481–526; Volkmann 1865; 1862; Hirzel 1871; and Blass 1865; 1868; 1874) and a *tradition of philosophy of language* (Gerber 1871–3, and via Gerber, nineteenth-century linguistics and philosophy of language). The combination of these two traditions is perhaps the most important fact about Nietzsche's lecture. In the field of classical philosophy, priority belongs to Leonhard Spengel, a great expert on Aristotle, who produced an entire series of writings on rhetoric and published important editions. Spengel did not limit himself to description, classification, and summary, but interpreted rhetorical works against their historical and logical background. Indubitably, Nietzsche took the intellectual substance of the discussion of rhetoric from Spengel and also followed him with regard to important questions of schematization. For historical questions, Nietzsche used Westermann's *History of Eloquence* as his handbook, but clearly found it outdated and replaced it, wherever possible, with the work of his coeval Friedrich Blass, which was still appearing one volume at a time. Especially for the systematic portions of his text, Nietzsche used the two rhetoric handbooks by Volkmann. The section on Plato in §1 includes selected quotations amounting to a near-summary of a Habilitationsschrift written by Rudolf Hirzel, whom Nietzsche likely knew from his time in Leipzig. All in all, it is apparent that Nietzsche had no desire to undertake his own study and interpretation of the sources, but nevertheless rigorously sought to share with his students the most current state of the scholarship.

Gustav Gerber's *Language as Art*, which Nietzsche borrowed from the university library in Basel in 1872 (Oehler [1942] 1975, 51), constitutes a somewhat different case, as this book had a direct influence on the philosophy of language Nietzsche expresses most poignantly in his "On Truth and Lies in an Extra-moral Sense." Like Volkmann, Gerber was also the director of a Gymnasium and already more than fifty years old when the first volume of *Language as Art* appeared. The second volume followed in two parts in 1873 and 1874, with a second printing in the year 1885. Gerber wrote two more books on the philosophy of language (Gerber [1884] 1976; 1893) as well as some smaller writings for schoolbooks. While he was clearly somewhat well known at the end of the nineteenth century, he has since been largely forgotten; Siegfried J. Schmidt assigns him, along with Otto Gruppe, Friedrich Max Müller, and Georg Runze, to the "forgotten philosophy of language of the 19th century," which, along with more recognized movements—comparative grammar, the Neo-grammarians, and the Leipzig School—held fast to Humboldt's philosophical foundations for linguistic doctrine and which, via Gerber, became important not only for Nietzsche but also for the language philosophy of the twentieth century (especially Wittgenstein).[16] Gerber's significance for Nietzsche is based firstly on the fact that it was through him that Nietzsche came to know not only this tradition (Wilhelm von Humboldt, Franz Bopp, Haymann Steinthal, Karl Wilhelm Heyse) but also the specific linguistic scholarship of the nineteenth century, whose findings (for instance, in the field of comparative grammar and semantics, the history of language and etymology—Jakob Grimm or August Friedrich Pott—as well as in phonetics and metrics) Gerber had carefully incorporated into his more philosophically oriented study. Moreover, Gerber possessed an extraordinarily rich, multilingual literary and philosophical education (Locke, Kant, Hamann, Herder, Schleiermacher, Hegel, Schopenhauer, Jean Paul, Grillparzer, and others). This education allowed him to assemble a unique constellation of textual examples that persuasively support his thesis—considered from many different angles (evolutionary-historical, semasiological, grammatical, phonetic, metric)—of the fundamentally tropological and figural character of language. This constellation constitutes a true poetic inventory that Nietzsche also used (not only in his lectures on rhetoric) and employed for his own poetic procedure.[17] At the same time, he distances himself from Gerber, who insists on maintaining a methodological distinction between, on the one hand, the "art of language" [Sprachkunst] and its (aesthetic) consideration and, on the other, the theory of language [Sprachlehre] (and thus rhetoric).[18]

However, it is difficult to determine the exact place of Gerber's *Language as Art* between linguistics and philosophy. Specifically, the forceful insistence on the *artistic* character of language—the single, often repeated and plausible thesis, which is resistant to *scholarly* classification, as is evident even in the confusing, unsystematic structure of the book—this insistence must have given the volume the appearance of a foreign entity in the new linguistic paradigm of Hermann Paul. For philosophers, on the other hand, Gerber's "critique of language" as a "critique of impure reason"[19] in the tradition of Hamann and Herder contained too much linguistic-poetic material and too little methodological rigor to meet such a high standard.

The only novelty in Nietzsche's lecture, in fact, is the juxtaposition of an old (classical) philological tradition with Gerber's relatively new theory of language, which relies on Hamann's and Herder's critique of Kant as well as on Wilhelm von Humboldt. While Nietzsche adopts this philological thinking rather directly, if in a considerably simplified and abbreviated form, with just a few strokes he radicalizes Gerber's impressive constellations and observations on the universally tropological and figurative nature of language. This gesture amounts to a totalization: Nietzsche quotes Gerber ("All words are, however, in and of themselves, with relation to their meaning, originally tropes") but adds the sentence: "This is the *first* consideration: *language is rhetoric*" (GA XVIII, 249).[20] With this single sentence, all of the quotations from Gerber take on a different orientation; with this supplement, it is clearly no longer *Gerber's* text. Indeed, the universal significance of rhetoric is established, every linguistic expression can now be deconstructed according to its inherent rhetorical structure, everything is rhetoric, everything language, but at the same time the scholarly foundation of Gerber's work is lost: the consistently postulated division of the art of language [Sprachkunst], the intellectual investigation of language [Sprachbetrachtung], and the theory of language [Sprachlehre][21] as well as the scrupulous distinction between the different fields within the investigation of language (grammar [Grammatik], semantics, phonetics, etc.). The phrase "language is rhetoric" indeed *reifies* the fundamentally tropological and figural nature of language, but loses itself in the same, whether metaphor, metonymy or synecdoche—remaining unusable as a basis for scholarly-philological activity, which it clearly undermines. It is therefore easily understandable that this fulgurous combination of classical-philological rhetoric and language theory would not be sustained: neither in Nietzsche's later work, nor in Classical Philology, nor in language theory. It is also easy to imagine that the compilation of the entire traditional inventory of rhetoric (tropes, figures, etc.) was henceforth purely compulsory for Nietzsche, which would explain the rather "borrowed" character of these portions of his text.

This should suffice for the general presentation of Nietzsche's lectures on rhetoric and their sources. Of course, we cannot claim to have found all sources—a detective's curiosity would, after all, prefer to be able to attribute *everything* to a source, but it is important to keep in mind what Nietzsche wrote in the posthumously published fragments of 1874: "It is even so for philology: the completeness of the material is something unnecessary in many cases" (KSA 7, 450). In this sense, the interpretation of the source material at hand is more important than speculation regarding further possible sources.

2

In the first part of this essay, we introduced the sources of Nietzsche's lectures on rhetoric. *That* he used these sources is not astonishing—it would, perhaps, have been astonishing had he used no sources. For at issue here is the scholarly presentation of classical theory known only, if at all, through written records. Without his sources, Nietzsche would have merely produced a phantasy, a historical novel of sorts.

That Nietzsche used sources, then, is uninteresting; what *is* interesting is *which* sources he used and, especially, *how* he used these sources. The concept of a source in philology indicates only that something is acquired, drunk, but completely ignores the various methods of acquisition and drinking. One might map the following varieties (the list of variants provided here certainly does not exhaust the possibilities):

1. *Quotation:* the conscious and obvious reproduction of the (almost) entirely unaltered wording of what has been read, either with or without an explicit reference to the source.
2. *Paraphrase:* the equally conscious and obvious reproduction of a slightly or heavily altered, but nonetheless recognizable wording of what has been read, either with or without an explicit reference to the source.
3. *Plagiarism:* the conscious but not openly acknowledged reproduction of the unaltered or altered wording of what has been read, as if it were the product of one's own thinking, suppressing any reference to the original author.
4. *Excerpt:* the conscious and acknowledged reproduction of the (almost) entirely unaltered wording of what has been read for the purposes of one's own research, without intent to publish it as such or pass it off as the product of one's own thinking, either with or without explicit reference to the source.
5. *Note:* the conscious and acknowledged reproduction of a slightly or heavily altered, but nonetheless recognizable wording of what has been read for the purposes of one's own research, without intent to publish it as such or pass it off as the product of one's own thinking, either with or without an explicit reference to the source.
6. *Inspiration:* the conscious use of the conceptual material of what has been read, abandoning the original wording, as a point of departure or in support of one's own text, normally without explicit reference to the source.
7. *Reminiscence:* the belated and unconscious effect of what was once read on one's own work, without explicit reference to the source.
8. *Allusion:* the conscious and explicit reference to a source through an abbreviated reproduction of the original wording, usually without explicitly naming the source.

It is obvious that this differentiation is fundamentally problematic and also difficult to implement in any individual cases for a number of reasons. (1) It brings together two criteria belonging to entirely different registers, namely the author's awareness, on the one hand, and the presence of certain textual markers (names, references, quotation marks, etc.) on the other.[22] Moreover, the concept of source (2) presupposes a difference between the original text and the derivative text, between source and river: yet, precisely this distinction is endangered in all of these cases, and in plagiarism it can even vanish. If a text consists completely of a copy of *a single* source, there should be little difficulty in identifying the first composer as the author: but what if a text is a complete copy of six different sources? And finally (3) this differentiation opens the door to a conceptual regressus ad infinitum, since there is no text that does not refer to others, no source that did not feed on other sources. When to stop? These are paradoxes of theoretical interest not only to us, but which also confronted Friedrich Nietzsche as a classical philologist with concrete methodological questions in his scholarly work, questions which he consistently subjected to sophisticated and subtle conceptual analysis. Indeed, one of the emphases of his scholarly research was the analysis of the sources of authors like Diogenes Laërtius, and in this field he came to conclusions that still have not been entirely surpassed today.

The analysis of sources is one of the most dominant research concerns of scholarship on antiquity in the second half of the nineteenth century. Essentially, it dates back to Friedrich August Wolf's intuition that Homeric epics had been pieced together from smaller, earlier songs;[23] philological research in the nineteenth century dedicated a great deal of energy and intelligence to the identification of Homer's supposed sources through the alleged contradictions and discrepancies in the text as it had been handed down. Around the middle of the century, these methods were applied by Karl Lehrs, explicitly following and refining Wolf's approach, to classical erudition and later increasingly to the history of classical philosophy (Lehrs 1837; 1873; 1875; 1882). In the years during which Nietzsche studied and worked on Classical Philology, source-critical analysis of post-Aristotelian philosophical texts was emerging as a highly contemporary approach to scholarship—one need only think of Usener (1834–905; cf. Usener 1912) and Diels (1848–922; cf. Diels 1870; [1879] 1969).

In the years 1866 through 1868, Nietzsche worked intensively on *De Laertii Diogineis fontibus* [*The Sources of Diogenes Laërtius*] for an essay competition,[24] researching not only the sources of Diogenes Laërtius but also those of late antiquity and Byzantine erudition (especially those of the Suda, but also Apollodorus, Athenaeus, Plutarch, Aulus Gellius, Eustathius, the *Etymologicum Magnum*, and Stobaeus) and of classical and Hellenistic Greek authors (Herodotus, Aristotle, the vita of Hesiod). In the case of Diogenes Laërtius, Nietzsche came to the conclusion that he had copied his book primarily from a single source, Diocles of Magnesia, but that he had also selectively brought in Favorinus of Arles and a further source, perhaps Theodosius, on the skeptic Pyrrho.[25] Here, though, we are less interested in the concrete findings that Nietzsche came to in his analysis[26] than in his method and the critical reflections on method that accompanied this work. Nietzsche's source-critical work reposes on three principles:

1. *The principle of laziness:*[27] one tends to suspect fewer sources than to suspect more; the author is imagined as a lazy individual, who stays with one source as long as possible and only changes to another when it becomes absolutely necessary. As Nietzsche writes of Diogenes Laërtius:

[...] is Laërtius meant to have suddenly spurned this same source that he had used with such satisfaction and ease? Would he have taken from it just one third of a coherent doctrine, suddenly to jump to something else and look around for other resources? (BAW 4, 225)

2. *The principle of secondhand erudition*: the more widely read the author appears to be, the less of this knowledge is attributable to his own reading; as Nietzsche once more writes of Diogenes:

He shared the belief of almost all scholars that a great number of quotations attests to erudition, the belief that one was justified in copying quotations he shared with many. It pleased him to astound his reader with his erudition: this is why he indulged in quotation so liberally. (BAW 4, 219)

3. *The principle of misleading reference*: the writer alludes somewhere to the authors he has copied so as not to be accused of theft, but he only mentions them in passing regarding trivia and mostly polemically in order to mislead the reader. For example, Nietzsche writes:

In general, though, we can be certain that the greater portion of §38–167 is indebted to a single source: with the exception of just a very few and not even certain examples. La[ertius] took care not to tell us this too clearly: rather, cunning as such compilers are, he only occasionally mentions the name Diocles in those places. "Someone is even less likely to suspect," he likely thought to himself, "that I owe this erudition to him alone." For nothing protects a thief better than a little honesty. If, for this reason, L[aertius] cites Diocles a few times in each section of his work, we must not be so naïve as to think that the indicated passages are the only ones he pillaged from the riches of Diocles. (BAW 4, 229–30)

What happens, then, if we employ the methodological principles of Nietzschean source-criticism to analyze Nietzsche's own lectures on rhetoric? We are in an infinitely better position to do so than Nietzsche was in his research, since we still possess his own sources, rather than merely being able to access and to reconstruct them through his texts. If we did not have access to his sources, no one would suspect that Nietzsche was as dependent on them as he in fact was.

A detailed analysis of the relationship between Nietzsche's lectures and their drafts demonstrates that, with regard to the construction of the lectures, Nietzsche depends on Volkmann's *Rhetoric of the Greeks and Romans* from 1872. But he arranges the material independently and supplements it with the new and unusual §3: "Relationship of the Rhetorical to Language" (GA XVIII, 248–51) as well as the aforementioned "Outline of the History of Eloquence." In this outline he relies on Westermann and, to the extent that it was already available, Blass.

The most utilized source for the main portion of the text is Volkmann's *Rhetoric* (Volkmann 1872), which provides the material for the traditional portions of the lectures (elocution, "dispositio," etc.). Spengel (1863) is also used in §1 ("The Concept of Rhetoric") for differentiation, especially with regard to Aristotle and the general classification of rhetoric. In this portion, Nietzsche also condenses Rudolf Hirzel's

Habilitationsschrift (Hirzel 1871), which had appeared a year earlier, in a one-and-a-half-page summary on this question. The first section contains a general reflection on speaking and writing that carries into later fragments and into the third part of the lectures on "The History of Greek Literature."[28] In the second section, Nietzsche summarizes his understanding of Gustav Gerber's *Language as Art* and opposes it to Aristotle's concept of rhetoric.[29]

This general dependency can be observed *visually* in the appendix to this study, where we reproduce two chapters (§§2 and 7) from Nietzsche's lecture course as examples and identify those passages taken from various sources with various kinds of underlines.[30] In a later investigation into Nietzsche's *Vom Nutzen und Nachteil der Historie für das Leben*, we were able to show how Nietzsche's use of sources developed later into a general technique of overwriting quotations and notes (Most and Fries 2008, 133–56).

It is clear from our appendix that Volkmann provides the framework for Nietzsche's text in the second chapter, whereas Spengel is added in here and there; in the seventh chapter, however, Nietzsche took his introduction from Gerber and his catalogue from Volkmann (with selective additions from Gerber). Inasmuch as Nietzsche is dependent on his sources (one should not forget that there are places in the appendix that are not underlined, which is to say, they are either original to Nietzsche or their sources have not yet been identified), he seems to have employed essentially two methods:

1. *Epitomacy*: Nietzsche's reproduction of his sources generally takes the form of an abbreviated excerpt. He tends to omit the following traits from the originals: stylistic fat (where the original uses two synonyms, he uses only one); complications, problems; some examples; Greek texts.
2. *Compilation*: Nietzsche composes his texts whenever possible out of a few sources, normally two or three in each chapter, usually employing one source for the framework and filling it in selectively with the others.

This is, however, precisely the method of the epitomes of late antiquity that Nietzsche analyzed and condemned. He wrote of Diogenes: "If we are strict, we must call this dissimulation and unreliability on the part of the author and keep this character trait in mind" (BAW 4, 219). Should we also condemn Nietzsche with his own judgment? Certainly not: he distinguishes himself from a thoughtless compiler, let alone a plagiarist, through two small methodological differences and an essential genre distinction. The methodological differences are: (1) Nietzsche does not merely excerpt but rather marshals the sources named in the texts he is considering and also adds something to them (for example, at the end of §2 he quotes Cicero from his own knowledge and at the end of the discussion of synecdoche in §7 he adds the second play of the *Oresteia*). (2) Nietzsche indeed compiles sources, but he does not merely put longer textual passages next to one another in a mechanical fashion. Instead he himself creates a kind of mosaic from smaller textual fragments (for example, at the beginning of §7, where he manifestly had both Volkmann and Gerber open before him and alternated between the two).[31] Far more important is the aforementioned genre distinction: Nietzsche never published his lectures or intended them for publication. Of course the problem of Nietzsche's dependency on his sources is relevant to other writings as well, and not only in regard to his essay "On Truth and Lies in an Extra-moral Sense," which was also never intended for publication; recent scholarship has increasingly acknowledged this problem as a genuine question in Nietzschean textual production.[32] But in the case of this lecture, the drastic dependency on a small number of sources is somewhat sharpened by the genre of the text. In any event, it can be designated as a collection of material, as a stockpile for Nietzsche's own use and the use of his audience: in terms of the classifications listed above, it would not be plagiarism but rather a collection of excerpts. Only the editorial decision to publish it posthumously could even call into question what sort of text it is. Moreover, it should be pointed out that we do not know exactly how Nietzsche expanded on these notes when speaking—that he acknowledged his sources there is perhaps not particularly likely but cannot be ruled out.

The conclusion remains, however, that at least in this chapter of his lecture, few sentences were conceived by Nietzsche himself. That most sentences were either taken verbatim from particular sources or at best slightly modified raises the question to what extent the lectures should be thought of *as a Nietzsche text*. Whose voice is it when we read this text? The editorial translation of this question is: should the editor of such a text add ["] at the beginning and ["] at the end of each quotation?

3

The problem of the status of this text has long been recognized (at least in certain circles) but never sufficiently studied and, most importantly, never even approximately reflected upon as such. Even Crusius, who first published the text in 1912 in the *Philologica* of the *Großoktav* edition, recognized Nietzsche's dependency, particularly on Volkmann and Blass (GA XVIII, 333), but neither documented this nor elaborated on it. In 1970, Nancy and Lacoue-Labarthe were the first to recognize that the entire text was assembled as a mosaic of quotations:

> One should also indicate [...] that the lectures on rhetoric are not "by Nietzsche" in the sense this would be understood by scholarship concerned with intellectual property, using the search for "sources" to establish the author's rights [...] In almost its entirety, this text is purely and simply recopied from other (at that time, mostly recent) works from which Nietzsche makes a judicious amalgam, what one might call a "collage." (Nancy and Lacoue-Labarthe 1971, 100)

And although Nancy and Lacoue-Labarthe refer to Volkmann and Gerber (they even allude to Spengel and Blass) and occasionally give specific examples in the annotations, they provide neither a systematic engagement with this insight nor does it have consequences for the interpretation of the text in Lacoue-Labarthe's accompanying essay "Le détour" (Lacoue-Labarthe 1971, 53–76). Indeed, the very fact that the French translation bears the easily misunderstood if not even misleading title "Friedrich Nietzsche: Rhetoric and Language" could leave a deeper impression on many readers than the somewhat hidden allusions to this problem. In 1988, then,

Meijers studied Nietzsche's dependence on Gerber (Meijers 1988, 369–90), but he limited himself to the study of rhetorical figures and tropology[33] on the one hand, and to this single source, on the other—leading to a rather distorted image of Nietzsche's influences.[34]

In general, the scholarship has responded to this problem with four different strategies:

1. by simply ignoring it;[35]
2. by merely paying lip service to its existence but then disputing its significance: one acknowledges that Nietzsche's text is dependent on sources, but then attributes what is already present in the sources to Nietzsche as if it were his own original contribution;[36]
3. through an "indeed ... but" strategy: Nietzsche's lectures are *indeed* dependent on previous sources, *but* are nevertheless so illuminating for Nietzsche, either through a kind of quarantine (some material is acknowledged as belonging to Nietzsche's sources, but the rest is attributed to Nietzsche himself)[37] or through compilation (all parts are indeed stolen, but have been combined by Nietzsche in an original manner)[38] or through emphasis (indeed, Nietzsche says the same thing as his sources, only that he says it louder);[39] or
4. by acknowledging the problem but finding in it only (another) reason to condemn Nietzsche.[40]

But the problem of intellectual property should not be oversimplified, especially not in the context of rhetoric. For questioning the concept of literary property, of an original author, is a defining characteristic of rhetoric. This question takes place systematically, for example, in the notion of "inventio," which invents nothing new but rather rediscovers what is already at hand in topoi and *loci*. Rhetoric does not teach us how to express novel, hitherto unconceived notions but rather how to make already known ideas relevant for a specific situation in a new form. "Locos appello [...] sedes argumentorum, in quibus latent, ex quibus sunt petenda" (Quintilian, *Institutio oratoria* V, 10, 20): to an extent, Gerber's and Volkmann's manuals are for Nietzsche the *loci* where he can come across his arguments and examples. The same difficulty with literary property is, however, found throughout the history of rhetorical theory: rules and examples are passed from one theorist to another; with Tisias and Corax it is already unclear what belongs to whom.[41] Many treatises of late antiquity are simply excerpts and compilations of earlier ones. And famous names consistently bring in foreign works.[42] Ultimately it is the same in classical rhetorical practice: since accusers and the accused were required by Attic law to speak for themselves, they read texts aloud that had been written for them by so-called logographers—mostly by Lysias, but also by almost all other great rhetoricians. Thus, the speaker was sometimes not even identical to the author (hence the importance of the teaching of "ethopoiia").[43] In this sense, Paul de Man's interpretation of Nietzsche's understanding of rhetoric as a deconstruction of the subject (de Man 1979, 103–18) is valid—but not only for Nietzsche: rather, it is true for the entire tradition of rhetoric, to which Nietzsche is far more indebted than has sometimes been acknowledged. Of course it is regrettable that de Man failed to recognize that this questioning of the subject was accomplished not only by the content but also by the form of Nietzsche's text in its compositional procedure. We can close this section of our essay with a few short implications:

1. For the specific statements made by this text, Nietzsche should be regarded less as an author than as an affirming reader. It is necessary to establish on a case by case basis who has written each sentence: before the text will be interpretable, an extensive analysis of sources, which has not yet occurred, must take place. Specific ideas are in many cases not Nietzsche's original contributions (to continue to question this would mean to be left behind the rhetorical tradition), but are, rather, already contained in the tradition before him. The more closely one reads Nietzsche's text, the more he disappears as the author and is replaced by the rhetorical tradition that is in fact perceived by the reader as the speaking subject.[44] This does not, however, make the text less interesting, but rather much more so—not least as an indication that we need not read only Nietzsche but also Gerber, Volkmann and his many other sources.
2. Nevertheless, Nietzsche exerted himself to engage in detail with these sources and to excerpt from them extensively. To some degree, they also reflect Nietzsche's own opinion, not only the opinion of his predecessors; and at least one of Nietzsche's rhetoric students, Louis Kelterborn, attests to how impressive and inspiring these lectures were.[45] Thus the questions that remain in the end are: why did Nietzsche engage so thoroughly with rhetoric and with what consequences for his later work? These questions open up to others: on the one hand, the question of the impact of public speeches (which was of great interest to Nietzsche at this moment and which he brought together with questions of education, educational institutions, and general culture) and, on the other hand, the question of the application of such rhetorical means in Nietzsche's own writerly practice.

4

This last section will address some consequences of what we have just written and pose the question of the influence—or perhaps better: non-influence—of rhetoric on Nietzsche's work and of his rhetoric on linguistics and philosophy.

At the origin of Nietzsche's engagement with rhetoric, besides the preexisting pedagogical tradition, is a genuine interest in the question of how one can achieve public impact, how one can effectuate something through writing and speaking: "The belief in truth is necessary, but the illusion is enough, which is to say that 'truths' prove themselves through their effect [...]" (NF 1872/73, 19[43]; KSA 7, 433). At the same time this interest accompanies *The Birth of Tragedy* and the lectures *On the Future of our Educational Institutions*, but in a different way for each work. Yet, unlike Greek tragedy or classical education, the question of rhetoric—aside from the totalitarian sentences declaring the inherently tropological character of expression or the rhetorical character of language—remains a *phenomenon of the past*, a fragmented hodgepodge of dead speakers and speeches, classifications, inventories, all apparently without consequence for contemporary life. The collage character of Nietzsche's lectures reflects his frustration over this reduction to a sterile and "antiquated" but "monumental" rhetoric and the apparent impossibility of a "critical"[46] rhetoric.

The only true trove of his research is Gerber's *Language as Art*. It aids him not only occasionally but systematically, in collation with the classical philological tradition, in his insight into the tropological character of interpretation and reference [des (Be)deutens] and in the figurative character of speech. This—now actually "critical"—discovery leads to pointed refinements of Gerber's careful and sophisticated observations, even of the sentence, "Language is rhetoric."[47] Gerber would not, however, have been capable of formulating *this sentence*, because the distinction between language and the intellectual investigation of language is for him, as already mentioned, an inalienable necessity (for the security of his own discourse as well) and because, even within this investigation of language, rhetoric is only one branch among others. The more radical sentence about rhetoric necessarily raises the question of its own tropological signification, thus bringing its own discourse back under observation. The possibility of rhetorical deconstruction, which, as a result of this totalitarian sentence, seems to offer itself up as a critique of any discourse in any field, effacing the borders between distinct fields of knowledge, is thereby related to its own preconditions—relegated to its own compensatory, active "poeticization." If it is here that we seek to locate Nietzsche's productive insight, it becomes apparent that this insight cannot carry forward as *scholarship*, as rhetoric in the traditional sense, or as philology. This insight puts everything in relation to everything else but at the same time revokes the foundation of individual disciplines, especially philosophy, which are publically defined and legitimized through differentiation and specification of the subjects of study. In this sense, the collation of classical philological and language-philosophical rhetoric, which we have understood as the deciding factor for Nietzsche's lectures on rhetoric, leads to a dead end.

That Gerber's and Nietzsche's insight was forgotten is thoroughly in line with the same: both (Nietzsche following Gerber) repeatedly emphasize the meaning of the repression and the forgetting of trope and figure for the progress of civilization.[48] It is therefore unsurprising that this encounter between rhetoric and linguistics went largely unnoticed in both fields and has had no progeny in either. It is also hard to imagine how a scholarly field—even an only passably recognized one—could be grounded on these foundations, and recent experiences with rhetorical deconstruction have, at least with regard to scholarship, been unable to allay these doubts.

Three indirect lines of influence can be drawn from Nietzsche, and all three cases *shift* the orientation of the lectures on rhetoric. The *first line*, which has already been alluded to a number of times, is the continuation and consummation of Gerber's and Nietzsche's insight in the 1873 treatise "On Truth and Lies in an Extra-moral Sense." As is well known, Nietzsche did not publish this essay and justified his reticence later in *Human, All Too Human*, with the estimation that it—clearly even more than his other non-philological writings—went beyond the scope of his work in Basel (KSA 2, 370).[49] Nietzsche's later statements must be understood not only in the context of his avoidance of a renewed philological shock after *The Birth of Tragedy* but also with regard to the Basel writings Nietzsche was then working on, specifically those addressed to and written about Richard Wagner. From the perspective of the later work, the essay thus appears to be an important deconstructive subversion even of Nietzsche's own efforts, and could, at least in *this* manner, leave no intellectual legacy.

The *second line* comes to be through the amplified poetic-poetological reflection on writing, specifically Nietzsche's *own* writing, in the posthumously published fragments of 1872 through 1874; here the infiltration of Gerber's concepts and arguments can be readily observed from 1872 onwards. All interpreters agree that this new language *practice* is of great significance for Nietzsche's entire oeuvre.[50]

The *third line* has not yet received sufficient consideration. It is a result of the continuation of Nietzsche's academic teaching. Nietzsche clearly saw the perpetuation or further development of the kind of collation practiced in 1872 and 1873 as impossible. This does not mean, however, that he gave up on rhetoric as an academic subject. Rather he continued his study in two very specific ways: namely, as a history of eloquentia on the one hand and in his engagement with Aristotle's *Rhetoric* on the other. The fact that Nietzsche carefully translated Aristotle's *Rhetoric* and prepared a neatly written fair copy might indicate the significance of this text for Nietzsche: specifically as the most important (and perhaps only) opponent whose methodological foundation of rhetoric—the separation of language and the investigation of language—surpasses all earlier and later depictions. In this sense, one could see the engagement with Aristotle as a corollary or a corrective to the essay "On Truth and Lies in an Extra-moral Sense"—and, moreover, in the interest of Nietzsche's own work as a professor, which he, at this moment in time, hardly considered concluded. But this is, as has already been noted, pure speculation. The lectures on the history of Greek eloquence from 1874 can be understood, in contrast, as *retreat*: a retreat to the history of eloquentia—and thus a genre history of public speaking with a purely narrative procedure again founded completely on excerpts, as is, *mutatis mutandis*, typical for both of the first parts of the lecture course on the history of Greek literature. Retreat, though, also with an eye to the *history* of rhetoric, since the concentration on eloquentia, which had influenced rhetoric far into the eighteenth century, was outmoded by the nineteenth. Nevertheless, this also leads to a discovery: namely, the question as to the—cultural, social, historical—conditions of the possibility of public speaking. Nietzsche expands this approach in an exciting, self-confident manner in the third part of the lecture course on the history of Greek literature.[51] A *literary theory* originates that can—between the poles of antiquity and modernity—be considered as important as the theories of tragedy, of history, and of classical education. But that would be another chapter.

Translated by Ian Thomas Fleishman

Notes

1   According to Curt Paul Janz, who lists the following courses: (1) winter term, 1870/71, seminar, "Quintilian Book I" [announced, but never took place]; (2) summer term, 1871, lecture, "Quintilian Book I" [announced; uncertain whether it ever took place]; (3) winter semester, 1871/72, lecture "Dialogus de oratoribus"

[announced; uncertain whether it ever took place]; (4) winter semester, 1872/73, lecture, "Greek and Roman Rhetoric" [announced as "Rhetoric of the Greeks and Romans"; with a supplement: "Outline of the History of Eloquence" (*Nachlaß*, P II 12a, 2–101)]; (5) summer term, 1874, lecture, "Presentation of Classical Rhetoric" [announced, uncertain whether it ever took place; presumably the same as the "History of Greek Eloquence" (*Nachlaß*, P II 13c, 230–148)]; (6) winter term, 1874/75, lecture, "Exposition of Aristotle's *Rhetoric*" [announced and took place (*Nachlaß*, P II 12a, 102–7, 219–146, first part)]; (7) summer term, 1875, lecture, "Aristotle's *Rhetoric* (Continuation)" [announced and took place (*Nachlaß*, P II 12a, 102–7, 219–146, second part; P II 12b, 51–38, incomplete)]; (8) winter term, 1877/78, lecture "The *Rhetoric* of Aristotle" [announced; uncertain whether it ever took place]; (9) summer term, 1879, lecture, "Introduction to Greek Eloquence" [announced, but never took place] (Janz 1974, 192–203). On Nietzsche's teaching in Basel, see also Stroux 1925; Meister 1948, 103–21; Gutzwiller 1951, 148–224.

2   Personal discussion with Professor Fritz Bornmann, Florence.

3   On November 7–8, 1872, he writes to Richard Wagner: "But there is a matter that is terribly unsettling to me at present: our winter term has begun and I have absolutely no students! Our philologists are keeping clear! Really it is a *pudendum* that should be fearfully hidden from everyone. I tell you, beloved master, because you should know everything. The reason is very easy to explain—I am, among my colleagues, suddenly so disreputable that our small university is suffering for it! This tortures me greatly [...]. Until last semester, the number of philologists was always growing—now suddenly as if deflated! But this corresponds to what I've heard of other university cities as well. Leipzig, of course, is once again blooming with envy and darkness, everything denounces me [...]" (KSB 4, 89). And on the same day to Malwida von Meysenburg: "With my Birth of Tragedy I have managed to become the most scandalous philologist of the day, and it would be a true miracle of audacity for one to advocate on my behalf, I am so unanimously condemned" (KSB 4, 81).

4   Born on September 24, 1853 in Basel, Kelterborn was a jurist (examining magistrate) and musician in Basel and, from 1884 onwards, a writer and musician in Boston. He died on December 17, 1910 in Waltham, Massachusetts. His son, Louis Kelterborn (1891–1933) later returned to Basel and is related to the composer Rudolf Kelterborn.

5   Max Oehler notes that the lecture notes are to be found in Nietzsche's library (Oehler [1942] 1975, 31).

6   Although at the time of writing it is still debated in the secondary literature.

7   The only sentences quoted verbatim by Kelterborn from §1 of the lecture are also to be found, with only minimal discrepancies, in Nietzsche's script.

8   It does not appear to be in Basel.

9   For instance, the bibliographic references at the end of §1 (GA XVIII, 245).

10   [Editors' note: Since 1994, the production of KGW II improves the GA edition in several respects. Nevertheless it is neither a perfect nor an indisputable replacement for the GA. Thus the authors' reliance on the text of GA remains vital.]

11   Their documentation includes Philippe Lacoue-Labarthe's essay, "Le détour (Nietzsche et la rhétorique)," in the same volume (Lacoue-Labarthe 1971, 53–76).

12   Their annotations frequently make reference to texts that Nietzsche only knew through his sources (as can be seen in these sources).

13   Both the German text and the translation contain so many omissions and errors that one can only wonder how a reputable publisher could permit such sloppiness.

Anton Bierl and William M. Calder III published a damning critique of this edition in *Nietzsche-Studien* Vol. 21 (Bierl and Calder 1992, 363–6) and included—in part as a counterexample and a real "first edition"—the appendix of the lecture, the "Outline of the History of Eloquence" (Bierl and Calder 1992, 367–89).

14 For example, "Applied Rhetoric" (winter term, 1866/67) and "Rhetorical Exercises" (summer term, 1870). Information provided by Klaus Weimar.

15 As is true of his time in Basel generally, the editions cited by Nietzsche (Aristotle, Cicero, Dionysius of Halicarnassus, Cornificius, Quintilian, and Seneca, as well as collections by Halm, Spengel, and Walz) show no evidence of his own examination of the primary sources. At best, he occasionally verifies a quotation, sometimes translating it to German or replacing the translation with the original text, sometimes inserting a spontaneous comment as well. This only occurs, though, for texts that Nietzsche knows well: for instance, Aristotle's *Rhetoric* or Cicero's *Academica*. Otherwise his evaluation of textual passages is bound to earlier editions and commentators.

16 More information on the reception of Gerber (including reviews and contemporary criticism) can be found in Meijers 1988, 372–6. On Gerber, see also Bettelheim 1901 and Schmidt 1968, 80–147.

17 Martin Stingelin, for instance, shows this in the example of Nietzsche's wordplay (Stingelin 1988, 336–49).

18 "If he [Locke] then only considers the art of public speaking [die Redekunst] permissible for the populace through speeches, condemns its use in scholarship and complains that people hire professors of eloquence in order to learn how they can deceive one another, but nevertheless thinks so much of the magic of eloquence that it would be audacity to speak against it ('Eloquence, like the fair sex, has too prevailing beauties in it to suffer itself ever to be spoken against; and it is in vain to find fault with those arts of deceiving, wherein men find pleasure to be deceived' [Locke, *An Essay Concerning Human Understanding*, III, 10, 34])—one must first remark that scholarship inevitably aspires to protect itself against the deceptions of imagistic and figurative discourse, but that it has no other means by which to express itself other than these same linguistic images and figures that it would like to overcome [...] Thus the teaching of elocution in rhetoric or in stylistics has less to do with the art of language [Sprachkunst] than with the *appropriateness* of the whole of the speech and of particular expressions to the goal a speech is intended to achieve in specific circumstances, in a specific environment, within specific borders, etc. Rhetoric is, for this reason, essentially *prescription*; it is, like stylistics, a product of grammatical-historical knowledge: both fields take their rules from their models, give instruction on how to prepare works of public speaking and can—should they seek to examine the works of language art that have already been naturalized in language [in der Sprache bereits eingebürgerten Werken der Sprachkunst]—only see these as a subservient accompaniment with relation to the effect of the whole. Aesthetics, however, and especially the art of language, comes to no prescriptions; it cannot recommend imitation but rather only observation, it does not desire to offer instruction but rather to point to artistic pleasure" (Gerber 1871–3, I, 77f.). To support this thesis, Gerber then refers to Herder and Goethe, but particularly to Hegel's *Aesthetics*.

19 "If, for that reason, scientific studies based on mere concepts and abstractions have come into disrepute today, and are received with incredulity, if empirical research is demanded as fundamental, then it is also clear that what Kant began as a 'critique

of pure reason' must be continued as a critique of impure reason—as a critique of language" (Gerber 1871-3, I, 262). Gerber then makes reference to Humboldt, Leibniz, and Herder.

20   Gerber writes already in his table of contents that "all words are originally tropes" (Gerber 1871, I, viii) and then specifies: "*All words are acoustic images and are, in relation to their meaning, originally tropes. Since the origin of the word was an artificial one, its meaning only essentially changes through artistic intuition. 'Real words,' meaning prose, do not exist in language*" (Gerber 1871, I, 333, original italics). Later he elaborates: "Nevertheless, the sense employed by an acoustic image aims at something specific, but the necessity to understand it in this way is minimal, and others take it in another sense to the extent that the difference of meaning can escalate to the point of antonymy. It is on this battlefield that people romp about. Every solitary individual longs to be connected to humankind and nature—and it is to this end that he acts, to this end that he speaks, but speech is and always remains a tropus and even action cannot overcome this and remains *parádeigma*" (Gerber 1871, I, 333, original italics).

21   Cf. footnote number 18.

22   A well-known literary treatment of this problem is Borges' short story "Pierre Menard, autor del *Quijote*."

23   Cf. Grafton, Most, and Zetzel's introduction to their translation of Wolf (Wolf [1795] 1985, 26ff.).

24   Of his work on this subject, Nietzsche published three long studies from 1869–70 (all in KGW II/1 and BAW 4 and 5): *De Laertii Diogenis fontibus, Analecta Laertiana, Contributions to the Study of the Sources and to the Interpretation of Laërtius Diogenes.*

25   Jonathan Barnes gives a good overview in his article, "Nietzsche and Diogenes Laërtius" (Barnes 1986, 16–40). [Editors' note: The references provided are to Barnes' originally printed version, not what is reproduced here.]

26   In Barnes estimation, Nietzsche's hypothesis is neither proven nor ruled out (Barnes 1986, esp. 34–5).

27   Barnes, in this context, also speaks of a "Principle of Indolence" (Barnes 1986, esp. 27).

28   Cf. KSA 7, 828–30 (37, 2–5) and GA XVIII, 129–98.

29   "It is not difficult to prove, though, that what one calls 'rhetoric' as an instrument of *conscious* art was already an instrument of *unconscious* art in language and its becoming, indeed, that *rhetoric is the recognition of the artistic qualities of language* [cf. Gerber 1871-3, I, 74ff., 112, 332, 356, 365, 387f.] by the bright light of the intellect. There is no non-rhetorical 'naturalness' of language to which one could take recourse: language itself is the result of entirely rhetorical arts [cf. Gerber]. The power that Aristotle calls rhetoric, the capability to find and utilize in everything that has an effect and leaves an impression, is, at the same time, the essence of language: language, like rhetoric, does not refer to truth, to the *essence* of things, it does not seek to instruct, but rather to stimulate a subjective response in others [...] This is the *first* point of view: *language is rhetoric*, since it only wants to communicate a dóxa, not an epistéme" (GA XVIII, 248ff.).

30   [Editors' note: In the original publication of this paper, there is a lengthy appendix that reproduces schematically the second and seventh sections of the lecture on rhetoric. Although we have opted not to reproduce that appendix here, for the original, see pages 41–6.]

31   Cf. *mutatis mutandis* Nietzsche on Horace's style in the chapter of *Twilight of the Idols* entitled "What I Owe the Ancients": "This mosaic of words, where every word exerts its force—as a sound, as a place, as a concept—to the right and to the left and throughout the whole, this minimum in the range and number of signs that aims at a maximum in the energy of signs" (KSA 6, 155).

32   Cf., for example, Martin Stingelin's work (Stingelin 1991, 400–32) on the excerpts from Albert Hermann Post quoted in Nietzsche's posthumous fragments the early drafts of *Beyond Good and Evil* and *On the Genealogy of Morals*.

33   Most likely because Cruisus only printed the manuscript up to §7 and left off §§8–16 and the historical appendix.

34   It was for this reason that Claudia Crawford, in her book *The Beginnings of Nietzsche's Theory of Language*, could polemically claim that Lange was much more important than Gerber (Crawford 1988, 198ff.).

35   For example Goth 1970 and Löw 1984.

36   For example, Schrift 1985, 371–95 (the deconstruction of philosophical errors through rhetoric) and especially Gilman, et al. 1989 (the centrality of rhetoric for language).

37   For example, Gilman, et al. 1989, xi. However, (1) there is hardly anything "original" in some sections, (2) the apparently "original" could quite possibly simply come from as of yet unidentified sources and (3) even what Nietzsche found in the work of others was copied down and spoken aloud by him, so that one cannot simply claim it was not his opinion.

38   For example, Gilman, et al. (Gilman, Blair. and Parent 1989, xvii) and Paul de Man in his "Rhetoric of Tropes" (de Man 1979, 104–5). This is completely true on the macroscopic level, where Nietzsche uncharacteristically combines a philological-historical observation of classic rhetoric with perspective gleaned from language philosophy, but certainly not on the microscopic level, where Nietzsche's procedure is essentially one of a compiler.

39   For example, de Man 1979, 104–6. But this is merely the effect of excerpting.

40   For example, Bierl and Calder 1992, 363–6. But this judgment is a hasty one and historically distorted: it repeats Nietzsche's naïve moral condemnation of Diogenes Laërtius without taking a genuinely scholarly standpoint.

41   Plato attributes the argument from probability to Tisias (*Phaedrus* 273a6ff.), Aristotle to Corax (*Rhetoric* 1402a18).

42   For example, Aristotle uses Anaximenes, and Cicero the anonymous *Rhetorica ad Herennium*.

43   Here as well famous names appropriated discourse taken from elsewhere: the corpus of almost every attic rhetorician contains something foreign (but the question of what, precisely, sometimes remains disputed). Cf., for example, Dover 1986.

44   The same is true of Diogenes Laërtius in Nietzsche's account.

45   See the first section of the present essay.

46   In the sense of the *Untimely Meditations. II: On the Uses and Abuses of History for Life* (KSA 1, 269).

47   And of the better known sentences of "On Truth and Lying in an Extra-moral Sense" (KSA 1, 873–90, particularly 878–86).

48   Cf. KSA 1, 878ff. and the posthumous fragments of 1872–3: "Every kind of *culture* begins by *disguising* a large number of things. The progress of mankind depends on this dissimulation" (KSA 7, 435).

49 One can understand the distancing from Schopenhauer and from Wagner in the same context. Cf. KSA 11, 248ff. and KSA 12, 233.
50 Cf. de Man 1979, 119–31 and Stingelin 1988, 336–49.
51 The script of this lecture is found in the same quarto notebook (P II 13 c) as the lecture on the history of Greek eloquence.

Works cited

Barnes, Jonathan (1986): "Nietzsche and Diogenes Laertius." In *Nietzsche-Studien*. Vol. 15, 16–40.

Bettelheim, Anton (ed.) (1901): *Biographisches Jahrbuch und deutscher Nekrolog* VI. Berlin (Georg Reimer).

Bierl, Anton and William M. Calder (1992): "Introduction" to "Friedrich Nietzsche: 'Abriß der Geschichte der Beredsamkeit.'" In *Nietzsche-Studien*. Vol. 21, 363–6.

Blass, Friedrich (1865): *Die griechische Beredsamkeit in dem Zeitraum von Alexander bis Augustus*. Berlin (Weidmann).

—(1868): *Die attische Beredsamkeit*. Vol. I: *Von Gorgias bis Lysias*. Leipzig (B. G. Teubner).

—(1874): *Die attische Beredsamkeit*. Vol. II: *Isokrates und Isaios*. Leipzig (B. G. Teubner).

Crawford, Claudia (1988): *The Beginnings of Nietzsche's Theory of Language*. New York (Walter de Gruyter).

de Man, Paul (1979): "Rhetoric of Tropes." In his *Allegories of Reading: Figural Language in Rousseau, Nietzsche, Rilke, and Proust*. New Haven (Yale University Press), 103–18.

—(1979): "Rhetoric of Persuasion." In his *Allegories of Reading: Figural Language in Rousseau, Nietzsche, Rilke, and Proust*. New Haven (Yale University Press), 119–31.

Diels, Hermann (1870): *De Galeni historia philosopha*. Bonn (dissertation).

—([1879] 1969): *Kleine Schriften zur Geschichte der antiken Philosophie*. W. Burkert (ed.) Darmstadt (Wissenschaftliche Buchgesellschaft).

Dover, Kenneth James (1968): *Lysias and the Corpus Lysiacum*. Berkeley (University of California Press).

Gerber, Gustav (1871–3): *Die Sprache als Kunst*. Bromberg (H. Hayfelder).

—([1884] 1976): *Die Sprache und das Erkennen*. Berlin (R. Gärtner).

—(1893): *Das Ich als Grundlage unserer Weltanschauung*. Berlin (H. Hayfelder).

Gilman, Sander L., et al. (eds) (1989): *Friedrich Nietzsche on Rhetoric and Language*. New York (Oxford University Press).

Goth, Joachim (1970): *Nietzsche und die Rhetorik*. Tübingen (Max Niemeyer Verlag).

Gutzwiller, Hans (1951): "Friedrich Nietzsches Lehrtätigkeit am Basler Pädagogium." In *Basler Zeitschrift für Geschichte und Altertumskunde*. Vol. 50, 148–224.

Hirzel, Rudolf (1871): *Über das Rhetorische und seine Bedeutung bei Plato*. Leipzig (S. Hirzel).

Janz, Curt Paul (1974): "Friedrich Nietzsches akademische Lehrtätigkeit in Basel." In *Nietzsche-Studien*. Vol. 3, 192–203.

Jens, Walter. "Von deutscher Rede." In Adam Müller: *Zwölf Reden über die Beredsamkeit und deren Verfall in Deutschland. Mit einem Essay und einem Nachwort von Walter Jens*. Frankfurt am Main (Insel-Verlag).

Lacoue-Labarthe, Philippe (1971): "Le détour (Nietzsche et la rhétorique)." In *Poétique*. Vol. 5, 53–76.

Lehrs, Karl (1837): *Quaestiones epicae.* Königsberg (Bornträger).

—(1873): *Die Pindarscholien. Eine kritische Untersuchung zur philologischen Quellenkunde.* Leipzig (S. Hirzel).

—(1875): *Populäre Aufsätze aus dem Alterthum, vorzugsweise zur Ethik und Religion der Griechen.* Leipzig (Teubner).

—(1882): *Aristarchi Studiis Homericis.* Leipzig (S. Hirzel).

Löw, Reinhard (1984): *Nietzsche, Sophist und Erzieher: Philosophische Untersuchungen zum systematischen Ort von Friedrich Nietzsches Denken.* Weinheim (Acta humaniora).

Marietti, Angèle (trans. and ed.) (1992): *Friedrich Nietzsche: Le Livre du philosophe: études théorétiques = Das Philosophenbuch: theoretische Studien.* Paris (Aubier-Flammarion).

Meijers, Anthonie (1988): "Gustav Gerber und Friedrich Nietzsche: Zum historischen Hintergrund der sprachphilosophischen Auffassungen des frühen Nietzsche." In *Nietzsche-Studien.* Vol. 17, 369–90.

Meijers, Anthonie and Martin Stingelin (1988): "Konkordanz zu den wörtlichen Abschriften und Übernahmen von Beispielen und Zitaten aus Gustav Gerber: *Die Sprache als Kunst* (Bromberg 1871) in Nietzsches Rhetorik-Vorlesung und in 'Über Wahrheit und Lüge im aussermoralischen Sinne'." In *Nietzsche-Studien.* Vol. 17, 350–68.

Meister, Richard (1948): "Nietzsches Lehrtätigkeit in Basel 1869–79." In *Anzeiger der Österreichischen Akademie der Wissenschaften, Phil.-Hist. Klasse.* Vol. 85, 103–21.

Most, Glenn W. and Thomas Fries (2008): "Von der Krise der Historie zum Prozess des Schreibens: Nietzsches zweite *Unzeitgemässe Betrachtung*." In Peter Hughes, Thomas Fries, and Tan Wälchli (eds): *Schreibprozesse.* Munich (Fink), 133–56.

Nancy, Jean-Luc and Philippe Lacoue-Labarthe (1971): "Friedrich Nietzsche, Rhétorique et langage." In *Poétique.* Vol. 5, 99–142.

Oehler, Max ([1942] 1975): *Nietzsches Bibliothek. Vierzehnte Jahresgabe der Gesellschaft der Freunde des Nietzsche-Archivs Weimar.* Nendeln-Lichtenstein (Kraus-Reprint).

Schmidt, Siegfried J. (1968): "Die vergessene Sprachphilosophie des 19. Jahrhunderts." In his *Sprache und Denken als sprachphilosophisches Problem von Locke bis Wittgenstein.* The Hague (Martinus Nijhoff), 80–147.

Schrift, Alan D. (1985): *Language, Metaphor, Rhetoric: Nietzsche's Deconstruction of Epistemology.* In *Journal of the History of Philosophy.* Vol. 23 (3), 371–95.

Spengel, Leonhard (1842): *Über das Studium der Rhetorik bei den Alten.* Munich (J. G. Weifs).

—(1851): *Über die Rhetorik des Aristoteles.* In *Abhandlungen der Philosophisch-philologischen Classe der K. Bayerischen Akademie der Wissenschaften.* Munich (Bayrische Akademie der Wissenschaften). Vol. 6.

—(1862): "Die rhetorica (des Anaximenes) ad Alexandrum kein machwerk der spätesten zeit." In *Philologus.* Vol. 18, 604–46.

—(1863): "Die Definition und Eintheilung der Rhetorik bei den Alten." In *Rheinisches Museum für Philologie.* Vol. 18, 481–526.

Stingelin, Martin (1988): "Nietzsches Wortspiel als Reflexion auf poet(olog)ische Verfahren." In *Nietzsche-Studien.* Vol. 17, 336–49.

—(1991): "Beiträge zur Quellenforschung. Konkordanz zu Friedrich Nietzsches Exzerpten aus Albert Hermann Post, *Bausteine für eine allgemeine Rechtswissenschaft auf vergleichend-ethnologischer Basis. Oldenburg 1881 (2 vols.)* im Nachlaß von Frühjahr-Sommer und Sommer 1883." In *Nietzsche-Studien.* Vol. 20, 400–32.

Stroux, Johannes (1925): *Nietzsches Professur in Basel.* Jena (Frommansche Buchhandlung).

Usener, Hermann (1912): *Kleine Schriften.* Vol. 1.: *Arbeiten zur griechischen Philosophie und Rhetorik. Grammatische und Textkritische Beiträge.* Leipzig (Teubner).

Volkmann, Richard (1865): *Hermagoras oder Elemente der Rhetorik.* Stettin (Th. von der Nahmer).

—(1872): *Die Rhetorik der Griechen und Römer in systematischer Übersicht.* Berlin (Ebeling).

Wackernagel, Wilhelm ([1873] 2003): *Poetik, Rhetorik und Stilistik.* New York (G. Olms).

Westermann, Anton (1833–5): *Geschichte der Beredsamkeit in Griechenland und Rom.* Leipzig (Verlag von Johann Ambrosius Barth).

Wolf, Friedrich August ([1795] 1985): *Prolegomena to Homer.* Anthony Grafton, Glenn W. Most, and James E. G. Zetzel (trans. and eds). Princeton (Princeton University Press).

Apollo and the Problem of the Unity of Culture in the Early Nietzsche

Douglas Burnham

1. Introduction

Early drafts of what would become central themes of *The Birth of Tragedy* date from 1870. The series begins with two public lectures, "Greek Musical Drama" and "Socrates and Tragedy," in January and February of that year. In addition, Nietzsche wrote the complete but unpublished essays "The Dionysian Worldview" (commenced in July, probably not finished until at least September) and "The Birth [or Development] of the Tragic Thought," which was a gift to Cosima Wagner at the end of that year. The book itself is written by spring 1871, and part of it printed for private circulation as "Socrates and Greek Tragedy," but the whole is not published until 1872. *The Birth of Tragedy* certainly seems a complete and self-contained piece of work, and the culmination of this series of shorter pieces; in fact it is only part of a continual series of reflections on tragedy, culture, language, art, and science. Indeed, completion of the tragedy book by no means put an end to Nietzsche's struggle with its view of Greek life and culture, or with its implications. The evidence of this is all through the notebooks, and Nietzsche's 1872 Christmas/birthday gift to Cosima were five prefaces to unwritten books, which included "The Greek State," "Homer's Contest"—both of which obviously continue to deal with these classical issues, and both of which exist in some draft form prior to the completion of the manuscript of *The Birth of Tragedy*—and "On the Pathos of Truth," the specifically Greek-centered analysis in which is not evident from the title. Also in 1872, Nietzsche lectured on Ancient Rhetoric at Basle. Moreover, he was busy working up his lectures on the Pre-Platonic philosophers into a book (Philosophy in the Tragic Age of the Greeks) which was largely completed by spring 1873 but never published, although Nietzsche worked on it as late as 1879. This work is framed by the claim that the enduring significance of these "refuted" philosophical systems is a cultural one. In brief, then, *The Birth of Tragedy* is part of a puzzle—albeit the part that happens to have been published. Most obviously it is part of a puzzle concerning ancient Greek culture. However, as we shall see there is a tight interconnection between this narrower topic and Nietzsche's other philosophical preoccupations. A proper understanding of that book is impossible without reflecting upon how Nietzsche develops his ideas, what connections they have to other problems with which he was grappling, and where he pursues them immediately after its publication.

Beyond the explicit concern with Greek cultural life, the most famous philosophical implications of this work have to do with the nature of language and truth. Of course, there is the widely anthologized, but unpublished, essay "On Truth and Lies in an Extra-moral Sense" (1873). Much of the content of that essay, though, is found in earlier work. For example, we will return below to Nietzsche's Basel lectures on Ancient Greek Rhetoric (first given at the end of 1872 and scheduled to have been repeated in 1874); the 1873 essay contains the philosophical substance from the third of these lectures. Likewise, the extraordinary first paragraph of that essay is found, in draft, in "On the Pathos of Truth" which as we know predates it by a year. Nietzsche also produces a set of five lectures on education, which again pursue the themes developed in connection with Greek culture towards an understanding of Nietzsche's contemporary Germany. The second half of *The Birth of Tragedy* makes exactly the same move: an analysis of contemporary Germany in terms of the as yet unrealized possibilities of culture. Accordingly, my claim—consistent with Nietzsche's career as a classical philologist—is that these early discussions of the nature of language, truth, education or contemporary cultural politics are in fact different ways of pursuing those *same insights* originally established on the apparently narrower ground of ancient Greek culture. It is thus no exaggeration to assert that Nietzsche's understanding of the mode of cultural life of the Apollonian is central to *all* his early philosophical work. Now, one can imagine a study that moved forward, as it were, from the problem of Greek culture to the bigger themes of Nietzsche's career. Here, we will make something of a start on such a study; however, the necessary preparatory work will be to establish firmly that understanding of Greek culture. So, we need to start by following these links *back* from Nietzsche's relatively well-known philosophical themes, in order to articulate the much less well-known, underlying insights concerning Greek antiquity.

The first step below will be to outline the key ideas of *The Birth of Tragedy*. This is essential for a number of reasons. It will help us to get rapidly past what "everyone knows" about this book. Thus we will be able to concentrate more effectively on what is novel about my interpretation of that work, and also to bring out what the problem is to which this essay hopefully will be an answer. Both the novelty and the problem concern the figure of Apollo. I want to argue for a slightly modified understanding of the Apollonian in Nietzsche's early work. In turn, this raises the problem of *why* Nietzsche might have arrived at this view, and with what implications. This paper will propose two ideas. First, a philological one, that Nietzsche arrived at the notion of the Apollonian only relatively late, *after* working out his concepts of the Dionysian and Socratic. Second, a philosophical one, that this late arrival of the Apollonian tells us a great deal concerning how the development of the idea allowed Nietzsche to articulate and resolve much bigger problems: the nature of cultural unity, and the nature and limits of science.

2. Overview of Nietzsche's ideas in *The Birth of Tragedy*

The Birth of Tragedy contains five major themes. The first is an account of the development of culture (in this case Greek culture) in terms of a set of drives. The two famous drives are the Apollonian and Dionysian. The former represents a cultural drive for form, clarity, individuation, calmness; the latter for intoxication, loss of identity, universal "oneness." My work on *The Birth of Tragedy* (much of it benefiting from being done with Martin Jesinghausen) demonstrates how this first thesis must be understood: we have to think of *three* separate drives (the Apollonian, Dionysian, and Socratic) rather than, say, the Socratic as a degenerate form of the Apollonian.[1] The Socratic represents an optimistic belief in logic and scientific enquiry. It is no less ancient than the others, but only begins to dominate the cultural landscape with Socrates, and thus its name.

The second thesis of Nietzsche's book is the claim that these drives not only determine cultural production, but implicitly contain metaphysical views about reality and about the place of human beings. Many, but not all, of these views Nietzsche takes from Schopenhauer. The Apollonian believes in the *value of* form and individuation as dream-like states, and as they are and not "corrected"; the Dionysian believes in the underlying unity of all things (what Schopenhauer called the Will); the Socratic believes in the straight-forward existence of the objects of its thought and bears a corresponding optimism in progress. In this, the most important difference between the Apollonian and the Socratic becomes clear: the former realizes the illusory character of its beliefs and its productions, but nevertheless ascribes them the highest value. The Socratic, by contrast, finds this unintelligible, both because it identifies illusion with the *absence* of value, and because it finds morally absurd the assigning of value to that which is. The Socratic finds the Dionysian worldview no less unintelligible.

Third, classical Greek tragedy is an important event in the history of European culture because it represents the union of the Apollonian and Dionysian drives—a unique moment of cultural unity. As we shall see below, this notion of the unity of culture then comes to predominate Nietzsche's philosophical work, both within *The Birth of Tragedy* and in his work for some years later. Fourth, tragedy rapidly declines as a cultural form because of the increasing dominance of the Socratic drive, the metaphysical view of which finds it impossible for there to be other drives. Socrates and Euripides simply did not understand those cultural drives that lie behind the tragedy of Aeschylus and Sophocles, and certainly did not understand the metaphysical principles for which they stood, and so reconceptualized and redesigned the nature of tragedy on the scientific optimism of the Socratic.

The fifth thesis leaves the Greek world behind and jumps to Nietzsche's late nineteenth-century Germany (and Europe, by extension). Here, Nietzsche analyzes under what conditions a "rebirth" of tragedy in the modern world would be possible. Nietzsche does not hide the fact that this fifth thesis is in fact an exploration of the cultural and metaphysical meaning of Richard Wagner.

Here we will focus on the development of the concept of Apollo, a proper under-standing of which will be our point of access to a richer understanding of Nietzsche's thought in this period. To isolate the concept of the Apollonian, however, is already to commit gross simplification. First, this is because the concept must be understood as part of the three-way dynamic mentioned above—that is, as one of a set of cultural drives which project distinct metaphysical views of reality and divergent cultural behaviors. Second, because the separation of the analysis of Greek cultural life from the investigation of broader philosophical, or contemporary, issues misses the *strategic* role of the relationship between them. Nietzsche writes,

> The Greeks as interpreters—when we speak of the Greeks, we involuntarily speak of today and yesterday: their widely familiar history is an unblemished mirror that always radiates back something that is not in the mirror itself. [...] In this way, the Greeks ease for modern men the communication of much that is difficult to communicate and curious. (AOM 218; KSA 2, 417)

This passage echoes what Nietzsche had said in the "Forward to Richard Wagner" in *The Birth of Tragedy* several years earlier (BT Foreword; KSA 1, 23–4). It is not, in other words, a lucky accident that led Nietzsche from his studies of classical Greece to all these other philosophical (and social or political) issues—it was planned, in outline if not in detail.

Simplify we must, though, in order to have something to say in a short space. As we said above, Apollo symbolizes one of several cultural drives, by which Nietzsche means at least a need of the Hellenic people to express themselves by way of a particular type of cultural production, and a corresponding interpretation of this need as a "Weltanschauung." As we noted above, the cultural production associated with Apollo is characterized above all by clarity and a certain calmness of imagery; it is exemplified by epic poetry, and the arts of architecture and sculpture, as well as central political, social, and religious institutions. The "worldview" of the Apollonian is slightly complicated, and often misunderstood. To be sure, Nietzsche identifies it with the principle of individuation in Schopenhauer. This principle asserts the *original* separation of one thing from other things. This notion Nietzsche finds in the "clarity" of the Apollonian in its concern with the outlines of things, in opposition to some underlying, fluid unity. However, for Nietzsche, the original Schopenhauerian idea has to be understood as mediated by an awareness of illusion. Famously, Nietzsche employs the notion of something like "lucid dreaming," which he seems to claim is not the exception but more like the essence of the dream-state. I dream, but I am at the same time aware that I am dreaming, that all I sense is an illusion; but I nevertheless value the illusion and have no wish but to carry on dreaming (BT 1; KSA 1, 25–30). The Apollonian drive, then, comprises a metaphysical worldview that is, in its essence, *not different* from the Dionysian. In both cases there is a commitment to the truth of the underlying oneness and lack of individuation of all things; in both cases there are quite appropriate attitudes of terror and desire towards that oneness. In the Apollonian, however, rather than giving itself over to the ecstatic dissolution of identity into the oneness of the world, I am content to—indeed, I require myself to and take calm delight in this requirement—remain at the level of illusions of individual forms. Importantly also, this is a claim about a whole people and the nature of their existence and whole cultural production, from top to bottom, not just a claim about what their philosophers or artistic geniuses think and do. It is, in other words, a historically specific but nevertheless fundamental ontological characterization of human being.

Now, of course, it is one thing to say classical Greek antiquity was characterized by clarity of imagery in many of its cultural products—indeed, various modes of clarity are the most obvious differences among Winckelmann's four periods of Greek art. Such a claim was already a cliché by the time Nietzsche is writing. Nietzsche also suggests that there is a connection between the visual values of Greek sculpture and architecture, on the one hand, and philosophical themes in Plato or Aristotle such as the Forms, species differentiation, dialectic or the syllogism. This claim, although perhaps original, might even have appeared rather old fashioned, since the idea has something of the intellectualized approach to aesthetics found in Wolff or Baumgarten—sensible beauty is perfection in the exhibition of the rational idea. However, compared to these two preliminary notions, it is quite a different matter to say that classical Greeks were fully cognizant of the illusory quality of this view of things, relative to the desperate pessimism of the Dionysian which Nietzsche illustrates through Silenus, and yet held onto these illusions for the sake of an aesthetic justification of their existence, their civilization, and their gods. This too may or may not be an entirely novel claim, but it certainly is an extraordinary one.

3. The birth of Apollo

This concept, however, did not spring fully formed from Nietzsche's head. Its gestation was nearly a year coming, from the autumn of 1869 to the summer or autumn of 1870, and is a very revealing story. To begin with, it is not too much of a stretch to say that Nietzsche was particularly pleased with the reception of the second of the public lectures he gave in Basel, in the new year of 1870, "Socrates and Tragedy," given on February 1, 1870. Letters (for example, to Erwin Rohde and Paul Deussen in February or March in KSB 3) talk of the "terror and incomprehension" that greeted the lecture.[2] Nietzsche evidently believed that this response meant he was on to something. This lecture, more speculative than the first, really represents a first draft of the ideas that would appear in *The Birth of Tragedy*. It is very unlikely that the terror and incomprehension came from the only mention of the "Apollonian," where Nietzsche says that Socrates possesses one side of the Hellenistic, its "apollonian clarity" (KSA 1, 544). It is certainly very tempting to see Nietzsche bringing together here the Socratic and Apollonian drives. This temptation precipitates in turn a great misunderstanding of the meaning of *The Birth of Tragedy*. It is the fact that the alleged meaning of this early passage is so out of kilter with *The Birth of Tragedy* (where it is entirely clear that Nietzsche does not conflate, in any sense, these two drives) that leads one to suspect its interpretation. In fact, there is *no evidence whatsoever* that the adjective "apollinische" is here used in any way other than as a *general* symbol of light and clarity—as if Nietzsche had written, for example, "sun-like." What looks like an explicit reference to the specific, technical concept of the Apollonian early in 1870, is not. Nowhere else in the lecture, or in Nietzsche's Notebook 2 from this period (NF 1869, 2), is the full concept of the Apollonian employed, or even gestured towards. The only candidate would be 2[31]. Here we find the nominal form, to be sure, but otherwise it is difficult to see this brief and cryptic fragment as anything other than a way of making the point (which we discussed above) that Socratic or rather Platonic dialectics belongs to the general tradition of Greek "clarity": "The development of the Apollonian towards

doctrine [Lehrsatze]" (NF 1869, 2[31]; KSA 7, 56). This sentence fragment is interesting, to be sure, but it is not yet the concept of the Apollonian as found in *The Birth
of Tragedy*.

In Notebook 3 (NF 1869, 3), discussion of Apollo starts to come thick and fast.
Nietzsche often had several notebooks on the go at the same time, and thus their
contents will frequently span six months or more. Although Notebook 3 seems to
have been started at the end of 1869, we can confidently date these thoughts to the
spring of 1870, since otherwise we would have to explain the almost complete absence
of the term elsewhere either in Nietzsche's two lectures, or Notebook 2. As part of its
heading, 3[12] reads "Apollo as the avenging god [Sühngott]" (NF 1869, 3[12]; KSA 7,
62)—perhaps a pun on "sun-god" is intended. Apollo is picked out as a distinct concept
here. It is difficult to see how the Old Testament idea of the vengeful god relates to how
Nietzsche thinks of the concept later, and thus this notebook entry is further evidence
that the concept of Apollo went through a long and delayed development. Entry/Note
3[25], however, contains a particularly important new move: "In the worldview of
Sophocles, Apollo just as much as Dionysus again came to victory: they became reconciled [sie versöhnten sich]" (NF 1869, 3[25]; KSA 7, 67). The notion of reconciliation
is the most obvious key advance. Less obviously, but equally important, for the first
time in Nietzsche we see Apollo and Dionysus viewed as similar kinds of things—
i.e. both thought as cultural forms or drives. Casting them in this way means that
tragedy could be their coming together. In fact, much of Notebook 3 is an account of
Nietzsche gradually, and with missteps, moving closer to the account of Apollo found
in "The Dionysian Worldview" and in *The Birth of Tragedy*. Key among those missteps
are those that resemble the widespread misinterpretation of *The Birth of Tragedy*
discussed above: considering the Socratic as a further development of the Apollonian.
So, at 3[33]: "Enchantment: it is the suffering that resounds, as opposed to the activity
of the epic: the 'image' of Apollonian culture is portrayed through enchantment by
man" (NF 1869, 3[33]; KSA 7, 69). And, more clearly, at 3[36] we read: "Dialectic,
as the art of 'appearance', annihilates tragedy. [...] In Plato, the supreme glorification
of things as original images; that is, the world viewed entirely from the standpoint of
the eyes (Apollo)" (NF 1869, 3[36]; KSA 7, 70). This is an extraordinary idea! For our
purposes here, however, we need to notice that, with respect to Nietzsche's full concept
of the Apollonian, this is still an oversimplification. Images and the visual are opposed
to feeling (particularly suffering), which are expressed primarily though musical
tones. When uninhibited by the Dionysian truth, the former lead directly to Socrates,
Plato, and science. Accordingly, Nietzsche writes, a few entries later concerning the
dissolution of tragic balance: "The overwhelming sense of beauty absorbed the idea
of truth, [then] gradually released it. The tragic world-outlook is the tipping point
[Grenzpunkt]: beauty and truth balance each other" (NF 1869, 3[45]; KSA 7, 73).
Now, assuming we identify Dionysus with truth, here, this fragment is a narrative
of the death of tragedy. In other words, after the delicate balance that is tragedy, the
Apollonian takes into itself the Dionysian truth, and then issues it again, but without
its basic Dionysian content. In brief, the Apollonian becomes Socratic. To be sure,
this is a no less thorough-going conception of the suicide of tragedy than that found
in *The Birth of Tragedy*. Nevertheless, this infection is what, in *The Birth of Tragedy*,

Nietzsche calls the "pathological" version of the Apollonian (BT 1; KSA 1, 28), and which he refuses to identify with the Socratic. The Socratic is a third drive, and one that predates tragedy, and already existed as a deep element of Greek culture. For example, "The Socratic is older than Socrates" he writes in "Socrates and Tragedy"; the same point is made in *The Birth of Tragedy* (BT 14; KSA 1, 95). Thus, although Apollo features heavily in this notebook, and finally as something like the partner of Dionysus, there is still no indication of the essential difference of the Apollonian from the Socratic. Instead, there is an unnecessary confusion of the concept of the Socratic; the clarity with which Nietzsche had earlier envisioned the death of tragedy (back in February of 1870) has become temporarily clouded. By "The Dionysian Worldview," these missteps are largely behind him.

Let us return to the passage concerning Socrates and his Apollonian clarity in the second lecture, "Socrates and Tragedy," given at the beginning of February 1870. If not the idea of Apollo, what *can* be taken from this passage? Certainly, it is true that Nietzsche's later characterization of Socrates as misunderstanding or twisting earlier Greek culture, and doing so in a way that led to the development of a specifically modern sense of the scientific, is already in place. In the second lecture, in the discussion of tragedy's death, we find an analysis of Euripidean tragedy in terms of a distortion of the healthy agonistic Greek culture. The rot set in, Nietzsche asserts, with dialogue. The original chorus, or chorus with single actor, developed into two actors. At this point, the deeply rooted Greek sense of competition between equals resulted in the temptation to treat dialogue as a contest of words and reasons. This conception of dialogue Socrates understands, and adopts as a philosophical practice: dialectic. In brief, then, the story of the *death* of tragedy at the hands of Socrates and Euripides is here, right at the beginning of 1870. *This* may have been of consternation to the audience in the *Rheinisches Museum*. Other candidates for shock value are the strongly Schopenhauer-influenced characterization of the Dionysian, considered as the core of tragedy, together with the enthusiastic gestures to Wagner. Both of these, though, are also to be found in the first lecture—even the title of that first lecture is a reference to Wagner—so my money is on the portrayal of Socrates as being the feather ruffler, and thus it is the first instance of Nietzsche being Nietzsche in public.

As we just saw, at the beginning of this period, Nietzsche is closer to his *Birth of Tragedy* notion of the Dionysian, and of the death of tragedy through the influence of Socrates and Euripides, than he is to the conception of the Apollonian. Surprisingly, that is, the Apollonian is the *last* piece of the puzzle. By the time he writes "The Dionysian Worldview" and "The Birth of the Tragic Idea" later in 1870, however, the puzzle is complete, at least in its broad outlines. All of which demands that we ask the question: what philosophical or other considerations may have led Nietzsche to develop, within six months or so, the full concept of the Apollonian? I am not interested in this question as a biographical or simply historical question. I am interested in it insofar as it reveals a philosophical idea, analysis or argument that might previously have been overlooked, and which thus enriches our understanding of Nietzsche's philosophy and especially his views on Greek antiquity. The answer to my question lies in what above we called a historical but fundamental ontological assertion—a drive that characterizes a whole people. Nietzsche's historical ontology was originally one-sided, it lacked an internal dynamic. The full concept of the Apollonian arrived to supply that dynamic.

During the early part of this period (the winter of 1869/70), there is no question but that he sees the Dionysian as a drive generally inherent in the Greek people, a standing if generally not visible part of their broad cultural life, and more significantly a way of existing. For example, in the lecture "Greek Music Drama" from January 1870, Nietzsche says: "However, the soul of the Athenian who came to view tragedy at the great festival of Dionysus, already had within it something of that element out of which tragedy is born" (KSA 1, 521); and again, "Something of this Dionysian natural life was, during the period of the flowering of Attic Drama, still in the soul of the audience" (KSA 1, 522). This Dionysian effect is not something that is initiated in the theater, then, but something that the audience brings with them, an existence the Greek people already are—and indeed *still* are, despite gradually emerging Socratic forces—and one that is at best *activated* through the performance of tragedy. To be sure, Nietzsche then oscillates on the question of whether the Dionysian mode of life is native to Greece, or whether it originates from Asia. In the earlier period, the only mention of Asian imports is the discussion of purely instrumental music in "The Greek Music Drama" (KSA 1, 529). By the time he writes "The Dionysian Worldview," Nietzsche writes of "Dionysus storming in out of Asia" (KSA 1, 556). So, briefly, Nietzsche expelled the origin of the Greek Dionysian some distance towards the Orient; the speculation is plausible that this idea arises as a way of supplying the dynamic reasons for historical changes which, we have argued, were missing in the previous version. However, thinking of the Dionysiac as arriving from outside is not an *internal* dynamic, not a story of the necessary development of culture but only of the accidental influence of one culture by another. By the time that he writes the full manuscript of *The Birth of Tragedy*, then, Nietzsche asserts the Dionysian to be a fundamental drive of all peoples, whether barbarian or Greek (KSA 1, 31f.). The reason for the cultural development of tragedy is now for the first time the notion of an original brotherhood of drives.

In contrast, as we have seen, Nietzsche's technical concept of the Apollonian is not to be found in this early work. So, it is hardly surprising for us to realize that a conception of the Apollonian as a characterization of Greek existence is missing too. Concepts of image and illusion are present, of course, but are not metaphysical claims nor are they general claims about a *people* (like the Dionysian and Socratic are)—rather, they are specific claims about artistic practices. A notebook entry like 1[49] contains a germ of Nietzsche's later idea of the plastic imagination of the poet and the generation of mythology (NF 1869, 1[49]; KSA 7, 24). The emotional content of Greek musical drama is universal, but the poet has to imagine a past that is the cause of these universal moods. This cause is mythology, "A mirroring of our most universal states, seen in an ideal and idealizing past." However, the discussion is quite specific (framed by the context of the development of absolute music), and the idea is confined precisely to the individual poet. There is no sense here that such a plastic imagination is central to Greek life as such, or that it is based upon a fundamental drive. Likewise, in that passage we find again the cliché of the Greeks as celebrating clarity and distinctness, but there is scant evidence that even this is thought of as a basic cultural drive of a whole people, as was the Dionysian. However, looking back from the point of view of *The Birth of Tragedy*, this absence is very surprising indeed, so much so that many readers of Nietzsche's notebooks and early lectures do not allow themselves to notice that it is missing.

So, between late winter 1869/70 and the summer or autumn of 1870, Nietzsche realized that his story of the high period of Greek culture was incomplete. The concept of the Apollonian is invented sometime in the spring as a fellow drive, the reconciliation of which with Dionysus is the event of tragedy. But this early version of the Apollonian on its own does not fit with the already worked-out conception of the Socratic, as we saw above; indeed, it just brings confusion to what had already been established concerning the Socratic. "The Dionysian Worldview" was started in July 1870 but, the war and Nietzsche's long convalescence intervened. Nietzsche served briefly as a medical orderly in August and September 1870 and was still suffering effects of the illness he contracted months later. Although he claims that it was written in the summer, Nietzsche does not mention the essay prior to a flurry of announcements in letters dated no earlier than November that year.[3] Thus, it seems likely that "The Dionysian Worldview" was not completed until later in the year, perhaps as late as October. This text formed the basis also of "The Birth of the Tragic Thought," a gift to Cosima Wagner in December. Thus, it is not simply for effect that Nietzsche (both in the "Preface to Wagner" and in the "Attempt at Self-Criticism") talks about *The Birth of Tragedy* being forged during the war. Indeed, it is tempting to speculate that reflections on the meaning of these political and military events precipitated the new idea of the Apollonian (cf. the reflections on war, the state, and art in Notebook 10, and also striking reflections such as "Germany as a backwards-processing [rückwärts schreitende] Greece: we have reached the period of the Persian wars" (NF 1870, 5[23]; KSA 7, 97).

Whatever events precipitated it, Nietzsche realized that the Dionysian drive needed a brother and sparring partner, one that lay at the same level of a historical-ontological character of the Greek people, and one that did not make nonsense of the concept of the Socratic. Moreover, the brother drive to the Dionysian could not be the earlier form of the Socratic drive, for that was everywhere and always only the annihilation of the Dionysian. He realized that there were too many problems with the earlier account of tragedy's development and its death that remained unsolved. Chief among these problems was the need for something that would explain the dynamism of Greek cultural production and thus account for the narrative of the development of culture. In Nietzsche's first lecture ("Greek Musical Drama") we find the now familiar description of the growth of tragedy from the chorus, what is missing is any *explanation* for such development. In the second lecture ("Socrates and Tragedy") explanations for developments are definitely not lacking. As mentioned above, there the *Birth of Tragedy* story concerning the Euripidean and Socratic failure to understand tragedy, and decisive modifications to tragedy which results in its "suicide," are clearly present.

The cliché of Greek sun-like clarity evolved (in Nietzsche's thought, that is) into the Apollonian, with its essential difference: awareness of illusion, and the valuing of illusion. This was the decisive step. Not only could Nietzsche now, as we just said, account for the development of Greek cultural forms (for example, the treatment of Homer and of Archilochus in the first third of *The Birth of Tragedy*), but a whole host of other philosophical consequences follows as well. Nietzsche can now (i) produce a much more detailed model of metaphysical and affective moments of that cultural innovation that was tragedy (*The Birth of Tragedy* from about sections 7 through 10); and (ii) solve the problem of "Greek cheerfulness [Heiterkeit]" in contrast to pessimism by showing the former to be a serious philosophical idea—the aesthetic justification of existence—and indeed a way of existing, rather than something that arises from mere ease and comfort; (iii) show what a truly epochal moment it was when the Socratic drive became dominant and thus misunderstood and repressed what had, for three centuries, been the essence of Hellenism (*The Birth of Tragedy*, sections 11 to 15); (iv) treat the contemporary "German problem"—the perceived stagnant or decadent culture, a view he shared with Wagner and with which he had been preoccupied since the beginning—with a new critical eye in terms of its relation to Socratism and the whole history of science. Moreover, in this regard the re-emergence of the Apollonian in the contemporary scene opens up the possibility of a reconciliation of science and art which Nietzsche envisions throughout the second half of *The Birth of Tragedy*. (v) As pointed out above, the notion of the "agon" as a feature of classical Greek cultural life is employed in the second lecture ("Socrates and Tragedy") early in 1870. However, because Dionysus has no sparring partner, there is no indication that Nietzsche is there employing the idea of the "agon" in a more fundamental fashion. That is, the idea of "agon" is not found here as the general mechanism of Greek cultural *development*, much less as a universal mechanism of culture. Arguably, at least, the discovery of the concept of the Apollonian allows Nietzsche to generalize the concept of the "agon" in these ways. Thus, as we have already noted, by "The Dionysian Worldview" in the late summer or early autumn of 1870, the struggle between Apollo and Dionysus now provides the dynamic mechanism behind the development of Greek culture. Further, it is clear that by the time he writes *The Birth of Tragedy* in 1871, Nietzsche intends this analysis to be an account of cultural development *in general*—for otherwise, the notion of a rebirth of tragedy in a contemporary setting would make no sense. Finally, (vi) Nietzsche can now solve the problem of what it means for there to be a unity of culture—a problem which he did not quite even realize that he had until the discovery of Apollo, but which then drives much of his work thereafter.

4. A genuine unity of culture

The ultimate aim of this paper is to explore the last of these implications. However, they are all closely interconnected, and thus it turns out that the natural starting-point will be the second. (Moreover, before the end we will also have to discuss the fourth.) Cheerfulness, on Nietzsche's new analysis, is no longer a historically accidental emotional state ascribed to the classic Greeks; it is the mode of existence of the Apollonian. Here I stress the Apollonian because it is the civic, productive, and above all visible side of Greek existence, while the metaphysics implicit in it are not at all different from and indeed assume the Dionysian "worldview." If the Greeks gave the *impression* of being cheerful, it is because they existed as Apollonian beings. We have here a whole people whose very existence is to be understood by the necessity and value attached, in full consciousness, to illusion, which in turn is understood to float above a terrifying abyss of the dissolution of all identity and with respect to which individuals including the gods themselves are, at best, tools in some single, inscrutable destiny. This cheerfulness is really a cultural issue—where "culture" for Nietzsche means the existence of a people as to their drives and values, such that their whole civilization becomes a mechanism for the production of greatness.[4] "Cheerfulness" of the Greeks was an important notion for Nietzsche[5] not just because he saw it as his most striking challenge to conventional wisdom and scholarship in the area, but also because it encapsulated his new understanding of the nature, importance, and possibilities of culture, whether Greek or any other. Greek culture was unified; modern culture is dissipated.

Above, we briefly mentioned some of the implications of the insights in *The Birth of Tragedy*, which Nietzsche started to pursue with vigour even before the book had appeared: political philosophy ("The Greek State" and "Homer's Contest"), educational philosophy ("On the Future of our Educational Institutions") and philosophy of language (lectures on Ancient Rhetoric, and "On Truth and Lies in an Extra-moral Sense"). "Philosophy in the Tragic Age of the Greeks" reflects all of these concerns, also. It is the philosophy of language that will detain me here. It interests me precisely because, although I will argue Nietzsche's conception of language is at bottom *the same issue* as that of culture, it is the *least obviously* so. Accordingly, Nietzsche's philosophy of language is most susceptible to misunderstanding. Again, the purpose is not to trace the lines of the development of thought forward; rather, I intend to move backwards from the later work towards what it illuminates concerning the concept of the Apollonian as developed for *The Birth of Tragedy*.

Nietzsche's philosophy of language, circa 1872/73, is in fact not primarily about language at all. The title of the essay "On Truth and Lies in an Extra-moral Sense" already tells us this. The issue is the possibility of truth, and the necessity of some set of untruths for any given culture; language is simply an element in the explanation of these phenomena. Moreover, at this stage, Nietzsche has a surprisingly naïve sense of language, entirely thought through semantics, a set of verbal signifiers for some mental content. To be sure, Nietzsche's account here is important in that it inaugurates a poetic conception of what philosophical writing would have to be. However, the primary importance of this work is its relation to the problem of the nature and unity of culture, and to the critical problem of the nature of truth. Let us then briefly work through the account of language in order to bring out these other issues.

What is it that words (or phrases or whole sentences, perhaps) refer to? Not to things as they are, to be sure, and not even in any unmediated way to nervous stimuli (sensations, broadly speaking). There is always some artistic or poetic twist between things, sensations and words—metaphor, metonymy, etc.—such that the whole fabric of language is an artistic illusion. With respect to the nature of language, the key novelties are that the signification relation is understood tropologically (as is, in turn, the relation of mental content to nervous stimulation), and that the development of concepts happens not prior to the utterance, but subsequently, from the need to repeat and reuse the word. The primary drive lying behind this artistic creation of illusion is pragmatic: our relations to things, and specifically relations of pleasure or pain and thus utility or danger, are what get expressed in language. Indeed, the key thing is not what in fact might lead to preservation, but what is believed to do so. Access to truth—which would be things as they are, unfiltered, unmodified—is strictly speaking impossible. Moreover, Nietzsche insists that language users persist in a naïve view of the relation of language to things, having forgotten the rhetorical tropes on which all language is founded, and thus also not noticing the implicit valuing function of actual language. Nietzsche writes, famously, "Truths are illusions, of which one has forgotten that they are illusions" (TL 1; KSA 1, 880f.). So, the truths of ethics, politics, science, and philosophy are more or less *useful* untruths. However, language is a communal phenomenon—we write or speak to each other employing a language that was already common to us all—and the pragmatic drive here is one of the preservation of the community, first and foremost. Language belongs to a people, and the particular "truths" that it embodies are primarily values—a sense of good and bad, right and wrong—those that serve (or appear to serve) that people in terms of survival and prosperity. The move from individual speakers to communities of speakers—and thus to a "people"—is the most evident link between the problem of language and the problem of culture. Now, there are two curious things we need to observe in "On Truth and Lies." The first is that, throughout, Nietzsche employs the language of illusion, dream, artistic production, individuation, and images. Since late in 1870, this was the established language of the Apollonian. This raises the question of what is the relation between the Apollonian and Nietzsche's account of language and truth. Second, we just saw Nietzsche using the language of forgetting. This, however, seems to entail the possibility of "remembering"—but what could that possibly mean?

The answers to these questions are not to be found in "On Truth and Lies." That essay presents a general or ahistorical set of claims, not confined to a specific historical period or group of people. It does not include any discussion of how, for instance, the Greek experience of language and truth might have been significantly different from the general rule. However, what Nietzsche discovered about the two phases of Greek cultural life (the pre- and post-Socratic) was in fact the basis for these more general analyses. To pursue this further, we look to the lectures on Ancient Rhetoric, which Nietzsche first gave at Basel in 1872. The third of these lectures is clearly a version of "On Truth and Lies," including many of the same analyses and even examples. There, Nietzsche writes, mirroring what is found in "On Truth and Lies": that "[R]hetoric is a further cultivation of those artistic means that are situated in language, in the clear light of understanding" (Gilman, et al. 1989, 20). Likewise, in the supplemental lecture on Greek eloquence, Nietzsche says of the rhetors: "The Rhetors have in their control [in der Hand] 'opinion concerning things' and hence the effect of things upon men; they know this" (Gilman, et al. 1989, 213). The "clear light" and "they know this," to be sure, makes it sound as if Nietzsche were describing the rhetor as "remembering" the basis of language, moreover remembering as an individual speaker and in isolation from his or her cultural life. But, remembering cannot be primarily an *individual* journey towards truth, since the recollection of what was forgotten (anamnesis) is a Socratic/Platonic notion of truth. Such a way of thinking about the rhetor would be entirely inconsistent with Nietzsche's critique of Socratic thought. In fact, Nietzsche consistently refuses to place the individual in that kind of foundational role; doing so signals the end of Hellenic culture and the beginning of modernity. Instead, in these lectures, we get a *collective* picture. Right up front in the lectures, Nietzsche says, "In this way what is specific to all Hellenic life is characterized: to grasp as play all business of the understanding, of life's seriousness, of necessity, even of danger" (Gilman, et al. 1989, 2). This is a generalization beyond the purely aesthetic realm of the notion of "play" found in Kant's aesthetics (Nietzsche gives a lengthy quotation from Kant just previously). The same idea is found in *The Birth of Tragedy*, this time in association with Goethe, whom Nietzsche quotes as claiming that subjects of intense pathos were merely "aesthetic play" for the ancients (BT 22; KSA 1, 142). In other words, we have the same insight in the rhetoric lectures as in the account of Greek cheerfulness in *The Birth of Tragedy*—namely, Greek culture is a mode of existence of a people, rather than a set of conceptual insights or tools in the hands of a few. Specifically, the Apollonian mode of existence is not one arrived at just by individuals (for example, great poets) under certain conditions, but one that must *already* belong to a people.

This is the same collective picture as is found in other texts of the period, regardless of the topic under discussion. For example, in "The Greek State" (one of the five prefaces to unwritten books that Nietzsche gave to Cosima Wagner at the end of 1872), he writes concerning the "shame" of labor, including artistic labor:

> The Greeks have no need of such conceptual hallucinations, among them it is expressed with shocking openness that work is a disgrace—and a more hidden, rarely spoken wisdom, but one everywhere alive, added that the human thing was a disgraceful and wretched nothing and a "shadow's dream." (KSA 1, 765)

It is not just, then, that the Greeks had different conceptual hallucinations—although no doubt they did—rather that there is a culture-wide attitude that all concepts (no matter how vivid or valuable) are such hallucinations. Similarly, in "Homer's Contest," Nietzsche writes concerning the Greek lack of self-delusion about the necessity of war and conflict, compared to modern hand-wringing: "Why did the whole Greek world rejoice over the images of war in the *Illiad*? I fear that we have not understood these in a 'Greek' enough way, indeed that we would shudder if once we had a genuine Greek understanding" (KSA 1, 784). Again, the point is not that the Greeks were particularly blood-thirsty, or that later people were not. Rather, the point is that the Greek mode of existence accepted the images of violence (and any images of some quasi-moral evaluation of violence) as, precisely, *images*—and perhaps images symbolizing something altogether more distressing.

Across all of these various topics, the theme of the unity of Greek culture stands out: a people whose unity is itself the mythic symbol of the underlying but turbulent oneness of the world, revealed through the Dionysian. The point is made most clearly, perhaps, in "Philosophy in the Tragic Age of the Greeks," which was Nietzsche's first full-scale project after finally publishing *The Birth of Tragedy*. The purposes of culture culminate in greatness, Nietzsche insists (this is the theme of several other early works also, including "On the Pathos of Truth"). This culmination in a Homer, Thales, Pericles, or Plato is not an aberration, though—not an individual who is "an accidental and arbitrary wanderer, dispersed now here, now there" (KSA 1, 809). The accidental and dispersed individual is an image of modernity, in which one "is assembled gaudily from bits" ("The Greek State"; KSA 1, 765). The image of the modern individual as having been pasted together from colorful scraps is one of Nietzsche's most persistent images. Just to mention two instances, he employs it again straightaway in the first *Untimely Meditation* (DS 1; KSA 1, 163), and then ten years later in *Thus Spoke Zarathustra*, "On the Land of Bildung." From the title of that section it is already apparent that "culture" ["Cultur"] is a problem not solved by "Bildung" ["cultivation" in the sense, above all, of *education*]. Thus, also, Nietzsche's early discussions of education (for example "On the Future of Our Educational Institutions" or "Schopenhauer as Educator") are found to be closely linked to the issues we have been discussing. Instead of these dispersed, patchwork, accidental individuals, Greek "geniuses" spring "from natural, native soil" (KSA 1, 806). Accordingly, Nietzsche can write, "If we were to correctly interpret the whole life of the Greek people, we would always find only the reflected image of that which radiates from their highest geniuses in more luminous colors" (KSA 1, 808). The Greek philosophers, and other "great" individuals, were not "untimely" (a notion shortly to become one of Nietzsche's favorites), but were deeply embedded in their properly unified culture so as to be both its original mold and its finest flowering.

Given this understanding of the unity of culture and its relation to the emergence of genius, it becomes impossible not to read the work on rhetoric and the philosophy of language accordingly. Nietzsche is arguing that, in ancient Greece though not elsewhere, extraordinary as it may sound, *everyone* is a rhetor. To be sure, there must be rhetors to a greater or lesser degree of skill, insight and creativity, but the basic conception of language as rhetorical through and through will be one that is culturewide. Nietzsche's claim is that the nature of language that modernity has failed to and could not remember was in ancient Greece *never forgotten*. Thus, the account of language as forgotten tropic distortion, given in "On Truth and Lies," is not something to be seen through by an individual act of remembering—or if this is possible, such an individual would remain untimely, probably ending in destruction, or at least very poor book sales. Rather, language must be rehabilitated in a cultural revolution that would bring the Apollonian out of the "cocoon" in which it has been concealing itself since the rise of Socratism, and allow the Dionysian to return from its exile in marginal cults. The insight into language provided by a civilization of rhetors goes hand in hand with a genuinely unified culture. It is this unified culture that modernity must somehow learn from the Greeks.

5. Critique, science and myth

To fully understand this idea of a unified culture, we need to go back a year to the last third of *The Birth of Tragedy*. Nietzsche had already established earlier in the book his theory of both the birth or tragedy and its demise. There remain a series of problems left for the later sections: above all, the conditions under which the re-emergence of tragedy might be possible. Since these conditions cannot simply erase two millennia of the Socratic, they must instead incorporate them, somehow. Here we need to look at just two aspects of this problem. First, the critical limits of science. Second, an issue which arguably Nietzsche never quite puts his finger on decisively in this book (but, as we just saw, certainly does so in the introductory sections of "Philosophy in the Tragic Age of the Greeks"): namely, the unity of culture.

This last phase of *The Birth of Tragedy* begins in section 17 with this sentence:

> If ancient tragedy was pushed off track by the dialectical drive to knowledge and to scientific optimism, then we would have to infer from this fact that there is an eternal struggle between the *theoretical* and the *tragic contemplations of the world*; and only when the spirit of science has been led to its limits, and its claim to universal validity negated through the proof of these limits, may one hope for a rebirth of tragedy: we have put forward the symbol of *Socrates driven to music*, in the sense discussed earlier, for this cultural form. (BT 17; KSA 1, 111)

The spirit of science, confronted with the evidence of its *intrinsic* limits, would be transformed; Socrates is driven to music. The next section (18) tells the story of the first stage of transformation. He writes: "Kant and Schopenhauer's tremendous courage and wisdom successfully achieved the most difficult victory, victory over that optimism concealed within the essence of logic, which in turn is the hidden foundation of our culture" (BT 18; KSA 1, 118). Critical philosophy, then, is science becoming aware of its own limits. But "limits" here might be a misleading expression. One might, for instance, argue that modern science—and perhaps ancient science also—was from the beginning a recognition of limits, in the sense of a careful consideration of what conclusions could be justified given the evidence, and also what constituted evidence. Such considerations in turn led to advances in the technological means of gathering reliable evidence—microscopes, clocks, thermometers, etc.—and mathematical advances in the analysis of evidence—statistics for example. That science knew its limits prompted it to find ways to look a little further, a little deeper, or around the corner. In other words, the situation is arguably opposite to what Nietzsche says: limits *fed* optimism. However, the properly *critical* notion of a limit is something different. What lies beyond the limits of scientific knowledge is not something that could be established by science; rather, it is something that could be established only by an investigation of the conditions of possibility of science. What Nietzsche here calls "wisdom" is the insight that what is "beyond" science is not beyond it because of the nature of the object with respect to scientific resources—e.g. the object of study is too small, far away, complex or rare—but because of the nature of science as inquiry into *constituted appearance*. By the latter phrase I mean the broadly Kantian philosophical insight that what appears is not just naïvely given, or as it is "in itself," but constituted through a series of "spiritual" acts.

Nietzsche's own neo-Kantianism—if we can call it that—centers on the kinds of analyses of language and truth found in the Rhetoric lectures and the "Truth and Lies" essay. The conditions for the possibility of sensible experience, as Nietzsche sees it, are physiological and cultural in nature. These analyses in fact borrow heavily from science (and from other philosophers who were themselves avid readers of contemporary natural science, such as Friedrich Albert Lange). Nietzsche's discussions of language as the transformations of "nervous stimulations" rely on Hermann von Helmholtz's work on physiology and acoustics. However, I do not here want to look at the details of Nietzsche's scientific acquisitions, but rather at the *conception of a critical science* that these borrowings show to be at work. Importantly, Helmholtz thought that his work, and the work of others such as his teacher Johannes Müller, was a practical demonstration of the broadly Kantian thesis that experiences are conditioned by the human faculty of sensibility. Accordingly, in the well-known lecture "On the relation between natural science and science in general," he writes: "Kant's critical philosophy sets out only to test the sources and the legitimacy of our knowledge, and to set up a standard for its intellectual labour with respect to any of the other sciences" (Helmholtz 1862, 3). This means two things: first of all, that critical philosophy is not the queen of the sciences, legislating principles for the others, but rather only for itself. On the other hand, Helmholtz here means both that Kant should be understood precisely as a physicist and psychologist—he says as much in the immediately preceding sentences—and more importantly that this Kantian mode of critical thinking is exactly what natural science itself must do. Not "critique" in the trivial sense we discussed above of evaluating its evidence, but in the properly Kantian sense of investigating its own conditions of possibility.

Much of Nietzsche's early philosophy of language is also influenced by Gustav Gerber. The transformations that unconscious stimuli undergo in becoming first word and then concept needs to be understood as a kind of unconscious artistic-creative process. Gerber too stood in a series of (neo-)Kantian influences on Nietzsche— provided we think, as indeed Nietzsche was happy to do, in terms of historical and physiological conditions, rather than purely transcendental ones. In a striking phrase, Gerber writes that it is now clear that what Kant began as a critique of pure reason has become "critique of impure reason," and therefore "critique of language" (Gerber 1871, 262).

A further example would be Nietzsche's study of Johann Zöllner's curious book on comets, published in 1872, which contains a long essay on Kant as a natural scientist. Zöllner abstracts that essay by writing: "The more perfectly developed is the keenness of the operation of the understanding, the less observational data there needs to be from which are derived proper inferences and conclusions about causal relationships in nature" (Zöllner 1872, XCV). This expresses Zöllner's characteristic rejection, as a proper method of scientific enquiry, of the mere accumulation of evidence and the repetition of experimentation. Nietzsche shared and often used this idea (e.g. NF 1873, 29[24]; KSA 7, 635). Zöllner is thus a proponent of proper experimental design. However, although Zöllner's essay mainly concerns Kant's pre-critical writings, the idea just expressed also reflects the key description of scientific method from the *Critique of Pure Reason*. Kant argues that science only began making progress when its practitioners realized that nature will only answer questions that scientific reason puts to it, because it is by the detour of nature that reason discovers its own contribution to the constitution of nature. Kant writes, "Reason approaching nature must do so with its principles in one hand, according to which alone arrangements of appearances could count as laws and, in the other hand, with the experiment that it has planned in terms of those principles" (Kant 1968, Bxiii). Again, the generally neo-Kantian outlook of many of the figures who influenced Nietzsche shines through. Zöllner's (and Nietzsche's) concerns with scientific method are not just that his contemporaries were wasting time and valuable equipment, but that they had grotesquely misunderstood the nature of scientific inquiry and knowledge.

Finally, let us turn to the most famous of Nietzsche's scientific borrowings, Ruggero Boscovich. Nietzsche read the eighteenth-century physicist in the early 1870s, but we will look at a discussion in print written more than ten years later in *Beyond Good and Evil*. To be sure, Nietzsche is a different philosopher at this point, but many of his thoughts concerning the science of his day show considerable continuity. He writes:

> For, while Copernicus persuaded us to believe, against all the senses, that the earth was not fixed in place, Boscovich taught us to abjure the belief in the last "fixed and certain" thing regarding the Earth, namely the belief in "material," in "matter," in the residue of Earth, the little lump that is the atom [an das Erdenrest- und Klümpchen-Atom]: this was the greatest triumph over the senses that had ever been achieved on Earth. (BGE 12; KSA 5, 26)

Now, again, if all Nietzsche means by a "triumph over the senses" is that what appeared to be obvious to our senses turns out to be a mistake, then this is not very interesting. Doubting the senses, or getting behind sensory evidence to what is real, is a very common philosophical and scientific move—indeed, it is arguably the core of Socratism and Platonism, and Nietzsche documents the precedents in pre-Socratic thought in "Philosophy in the Tragic Age of the Greeks." Within the modern scientific sphere, distinguishing between relative and absolute measurement of temperature or color is a good example, since it relates to often-used skeptical arguments.[6] However breath-taking and revolutionary such developments end up being, they remain part and parcel of scientific enquiry. So, what then is Nietzsche's point? His choice of Copernicus as an example here is important, since of course that is also Kant's choice in his discussion of scientific revolutions. Kant uses Copernicus in two ways, and I think Nietzsche is doing the same. First, by *analogy:* Kant's transcendental idealism is a similarly dizzying displacement of point of view (see Kant 1968, Bxxiin, where he makes this explicit, and also makes the point, identical to Nietzsche's, about Copernicus' hypothesis being "against the senses"). The second use, however, is much more than analogical. In order for the first usage to carry any weight, we must understand that for Kant Copernicus is a *critical scientist* who realized the nature of scientific method, and was thus one of those who put physics on the "high road of science" (Kant 1968, Bxii). Nietzsche's use of Boscovich has this same content. Rethinking atoms without the notions of matter or substance (or even spatial extension) is a revolutionary idea, to be sure. However, Nietzsche's point must be more than that. Nietzsche's claim is that substance materialism had been, until very recently, part of the historical but no less rigid conditions of thought, which have been at work even in the physiological basis of thought *in our bodies*, constituting our most basic experiences of the world. Thanks to physicists like Boscovich, and their philosophical fellow travellers such as Kant or Schopenhauer, science had begun to be an inquiry into its own conditions, dragging culture with it.

The above brief excursion into the influences on Nietzsche during this period, and their more or less Kantian view of the proper vocation of science, has served to set up the final phase of this paper. The last third of *The Birth of Tragedy* concerns the possibility of a rebirth of tragedy; that in turn requires that the dominance of the Socratic be overcome (not simply nullified). More specifically, it required that Nietzsche have in hand the difference between the Dionysian and the Socratic—which as we have seen he worked out by February 1870—and also both the brotherhood of Apollo and Dionysus, together with the difference between the Socratic and the Apollonian—which advances took at least five further months. Without the last of these, a rebirth of tragedy looks suspiciously like some naïve reversion to a Greek mode of life. With the Apollonian in play, Nietzsche can now describe the way in which Socratic modernity must be thought through to its end. Nietzsche's interest in science during this period stems from his analysis of Socratic modernity. The vaguely neo-Kantian flavor of Nietzsche's views on the nature of science is key here. As part of the cultural revolution, science must recognize its new, and proper, status as *rhetoric* or *art*.

How, though, does the significance of the Apollonian concept manifest itself in the final few sections of *The Birth of Tragedy*? By way of the concept of myth. Above, we have shown how the notion of unity of culture animates much of Nietzsche's work after *The Birth of Tragedy*. Likewise, we have examined some of the *effects* of the Greek unity of culture: effects on how the Greeks experienced language, for instance. But on what ground does a genuine unity of culture arise? To solve this problem, in *The Birth of Tragedy* Nietzsche employs the concept of "myth," first in sections 9 and 10, but most fully towards the end of the book. By myth broadly speaking Nietzsche means the idealized projections of the values, beliefs, and drives of a culture, both its achieved beauty and the terror beneath or behind it. That is approximately the account he gives at the beginning of *The Birth of Tragedy* (BT 3; KSA 1, 34–6). Thus, the unity of myth is or should be correlative to the unity of culture. In the modern period, under the dominance of the Socratic, we have no "native myth." He continues by way of consequence: "[T]hink of a culture with no secure, holy, native seat, but which instead is condemned to exhaust every possibility, and feed meagrely off all cultures" (BT 23; KSA 1, 146). The metaphor of motley patchwork has expanded from being about individuals: here is a whole "culture" made up of scraps.

However, this analysis sits side by side with Nietzsche's final discussion of the overall effect of tragedy. Myth, Nietzsche seems to think, is the final piece of a puzzle concerning the possibility of tragedy in a post-Socratic age. So, he returns to tragedy in the ancient period, in order to recast one last time the theory of the birth of tragedy, now in terms of myth. What tragedy reveals about Greek civilization—and also returns to it as a gift—is a state where the Apollonian "negates itself" and speaks with "the voice of Dionysus" (BT 21; KSA 1, 139–40). It is this condition Nietzsche calls "myth." However, it is far from clear what this means, and thus it is important that we pause and ask: what could it mean for a state of existence that takes and values images as merely images to "negate itself"? First of all, the negation of the image *as such* would mean dissolution into the Dionysiac—as even the pretence of individuation falls back, only Dionysiac ecstasy remains. So that cannot be what Nietzsche means. On the other hand, though, negation of the *value* of the image would cancel the healing power of the Apollonian. That is to say, the tragic state would fall *forward*, so to speak, into the Socratic conception of illusion as mere deception. There is a third alternative, also impossible: negation of the *awareness* of illusion leads as we know to pathological consequences. Moreover, this mode of negation would take us further from the enchantment in the Dionysiac, by erecting a fixed barrier of images.

So, what does it mean for the Apollonian to negate itself and thereby speak with the voice of Dionysus? By negation here Nietzsche can only mean the negation at some level of the *demand* of individuation. We already know that the basic metaphysical outlooks of these two drives are not in fact different—because the Apollonian artist or spectator is aware of his or her own image making, the Apollonian as a worldview reduces to the Dionysiac. However, they are *as if* different, because the Apollonian presents and values the image as such. Still, we can analyze this concept of "image" in Apollo into two phases. The first phase is the arising of the images of individual things as if they were real; the second phase is the arising of these as if these images qua individual entities were in fact *the basis of* the real. In both cases, as we have argued, awareness of the "as if" is essential to the Apollonian. The latter is Nietzsche's version of Schopenhauer's original conception of the order of representation: reality is understood to be comprised of individual entities from out of which the fabric of the real is constructed. What these last few sections of the *Birth of Tragedy* are working out, then, is in what way the as if metaphysics of the Apollonian changes under the condition of its partnership with Dionysus. This fits nicely with the emerging concept of myth. Tragic myth is the Apollonian presentation of images as *symbols of* the underlying Dionysiac oneness of things.

Accordingly, for Apollo to speak with the voice of Dionysus thus means that the "visible" culture of myth is "rescued from its indiscriminate meandering" (BT 23; KSA 1, 145). Artistic imagination—and indeed, much more broadly, any cultural production—would otherwise consist of individual images in an unending parade, but without relation or overall destiny. It is likely Nietzsche has in mind here the fact that in Euripides the trilogy of tragedies were unrelated, whereas in early tragic practice the trilogies told a continuous mythic narrative. (He clearly also has in mind those images of dispersion and patchwork in modernity.) The Dionysian lends its primordial oneness to the Apollonian, to be expressed symbolically, and this is the self-negating of the Apollonian. Through this negation, myth finds a way *symbolically* "to flee back again into the womb of the true and one reality" (BT 22; KSA 1, 141). This must be symbolic, because to *actually* do so would be, again, Dionysian dissolution. On the other hand, for the symbolic system to remain a set of *individual* images—images that are contemplated not just as if real but as if the basis of the real—would fail to reveal that "one and true reality." In the tragic effect as a whole, the negation of the Apollonian, the mythic images remain individual, but as a whole they become unified. That is, as a whole, they become mythic symbols of the underlying oneness of the world. Such an effect surpasses the possibilities of Apollonian art—which presents no holism other than the repeated, individual creation of beauty. This shows the Dionysian to be the more fundamental drive. However, of course, none of this production would be possible at all without the "brotherhood" of the two drives, and this solution both to the nature of tragedy and the nature of myth thus had to await Nietzsche's discovery of the Apollonian. Moreover, if myth is the projection of a culture, then a unified myth entails a unified culture. Critical science, reconceived as rhetoric or art, supplies what we might call an intellectual mythology. Accordingly, Nietzsche's portrait of the pre-Socratics in "Philosophy in the Tragic Age of the Greeks"—it is now clear why it had to mention tragedy in the title—is a sketch of what such an "intellectual mythology" would be like. The most profound of philosophical-scientific disagreements merely serves as an agonistic symbol of the multiplicity-within-wholeness of the forms that can be taken by the will. This cultural wholeness is what tragedy reveals to and about the Greeks, and also what as a cultural production it seeks to further.

This paper has presented and defended two hypotheses. First, that the development of the concept of the Apollonian came somewhat later than the first drafts of the theory of tragedy. Specifically, it arrived later than the fairly worked-out notions of the Dionysian and the Socratic, including the account of the death of tragedy by way of the Socratic. This delay reveals a story about the role of Apollo in *The Birth of Tragedy*, such that Nietzsche is for the first time able to give a general account of the dynamics of cultural development. Second, that one of the most important new philosophical vistas opened up by the role of the Apollonian in the full theory of tragedy is the notion of a genuine unity of Greek culture. This second hypothesis is more complicated, and needed to be fleshed out in several stages that passed through a variety of Nietzsche's writings during the period of 1870–3. In particular, we explored—all in conjunction with the problem of a unified culture—Nietzsche's philosophy of language and truth, of the nature of critical science, and finally of myth.

Notes

1   In 2009 Martin Jesinghausen and I published a commentary to *The Birth of Tragedy*. One of the chief novelties of this work was to argue for an original and continuing *three-way* external dynamic among those Greek cultural drives that Nietzsche designates Apollonian, Dionysian, and Socratic. Later, we wrote a paper which extended this analysis to how Nietzsche modifies the figure of Apollo in later works (especially *Thus Spoke Zarathustra*) to articulate an *internal* dynamic to that ideal he now identifies with Dionysus (cf. Burnham/Jesinghausen 2011).

2   To Erwin Rohde, January and February 15, 1870; KSB 3, 93–6. To Paul Deussen, February, 1870; KSB 3, 97–9.

3   To Carl von Gersdorff, November 7, 1870; KSB 3, 154–6. To Erwin Rohde, November 23, 1870; KSB 3, 158–60.

4   We will return to the concept of "culture" below, and especially to the notion of a unity of culture.

5   See the original title of *The Birth of Tragedy*, the first draft of the Forward to Wagner, 11[1], and 15 years later this is acknowledged in the "Attempt at Self-Criticism"; KSA 1, 11.

6   E.g. Descartes follows ancient skeptics such as Sextus Empiricus in talking about jaundice and color perception in *Discourse on the Method*, Part IV (Descartes 1964, 39–40).

Works cited

Burnham, Douglas and Martin Jesinghausen (2009): *Nietzsche's* The Birth of Tragedy. London (Continuum/Bloomsbury).

—(2011): "Of Butterflies and Masks." In Andrea Rehberg (ed.): *Nietzsche and Phenomenology*. Cambridge (Cambridge Scholars).

Descartes, René (1964): *Oeuvres de Descartes*. Paris (Vrin). 2nd edn. Vol. 6.

Gerber, Gustav (1871): *Die Sprache als Kunst*. Bromberg (Mittler'sche Buchhandlung/H. Hayfelder). Vol. 1.

Gilman, Sander, et al. (eds) (1989): *Friedrich Nietzsche on Rhetoric and Language*. Oxford (Oxford University Press).

Helmholtz, Hermann Ludwig von (1862): *Über das Verhältnis der Naturwissenschaften zur Gesammtheit der Wissenschaft*. Heidelberg (Georg Mohr).

—(1863): *Die Lehre von den Tonempfindungen als physiologische Grundlage für die Theorie der Musik*. Brunswick (F. Vieweg).

Kant, Immanuel (1968): *Werke: Akademie-Textausgabe*. Berlin (Walter de Gruyter). Vol. 3.

Zöllner, Johann Carl Friedrich (1872): *Über die Natur de Kometen: Beiträge zur Geschichte und Theorie der Erkenntnis*. Leipzig (Wilhelm Englemann).

Part Three

Scholarly Achievement

5

Nietzsche's Valediction and First Article: The *Theognidea*

Anthony K. Jensen

The *Theognidea* is a thematic cluster that holds a privileged place among all Nietzsche's early projects.[1] The *Theognidea* was Nietzsche's first major scholarly project. It was his *Valediktionsarbeit* and his first publication. It endured as a project from 1863–9; thus, it was the work that gained Nietzsche recognition at Schulpforta, helped him into a comfortable seat at Bonn, made him a favorite of his mentor Ritschl at Leipzig, and facilitated his hiring at Basel. It was arguably the project for which he conducted the most "scholarly" research, dealing with centuries-old manuscripts, codices, stemmata, and the other official tools of nineteenth-century philology. It is a piece that, had Nietzsche never written another word, would have assured his place, albeit a quite minor one, in the history of German philology.

And yet, for all that, Nietzsche's *Theognidea* project has been, with one glad exception, entirely ignored in both Anglophone and European Nietzsche scholarship.[2] To redress this lacuna in the literature, it is my purpose here, first, to examine the genesis of his Theognis project, specifically, the biographical circumstances in which Nietzsche composed his essay, the philologists he read, and those who would later rely on him. Second, I will explicate Nietzsche's contribution to the so-called Theognidean question, the philological problem he located, the solution he proposed, and the reactions of scholars to it. Finally, I will weigh the value of Nietzsche's article on Theognis as a paradigm of his early philological methods.[3]

1. Nietzsche's Schulpforta Valediktionsarbeit

Before Wagner, before Schopenhauer, before Burckhardt, Ritschl, Jahn, Rohde, and Overbeck, and indeed before Bonn, Leipzig, and Basel, Nietzsche showed genuine talent and interest in philology from his time at the well-respected Schulpforta, which Nietzsche attended from 1858–64.[4] There it was not uncommon that students, who today would be considered high-schoolers and collegiate lower-classmen, were expected to compose an extensive and original piece of research (often in Latin) that served as a sort of exit-thesis or Valediktionsarbeit. Less common, though not completely unique, was the technical aptitude Nietzsche showed in his essay "De Theognide Megarensi" (BAW 3, 21–64; hereafter DTM). By the summer of 1864, after a frantic schedule, Nietzsche had completed three sections (to Deussen, July 8, 1864; KSB 1, 290; see also Janz 1993, 123). Rushed for graduation in September, Nietzsche writes with some embarrassment to his friend Wilhelm Pinder, "This afternoon I began my work on Theognis, five columns are already finished; the Latin style is laughable [scherzhaft]; today I've already had a few chances to mock all those short little questions" (to Pinder, July 4, 1864; KSB 1, 287–8).

Despite his characteristic private reservations at this stage in his career, the piece was well regarded, even praised by his Schulpforta teachers Wilhelm Corssen and Dietrich Volkmann. Nietzsche repeatedly composed letters to family and friends citing the unexpected generosity both teachers showed him in their corrections and advice, and in using their professional connections to procure otherwise hard-to-find sources. And Volkmann's cordiality with his former teacher Friedrich Ritschl was possibly a contributing factor to Nietzsche's matriculation at Bonn. Even two years after Nietzsche had left Pforta, both scholars continued to help Nietzsche with revisions towards the published version. "I am walled in by books—thanks to Corssen's uncommon generosity. I must also mention Volkmann, who has freely helped me, especially with the whole Suidas [sic.] literature, on which he is the leading expert" (to von Gersdorff, April 7, 1866; KSB 2, 120). And again, "Corssen's been pulled into the mystery [too;] he's been very eager and very active; we scramble around the library together for hours" (to Mushacke, March 14, 1866; KSB 2, 115).

The first part of the 1864 DTM essay dealt with the life and times of Theognis in his native Megara. As a conservative of the old guard in a time of radical upheaval resulting from the town's newly won independence from Corinth and subsequent thrall under Theagenes the Tyrant, Theognis' original elegiac poetry—though what exactly that was will require substantial philological analysis in our next sections—was a blend of encomia for times gone by, laments for what things have become, and exhortations that his male confidant, a youth by the name of Kyrnos, remain stalwart and endure through the turmoil (Davies 1873, 130).[5] In verses 53–60, we read:

> This city is the same, Kyrnos, but the people different.
> Those who once knew neither laws nor justice,
> And wore tattered goatskins around their bellies,
> And lived outside the city walls like deer,
> Now they are considered noble, son of Polypaos,
> While those who were noble once are now base.
> Who can endure to witness such a scene?
> They deceive and mock one another,
> Knowing not the principles of good and wicked.[6]

The second part of the 1864 DTM treats the work of Theognis as to its formal and contextual point of view, and with an eye towards questions of manuscript transmission.[7] In the third section, Nietzsche distinguishes the political, moral, and religious aspects of Theognis' work. In his portrait, Theognis is made to appear a partisan of the sixth-century Doric nobles, a stalwart of "archaic" wisdom, and a model of aristocratic values. Nietzsche even compares Theognis to the Marquis of Posa in Schiller's drama *Don Carlos*—the relationship between Theognis and Kyrnos is to parallel that between the Marquis and Carlos (BAW 3, 41).[8] In sum, to the 20-year-old Nietzsche, Theognis' poetry symbolized the very "Glaubensbekenntniß des Adels" (BAW 3, 18; cf. Cancik 1995, 10), or, said in his Latin, "Habemus igitur illam superbam Doriensis nobilitatis persuasionem" (BAW 3, 60).

For all the enthusiasm, something here was not quite right. In the course of his research for this 1864 offering, Nietzsche was made aware that this portrayal was not always confirmed by other authorities. There seemed to be certain inconsistencies in the writings of Theognis that lent themselves to a bizarrely wide variety of interpretations, both in later Hellenistic writers and among contemporary authors. Among those who considered Theognis the paradigm of aristocratic moral values the foremost authority is Plato. At *Laws* 630a2–b1, Plato writes, "We have a poet to bear witness to this [viz., gallantry in war]: Theognis, a citizen of Megara in Sicily, who says, 'Kyrnos, find a man you can trust in deadly feuding: he is worth his weight in silver and gold'" (Plato is referencing Theognis vv. 77–8). Isocrates named him ἄριστος σύμβουλος [the best measure] (BAW 3, 71; following Isocrates *Ad Nicolem*, c. 12).[9] But, on the other hand, certain authors bore little but disdain. The encyclopedian Wilhelm Teuffel would find him "embittered by society" and "vengeful toward the commoners." As Nietzsche quotes him, "because of dull experiences, his tone is embittered against the people; and the more he believes it in principle the more he concedes it in practice— that he alone salvages the glory of existence over and against the debasement of life, and through his poetry he wants to avenge himself against it" (BAW 3, 52).[10] Goethe would write, "He appears to us as a lugubrious Greek hypochondriac" (BAW 3, 36).[11] What could account for such a discrepancy? Moreover, what could account for Theognis' seemingly first-hand references to events that would have happened outside the span of his life? For example, Theognis' "floruit" is placed confidently in the sixth century BC, and yet certain verses claim eye-witness knowledge of the Persian foray into the Megarid in 479 BC (Theognis vv. 757–64).[12] While Nietzsche even now suspected that something was amiss in the manuscript tradition, the full solution to this riddle would only be expounded in his first article.

2. Constructing "Zur Geschichte der Theognideischen Spruchsammlung"

In 1867, Nietzsche published in his mentor Friedrich Ritschl's renowned journal *Das Rheinische Museum für Philologie* a revised and more extensive version of DTM: "Zur Geschichte der Theognideischen Spruchsammlung" (hereafter GTS).[13] Having left Bonn and matriculated at Leipzig, Nietzsche had resumed his research on Theognis in the summer of 1865. Now focused on the issues of manuscript transmission left over from his earlier work, he writes to Hermann Mushacke in August that "Theognis was frightfully mistreated. Hanging from a long methodical string, every day I cut some fraying tinsel from him with critical scissors" (to Mushacke, August 30, 1865; KSB 2, 81). By January of 1866, Nietzsche presented his work to the Leipzig philology club, and, after adding marginal notes that took account of the questions and comments entertained at the meeting, gave the text to Ritschl following one of his class lectures. Less than a week later, the renowned professor called Nietzsche to his study to tell him that, "never before had he encountered such a sureness of approach and such a mastery of analytical technique in a third-semester student" (Cate 2002, 69). By July 1866, Ritschl commissioned a further revised version to be printed in his journal. As the first student article published in the *Rheinisches Museum*, the event marked a turning point in Ritschl's relationship with Nietzsche, which had been rather cool at Bonn. For his part, though, Nietzsche's response was somewhat ambivalent. On the one hand Nietzsche was elated by Ritschl's encouragement. "Ever since that day when Ritschl assessed my Theognis paper so favorably, I have been very close to him. I go to him almost weekly at noon and find him always prepared, and always a serious and lively conversation ensues" (BAW 3, 304). On the other hand, Nietzsche was also rather overwhelmed by the master's trust, revealing in a letter, "I can't denounce being the tyro; but I have no practice with such things. Meanwhile I work from dawn till dusk like a stooge [Handlanger]; how far I still am from a real composition!" (to Mushacke, March 14, 1866; KSB 2, 116).

From his friend Mushacke, Nietzsche requested the following manuscript editions out of the University of Berlin library: the γνωμολογίαι παλαιοτάτων ποιητῶν edited by Turnebus (1553), and the *Theognis Codex* editions produced by Camerarius (1559), Seberus (2nd edn., 1620), Vinetus (1543), and Stephanus (1566 and 1588) (to Mushacke, March 14, 1866; KSB 2, 115–16).[14] Of modern manuscripts and codices, Nietzsche was familiar with the key works: those by Immanuel Bekker (1815, 1827), Schneidewin (1838), and three shorter publications of Bergk (1843, 1853, 1866). He knew well the critical work of Gottfried Bernhardy (1867), that of Carl Dilthey (1863),[15] and the Habilitationschrift of Karl Rintelen (1858). Nietzsche even wrote a critical review of Christopher Ziegler's then-recent edition of the *Mutinensis* manuscript (Ziegler 1868; BAW 5, 242–3). Nietzsche's own portrait of Theognis is posed in part as a response to Karl Otfried Müller's *Geschichte der griechischen Literatur* (1841), which had already by then been lambasted by Bergk (1843, 225–9).[16]

Among the scholarship Nietzsche most closely engaged is that found in Friedrich Gottlieb Welcker's *Theognidis Reliquiae* (Welcker 1926) and Theodor Bergk's *Poetae Lyrici Graeci* (Bergk 1843, 117–236),[17] both of which were procured for him with the help of his teacher Volkmann.[18] Welcker was Ritschl's co-editor on the *Rheinisches Museum* and a champion of the hermeneutical methods propounded by the great philologist August Boeckh. Bergk was the student of Boeckh's rival, Gottfried Hermann, under whom he and Ritschl had both studied at Leipzig. Bergk's two-part article "Ueber die Kritik im Theognis" was also published in the *Rheinisches Museum* (Bergk 1845, 206–33, 396–433), and Nietzsche refers to it critically in his own essay.

"Walled-in" by his Schulpforta teachers' books, by Muschacke's faithful shipments from Berlin libraries, and by Rohde's and Ritschl's corrections and advice, Nietzsche worked tirelessly on his Theognis publication. Since "Ritschl considers the publication of my study necessary [...], my little room is generally filled up with books" (to Franziska and Elisabeth Nietzsche, March 3, 1866; KSB 2, 113). In keeping with Ritschl's expectations, Nietzsche conducted his investigation with as much philological rigor as could be mustered. As he wrote excitedly to his friends Krug and Pinder about his Valediktionsarbeit,

> I have allowed myself a certain quantity of supposition and fantasy, but I plan to carry the work out to the end, and set it upon a true philological foundation and *in a manner as scientific as possible.* I've already reached a new view regarding the observation of this man, and in most things judge him quite differently than most do. (To Krug and Pinder, June 12, 1864; KSB 1, 282; my emphasis)

But the serious attitude of a professional scholar only ever fitted Nietzsche awkwardly. Shortly after the composition of his GTS in 1867, he writes to his friend Carl von Gersdorff that, "I never again want to write in so wooden and dry a manner, so logically straitjacketed, as I did for example in my essay on Theognis: along this path no grace is seated" (to Gersdorff, April 6, 1867; KSB 2, 209). The development in Nietzsche's thought between these years (1864–7) marks his transformation from a philological tyro to an emerging philosopher along the lines of his increasing concern for the value of these fields of study. Were it all one read, one could hardly imagine the same man was the author of GTS and the brazenly speculative and highly styled composition of the *Birth of Tragedy*. Indeed, Ritschl hardly could: after the appearance of the *Birth*, he would write to Wilhelm Vischer, Nietzsche's erstwhile boss at Basel:

> It's remarkable how in one person two souls live next to each other. On the one side, the strictest method of academic scientific research ... on the other this fantastically-overreaching, over enthusiastic, beat-you-senseless, Wagnerian-Schopenhauerian art-mystery-religion-nonsense [Kunstmysterienreligionsschwärmerei]! [...] What really makes me mad is his impiety against his true mother, philology, who had suckled him at her breast. (KSA 15, 46f.)

3. Nietzsche's contribution to the "Theognis-question"

With his 1867 publication, Nietzsche would give a complete philological exposition to the problem posed in his 1864 dissertation. Nietzsche's main argument is that the massive train of elegiac verse attributed to Theognis was actually the arranged product of a later redactor. The grouping of gnomic apothegms that we have inherited reflects an intentional method of organization by this redactor according to certain "Stichwörter" or "keywords" of shorter poems written by Tyrtaeus of Sparta, Mimnermus of Smyrna, Solon of Athens, and Phokylides of Miletus (KGW II/1, 16–26). The frequency of their repetitions cannot be accidental. The lines must have been linked together intentionally in order to form a single elegiac chain out of what was once a thematic but not compositional series of apothegms. Nietzsche contends, "Our collection is arranged neither thematically nor alphabetically. But surely it is arranged according to words. The fragments are linked together by keywords, such that each pair of fragments has the same or a similar word in common" (KGW II/1, 17). Nietzsche lists hundreds of these repetitious chains of keywords that occur throughout the poem. Note the explicit repetitions that would allow for convenient linking of the following stanzas:

Verses 73–76:	πιστὸν
77–78:	πιστὸς
80–86:	πιστοὺς
	γλώσσῃ
87–92:	γλώσσῃ
93–100:	γλώσσῃ
	ἀνὴρ φίλος
101–112:	ἀνὴρ φίλος
113–114:	ἄνδρα φίλον

Given the evident schematization of the poem's keywords,[19] Nietzsche suggests that lines which contained one of these words were grouped together intentionally and by editors other than Theognis. Later copyists evidently took these topical similarities to be title-headings for the various stanzas, and embedded the reduplicated words within subsequent editions of the text. Thus, when the redactor located phrases containing words like φίλος or γλώσσῃ, he cut them from their original thematic context and tied them to other apothegms irrespective of their style or original context. And if no suitable keyword could be found in Theognis, the redactor would evidently borrow phrases or even entire stanzas from other authors, weaving them in without attribution. We find phrases in Theognis at various points that are elsewhere attributed to his contemporaries Solon, Mimnermus, and Tyrtaeus. What we now possess under the name "Theognis" is not his original composition, but a later-arranged combination of redundant phrasings, awkward thematic assemblages, and even intrusions from other poets. The fact that no ancient writer before the fifth century AD notices these oddities suggests that they were inserted sometime thereafter.

To see the problem more clearly, examine the first set of keywords situated in the lines referenced above:

Verses 73–78:

Do not discuss any such matters, even with all those friends,
for indeed few of those many have a trustworthy mind.

Trust few when attempting great works, Cyrnus,
Lest you come to endure unceasing hardship.

A trustworthy man in times of civil strife, Cyrnus,
is worth his weight in gold and silver.

As is apparent, there is no poetic cohesion in these lines beyond the superficial word "trust." While the theme is "trust" in a rudimentary sense, the context in which it appears is different in each case: trusting friends in "those matters," trusting anyone in constructing "great works," and trusting political allies in times of upheaval. It would surely have made for better poetry to situate these apothegms in settings which better define "those matters" and "great works," which better indicate the situation which gave rise to that "civil strife." The awkward repetitiveness of the above phrasing, which is but one example among hundreds, is not the product of an inferior poet, but that of a later redactor with his own editorial intentions. To a philologist's critical eye, the text suggests a later alteration made not for poetic reasons, but for some other end.

Nietzsche's contention is that the text as we now have it is not simply a bad patchwork of foreign materials,[20] nor an arrangement based on an innocent misinterpretation,[21] nor clumsy and mindless interpolations,[22] nor a collection of drinking songs,[23] nor even—the reigning thesis today—a cumulative synthesis of Megarian folk poetry from different generations (cf. Nagy 1985, 33), but an extended elegiac, written originally by a single author, which from a specific time was intentionally rearranged and transformed by this later redactor. Nietzsche concludes, "It is a fact, that very many of the fragments (more than half), are connected by keywords; it is a supposition, that the entire collection was arranged in this way" (KGW II/1, 19). Therefore "trust" is evidently the keyword that the redactor used in assembling the long text we now possess, unnatural as the verse may now sound. At this point two interconnected questions suggest themselves: when precisely was this edition of Theognis constructed, and why was it done so?

As a good philologist, Nietzsche turns instinctively to the manuscript tradition, which he classifies into three families. The oldest manuscript available to Nietzsche (and it remains so to us) is the tenth-century *Pariser Pergamenthandschrift* (A), which Immanuel Bekker labeled the *Codex Mutinensis* in 1815. Manuscript (A) is the only one to include a collection of apothegms dubbed the *Musa Paedica*, which, as the name suggests, consists in a rather lurid encomium to pederasty (KGW II/1, 4–5). Second, the *Codex Vaticanus* (O) from the thirteenth century and the *Codex Venetus Marcianus* (K) from the fifteenth are traceable to a common source and contain some copy errors and omissions, but no additional editorial interpolations beyond what is contained in (A) (KGW II/1, 5–7). Nietzsche's third group contains the rest of the late-medieval manuscripts, which are each severely corrupted and evince some common peculiarities between them (KGW II/1, 7–14).

The transmission of the *Theognidean* manuscripts from medieval times to modern bears several oddities. Most problematic is that the *Codex Mutinensis* contains far more Stichwort repetitions than later editions, which belies the reflexive expectation for older texts to be truer to their author's intentions than those that have been copied and edited repeatedly. It would be bad enough to find semantic or syntactical changes. But in the case of Theognis' *Codex Mutinensis* there are evident additions of structures, phrases, and even entire sentences (KGW II/1, 4). These very obvious repetitions are never mentioned before the fifth century AD, but are frequently cited thereafter. This led Nietzsche to doubt the authenticity of large sections of the inherited manuscripts. And it led him to question the lurid *Musa Paedica* as an editorial interpolation since it is found only in the earliest edition and plainly does not match stylistically with either the rest of Theognis' writings or with the reputation allotted him by antiquity.

Given the propensity of older manuscripts to contain more repetitions and errors, and to contain them in a more rigorous and frequentative pattern, Nietzsche believes that their arrangement was not the product of later copyists, but was a characteristic of the originally redacted text, however many centuries before the *Codex Mutinensis*.[24]

Because Julian Apostate and Stobaeus seem to be referring to different Theognis texts in their own writings, Nietzsche thinks this older—but now lost—source of the *Codex Mutinensis* must be dated to some time between the late fourth and mid-fifth centuries AD. The later medieval manuscripts, having fewer repetitions than the *Codex Mutinensis*, suggest that later editors not only refrained from new additions but even sought to repeal the redactions of the original redactor, opting to marginalize an increasing number of what they perceived were unnecessary emendations due to the Stichwörter repetitions.

As Nietzsche concludes to his fellow philologist Carl Dilthey:

> I have proven that the repetitions become continually more numerous proceeding from the youngest back to the oldest, and that buried therein is a definite intention of the redactor. And I believe to have finally found the principle of this redaction, which also explains the repetitions. The individual fragments are ordered by Stichwörter, about which Welcker had already remarked in a number of places [...] This also counts for the attachment of the *Musa Paedica*. In between the original and the redaction, Stobaeus used our Stichwörter principle; I have located the period of development of this redaction to the period between Julian and Stobaeus. (To Carl Dilthey, April 2, 1866; KSB 2, 117f. Following Porter 2000, 386n. 23)

With this, Nietzsche contents himself with having answered the "when" question. As to the "why," Nietzsche is equally confident.

> Since we now know that the redactor had a hostile tendency toward Theognis, we should no longer believe [the corruption] was a harmless oversight. He sought weapons to hurt [Theognis]: he intentionally introduced shadows here and there in the pure character portrait of Theognis. Hence, he assembled parodies of Theognis, and *added verses of Mimnermus*, which, mushy in tone, oddly contrasts the hard, energetically powerful, often foreboding and grim thoughts of Theognis. (KGW II/1, 37; Nietzsche's emphasis)[25]

But there is a glaring weakness in Nietzsche's argument. As Thomas Hudson-Williams justly criticizes, "It must first be proven that the poems were *intentionally* arranged on this principle" (Hudson-Williams 1910, 14). But what can be proven about a hypothetical figure whom a philologist only posited in order to conveniently explain problems that he himself uncovered? The redactor is not a historically verifiable person, but Nietzsche's scholarly hypothesis. Anything that Nietzsche could say about his intentions would remain on the level of pure speculation, one without possible confirmation or disconfirmation. And this was noticed almost immediately by Theodor Bergk, too, who in the 1882 edition of his *Poetae Lyrici Graeci* claims that Nietzsche can only argue with "the kinds of reasoning by which even the most vacuous comment compels assent" (Bergk 1843, 236).

4. The "real" Theognis

The character portrait of Theognis, as it has been transmitted to us by the editorial tradition, appears impossibly ambivalent. In some verses, those held up by Plato or Isocrates, he is manifestly the proud inheritor of a prouder aristocratic tradition. "Expend yourself in the pursuit of excellence, hold justice dear to you, but let no shameful advantage take hold of you" (Theognis vv. 465–6). "Good judgment and discretion accompany the noble man" (Theognis v. 635). Yet in those highlighted by Teuffel or Goethe, he appears no more than a Junker (BAW 3, 74), a tired old moralizer whose time of influence has long since past—and worse, a miser, a drunk, and even a pederast.[26] "My head is drunk with wine [...] it overpowers me; I'm no longer in control of my judgment, and the room is spinning" (Theognis vv. 503–5). "Often I'm wracked with helplessness, distressed in my heart, for never having risen beyond poverty" (Theognis vv. 1114f.). "I'll drink my fill, without a thought for soul-destroying poverty or enemies who speak ill of me. But I lament the lovely boy who is leaving me, and weep at the approach of grim old age" (Theognis vv. 1129–32). "Happy is the man who at home engages in erotic exercises, sleeping all day long with a pretty boy" (Theognis vv. 1335–6). And to this decaying world, Theognis can apparently only respond with the tragic wisdom of Silenus, which Nietzsche would later co-opt for the third chapter of his *Birth of Tragedy* (1872):

> Best of all for those on earth is never to be born,
> never to look upon the rays of the keen-burning sun.
> Once born, however, it is best to pass most quickly through Hades' gates
> and to lie beneath a great heap of earth.
>
> (Theognis vv. 425–8)

What is to account for this inconsistency of character? Nietzsche's answer is that, "our collection is apparently not what determined antiquity's judgment on Theongis: it isn't moral enough. The verses cited in antiquity were just not cited as they stand here" (BAW 4, 200). As with the peculiarites in Theognis' compositional style, the solution to the question of Theognis' seemingly inconsistent character again lies in the manuscript transmission. This time, however, Nietzsche believes there are three main phases of alteration dating from the thousand years between the "floruit" of Theognis and the writing of Stobaeus. Rather than building his argument philologically upon the evidence of still-extant medieval manuscripts, Nietzsche must now rely upon the second-hand testimony of ancient authors and, in no small measure, upon armchair psychology.

As Nietzsche reckons, the authentic text written in Theognis' hand appeared shortly before his exile from Megara. The first augmentation came shortly thereafter by the edition of about 2,800 gnomic verses called the Γνωμολογία πρὸς Κύρνον (BAW 4, 201). Given the practical currency of his philosophical speculations on the character of virtue and vice, the gnomology became a rallying cry to the youth of Megara to remember their noble heritage and to remain virtuous in the face of Theagenes' tyranny. Philosophical speculation on the nature of the good was thus transformed into practical advice in order to better fit the needs of a transformed literary audience.

During the second phase of the ancient transmission, this "effective and unharmed" image of Theognis was utilized in the writings of Plato, in Xenophon,[27] and by Isocrates.[28] But since this was centuries after the fall of Megara, Theognis' political point of reference was irrelevant. The revolutionary was again transformed, this time into a moral pedagogue. The text of Theognis familiar to these classical authors was a chrestomalogical (student handbook) gnomology of around five thousand to six thousand verses (BAW 4, 206),[29] incorporating lines originally written by Callinus, Tyrtaeus, Solon, and Phokylides (KGW II/1, 29). Although this new round of emendations had not made something "intolerable" out of Theognis, "[o]ne no longer reads Theognis; he became a schoolbook!" (KGW II/1, 29).

By the third phase of transmission, in the time of Cyril and Julian, Nietzsche thinks the image of Theognis became further confused, as these foreign intrusions were made regular (KGW II/1, 30–6). At this point, however, there is yet no evidence that the Stichwort arrangement had been employed.[30] Sometime between Plato and these later writers there came to exist an anthology of Theognis' gnomics, the so-called "theognideische Gnomensammlung," which Nietzsche assumes could not have contained the lurid eroticism prominent in the *Musa Paedica* (KGW II/1, 42).[31] Because it was used in the schools, there arose increasing need to codify the scattered advisory remarks interpolated into Theognis' text. This gave license to Nietzsche's nefarious redactor to then rearrange the text along a convenient principle of classification— the Stichwort principle—and to add or subtract verses where he saw fit. And so, by the time of Stobaeus, we find the substantially same version of the *Theognideischen Spruchsammlung* that we find in the *Codex Mutinensis*, where the keyword principle is established, the pederasty and drunkenness is included, and the original intentions of Theognis have all but disappeared.

Finally, we conclude the manuscript history. "Therefore, if Athenaeus, Julian, and Cyril—433 AD at the latest—did not know our redaction, but if it was used by Stobaeus, *then it follows that its appearance must fall between 433 and* [the writings of] *Stobaeus, within the fifth century AD*" (KGW II/1, 35–6; Nietzsche's emphasis). Subsequent copyists had ignored the textual emendations made around that time, and with the passing of the centuries, the error became ever more firmly entrenched. Hence, the Theognis text out of which *Codex Mutinensis* was made actually dates from a fifth-century AD version. And in that century, Nietzsche notes, the moral intentions of the Christian editors could not have been further from the original authorial motivations of Theognis (KGW II/1, 38). For at that time one did not credit ancient pagan sources with an upstanding moral doctrine, unless it was consistent with the teachings of the early church. Even the later gnomological handbook of Theognis was far from that; and thus an effort was made to slander his name while at the same time revealing Plato and Isocrates as "heathens" for their praise. The real Theognis, and even the later pedagogical Theognis, was made to appear as a drunk, a pederast, and a cheat. "One might believe that he [the redactor] had assembled everything; out of what was somehow put into circulation under the name of Theognis, he constructed a new Theognis from the disiectis membris poetae" (KGW II/1, 29).

In this way, the work preserved under the name of "Theognis" is actually a parody of the "real" Theognis' true intentions. "All the more do I ardently believe the redactor had a hostile, indeed a *parodistic* tendency towards Theognis. According to this collection, Theognis the pedagogue should only appear as a *bon vivant*, as a drunk, a lover, even as a pederast, as the proxy of a flaccid morality; in short, the redactor loaded him with every fault from which a pedagogue should be free" (KGW II/1, 29).

5. Reception and influence

The reception of GTS was mainly positive. Three years after Nietzsche's publication, Theodor Fritzsche (1870) defended the main contribution of Nietzsche's scholarship (Fritzsche 1870, 521ff.).[32] In 1875, the Italian scholar Felice Ramorino argued to emend a passage in the Suidas in order to substantiate Nietzsche's contention that Hesychius of Miletus categorized Theognis in two separate articles, once as a poet and once as a philosopher (KGW II/1, 45–50). Ramorino found Nietzsche's study to be extraordinary for someone of his age, but sided with Bergk against both Nietzsche and Welcker as to Theognis' dating (Ramorino 1875, 238–49). Christopher Ziegler cites Nietzsche's GTS in the second edition of his *Theognidis Elegiae* (1880) with favor, noting that Nietzsche's was one of those "praeter editiones consului atque in usum meum converti" (Ziegler 1880, vi). Jacob Sitzler claimed that of all the more recent commentators, Nietzsche most accurately schematized the repitions (Sitzler 1880, 6). Sitzler is also sympathetic to dating the original redaction to approximately AD 433 (Sitzler 1880, 24). Though critical of the Stichwörter principle, Arthur Corsenn lists Nietzsche's "Zur Geschichte der Theognideischen Spruchsammlung" in the bibliography of his *Quaestiones Theognidiae* (Corssen 1887, 26–30). While critical of Nietzsche's scholarship generally, Hudson-Williams nevertheless does consider his *Theognidea* to be on an equal footing with the work of other, more canonical philologists. He confirms that Nietzsche's interpretation was defended by Fritzsche and, even with some problems, is still influential for contemporary studies (Hudson-Williams 1910, 14n. 1). What stood out in the eyes of these philologists—and still stands out— was the implausibility of Nietzsche's psychological reconstruction of the motives of Theognis and the redactor.

   One final word must be said about Nietzsche's relationship to Theognis. It cannot be doubted that the studies on Theognis, due to their chronological primacy alone, were a foundational source for Nietzsche's conception of antiquity generally, and especially for that of archaic, aristocratic socio-political thought. Moreover, Nietzsche was sympathetic throughout his career to the thought that behind Judeo-Christian morality there lay a fundamentally healthier set of values, long covered up by just such editorial manipulations. That the critical methods employed here have certain echoes in his later genealogical efforts is at least plausible.[33] These facts of themselves guarantee the importance of Theognis to Nietzsche studies.

   But we must also admit the limitations of this influence. There is a grand total of one passage in Nietzsche's published philosophical corpus where Theognis is mentioned by name: GM I, 5, where Nietzsche puts key Theognidean terms to use in his own construal of "noble" values.[34] His absence is conspicuous elsewhere in the mature corpus, especially in the "What I Owe the Ancients" chapter of the *Twilight of the Idols*. Even in his notes from the 1870s, only scattered references are found in lists of planned Basel lecture courses or potential projects. May 10, 1869 marks the last occasion on which the name Theognis appears in Nietzsche's correspondence.[35] He is mentioned only twice in the *Nachlaß* of the 1880s (KGW VII/1, 304 and KGW VII/3, 293), and neither of these references would suggest a renewed interest. Thus, while many themes in Nietzsche's later thought bear a tantalizing similarity to themes in Theognis, it is fair only to say that he has a quite marginal influence in the mature corpus. Hopefully, though, the accurate assessment of a marginal influence will be worth more to scholars of Nietzsche than an exaggerated assessment that would suggest a major one.

What is of more relevance in appreciating Nietzsche's value as a scholar of antiquity is just what we have demonstrated about the *Theognidea*. From what we have seen, it must be admitted that the work presents a brilliant, highly creative, and industrious author whose work would make any advisor proud and deserved publication in a highly regarded professional journal. We see, too, Nietzsche's early tendency to combine critical linguistic analysis—showing that the text must have been corrupted, when it was, and in what stages it was—with highly speculative if not outright fanciful motivational explanations about the characters of Theognis and his redactor. We see a certain unspoken preference for the archaic period, for poetry, and for explaining the historical developments of ideas against a socio-political backdrop. And we see an unspoken faith in the historian's ability to repair the lacunae in historical records that re-present a real and independently existing history in a generally naturalistic (appealing to psychological motivations rather than to Geist or some other unseen hand that propels history). What we do not encounter is the disciple of Schopenhauer, the friend and promulgator of Wagner, or the philosopher who wrote the *Birth of Tragedy*. It is not appropriate to say that Nietzsche had not yet "become who he was"; such a sentiment reads the story backwards, hoping to find foreshadowing in a story that in truth had not yet been written. Nietzsche had indeed become precisely who he was at that time of his life—how could it have been otherwise?—and what he was, was a classical philologist.

Notes

1   Revised portions of this paper appear in Jensen 2008 and 2013a. All translations are my own.

2   That exception is Antimo Negri, who did an admirable job translating Nietzsche's German and Greek into Italian and in offering a worthy introduction and commentary. See Negri 1985. Negri has also provided a detailed analysis of Nietzsche's 1864 dissertation in his 1993, 15–85. Much of what I say here would not have been possible without his groundbreaking research. And to the memory of his work on Nietzsche's scholarship, I would like to dedicate this essay. There have, of course, been a number of offerings that make some mention of Theognis. However, this is usually in connection with other themes in Nietzsche the author wishes to illustrate by showing a connection with Theognis. Among the more recent are: Collins 1997, 276–99 and Porter 2000, 231–40. For a useful, if brief summary of the 1864 dissertation, see Cancik 1995, 9–11.

3   What will be conspicuous by its absence here is an evaluation of the *Theognidea*'s influence on Nietzsche's later philosophical thinking. Especially with respect to Nietzsche's political thinking and conception of "Agon," Theognis figures prominently. For a thorough treatment of this theme, see Jensen 2008, 281–307.

4   The very first thematic compilation (though not a publication) on a philological theme was on the saga of the Ostrogoth king Ermanarich. Nietzsche sketched various creative forms to express his thoughts on this theme—from opera, to music, to scholarly essays—though it did not amount to anything disseminated for the public. For elucidation of the philological character of this piece, see Jensen 2013a, 7–12.

5   Throughout this summary of Theognis, I have consulted the standard work of Davies, along with that of Hudson-Williams 1910 and Negri 1993.

6   The Greek text used throughout is Young 1961.

7   The chronology is more detailed in 1867's GTS, so I will postpone discussion for the moment.

8   Negri is certainly correct that Nietzsche makes quite a stretch here. See Negri 1993, 20. The similarity to be found rests on Don Carlos' perceived slight by his father, King Philip of Spain. This, roughly, runs parallel to Kyrnos' perceived slights by the lower classes. The Theognis/Marquis von Posa character is the moral advisor and friend for each, though that is where the similarity ends. For one, the Marquis and Don Carlos are childhood friends of about the same age, whereas Theognis is much older than Kyrnos. Two, Carlos is the heir to the Spanish throne, whereas Kyrnos has only sparse ties with nobility. Three, Don Carlos is in love with his stepmother, Queen Elizabeth, whereas nothing of the sort is mentioned for Kyrnos. Most obviously, Posa gives his life for Don Carlos, while Theognis certainly does not for his young advisee. Thus, Nietzsche's suggestion of a parallel is interesting but fantastical.

9   A σύμβουλον, at the time of Isocrates' writing, would not have meant the etymologically derivative "symbol." It would have been regarded as a "measure" in the sense of "measuring stick."

10   Nietzsche's quotation comes from Teuffel's article on Theognis in the *Real-Encyclopedia*.

11   Nietzsche cites "Goethe: Werke. V, 549." The opinion, however, is not likely Goethe's own. The mention of Theognis is found in a review of Weber 1826. Here Goethe is simply paraphrasing Weber. See Goethe 1887–1919, 212f.

12   On the probable dating of individual verse intrusions, see West 1974, 67–8 and Oost 1973, 188–96.

13   The work was published in *Das Rheinisches Museum für Philologie* 22 (1867), 161–200.

14   Nietzsche did not cite the correct years of the editions of Camerarius, Vinetus, and Stephanus in his letter to Mushacke; those provided are my own emendations. Nietzsche mentions that he would need several other editions as well, but was unsure as to whether the Berlin library could provide these.

15   Carl was the brother of the philosopher and one-time Basel professor Wilhelm Dilthey. Volkmann had recommended that Nietzsche write to Dilthey in order to ask his thoughts on the Theognis problem, specifically with its treatment in the Suda. Cf. to Carl Dilthey, April 2, 1866; KSB 2, 117.

16   Porter is right to emphasize the importance of Müller's work for Nietzsche's own portrayal. See, Porter 2000, 233.

17 There were several editions of this work in Nietzsche's lifetime: 1843, 1853, 1866, and 1882. The last of these references Nietzsche's own essay, about which I will say more momentarily. Nietzsche had occasion to actually hear Bergk, though he does not seem to have been much interested in what the elder scholar had to say. Cf. to Erwin Rohde, August 6, 1868; KSB 2, 305.

18 While Volkmann wrote the request, it was sent by Nietzsche. Cf. to Hermann Kletschke, April 5, 1864, KSB 1, 277.

19 Nietzsche's schematic chart begins at KGW II/1, 20. His manuscript chronology is consistent with the research of his day. Recent scholarship, however, suggests a more complex tradition. Compare Nietzsche's Stemma at KGW II/1, 11 with that of Young 1961, xix.

20 The conclusion of Bergk.

21 The conclusion of Welcker.

22 The conclusion of Teuffel 1839–52, 1848–50.

23 The conclusions of Reitzenstein 1893, 43ff., 264ff.; Wendorff 1902 and 1909; and Wilamowitz-Moellendorff, U.v. 1913, 268ff. This and the preceding follows Porter 2000, 387nn. 33, 37.

24 There was then no clear consensus on the dates of the redactor. Welcker supposed the first redaction was due to Byzantine activity. Welcker 1826, cx. Bergk was indecisive, but eventually concluded it was the first century AD. Bergk 1845, 406. Following KGW II/1, 26.

25 Nietzsche's supposition concerning Mimnermus has now been largely accepted. It is believed that Theognis vv. 1019–22 were borrowed from Mimnermus, that vv. 935–8, 1003–6 belong to Tyrtaeus, and that vv. 153–4, 221–6, 315–18, 585–90, 719–28 are originally lines of Solon. See Carrière 1948, 10.

26 The quotation is highlighted in Janz 1978, 124; Negri 1985, 9; Porter 2000, 232; Jensen 2008, 336.

27 Cited in Stobaeus: *Sermones* 88, 499.

28 Nietzsche cites Isocrates: Ad Nicolem. c. 12. KGW II/1, 30. Cancik follows him. Cancik 1995, 10. The citation, though, is incorrect; most likely Nietzsche means Ad Nicolem. c. 42, where Isocrates mentions Theognis, along with Hesiod and Phokylides, as the "best teachers of practical morality."

29 Nietzsche borrowed the term "Chrestomathie" from Bergk, who believed that this was all Theognis' text could have ever been.

30 On this point, Nietzsche sides more closely with Welcker than with Bergk. The argument, however, is *ex silentio*: the Stichwörter are for Nietzsche so obvious that someone would naturally have mentioned them. Because no author does, it is presumed that they were not in the text at that time.

31 Nietzsche's evidence rests mostly on the Suda. Cf. KGW II/1, 42–50. Contemporary scholars tend to agree that, contra Nietzsche, the *Musa Paedica* is both stylistically and thematically consistent with the rest of the Theognidean corpus, and that therefore we lack sufficient evidence to suggest it was interpolated in the fifth century. See, for examples, West 1974, 43 and Vetta 1980, xi. Nietzsche's general assumption that pederasty was incompatible with the image of Greek nobility reflects the conservative scholarly attitude towards Greek sexuality in the nineteenth century. It is now usually agreed that drunkenness and pederastic tendencies were far more regular than Nietzsche and his colleagues were inclined to believe. As Nietzsche's argument about the parodistic tendencies of the redactor depends upon the incompatibility of these qualities with the image of

nobility, this modern finding has substantial negative consequences for Nietzsche's reconstruction.

32   Fritzsche's main position is that Nietzsche made a serious positive advancement upon Welker and Bergk, but that there are certain pairs of Stichwörter that Fritzsche finds dubious.

33   Many scholars have held this position. See especially, Porter 2000, 4 and Benne 2005, 101. On the contrary, in my 2013b I argue that Nietzsche's genealogical method is in fact inconsistent with his early philological efforts.

34   For an analysis of this passage, see Jensen 2008, 321–4.

35   It is found in a letter to Ritschl which declares that his work on Theognis has finally come to its end. See letter to Friedrich Ritschl, May 10, 1869; KSB 3, 7. In a letter to Rohde, Nietzsche makes a passing remark about the "Theognisberichte" of Ernst von Leutsch, then editor of the journal *Philologus*. See letter to Erwin Rohde, October 25, 1872; KSB 4, 71. Neither of these references would suggest anything more than a minimal interest in Theognis.

Works cited

Benne, Christian (2005): *Nietzsche und die historisch-kritische Philologie*. Berlin (Walter de Gruyter).

Bergk, Theodor (1843): *Poetae Lyrici Graeci*. Leipzig (Teubner).

—(1845): "Ueber die Kritik in Theognis." In *Das Rheinische Museum für Philologie*. Vol. 3, 206–33, 396–433.

Bernhardy, Gottfried (1867): *Grundriss der griechischen Literatur*. Halle (Eduard Anton). Vol. 2, Part 1.

Cancik, Hubert (1995): *Nietzsches Antike: Vorlesung*. Stuttgart (J. B. Metzler).

Carrière, Jean (1948): *Théognis de Mégare: Etude sur le recueil élégiaque attribué à ce poète*. Paris (Bordas).

Cate, Curtis (2002): *Friedrich Nietzsche*. London (Hutchinson).

Collins, Derek (1997): "On the Aesthetics of the Deceiving Self in Nietzsche, Pindar, and Theognis." In *Nietzsche-Studien*. Vol. 26, 276–99.

Corsenn, Arthur (1887): *Quaestiones Theognideae*. Leipzig (Klinkhardt).

Davies, James (1873): *Hesiod and Theognis*. Philadelphia (J. B. Lippincott & Company).

Dilthey, Carl (1863): "Theognis bei Suidas." In *Das Rheinisches Museum für Philologie*. Vol. 18, 150–2.

Goethe, Johann Wolfgang von (1887–1919): *Werke*. Weimar (Weimarer Ausgabe). Div. 1, Vol. 41, Part 2.

Hudson-Williams, T. (1910): *The Elegies of Theognis*. London (G. Bell & Sons).

Janz, Curt Paul (1993): *Friedrich Nietzsche: Biographie*. Munich (Carl Hanser Verlag). Vol. 1.

Jensen, Anthony (2008): "Anti-Politicality and Agon in Nietzsche's Philology." In Herman Siemens and Vasti Roodt (eds): *Nietzsche, Power and Politics*. Berlin (Walter de Gruyter), 281–307.

—(2013a): *Nietzsche's Philosophy of History*. Cambridge (Cambridge University Press).

—(2013b): "Meta-Historical Transitions from Philology to Genealogy." In *Journal of Nietzsche Studies*. Vol. 44 (2), 195–211.

Nagy, Gregory (1985): "Theognis and Megara: A Poet's Vision of his City." In T. Figueira and G. Nagy (eds): *Theognis of Megara: Poetry and the Polis*. Baltimore (Johns Hopkins University Press), 22–81.

Negri, Antimo (1985): *Friedrich Nietzsche: Teognide di Megara*. Rome and Bari (Biblioteca Universale).

—(1993): "Il destino della Polis: Nietzsche legge Teognide." In Negri (ed.): *Nietzsche nella pianura: gli uomini e la città*. Milano (Spirali), 15–85.

Oost, Stewart I. (1973): "The Megara of Theagenes and Theognis." In *Classical Philology*. Vol. 68, 188–96.

Porter, James I. (2000): *Nietzsche and the Philology of the Future*. Stanford (Stanford University Press).

Ramorino, Felice (1876): "Theognide di Megara." In *Rivista di Filologia*. Vol. 4, 1–49.

Reitzenstein, Richard (1893): *Epigramm und Skolion: ein Beitrag zur Geschichte der Alexandrinischen Dichtung*. Giessen (J. Ricker).

Sitzler, Jacob (1880): *Theognidis Reliquiae*. Heidelberg (Carol Winter).

Teuffel, Wilhelm S. (1839–1952): "Theognis." In *Pauly's Real-Encyclopädie der classischen Alterthumswissenschaft*. Stuttgart (J. B. Metzler). Div. VI, Vol. 2, 1848–50.

Vetta, Massimo (ed.) (1980): *Theognis: Elegiarum Liber Secundus*. Rome (Edizioni dell' Ateneo).

Weber, Wilhelm E. (1826): *Die elegischen Dichter der Hellenen*. Frankfurt (Hermann).

Welcker, Frederick G. (ed.) (1826): *Theognidis Reliquiae*. Frankfurt (Broenner).

Wendorff, Franz (1902): *Ex usu convivali Theognideam syllogen fluxisse demonstratur*. Berlin (University Dissertation).

—(1909): *Die aristokratischen Sprecher der Theognis-Sammlung*. Göttingen (Vandenhoeck & Ruprecht).

West, Martin L. (1974): *Studies in Greek Elegy and Iambus*. Berlin (Walter de Gruyter).

Wilamowitz-Moellendorff, Ulrich von (1913): *Sappho und Simonides*. Berlin (Weidmann).

Young, Douglas (1961): *Theognis: Bibliotheca Scriptorum Graecorum et Romanorum*. Leipzig (Teubner).

Ziegler, Christopher (ed.) (1868): *Theognidis Elegiae: Ex codicibus Mutinensi Veneto 522, Vaticano 915*. Tübingen (Laupp).

Nietzsche and Diogenes Laertius*

Jonathan Barnes

Den grössten Einfluss haben einige schöne Irrtümer erlangt.

1

In 1869 and 1870 Nietzsche published three long studies on Diogenes Laertius: *de Laertii Diogenis fontibus, analecta Laertiana*, and *Beiträge zur Quellenkunde und Kritik des Laertius Diogenes*.[1] The *Beiträge* contains a short index to all three papers, which Nietzsche evidently regarded as parts of a single work; and indeed the second and third studies can properly be treated as a series of appendixes to the first. Even as the studies were in press Nietzsche wrote of his intention to revise and publish them in book form (to Ritschl, October 16, 1869; KSB 3, 65; to Ritschl, March 28, 1870; KSB 3, 109). Curt entries in his notebooks probably indicate that the intention was still alive in 1874.[2] A letter written to Erwin Rohde in the summer of 1869 reveals a further Laertian project: "Usener and I plan a corpus on the history of philosophy in which I will deal with Diogenes and he with Stobaeus, pseudo-Plutarch, etc." (to Rohde, June 16, 1869; KSB 3, 18). The corpus was to be a critical edition of the Greek texts, and in the same year Nietzsche wrote to Curt Wachsmuth to ask for his collations of some of Diogenes' manuscripts (to Wachsmuth, October 14, 1869; KSB 3, 64). But these plans and projects were never realized, and Nietzsche published nothing on Diogenes after 1870.[3]

The three studies on Diogenes together constitute one half of Nietzsche's published philologische Schriften. (*The Birth of Tragedy*, whatever its merits and demerits, is not a work of philology or classical scholarship in the strict sense of those terms, nor did Nietzsche himself regard it as such.) The unpublished notes on Diogenes constitute

---

*   [Editors' note: This chapter was first published in *Nietzsche Studien* 15 (1986), 16–40. We gratefully acknowledge the author's and publisher's permission to reprint it here. Several of the footnotes in the original publication have been incorporated into the text for this reprinting. The citation and reference system has also been altered for the sake of the present volume's consistency.]

more than one half of Nietzsche's unpublished philological writings. Moreover, the work on Diogenes represents Nietzsche's most sustained effort in the field of scholarship. His standing as a scholar is therefore largely determined by his Laertian lucubrations.[4]

2

Diogenes Laertius probably wrote at the end of the third century AD. Nothing is known about his life or circumstances. His one surviving work, the *Lives of the Philosophers*, which runs to some five hundred modern pages, is a compilation of information—biographical, anecdotal, doxographical—on the earlier Greek philosophers. The vicissitudes of fortune have secured for Diogenes a considerable importance in the history of ancient philosophy; for he often preserves the only surviving evidence on capital points of biography or of doctrine.[5]

The work is not universally attractive. Its style is usually pedestrian. Its train of thought is frequently broken and sometimes incoherent. Its assertions are often of dubious value. Moreover, the Greek text is poorly transmitted, and corruptions mar every page.[6] But what repels the layman attracts the scholar. And of the many scholarly problems raised by Diogenes' text, the question of his sources, immediate and remote, has usually seemed the most pressing. For on this depends his value as a historian of philosophy: which and how many earlier authorities did he use? How accurately did he report their views? How carefully did he sift their various stories? How judiciously did he select and synthesize their testimonies? The *Lives* presents an appearance of scholarly learning: numerous sources are frequently referred to or cited, either to support the account which Diogenes himself decides to follow, or else to document disagreements which Diogenes does not see fit to resolve. On closer inspection matters assume a different aspect: it becomes clear that some, at least, of Diogenes' learning is second-hand—he cites texts which he has not himself read and he lifts references from earlier compilers. Moreover, the suspicion soon arises that much of Diogenes' work consisted in copying or epitomizing his predecessors, so that his claim to be a historian of philosophy is itself called into question. These issues are important, and they are still controversial: for over a century Quellenforschung has dominated Laertian scholarship.

3

As a schoolboy at Schulpforta, Nietzsche had acquired a love for classical studies (see Nietzsche's "Mein Leben" in BAW 3, 66–8), and his teachers there, so different from the "narrow-minded, cold-blooded pedants, who know nothing of learning but its scholarly dust," had inspired him with their own scholarship (see his autobiographical fragment of 1868/69 in BAW 5, 253). As a student at Bonn, where he heard Otto Jahn and Friedrich Ritschl, he continued his classical work. But it was not until he removed to Leipzig, in 1865, that he determined to follow a philological career himself.

In Leipzig, Ritschl, who had been called to the Greek chair, became Nietzsche's friend, his patron, and his "scholarly conscience" (to Deussen, April 4, 1867; KSB 2, 205).[7] On Ritschl's urging, Nietzsche joined in the foundation of a Philological Society, before which, on January 18, 1866, he gave a paper on Theognis.[8] Ritschl read the manuscript and enthused over it: Nietzsche was exalted, and felt himself born as a philologist (see his "Rückblick auf meine zwei Leipziger Jahre"; BAW 3, 291–315; here, 300). He gave three further papers before the Society, and his philological ambitions settled and strengthened.[9]

The third of Nietzsche's papers discussed the surviving ancient catalogues of Aristotle's writings (BAW 3, 212–26).

> As background to this paper I made an examination of the sources of Diogenes Laertius. From the start I felt myself attracted to this work, and in my first Leipzig semester I had already put together much relevant material. I also spoke at length to Ritschl on the subject. And so it happened that one day [in November 1866] he asked me, with dark hints, whether I would undertake a study of the sources of Diogenes if I received a certain encouragement from another quarter. I puzzled for a long time over the meaning of these words, until, in a moment of enlightenment, I became convinced that the next University Prize would have that particular question as its topic. On the morning when the topics were published, I ran to Kintschy's and eagerly picked up the Leipzig News. I was right: my eyes fell on the words I longed to see—*de Fontibus Diogenis Laertii*. (BAW 3, 311)[10]

Nietzsche set to work at once. Day and night he thought only of Diogenes' sources, and by January the main lines of the study were written down (to Mushacke, January 4, 1867; KSB 2, 193). In April he began to compose the final version (to Deussen, April 4, 1867; KSB 2, 205; and to von Gersdorff, April 6, 1867; KSB 2, 208). But difficulties emerged;[11] his energies were not boundless; other philological sirens called; and the spring of 1867 was balmy.

> At last, when there was no more time to lose, I settled down to my work on Diogenes and put together my results as simply and plainly as I could. The fateful last day of July began. I spurred myself on with all my powers, and at ten o'clock in the evening I was able to run to Rohde through the dark, rainy night with the finished manuscript. My friend was waiting for me and he had set up wine and glasses to restore me to life. (BAW 3, 311–12)

The essay was submitted, and on the last day of October Nietzsche was awarded the Prize (to Rohde, November 3, 1867; KSB 2, 230). By his own account he won "in competition with Mr. Nobody" (Ibid.); and he had always been confident of winning—Ritschl had, after all, set the theme with him in mind (to Gersdorff, January 16, 1867; KSB 2, 196). But although he professed a becoming nonchalance—"tant de bruit pour une omelette" (to Rohde, February 1–3, 1868; KSB 2, 248)—he was elated by the result.

The first part of *de Fontibus* was eventually published in the autumn of 1868. On the strength of it—and of an extravagantly laudatory testimonial from Ritschl—Nietzsche was offered an extraordinary Professorship of Classical Philology at Basel University. In March 1869 the second part of *de Fontibus* appeared,[12] followed in March 1870 by the *Analecta*.[13] The *Beiträge* were printed in May of the same year.[14]

4

Nietzsche was engrossed by his work on Diogenes, but he was not in love with his author. The studies contain a string of scornful remarks: Diogenes was a sleepy-head (KGW II/1, 80), he was stupid (Ibid., 89), he was an impudent and imprudent thief (Ibid.), he was "wretched little Laertius" (Ibid., 131), he was hasty and careless (Ibid., 197), vain and pretentious (Ibid.,189).

Yet Nietzsche had a clear—even an exaggerated—idea of the historical importance of Diogenes:

> What is Diogenes to us? No-one would waste a word on the philistine features of this writer were he not, by chance, the guardian of jewels whose value he does not recognize. He is in fact night-porter to the history of Greek philosophy: no-one can enter unless Diogenes has given him the key. (BAW 5, 126)

Moreover, there were worse scholars than Diogenes. In a scornful denunciation of the learned writings of Ritter and Brandis and Zeller, Nietzsche exclaims: "I at least would rather read Diogenes Laertius than Zeller; for in Diogenes at least the spirit of the old philosophers lives on, whereas in Zeller you will find neither that spirit nor any other" (SE 8; KSA 1, 417; see also KGW III/4, 396).

Nietzsche's scorn for Diogenes was, to some extent at least, conventional: that is how scholars wrote. The fact that Nietzsche continued to busy himself with Diogenes after the Leipzig prize was won suggests that he found the *Lives* not only important but also in some fashion congenial.

The Preface to Nietzsche's booklet *Die Philosophie im tragischen Zeitalter der Griechen* ends as follows:

> In philosophical systems which have been refuted, the only thing that can still interest us is the personal element; for that is eternally irrefutable. With three anecdotes one can give a picture of a man: I try to extract three anecdotes from each system, and I ignore the rest. (PTAG P; KSA 1, 803)

That passage, which betrays a strange misconception of the history of philosophy (and also of philosophy itself), harks back to Diogenes. It was surely in the anecdotal aspect of the *Lives* that Nietzsche found "the spirit of the old philosophers," and it was that aspect which made the *Lives* congenial to him. The stimulatingly capricious misinterpretations of Nietzsche's booklet have, in the end, little in common with the prosaic reportage of Diogenes; but it is not outlandish to surmise that the *Lives* helped to form Nietzsche's own notions of how to write the history of Greek thought.

5

Nietzsche's three Laertian studies are rich in detail: they contain numerous textual suggestions, historical conjectures, chronological proposals, exegetical essays. Many of the points of detail repay close study.[15] But the details are embellishments to a single thesis, which Nietzsche called his Grundhypothese (KGW II/1, 203): "the thesis, strong and clear, holds the essays together and gives them their argumentative unity. Here I shall restrict my attention to the Grundhypothese, first describing it and then briefly discussing its primary and most challenging contention."

The thesis is usually summarized in half a dozen words: "Diogenes Laertius is an epitome of Diocles of Magnesia." And Nietzsche himself allowed and used the summary (KGW II/1, 131 and 203). But in fact the main thesis of the studies was always a little more complicated than that; moreover, it underwent one significant modification. Nietzsche never argued that Diogenes used a unique source. Originally, he claimed that Diogenes depended on two sources: Diocles and Favorinus.[16] The dependency was close—indeed, Diogenes was often merely a slavish copyist. To this stolen material Diogenes occasionally added something of his own, notably his frightful epigrams. Later on, Nietzsche came to believe that the account of Pyrrhonian skepticism in Book IX of the Lives could not come either from Diocles or from Favorinus, and he posited a third, skeptical, source, tentatively identified as Theodosius (KGW II/1, 207).[17]

But although Diocles is thus, strictly speaking, one source among three, he is by far the most important source:

> If we take from Diogenes' book everything which belongs to Diocles, only a little remains: Diogenes' own additions from his *Pammetros*, a number of notes taken from his reading of Favorinus and inserted here and there, and finally ... an account of skepticism and of the skeptical διαδοχή. (KGW II/1, 206)

Diocles has overwhelming importance in the only *Life* which Nietzsche analyzes as a whole. The *Life* of Democritus (IX 34–49) occupies nine and a half pages in the Oxford Text. Apart from five lines taken from Favorinus (§§34–5) and Diogenes' own four-line epigram (§43), the rest is allegedly Diocles (KGW II/1, 218–21).[18]

The main thesis has two supplements. The first is a detailed survey of the sources used by Diogenes' sources. In particular, Nietzsche spends much time on Diocles' sources, in the hope of showing what authors he used, how faithfully he followed them, and with what skill he combined them. Secondly, Nietzsche offers a brief explanation of Diogenes' modus operandi: Diogenes was a poet; he wanted his poems to be preserved for posterity; and he constructed the *Lives* as a vehicle to carry a selection of his epigrams (KGW II/1, 193–201).

A summary of Nietzsche's major contentions in his Laertian studies would therefore run as follows: Diogenes was a poet. Wanting to preserve his work, he hit upon the idea of embedding it in a series of philosophical biographies. Most of this matter he copied from a single work, Diocles of Magnesia's *Summary of the Philosophers*; and since Diocles was a learned man who frequently cited his many sources, Diogenes' *Lives* assumed a vicarious learning. But Diogenes had also read Favorinus' miscellanies, and occasionally added a few choice passages from that source (KGW II/1, 23). In addition, he found a wholly different source, perhaps Theodosius, for his *Life* of Pyrrho.[19]

6

Most scholars will accept that Diogenes used Diocles[20] as a first-hand source (cf. Mejer 1978, 42): He mentions him some twenty times, and at least three times purports to quote him (*Lives* VI 12, VI 36, VII 48). Such citations do not strictly prove that Diogenes had himself read Diocles; for he might have lifted the references to Diocles from some other, later work—just as, on Nietzsche's own view, the other sources "used" and even "quoted" by Diogenes were all lifted from Diocles or from Favorinus. Yet such superfine caution may here reasonably be ignored: let us grant Nietzsche that Diogenes had Diocles' book to hand. The crucial question is: how often and how widely did he borrow from the book?

Diogenes nowhere hints that Diocles was his main source—indeed there are other authors who are mentioned more often than Diocles.[21] But there is nothing inherently objectionable in the idea that Diogenes used Diocles without always confessing the fact: ancient authors were never punctilious in naming their sources. And Nietzsche presents a sequence of arguments designed to show that Diogenes, despite his silence, did indeed regularly copy Diocles.

He first contends that Diocles is the source for the Stoic material in Book VII of the *Lives*. Then he argues to the same conclusion about the Epicurean material in Book X. Next comes a complex argument: Diogenes often uses Demetrius of Magnesia; but it can be shown that he knew Demetrius only through Diocles: therefore a further quantity of stuff in the Lives derives directly from Diocles. Into this argument Nietzsche interpolates a proof that the material on Cynicism came from Diocles, and after it he adds a proof that the Preface in Book I is Diocles' work. In the *Beiträge* Nietzsche adds special arguments for the Dioclean origin of the material on Democritus and on Menippus.[22]

Even were all those specific arguments sound, they would not amount to a proof of Nietzsche's Grundhypothese; for over half of Diogenes' *Lives* remains undiscussed. Nonetheless, the arguments might be thought to give the Grundhypothese a high degree of probability: if Diogenes copied so much from Diocles, it is only economical to suppose that most of the rest of the material in the *Lives* came from the same source. For why should Diogenes trouble to change horses, when the nag he was riding served him so well?

It would be a long task to examine each of Nietzsche's arguments in all its detail. But it will suffice to consider the main points in the three main arguments. I shall take the arguments, for reasons which will become evident, in reverse order: Demetrius, the Epicureans, the Stoics.

7

Diogenes certainly used Demetrius, directly or indirectly, in a number of places. I shall not here examine Nietzsche's disputable contention that all the book catalogues in the *Lives*, with the exception of those of Democritus and of Plato, came to Diogenes from Demetrius' work *On Homonyms*.[23] The vital question for Nietzsche is this: did Diogenes use Demetrius directly, or did he rather read him only in the pages of Diocles?

Nietzsche offers two arguments for his claim that the Demetrian book catalogues came to Diogenes via Diocles. First, he observes, correctly, that Diogenes often makes a close connection between the doxography of a given philosopher and the catalogue of his books. He remarks: "it is highly probable that this mode of connection came to Diogenes from Diocles" (KGW II/1, 130). That is Nietzsche at his most feeble. Why is it "highly probable"? Any writer, however untalented, will make some connection between the list of a philosopher's works and the description of his thought. The connections in Diogenes are in general banal: "These are his books, and in them he says ..." or "He says this. And these are his books ..." There is no reason at all to ascribe those "connections" to Diocles. Nothing in them tells against the supposition that Diogenes copied the lists from one source—from Demetrius, if you will—and turned to other, doxographical, sources for the philosophy. That supposition may turn out to be false; but Nietzsche's appeal to probability is valueless.

However that may be, Nietzsche has a second argument, which, he boldly claims, "cannot be refuted" (KGW II/1, 130). The argument bears specifically on the connection between book-list and doxography in the *Life of Epicurus*. According to Diogenes, Epicurus was more productive than any other philosopher; but the catalogue of his works in X 27–8 is selective: it lists 41 items,[24] Epicurus' "best" books. This list, Nietzsche assumes, came, at least indirectly, from Demetrius. The list is followed by the Epicurean doxography. This refers explicitly to 20 of Epicurus' writings; and, by what Nietzsche calls a "remarkable congruence" (KGW II/1, 130), all the 20 are included in the selective Demetrian list. Why does the doxography not refer to any of the other 250 works of Epicurus? Clearly, because the doxographer was using, and had transcribed, Demetrius' list. But the doxographer was Diocles. Therefore the Demetrian list of Epicurus' works was transcribed by Diocles. Hence Diogenes knew the list (and, by a heady generalization, all the other Demetrian lists) only through Diocles.

The argument is elegant, but despite Nietzsche's boast it can easily be refuted. First, it is not true that all the works referred to in the doxography are present in the selective list. The doxography—the term is hardly apposite here—consists primarily of transcriptions of three of Epicurus' letters (to Herodotus, to Pythocles, to Menoeceus) and of his *Kuriai Doxai*. The transcriptions are supplemented by short pieces of genuinely doxographical material. The Demetrian list mentions *Letters*, but it does so baldly: it does not mention individually the three letters which are later transcribed; nor does it mention specifically the *Letter to Friends in Mytilene* which is referred to at X 136. The list contains an *Epitome of the Books against the Physicists*. The doxography refers three times to the *Large Epitome* and twice to the *Small Epitome to Herodotus*. Even if the *Large Epitome* is the same as the *Epitome* of the list and the *Small Epitome* is the *Letter to Herodotus*, it remains true that the list does not refer to those works by the titles under which the doxography knows them. In any case, the doxography refers to *Twelve Elements* (X 44): no such title appears in the catalogue.

Those facts tend, I think, to support the opposite of Nietzsche's conclusion: they suggest that the Epicurean doxography and the selective book list were not found together in the same source.

Secondly, we may wonder how remarkable Nietzsche's "congruence" really is. The list purports to give "the best" of Epicurus' works (X 27), and the doxographer seems to rely largely on works which are on the list. But what is striking about that? Might we not expect a doxographer to rely largely on the best works of an author, works which would also tend to appear in any selective list of the author's writings?

Thirdly, even if the Epicurean doxographer actually consulted the selective list, why suppose that he also transcribed it? Allow, for the sake of argument, that Demetrius wrote the list and that Diocles employed it while writing the doxography: it does not follow—and it is not particularly plausible to infer—that Diocles also himself transcribed the list. Yet Nietzsche's argument demands that implausible inference.

8

The argument about Demetrius presupposes that Diocles was Diogenes' source for the *Life* of Epicurus. It thus depends on the conclusion of Nietzsche's second main argument.

At X 3–4 Diogenes lists a number of authors who attacked Epicurus. One of them was a certain Sotion, who entitled his book *Refutations of Diocles*. Diocles, therefore, had written a defense of Epicurus. A fragment of the defense is quoted by Diogenes a little later, at X 11. Nietzsche argues as follows:

> We have proved that Diocles expounded, at length and with learning, the doctrines of the Stoa to which he was not himself committed. Is it not highly probable that he showed even more learning and industry in explaining the views of Epicurus?—for his soul would rather relax in the gardens of Epicurus than in the cold Stoa. (KGW II/1, 89)

The argument is not compelling, but the conclusion is surely correct. Diocles' work was entitled *Summary of the Philosophers*. It contained, as we shall see, a reasonably detailed account of Stoicism: it will certainly also have contained a reasonably detailed account of Epicureanism—whatever Diocles' own philosophical predilections may have been.

But why think that Diogenes' *Life* of Epicurus draws on that account? So far as I can see, Nietzsche has two reasons for thinking that Diocles lies behind the *Life*. First, he suggests that we can then understand a puzzling statement at X 9: in the course of the defense of Epicurus against his calumniators, Diogenes reports that the Epicurean school, alone of the great Hellenistic schools of philosophy, is still flourishing, and that its headship has been handed down in unbroken succession from Epicurus himself. Such a statement is false of the third century AD: it must, Nietzsche claims, have been written by an author of the *first* century, whose words Diogenes then unthinkingly transcribed. Such an author was Diocles.

Secondly, Nietzsche adverts to X 29. Diogenes explains that he will transcribe Epicurus' three letters, together with the *Kuriai Doxai*: "thus you will be able to get a rounded view of the man and will know how to judge me [κἀμὲ κρίνειν εἰδέναι]." According to Nietzsche, we have no reason to suppose that *Diogenes* was an Epicurean, or that *he* is asking his readers to "judge me." Rather, he is again transcribing an Epicurean source, and the "me," which he has thoughtlessly copied, in fact refers to that source. And surely the source was Diocles.

The text at X 28 is disputed: Usener proposed "κἂν" for "κἀμέ," and he has been generally followed. (Bignone preferred "'καὶ ἅμα," Marcovich prints "καί.") If the text is emended, the apparent reference to the author as an Epicurean is lost, and Nietzsche's case falls.

But emendation, though tempting, is required neither by syntax nor by sense: the manuscript reading, which Nietzsche retains, seems to me to be perfectly acceptable. Furthermore, it is not implausible to suppose, with Nietzsche, that Diogenes is not here speaking in *propria persona*. Apart from X 29, there is no evidence that Diogenes was an Epicurean—or that he held any other philosophical views. The *Lives* do not betray their author. They are almost wholly impersonal works.[25] The sudden and perfectly casual intrusion of a self-reference would be out of character with the rest of Diogenes' book: for that reason, it is not wholly wild to suspect that Diogenes may have thoughtlessly copied someone else's appeal to his readers.

But why should that someone else be Diocles? Nietzsche has no reason for introducing Diocles beyond what might be called a Principle of Indolence: Diocles wrote about Epicureanism, Diogenes knew and used his writings—as an indolent copyist, eager not to multiply labor *praeter necessitatem*, he will have used him in X 29 as well. It is difficult to assess such an argument. Certainly, Diocles is a possible author for X 29, and he cannot be ruled out. Equally certainly, there are many other possible authors. I do not see that the Principle of Indolence gives Diocles any edge over the rival candidates; for I cannot see any particular plausibility in a general principle of that sort. (Is a Principle of Indolence any more plausible, in general, than a Principle of Boredom? "Diogenes had already copied a vast quantity of Diocles by the time he reached Book X, and copying is appallingly tedious: were he a normal human being, Diogenes would have used any source but Diocles in X 29.")

Much the same is to be said of the passage at X 9. Again, one half of Nietzsche's argument is not implausible: it seems likely that Diogenes is here reporting some earlier author's judgment on the perennial endurance of the Epicurean school.[26] But, again, why Diocles? There is no reason, beyond the Principle of Indolence, to select him as the earlier author.

9

Nietzsche's argument about Demetrius depends in a strong sense on his argument about Epicurus: if the latter falls, so must the former. The argument about Epicurus in turn refers to the argument about the Stoics; but here the dependence is weak—even if the latter falls the former may in principle be able to stand unaided. Nonetheless the contention that Diocles was Diogenes' source for the Stoic doxography in Book VII of the *Lives* is the *fons et origo* of Nietzsche's whole enterprise, and it is supported by the best and most subtle of his analyses.[27]

He begins from a passage at VII 48, where Diogenes explicitly names Diocles as his source for Stoic logic. The text, according to Nietzsche, implies that Diogenes has already quoted Diocles *verbatim*. Nietzsche thinks he can identify two earlier quotations. He then argues that Diocles must have written accounts of Stoic ethics and Stoic physics, and that Diogenes used Diocles for all three parts of Stoic philosophy and not just for Stoic logic. Finally, Nietzsche finds confirmation for his thesis at VII 160.

In the central passage, VII 48, the text is controversial. It will be best to begin by quoting Nietzsche:

> [Diogenes] then explains the view of Zeno and the Stoics on dialectic, and is not content with a summary exposition:
>
> ἐν οὖν τοῖς λογικοῖς ταῦτά τε αὐτοῖς δοκεῖν κεφαλαιωδῶς. καὶ ἵνα καὶ κατὰ μέρος εἴπωμεν, καὶ τάδε ἅπερ αὐτῶν εἰς τὴν εἰσαγωγικὴν τείνει τέχνην καὶ αὐτὰ ἐπὶ λέξεως τίθησι Διοκλῆς ὁ Μάγνης ἐν τῇ Ἐπιδρομῇ τῶν φιλοσόφων, λέγων οὕτως· ἀρέσκει τοῖς Στωϊκοῖς [...] [VII 48].
>
> If Diogenes confesses that he owes καὶ τάδε to Diocles, then he has already drawn other things from the same source: what could be plainer? And we might ask after the meaning of καὶ αὐτά. If you take those words to have the same force as καὶ τάδε, I will not agree. Rather, καὶ αὐτά is very closely connected to the following ἐπὶ λέξεως, and should be understood as follows: "If we are to give a detailed account, Diocles of Magnesia in his *Summary of the Philosophers* sets them down too—in so far as they bear on the introductory art—and them too *verbatim*, as follows."[28] Thus Diogenes indicates that he has already transcribed Diocles *verbatim*. (KGW II/1, 78)

Unfortunately, Nietzsche's interpretation of the Greek he cites is quite certainly mistaken. Hermann Diels, in his brief but trenchant criticism of Nietzsche's Laertian hypothesis, made the killing point (Diels 1879, 162). Nietzsche does not translate or explain the word "τε" after "ταῦτα." His punctuation of the passage, with a full stop after "κεφαλαιωδῶς," in fact makes the "τε" inexplicable. But the punctuation is essential to Nietzsche's interpretation of the passage as a whole. Therefore on Nietzsche's interpretation the "τε" is inexplicable. Therefore the interpretation is false.

Diels' own construal of the text has won general support. He takes the "τε" after "ταῦτα" to be correlated with the "καί" before "ἵνα." The core of the sentence is thus: "ταῦτά τε αὐτοῖς δοκεῖν [...], καὶ [...] τάδε." The "ἅπερ" clause then depends upon "τάδε"; and the "καί" before "αὐτά" introduces the second conjunct of this complex relative clause.[29] Thus: "In logic they believed both these things, summarily put, and—if we are also to give a detailed account—also the following things, which bear upon their introductory art and which Diocles sets down *verbatim* as follows." That is cumbersome (in Greek as in English), but it makes intelligible sense and can be paraphrased as follows: "In logic the Stoics held (a) the summary view we have just given, and also (b) the detailed views we are about to give—these detailed views bear on the introductory art and are expounded by Diocles in the following words." The important thing is this: Diels' interpretation of the text nowhere implies or suggests that Diogenes has *already* used Diocles.

The difference between Nietzsche and Diels is syntactical: "τάδε" is, on Nietzsche's view, the object of "τίθησι" and, on Diels' view, the subject of "δοκεῖν." Diels' interpretation is demanded by the "τε" after "ταῦτα." But the syntax of the Dielsian sentence is at best tortuous. The problem is this: there are too many "καί's" in the Greek. In particular, the "καί" before "τάδε" is strange. The "καί" before "ἵνα," answering "τε," connects "τάδε" to "ταῦτα"; the "καί" before "τάδε" means "also." These two "καί's" are separated by a parenthetical clause. Remove the clause and you find: "ταῦτά τε αὐτοῖς δοκεῖν κεφαλαιωδῶς καὶ καὶ τάδε" where the repeated "καί" is not Greek. With the insertion of the parenthetical "ἵνα" clause this solecism disappears—or is disguised; for, as it seems to me, it is still present as an undertone in the sentence, and it makes the sentence stylistically and perhaps even grammatically dubious.[30]

The point cannot be pressed. Diogenes was not a consummate writer, and although the tics and quirks of his style are still inadequately known, it is certain that his use of "καί" is often strange or erratic (see Freudenthal 1879, 309; Barnes 1992, 4288n. 246). Nonetheless it must be remarked that the "τε" after "ταῦτα," which is the cause of the difficulties with the "καί's" is not found in all our manuscripts. The textual tradition of Diogenes is complicated; but it appears that the surviving manuscripts can be reduced to three, B, P, and F (see Egli 1981, 1–5; Knoepfler 1991). B reads "ταῦτά τε." F reads "ταῦτα τά." P originally read "ταῦτ'" and was corrected by a later hand to "ταῦτά τε."[31] Perhaps Diogenes wrote "ταῦτ'" and not "ταῦτά τε"?[32]

In that case, the syntax of the sentence becomes much easier.[33] Place a full-stop after "κεφαλαιωδῶς," as Nietzsche does. The "καί" before "ἵνα" is now a standard sentential connective; the "ἵνα" clause is no longer parenthetical; and the "καί" before "τάδε" no longer seems solecistic. Next, "τάδε" needs a verb; and in fact it is easily construed as the object of "τίθησι": "And so that we may also give a detailed account, Diocles sets down the following things too." But now the "καὶ αὐτά" clause cannot represent a second limb of the relative clause, as it does on Diels' interpretation; for "αὐτά" must refer back to "τάδε" and fall within the main clause of the sentence. It is then clear, as Nietzsche remarks, that "καὶ αὐτά" goes closely with "ἐπὶ λέξεως"; and the "καί" can certainly be taken in the sense of "also." Thus we get: "And so that we may also give a detailed account, Diocles sets down the following things too, which bear on their introductory art—these too verbatim, thus: [...]" And so we have returned to Nietzsche's interpretation of VII 48: his interpretation will not fit the Greek text he read, but it will fit a Greek text which is at least as plausible as the text he read.

Yet even if we grant all that, Nietzsche's argument is still less than probative.[34] First, his reading of the "καί" before "αὐτά" is not obligatory. We might, for example, take it to be emphatic—to mean "indeed" rather than "also."[35] In fact, this strikes me as the better reading: "Diocles sets down the following things too, [...] and verbatim at that [...]" If that is correct, then the text provides no evidence that Diogenes had already offered other verbatim transcriptions of Diocles.[36]

Secondly, we might question Nietzsche's reading of the "καί" before "τάδε." Certainly, this "καί" means "also"; but the "also" need not imply that Diocles had said something else on the subject. If you say "Diogenes tells us X about Stoic logic, and Cicero also tells us Y," you do not imply that Cicero tells us X. The function of the "also" is to indicate that you offer additional information, not that Cicero offered two pieces of information. And so it is—or so it may well be—with our text. Diogenes means this: "I have already given the summary account; now read this too, which Diocles tells us."

None of that shows Nietzsche's interpretation of VII 48 to be wrong: at most we may conclude that the interpretation is not uniquely determined by the text.[37] But Nietzsche offers, in effect, two supplementary arguments, which perhaps give his interpretation an edge over its rivals.

He argues that Diocles was already quoted in VII 39–41, on the parts of philosophy, and that he was already quoted in VII 41–8, the summary account of logic. "For, first, the author of the remarks on the division of philosophy appeals to the same sources which Diocles uses in the λογικὰ κατὰ μέρος" (KGW II/1, 79). That is hardly a powerful argument. In any case, its premise is false: the λογικὰ κατὰ μέρος refer to three authorities who are not mentioned in VII 39–41; conversely, VII 39–41 appeals to seven authorities who are not mentioned in the λογικὰ κατὰ μέρος (see Maass 1880, 12–13). Perhaps aware of the falsity of his premise, Nietzsche immediately modified the argument: in VII 39–41 no Stoics later than the pupils of Posidonius are mentioned; therefore Diogenes is using a source who was a contemporary of those disciples—"and here the finger points, so to speak, to Diocles" (KGW II/1, 79). The premise of the modified argument is true; but the argument itself is evidently impotent. Diocles is at best one among several possible objects of the pointing finger.

Secondly, Nietzsche observes "that in several dialectical examples the name of Diocles himself is used, e.g. ζῇ Διοκλῆς. Whence could Diogenes have taken this if not from Diocles himself?" (KGW II/1, 79). The name of Diocles does indeed appear, once, in the λογικὰ κατὰ μέρος (VII 75). Its presence there shows, what in any event Diogenes says, that Diocles is a source for the detailed account of Stoic dialectic.[38] But Diocles' name occurs nowhere else as an illustrative example. In particular, it does not occur in VII 41–8, and so cannot provide evidence that the summary account of logic comes from Diocles. Nietzsche has made a careless mistake.

Nietzsche has therefore failed to show that there is Dioclean material in Diogenes before VII 48. What of his argument that Diocles is responsible not only for Stoic logic but also for the other two parts of the Stoic doxography? The argument is simple: Nietzsche supposes, surely rightly, that Diocles' *Summary* contained a complete Stoic doxography; he notes that Diogenes cites no other source for Stoic ethics and Stoic physics; and he asks, rhetorically, why we should think "that Diogenes abandoned without cause the source on which he had just been drawing" (KGW II/1, 79).

The rhetorical question assumes something which Nietzsche has no right to assume, namely that Diogenes had "no cause" to abandon Diocles. We know almost nothing about Diocles' *Summary*: perhaps Diogenes did have cause to abandon it—it was too long or too short for his uses; it was too simple or too obscure; a better source was easily available; Diogenes was simply bored with copying Diocles, or embarrassed by the fact that he had already pillaged so much. A hundred such reasons could be imagined: none has any claim on our credence; but equally we have no right to assume that there was no reason at all.

There remains the confirmatory evidence which Nietzsche found at V 160. There Diogenes ends his Stoic doxography with the following comment: "Such were their views on physics: the account we have given is sufficient considering our aim to preserve the balance of our work." Nietzsche claims that Diogenes himself could not have composed those words for the long Stoic doxography in fact destroys what balance the *Lives* may have aimed at, if indeed balance was ever an aim of Diogenes. Hence the words were taken from Diogenes' source, and that source must therefore have given a balanced account of all three parts of Stoic philosophy. Since the logic is known to have come from Diocles, the words at VII 160, and with them the whole Stoic doxography, are Dioclean.

It is not clear that the words in VII 160 cannot have been composed by Diogenes. When he speaks of the "balance of my work," he may have in mind simply the Stoic doxography, where balance is in fact more or less preserved: he need not be worrying about the balance between, say, the Stoic and the Peripatetic doxographies. Nonetheless, VII 160 does strike me as odd, and I am not averse to Nietzsche's suggestion that it was carelessly lifted from a source.[39]

Even so, and even if we suppose that Diogenes' source for Stoic physics had also written on Stoic ethics and Stoic logic, it does not follow that Diogenes used the same source throughout. He may, for example, have used Diocles for logic, X for ethics, and Y for physics, even though each of his three sources had written on all three parts of Stoicism.[40] We should then take the comment in VII 160 to refer to the balance of Y's Stoic doxography (or of Y's book, whatever that may have been).

There is, moreover, a relevant text which Nietzsche did not consider. VII 83 is a bridge passage between logic and ethics. It begins with the formula "such are the Stoics in matters of logic," and it ends with the formula "such is their account of logic." The sentences between the two formulas are ill-composed and in places textually corrupt. The two formulas seem to be doublets: why are they both there? One possible explanation is the following. The first formula is from Diocles: from VII 48 to VII 83 Diogenes has copied Diocles' account of Stoic logic; and he ends his quotation in §83 with Diocles' own coda. The second formula is then from Diogenes: it indicates that his own account of Stoic logic is over (so Egli 1981, 8). In that case Diocles is abandoned in §83, and some new source is used for the remainder of the Stoic doxography. Once again, that argument is far from decisive; but it provides some evidence against Nietzsche's Dioclean claims.

10

What, in the end, can be said of Diocles as a source for Diogenes? Most of Diogenes' references to Diocles are, on the surface, supplementary: Diocles is adduced as one of several authors who can testify for or against some biographical or doxographical contention. Only once, in the case of Stoic logic, is Diocles explicitly adduced in a more generous and extensive way. A simple-minded reading of Diogenes' *Lives* will say no more than that about Diocles.[41]

Nietzsche's arguments do not prove that such a simple-minded view is false. His arguments form a connected chain. Starting from the indubitably Dioclean material in VII 48–83, Nietzsche moves first (1) to VII 37–48, then (2) to VII 84–160, and finally, by a variety of means, (3) to the *Lives* as a whole. His detailed arguments at stage (3) are all frail: the main case for (3) can only be the Principle of Indolence—and that principle, as I have remarked, is of little merit. At stage (2) Nietzsche is less implausible; but he fails to consider, let alone to eliminate, the numerous alternatives to his own view. At stage (1) Nietzsche is at his best, and his interpretation of VII 48 at least deserves respectful consideration. But even here he cannot be said to have proved anything, or to have done more than raise an interesting possibility.

I do not believe that Nietzsche's Grundhypothese has been refuted, and I doubt if, in the present state of Laertian scholarship, it is refutable. In that respect it is at least superior to several other Grundhypothesen which have subsequently been advanced. On the other hand, it is no better than many similar hypotheses, unrefuted and unproved, which have been or could be proposed.

11

What, in the end, can be said of Diogenes as a historian of early Greek philosophy? Since Nietzsche published his *de Fontibus* several scholars, many of them eminent, have written with subtlety on the problem of Diogenes' sources. None of those studies has been more successful than Nietzsche's: each, like Nietzsche's, has incidentally contributed to our understanding of Diogenes, but none has yet produced a compelling or even a plausible proof.

A skeptic might think he had evidence enough for a skeptical conclusion; and I cannot show that he would be mistaken. In writing about Diogenes we float in a sea of possibilities, none obviously preferable to its rivals. But there are two things which, the sanguine will hope, may eventually change that: we need a proper critical edition of Diogenes' text;[42] and we need some serious study of his language and style. In VII 48, the interpretation turns first on the presence or absence of a "τε" in the text, and secondly on the possible uses of "καί" in Diogenes. We cannot yet discuss either of those issues with any confidence, for the philological groundwork is not yet done. There is of course no guarantee that the philological work on Diogenes which Nietzsche did not in the end undertake will provide the answers to the problems of *Quellenforschung* which he did investigate. But, so far as I can see, scholarship will not be able to advance in this area until a new text is available and detailed linguistic studies have been made.[43]

Those dry little things are not trivial. Our knowledge of Stoic logic depends partly on Diogenes Laertius. It therefore depends in part on the existence of a "τε" and the interpretation of a "καί".

12

What, in the end, can be said of Nietzsche as a classical scholar? "The history of philology has no place for Nietzsche: he did not make enough positive contributions" (Reinhardt 1966, 345). Karl Reinhardt's brisk condemnation is often quoted.[44] Twenty years before Reinhardt, Ernst Howald had similarly dismissed Nietzsche's classical studies as "average performances," and had declared that "by and large, the results of all his work have been proved false" (Howald 1920, 7). Such sweepingly general judgments are frequently parroted; but they are, in truth, of little interest and little value.[45]

In the particular case of Diogenes Laertius, Nietzsche's reputation is not remarkably high. The most recent monograph on Diogenes (Mejer 1978) has little to say about him, and the best modern account of Diogenes relegates him to a footnote (Gigante 1972).[46] The modern attitude derives, I suspect, from Hermann Diels. In the preface to his magisterial *Doxographi Graeci* Diels attacked Nietzsche with some lines of patronizing contempt, and proceeded to "prove that Nietzsche's opinion is not only highly uncertain and more frail than a spider's web, but also palpably false" (Diels 1879, 162; for the proof, see above, pages 17–20).[47]

Diels' opinion was shared by Wilamowitz.[48] A short passage from Wilamowitz's bilious *Memoirs*, written in 1928, has probably had more effect than anything else on the attitude of classical scholarship to Nietzsche's work:

> He followed Ritschl from Bonn to Leipzig (hence the attack on Jahn) and with his help got the Chair at Basel and the honorary doctorate. I do not understand how anyone can excuse such nepotism. It was an unparalleled promotion of a tyro which could in no way be justified by the things which Nietzsche had published in the *Rheinisches Museum*—things which contained very little truth and so answered to a very good doctoral dissertation. At the time I could not judge them; for Usener had praised them highly in his seminar, and in addition I was proud of the success of someone from my own school. (Wilamowitz 1928, 129)[49]

Wilamowitz's sneers and insinuations are merely bad-tempered.[50] His reference to Usener's praise is more interesting.

For there is other evidence that Usener admired Nietzsche's early work: he saw in the first *Rheinisches Museum* publications "a youthful freshness and a penetrating insight" (quoted by Vogt 1962, 108n. 21). Nor was Usener alone. Freudenthal asserts that Nietzsche's Grundhypothese had been widely accepted, and he observes that it had found its way into Überweg's standard handbook to Greek philosophy (Freudenthal 1879, 305). Maass records that the theory had commended itself to Susemihl, Volkmann, Rohde, and Kern (Maass 1880, 6); and to his list we may add the names of Zeller (see from Zeller, May 22, 1870; KGB II/2, 211–12; cf. to Ritschl, June, 1870; KSB 3, 124) and, of course, Ritschl (see to Gersdorff, December 1, 1867; KSB 2, 237–8; cf the official judgment of the Leipzig faculty, quoted by Nietzsche in a letter to Rohde, February 3, 1868; KSB 2, 247–8).

At first, Nietzsche's Laertian studies were received with admiration and assent—indeed, anyone acquainted with the history of classical scholarship and the nature of classical scholars must be surprised by the warmth and the width of the early reception. Later, Nietzsche's studies were harshly attacked: they were not merely false—they were stupid, ignorant, unscholarly, despicable. The *volte face* is remarkable.[51]

Usener, who had praised Nietzsche in 1869, announced to his students in 1872 that "anyone who has written a thing like that is dead as a scholar."[52] The "thing like that" was the *Birth of Tragedy*. The infantile tantrums which followed the birth are a familiar history. In the controversy Wilamowitz carried the scholarly world with him, and Nietzsche was sunk as a philologist.[53] He himself ensured that he never re-emerged. His attacks on the contemporary world of scholarship, peopled by mere "Konjekturenwüstlingen," did nothing to persuade scholars that the *Birth of Tragedy* was merely a temporary aberration. Nietzsche continued to denounce philology, he abandoned his scholarly studies, and he eventually came to disown his earlier philological exercises.[54] It might well seem that, in the words of Howald, "whenever they came into contact with one another, Nietzsche and philology were (with the exception of a brief armistice) fundamentally enemies" (Howald 1920, 1).[55]

It is tempting to believe that Nietzsche's personality rather than his scholarship was responsible for the contempt in which his philological writings have often been held. How could a man who himself despised philology and who had been fatally savaged by the great Wilamowitz have made any worthwhile contribution to classical scholarship?

Nietzsche was never a wise old scholar. His philological studies were all written in his youth. The *De fontibus* was composed by an author of 23 who wrote it in the space of a few months. It is not remarkable that the work shows signs of haste, that it contains numerous minor errors, that it offers exuberantly reckless conjectures, that its argument sometimes substitutes rhetoric for logic.[56] On the contrary, the Laertian studies are remarkable for their virtues, not for their vices.

First of all, the studies are brilliant. Nietzsche's subject is esoteric, he is obliged to argue in complex and tortuous turns, he carries a heavy burden of erudition. Yet the studies proceed with astonishing clarity and penetration. Their style is plain— sometimes pugnacious, sometimes witty, but never bombastic and never obscure. The argument is elegantly articulated, and its flow is sustained with unusual skill and sinew.[57] The Grundhypothese is always at the center, but the studies also contain a great richness of detail. Whatever the truth about the Grundhypothese, the Laertian studies are astounding works which fully explain Ritschl's extravagant opinion of his *protégé*: nineteenth-century Germany produced many precocious scholars, but none made a more brilliant debut than Nietzsche.[58]

Secondly, the studies are original.[59] Nietzsche opened up new territory to scholarship. The study of Diogenes took a new turn after his work, which has had, indirectly, a deep effect on our understanding of the history of ancient philosophy. Nietzsche's approach and his methods have been widely copied; his general attitude to Diogenes has been widely shared; and even if all his particular suggestions were to be rejected, he could still claim to have originated a new and important phase in the study of ancient philosophy.

I have no desire to exaggerate Nietzsche's philological contributions or to argue that he was a great scholar. In any case such evaluations are childish and ultimately uninteresting. But both classical scholars, who tend to think of Nietzsche as the author of ill-grounded ravings on Greek tragedy, and also philosophers, who tend to think of him as the antithesis of a hard-working scholar, should recognize that the Laertian studies were written by an industrious, erudite, disciplined, and brilliant young mind.[60]

Notes

1   All found in KGW II/1. Nietzsche's Nachlaß contains a vast number of notes, essays, and preliminary sketches on Diogenes: the texts are printed, with annotations, in BAW Vols. 4 and 5. All translations are my own.

2   See KGW III/3, 40, 45, 54, 61 (all from winter 1869/70), and 328 (1871); KGW III/4, 369, 445 (1874). The entry at KGW III/3, 45, says that Diogenes "should be ready" in autumn 1871; the other entries simply list Diogenes' name among other philological projects. As late as 1875/76 Nietzsche gave a seminar at Basel on "Diogenes Laertius *Democrit*." See Janz 1974, 200.

3   Not that Nietzsche ever forgot his Diogenes: there are occasional allusions or reminiscences in many of his later writings (see the Index to Janz 1978/79).

4   For descriptions and assessments of Nietzsche as a classical scholar see Svoboda 1919, 657–73; Howald 1920; Cervi 1960, 199–235; Vogt 1962, 103–13; Adrados 1970, 87–105; Gigante 1974, 196–224; Lloyd-Jones 1976, 1–15; Pöschl 1979, 141–55; Figl 1984, 111–28.

5   For a general account, with supplementary bibliography, see e.g. the introduction to Gigante 1983; Meier 1994, 824–33.

6   The point deserves stressing: Nietzsche did not have a decent critical edition of Diogenes before him (and his plan to produce one was timely). We are not yet much better off than Nietzsche in the case of most of the *Lives*; for the only complete modern editions of the Greek text are unsatisfactory.

7   The letter contains a moving tribute to Ritschl, on whom see e.g. Howald 1920, 3–5.

8   "Die letzte Redaction der Theognidea," in BAW 3, 150–73. Nietzsche had written on Theognis at Schulpforta. His various studies eventually turned into his first published paper: (1867): "Zur Geschichte der Theognideischen Spruchsammlung." In: *Rheinisches Museum*. Vol. 22, 161–200 (= KGW II/l). [Editor's note: On the details of this piece, see Jensen's contribution to the present volume.]

9   Full details in the relevant pages of Janz 1978/79; see also Schlechta 1948.

10   This is an elaborated version of the account Nietzsche gave to Hermann Mushacke. See to Mushacke, November 1866; KSB 2, 182–3.

11   The problems were, surprisingly, stylistic. Nietzsche decided to write the essay in German (it is unclear why) and then to translate it into the scholarly Latin which the Prize Essay demanded—"but in German I have absolutely no style" (to Mushacke, April 20, 1867; KSB 2, 214). There is a draft of the German text at BAW 4, 217–68.

12   *Rheinisches Museum* 23, 1868, 632–53; 24, 1869, 181–228.

13   *Rheinisches Museum* 25, 1870, 217–31.

14   Published in Basel, 1870, as a Gratulationsschrift for F. D. Gerlach, who had held the chair of Latin at Basel since 1820. Gerlach was an opponent of Ritschl and had campaigned vigorously against Nietzsche's appointment: Janz 1978/79, I, 309–11.

15   And the Nachlaß contains a vast quantity of stimulating stuff as well.

16   But at least once he asked himself: "Why may not Diocles have been simply excerpted from Favorinus?" BAW 4, 416.

17   On the "skeptical source" see also BAW 5, 41–3, and 130–1.

18   Nietzsche dated Diocles to the end of the first century AD (cf. KGW II/1, 85–8, and
     204–5), and this relatively late date is of some importance for his Grundhypothese.
     In fact, a date in the first century BC is almost certain: see the careful arguments
     in Maass (1880), 15–19. Maass' argument is severely criticized, however, by Goulet
     1994, 775–7.

19   It is of interest to compare the Grundhypothese advanced by Maass: "If you except
     the Skeptical διαδοχή and doxography, Diogenes made particular use of Favorinus
     and Diocles. To Diocles we should ascribe a few passages in the biographies and the
     more detailed doxographies; to Favorinus the summary doxographies and the major
     part of the biographies. Diogenes abbreviated what he found in the *Miscellaneous
     History* and interpolated a few little stories gleaned from the *Commentaries*; from
     this source he derived his rich store of references as well as the catalogues of books
     and the lists of homonyms" (Maass 1880, 103). Although Maass is generally critical
     of Nietzsche, the similarities between the two scholars are more remarkable than
     their differences, and the general method and approach of Maass is the same as that
     of Nietzsche. I say more on this below.

20   In what follows I limit myself to the question of Diocles, and in particular to the
     relation between Diogenes and Diocles: I have nothing to say about Favorinus (on
     whom see Mejer 1978, 30–2). On Theodosius see Barnes 1992, 4282–9. The thesis
     about Diogenes' poetical ambitions was explicitly borrowed by Nietzsche from
     Francesco Patrizzi. Nietzsche himself offers no arguments in its favor—and there are
     none.

21   Favorinus is in fact referred to more than twice as often as Diocles.

22   He twice says that he has proved that the material on Plato derives from Diocles
     (KGW II/1, 203, 221); but no such arguments are to be found in his texts.

23   On this difficult issue see especially Maass, 1880, 23–36; Mejer 1978, 38–9.

24   Nietzsche makes the total 44 (KGW II/1, 130); I have no explanation for the error.

25   For an attempt to discern the personality of Diogenes see Mejer 1978, 46–59.

26   So, implicitly, Glucker 1978, 342. (On page 336, Glucker explicitly refers to
     Nietzsche, with what I think is intended as praise.)

27   The argument is repeated, without significant additions, in the *Beiträge* (KGW II/1,
     201–3).

28   That is more cumbersome in my English than in Nietzsche's Latin (or in Diogenes'
     Greek). A paraphrase might run thus: "If we are to give a detailed account of Stoic
     logic in addition to the summary account we have just given, then we can find
     that too set down in Diocles' book (insofar as it bears on the introductory part of
     logic)—and that too is set down *verbatim* as follows."

29   As Diels notes, this use of "αὐτός" is standard in Greek, which does not normally
     repeat the relative pronoun; see e.g. Plato, *Meno* 90E5 (with Bluck's note).

30   This emerges very clearly from the way in which the text is presented in Hulser
     1987, I, 248.

31   At any rate, that is the information given by the critical appendix to the OCT and
     the Teubner editions.

32   Palaeographically "ταῦτά τε" might be thought more likely to be correct: an
     original "τε" was corrupted to "τά" in one tradition and omitted in another. And
     some will say that "ταῦτά τε" is the *lectio difficilior*. Neither point is negligible,
     neither is powerful; even together they do not seem to me to outweigh the
     grammatical difficulty which the "τε" raises.

33 With Cobet (and Nietzsche) we should read "εἴπωμεν" for the transmitted
    "εἴποιμεν"; and with Roeper we should read "δοκεῖ" for the transmitted
    "δοκεῖν." Neither change affects the sense of the passage. Egli 1981 proposed
    "τὴν εἰσαγωγικὴν διαλεκτικὴν [...] τέχνην"; but I do not know if that is Greek.
    Marcovich, in his Teubner edition, prints "ταῦτα δή" rather than "ταῦτα" or
    "ταῦτά τε"; and "τὰ δή" for "τάδε" (which is scarcely Greek).

34 A different construal of VII 48 is also possible: place a comma after "τέχνήν,"
    remove the comma before "καὶ τάδε," and read this "καί" as epexegetic. The "αὐτά"
    then refers back to "τάδε," i.e. to "τὰ κατὰ μέρος," and the whole sentence runs
    like this: "And so that we may also give a particular account, i.e. an account of the
    things which bear on their introductory art, Diocles sets down these things too
    verbatim." Nietzsche rejected that construal (KGW II/1, 78), for inadequate reasons.
    In fact, it gives the same conclusion as his own construal, namely that Diogenes has
    already quoted Diocles *verbatim*. The real difficulty is the reading of "τάδε": "τάδε"
    and "ταῦτα" must surely be taken as a contrasting pair, "ταῦτα" referring to the
    material Diogenes has just given and "τάδε" to the material he is about to give. But
    on the suggested construal "τάδε" is merely a pale and unnecessary antecedent to
    "ἅπερ" and no longer enjoys syntactical parity with "ταῦτα."

35 So Freudenthal 1879, 309. Freudenthal's Appendix on the sources of Diogenes
    (pages 305–15) contains a lucid exposition and a trenchant criticism of Nietzsche's
    Grundhypothese.

36 Should we speak of *verbatim* transcriptions by Diogenes at all? Egli 1981, 8–9,
    maintains that "ἐπὶ λέξεως τίθησι" means that Diocles transcribes the Stoics
    verbatim, not that Diogenes transcribes Diocles *verbatim*. That is a point of capital
    importance, not only for our understanding of Diogenes' methods but also for our
    knowledge of Stoic logic; for if Egli is right, we possess in the "Diocles fragment"
    a *verbatim* report of some Stoic texts on logic. (In point of fact Egli assumes
    that Diogenes *is* transcribing Diocles—and hence some Stoics—*verbatim*. But
    the assumption rests not on "ἐπὶ λέξεως" but on "οὕτως λέγων"; and if Egli's
    reading of "ἐπὶ λέξεως" is correct, then it is not clear that Diogenes is transcribing
    Diocles—for "οὕτως λέγων" may introduce a paraphrase or an epitome rather
    than a citation.) I am inclined to think that Diogenes' words are, strictly speaking,
    ambiguous; but I also think that they are more readily construed in Nietzsche's way
    than in Egli's way. After all, if I say "X sets this down *verbatim* as follows," then I am
    naturally taken to be reporting X *verbatim* and not to be commenting on X's mode
    of reportage. That impressionistic argument is perhaps supported by VII 75: see note
    38.

37 There is yet another uncertainty in the Greek text: what is the syntax and what is
    the reference of "αὐτῶν"? Nietzsche implicitly takes "αὐτῶν" to be partitive and
    to refer to "τάδε," thus: "Diocles also sets down these things, namely the parts of
    them which bear on the introductory art." Others construe "αὐτῶν" with "τέχνην"
    and take it to refer to the Stoics: "Diocles also sets down these things, which bear
    on their introductory art." The position of "αὐτῶν," and the general sense of the
    passage, seem to me to favor Nietzsche's interpretation.

38 Moreover, the presence of Diocles' name makes it unlikely that Diocles was
    transcribing Stoic text; for why should a Stoic have used Diocles' name? This seems
    to me to tell in favor of Nietzsche's interpretation of "ἐπὶ λέξεως" (above, note 36).

39 Maass 1880, 13, argues that Diogenes' text shows no asymmetry of the sort
    Nietzsche alleges, provided that we compare not the doxographies but the

biographico-doxographical accounts as wholes. Even if Maass' proviso is allowed, his claim is false: the Stoic biography-doxography is somewhat longer than the Epicurean, it is almost twice as long as the Platonic, and it is two and a half times as long as the Aristotelian. Handbooks regularly strive for συμμετρία (see Diels 1879, 242n. 1). Diogenes gives no indication elsewhere of such an ambition. It is therefore plausible that his solitary reference to συμμετρία was unthinkingly copied from a handbook.

40   Mejer 1978, 5–7 holds that the Stoic doxography is unitary and was copied as a whole by Diogenes from an earlier source; but he thinks that this earlier source was later than Diocles: the source compiled a doxography from Diocles' account of Stoic logic and from non-Dioclean accounts of ethics and physics.

41   See Freudenthal 1879, 312–13; cf. e.g. Diels 1879, 163 and Meier 1994, 42–5.

42   Since this paper was first published, Miroslav Marcovich's long-awaited Teubner text has appeared: for a review, see my 2002, 8–11.

43   Cf. the closing paragraph of Freudenthal 1879. It is depressing to reflect that the *desiderata* he catalogued in 1879 remain *desiderata* over a century later.

44   The paper was given as a lecture in 1941.

45   See Vogt 1962; and note the favorable judgments in Svoboda 1919 and in Pöschl 1979.

46   But note that in "Dal Wilamowitz" Gigante maintains that Nietzsche "has acquired an honorable position in our subject." Gigante 1974, 208.

47   In his *Festrede* of January 23, 1902 Diels spoke more generally and at greater length about Nietzsche: the pages of measured spleen repay a reading. Diels 1902, 35–9.

48   In his *Epistula ad Maassium*, published as an Appendix to Maass 1880, Wilamowitz paid grudging tribute to Nietzsche for his remarks on the relations between Hesychius and Diogenes: *propter turbas ab hominibus insulsis excitatus praemitto me, ut par est, Nietzschei de Hesychio disputationem summis laudibus dignam habere* (Wilamowitz 1880, 148). But he had already (pages 145–6) accused Nietzsche of ignorance of Greek and repeated (without acknowledgment) Diels' comparison of Nietzsche's arguments to a spider's web.

49   Nietzsche was not mentioned in Wilamowitz's *Geschichte der Philologie* which first appeared in 1921.

50   Maass 1880, 6, says that the first attacks against Nietzsche's Grundhypothese came from Wilamowitz, Diels, and Freudenthal. (i) For Wilamowitz he refers to lectures and to a paper published in *Hermes* 11, 1876: there, without mentioning Nietzsche, Wilamowitz simply moots the suggestion that Favorinus may have been Diogenes' main source. (ii) For Diels he refers to *Doxographi Graeci*, the contentions of which I have already discussed, and to a footnote to a paper in *Rheinisches Museum* 31, 1876; but there Diels takes sides *with* Nietzsche (on a relatively minor point). (iii) Freudenthal's *Albinos* does contain a lengthy critique of Nietzsche. (iv) Maass himself (esp. Maass 1880, 9–23) is the author of a long and not wholly unsympathetic critique of Nietzsche's hypothesis. (Even so, his arguments are often distressingly rhetorical, and he frequently contents himself with debating-points.)

51   It was not universal: in 1883, Bursian gave ten lines of moderate praise to Nietzsche's Laertian studies: Bursian 1883, 929.

52   Quoted by Nietzsche himself, on hearsay, in a letter to Rohde, October 25, 1872: KSB 4, 70–1.

53   On the dispute see e.g. Howald 1920, 22–30; Groth 1950, 179–80; Lloyd-Jones 1982, xi–xiii.

54 "Of course, there are also philological writings of mine—but they no longer concern either of us." To Brandes, April 10, 1888; KSB 8, 288.

55 But Howald's judgment is too crude: the war was not between Nietzsche and philology but between the "philosophical" Nietzsche and the "philological" Nietzsche. This internecine struggle is well documented in the letters and the Nachlaß: on it see e.g. Schlechta 1948; Campbell 1937, 251–66.

56 The Nachlaß shows how Nietzsche frequently changed his mind: ideas and suggestions are advanced and then later withdrawn; the overall structure of the Laertian studies undergoes numerous alterations; the mass of notes and remarks reveals not a single, dogmatically held theory but rather a sequence of flexible and developing hypotheses. Changes of mind are also present in the published works. I mention two of them here. (1) The third, "skeptical," source (referenced above) is introduced abruptly, without preparation, and without apology. Nietzsche does not consider what implications it may have for his general Grundhypothese: if Book IX is suddenly found to require a non-Dioclean source, may not similar discoveries be made for other parts of the *Lives* to which Nietzsche devotes relatively little attention? And in that case, may not a completely different picture of Diogenes' sources come to be painted? (2) In *De fontibus* (KGW II/1, 133–4) Nietzsche argued that one of Demetrius' sources was Hippobotus, i.e. that the "citations" of Hippobotus in Diogenes are in fact citations of Diocles' citations of Demetrius' citations of Hippobotus. Nietzsche's argument was simply this: in Diogenes, Hippobotus is frequently named in conjunction with Demetrius (or with one of Demetrius' supposed sources). In the *Analecta* (KGW II/1, 181), Nietzsche recants, making Hippobotus a direct source for Diocles. The earlier argument is dismissed in a single sentence. Although the case is in itself of little consequence, the argument in question—which Nietzsche first briskly advances and then brusquely rejects—is similar to many of Nietzsche's other reasonings. The ease with which Nietzsche himself was able to make such a *volte face* indicates how frail much of his argument was.

Some will conclude that Nietzsche did not take his studies very seriously—that he approached Diogenes in a spirit of unscholarly levity. (So e.g. Maass 1880, 51n. 52; 54n. 57.) But a different and a kinder conclusion should be drawn. Nietzsche himself was well aware of the weaknesses of the published studies, as a letter to Rohde of October 8, 1868 shows: "It is really silly to allow this newly hatched wisdom to be published so soon, and it causes me nothing but vexation" (to Rohde, October 8, 1868; KSB 2, 323–4). The Prize Essay was a preliminary report of Nietzsche's results; he was pushed, by Ritschl, into premature publication; his unpublished notes indicate that his thought never hardened into a rigid theory, despite the appearance of certainty which the published studies give. We should read Nietzsche's Laertian essays not as polished works of scholarship, as the fruits of long and mature consideration, but rather as reports of work in progress. So read, they are testimony to a vivid scholarly imagination, a keen analytical mind, and a flexibly audacious power of reasoning.

57 Nietzsche explained how he hoped to present his work in a letter to Deussen of April 4, 1867 (KSB 2, 205–6): the explanation is in effect a fine description of the style of the finished essays.

58 Much of the secondary literature on Diogenes is pedestrian and some of it is tenth-rate: in the history of Laertian studies two scholars stand out—Menagius and Nietzsche. The modern student will find more of value in Menagius' edition and in Nietzsche's various essays than in all the rest of the secondary literature put together.

59   See Maass 1880, 3–4. Maass attacks Nietzsche on numerous points, and he has harsh things to say about his work. But he rightly states that Nietzsche is "*de Diogene omnium longe optime meritus*," he records that he himself was captured by Nietzsche's vigorous and delectable style, and he pays Nietzsche the tribute of taking his studies as the starting-point for all of his own enquiries. See Maass 1880, 4–5.

60   This paper owes its existence to the gentle encouragement and unobtrusively helpful advice of Mazzino Montinari. My understanding of the crucial passage in Diogenes VII, 48, was aided by discussion with Jacques Brunschwig, Michael Frede, and Günther Patzig. And I thank the Sekretariat of the Wissenschaftskolleg zu Berlin for the charm and celerity with which they mastered a vile manuscript.

Works cited

Adrados, F. A. (1970): "Nietzsche y el concepto de la Filologia Clasica." In *Habis*. Vol. 1, 87–105.

Barnes, Jonathan (1992): "Diogenes Laertius IX 61–116: The Philosophy of Pyrrhonism." In *Aufstieg und Niedergang der römischen Welt II*. Vol. 36 (6), 4241–301.

—(2002): "Review of M. Marcovich (ed.) (1999): *Diogenes Laertius. Vitae philosophorum. Vol. 1: Libri I–X. Vol. 2: Excerpta byzantina*. Stuttgart and Leipzig (Teubner)." In *Classical Review*. Vol. 52 (1), 8–11.

Bursian, Conrad (1883): *Geschichte der classischen Philologie in Deutschland*. Munich and Leipzig (R. Oldenbourg).

Campbell, T. M. (1937): "Aspects of Nietzsche's Struggle with Philology to 1871." In *Germanic Review*. Vol. 12, 251–66.

Cervi, A. M. (1960): "La storiografia filosofica di F. Nietzsche." In *Studi in onore di Luigi Castiglioni*. Florence (G. C. Sansoni). Vol. 1, 199–235.

Diels, Hermann (1879): *Doxographi Graeci*. Berlin (Walter de Gruyter).

—(1902): *Sitzungsberichte der königlichen preussischen Akademie der Wissenschaften zu Berlin*. Berlin (Georg Reimer).

Egli, Urs (1981): *Das Dioklesfragment bei Diogenes Laertios*. Konstanz (Sonderforschungsbereich 99 Universität Konstanz).

Figl, J. (1984): "Hermeneutische Voraussetzungen der philologischen Kritik. Zur wissenschaftsphilosophischen Grundproblematik im Denken des jungen Nietzsche." In *Nietzsche-Studien*. Vol. 13, 111–28.

Freudenthal, Jacob (1879): *Hellenistische Studien III: Der Platoniker Albinos und der falsche Alkinoos*. Berlin (S. Calvary & Co.).

Gigante, Marcello (1974): "Dal Wilamowitz al Pfeiffer storici della filologia classica." In *La parola del Passato*. Vol. 29, 196–224.

—(1983): *Diogene Laerzio: Vite dei Filosofi*. Bari (Laterza).

Glucker, J. (1978): *Antiochus and the Late Academy*. Göttingen (Vandenhoeck & Ruprecht).

Goulet, Richard (1994): "Dioclès de Magnésie." In *Dictionnaire des philosophes antiques*. Vol. 2, 775–7.

Groth, J. H. (1950): "Wilamowitz-Moellendorf on Nietzsche's *Birth of Tragedy*." In *Journal for the History of Ideas*. Vol. 11, 179–90.

Howald, Ernst (1920): *Friedrich Nietzsche und die klassische Philologie*. Gotha (F. A. Perthes).

Hulser, Karlheinz (1987): *Die Fragmente zur stoischen Dialektik*. Stuttgart/Bad Cannstatt (Frommann-Holzboog), 4 vols.

Janz, Curt Paul (1974): "Nietzsches Lehrtätigkeit in Basel 1869–79." In *Nietzsche-Studien*. Vol. 3, 192–203.

—(1978/79): *Friedrich Nietzsche: Biographie*. Munich (Carl Hanser Verlag), 3 vols.

Knoepfler, Denis (1991): *La vie de Ménédème d'Érétrie de Diogène Laërce: contribution à l'histoire et la critique du texte des 'Vies des Philosophes'*. Basel (Schweizerische Beiträge zur Altertumswissenschaft 21).

Lloyd-Jones, Hugh (1976): "Nietzsche and the Study of the Ancient World." In J. C. O'Flaherty, et al. (eds): *Studies in Nietzsche and the Classical Tradition*. Chapel Hill (University of North Carolina Press), 1–15.

—(1982): "Introduction" to U. von Wilamowitz-Moellendorff, *History of Classical Scholarship*. Baltimore (Johns Hopkins University Press).

Maass, Ernst (1880): *Philologische Untersuchungen 3: de biographis graecis quaestiones selectae*. Berlin (Weidmann).

Meier, J. (1994): "Diogène Laërce." In *Dictionnaire des philosophes antiques*. Vol. 2, 824–33.

—(1978): *Diogenes Laertius and his Hellenistic Background: Hermes Einzelschriften 40*. Wiesbaden (Franz Steiner).

Pöschl, V. (1979): "Nietzsche und die klassische Philologie." In H. Flashar, K. Gründer, and A. Horstmann (eds): *Philologie und Hermeneutik im 19. Jahrhundert*. Göttingen (Vandenhoeck & Ruprecht), 141–55.

Reinhardt, Karl (1966): "Die klassische Philologie und das Klassische." In his *Vermächtnis der Antike: Gesammelte Essays zur Philosophie und Geschichtsschreibung*. Göttingen (Vandenhoeck & Ruprecht), 334–60.

Schlechta, Karl (1948): *Der junge Nietzsche und das klassische Altertum*. Mainz (Florian-Kupferberg Verlag).

Svoboda, K. (1919): "Friedrich Nietzsche als klassischer Philolog." In *Zeitschrift für die deutsch-österreichischen Gymnasien*. Vol. 69, 657–73.

Vogt, E. (1962): "Nietzsche und der Wettkampf Homers." In *Antike und Abendland*. Vol. 11, 103–13.

Wilamowitz-Moellendorff, Ulrich von (1880): "Epistula ad Maassium." In *Philologische Untersuchungen*. Vol. 3, 142–64.

—(1928): *Erinnerungen 1848–1914*. Leipzig (K. F. Koehler).

Nietzsche's Influence on Homeric Scholarship

Alexey Zhavoronkov

Whenever one thinks about the writings, which—at least partially—can be considered as bearing the fruits of Nietzsche's occupation with Homer, one first of all thinks of his inaugural speech *Homer and Classical Philology*. One may also refer to the short treatise *Homer's Contest*, as well as—with certain reservations—to the two-part essay *The Florentine Manuscript Concerning Homer and Hesiod, Their Ancestry and Their Contest*.[1] To understand Nietzsche's stance towards Homer in its entirety, however, it would not be sufficient to limit oneself to these texts: Homer, Homeric figures, and quotes as well as allusions to Homer appear in all of Nietzsche's philosophical works—in the early (*The Birth of Tragedy*; the notes before 1879), as well as in the middle (*Human, All-Too Human*) and late period (*Thus Spoke Zarathustra*; *Beyond Good and Evil*; *On the Genealogy of Morals*; and the late notes). Homer belongs to the earliest and most consistent strata of Nietzsche's thinking, and is repeatedly woven into his wider theoretical constructions (e.g. in the context of Nietzsche's critique of Christianity or Plato). In this text I will deal with some aspects of Nietzsche's relation to Homer in the context of his influence on Homeric studies in the twentieth century.

1. Nietzsche and the methods of Homeric scholarship

Nietzsche investigates the methods of Homeric scholarship in his inaugural speech, which he held at Basel on April 25, 1869. The title—*On the Personality of Homer*[2]— already reveals the contrasted setting of the speech in regard to common tendencies in Homeric scholarship of the time, i.e. to no longer speak of the person of Homer, but to view the texts of the *Iliad* and the *Odyssey* from perspectives of their possible (in)consistency. Most likely this was a first signal for Nietzsche's audience that they can neither expect a philological report on the state of the art in Homeric scholarship nor on the crucial points in the analysis of the *Iliad* and the *Odyssey* (above all on the "Homeric question"). Thus the problem with which Nietzsche begins his lecture and (even more importantly) the manner in which he views these problems must strike one as rather unusual.[3]

Rather than speaking of Homer, Peisistratos, or the Alexandrian philologists from the start, Nietzsche begins with critical observations concerning Classical Philology as a historical science, which at the same time raises a pedagogical claim about the foundations of the field. Classical Philology is said to be "a magic potion made from strange juices, metals and bones" and is from its origin "at the same time pedagogy" (HCP; KGW II/1, 250) (and thus it is not an Edelwissenschaft which has a special standing among the historical sciences). According to Nietzsche, Classical Philology also has a great number of enemies, which can be divided into two groups: (1) the mockers of philology and (2) those who, in "happy admiration of themselves," kneel down and view Hellenism as "a transcendent, therefore quite indifferent stand-point" (HCP; KGW II/1, 251). Some are even of the opinion that "philologists were themselves the actual enemies and destroyers of antiquity and ancient ideals" (HCP; KGW II/1, 252).

In this context Nietzsche performs a critique of Friedrich August Wolf's methodo-logical attitude—not, however, from the narrower perspective of his opponents among classical philologists. Instead, Nietzsche refers to Goethe's accusations: from Wolf's perspective the *Iliad* and *Odyssey* no longer exist as works of art or as objects of aesthetic admiration insofar as they no longer seem to appear as a coherent whole.[4] At the same time Nietzsche points to Schiller's critique by indirectly quoting his epigram to the *Iliad*:[5] "Schiller accused the philologists of having torn the *crown of Homer*" (HCP; KGW II/1, 252).[6]

The "possibility" of viewing Homer as an actually existing person, as the "flawless and infallible artist" (per Aristotle),[7] has, according to Nietzsche, the psychological origin of "wanting to identify a tangible personality, instead of a supernatural creature" (HCP; KGW II/1, 256f.). But if we go even further back in time (beyond Aristotle) we realize that the impossibility of grasping Homer as a person increases steadily: The Greeks of the older periods do not only identify him with the *Iliad* and the *Odyssey*, but also with an "immense torrent of great epics" (HCP; KGW II/1, 257).

The original "Homeric question" is thus restated by Nietzsche and split into two parts: (1) What did the word "Homer" refer to during this specific period and (2) whether "*accordingly a term was made from a person or a person from a term*" (HCP; KGW II/1, 257).[8] Thus the question is stated in the broader context of the problem of individuality of poetic genius and the conception of folk poetry. Nietzsche's proposal to view the topic of his lecture from a contemporary aesthetic position allows him to see the danger of the juxtaposition "of *folk poetry and individualized poetry*," to see that this was merely a "superstition," which "followed from the [...] discovery of the historic-philological science, the discovery and evaluation of the *Volksseele*" (HCP; KGW II/1, 260). In reality the difference between folk poetry and individualistic poetry does not exist: "all poetry, indeed, requires [...] a conveying single individual" (HCP; KGW II/1, 261). Concerning the name Homer, it "from the start had neither a necessary relationship to the conception of aesthetic perfection, nor to the *Iliad* and the *Odyssey*. Homer as the author of the *Iliad* and *Odyssey* is not a historic tradition, but rather an *aesthetic judgment*" (HCP; KGW II/1, 263). Furthermore, we believe "in the one great author of the *Iliad* and *Odyssey*—but don't believe that *Homer is this author.*" So Homer only designates a "substantial singularity" (HCP; KGW II/1, 266).

It is quite obvious that Nietzsche is addressing an ostensibly pure philological problem, yet indeed not from the standpoint of a philologist aided by the methods of critical analysis. He instead investigates the Homeric question from a philosophical and psychological viewpoint. In trying to defend Classical Philology,[9] he actually demonstrates its lack of reflection upon its own methodological foundations.[10] When Nietzsche says "all and every philological activity [must be] surrounded and enclosed [...] by a philosophical worldview" (HCP; KGW II/1, 268), to such a conservative discipline as Classical Philology of that time, it must have sounded like a provocation.

Nietzsche's methodological ideas in regard to Homer have received relatively little interest among classical philologists. Even Karl Reinhardt, one of Wilamowitz's best students, who also in his early years was Nietzsche's student at the University of Basel and was strongly influenced by his thoughts,[11] does not mention him explicitly in this respect. There are, however, intimations that Nietzsche's approaches, both in his lectures and in his more developed philosophical works, have been recognized by representatives of a unitarian or single-author position, in contrast to the Analysts.

The best example of such influence is Wolfgang Schadewaldt, one of the most prominent Homeric scholars of the twentieth century. In the introduction to a collection of his writings *Von Homers Welt und Werk* he writes that the Homeric question revolves "around a simple question basically," namely, "the essence of the poetic creator and the poetic work" (Schadewaldt 1944, 10) in their relation to "historic reality" (Schadewaldt 1944, 25).[12] This statement looks like an indirect quote from Nietzsche, whom Schadewaldt mentions earlier in his book.[13] Schadewaldt— just like Nietzsche—describes the Homeric question as very distinct proof for the necessity of a "mutual impregnation" within the humanities, i.e. the "interlocking of ideas, methods, and discoveries" (Schadewaldt 1944, 16). Nietzsche's influence on Schadewaldt, however, reveals another dimension. Schadewaldt's critique of Wolf's belief "in this exceptionally gifted youthful age of the Greeks, this paradisiacal font of man [...], where man out of a secret harmony of the soul lived and created childishly-unaware [kindisch-bewusstlos]" (Schadewaldt 1944, 25), is brought into an explicit connection with Nietzsche's position:[14] together with Nietzsche, Schadewaldt criticizes the reigning classicistic "ideal of Greek beauty [Griechenschönheit]" in the nineteenth century, which "more and more congealed into a larva" (Schadewaldt 1944, 25).

Proponents of oral poetry studies, a field which had developed at the end of the 1920s and which lent a lot of attention to the genesis and formation of the Homeric epics, have also shown an interest in Nietzsche's comments on the character of Homer as well as on his context in Greek culture as they are expressed inside and outside of his Basel speech.[15] In his landmark study *Die typischen Scenen bei Homer* Walter Arend quotes an infamous passage from *The Wanderer and his Shadow*, where Nietzsche— according to Arend—"makes the attempt" to "explain" the Homeric "repetitions positively" (Arend 1933, 2):[16]

> *To dance in chains.* [...] One can notice a variety of inherited formulas and laws of epic narration already in Homer, *inside of* which boundaries he had to dance: And he himself developed new additional conventions for those to come. This was the educational school of Greek poets: to thus first have a manifold constraint be

placed upon oneself by earlier poets; to then invent a new constraint, place it upon
oneself and gracefully overcome it: so that constraint and victory will be noticed
and admired. (WS 140; KSA 2, 612)

We can explain Arend's interest in Nietzsche, at least partly, by the fact that Nietzsche
belonged to those who did not view the Homeric repetitions as interpolations or proof
of the existence of several authors (as many Analysts claim), but as something natural
and traditional. Therefore, in Arend's interpretation, Nietzsche serves as a predecessor
to oral poetry studies.[17] Whereas the general methodological questions deal with small
but nevertheless important allusions and indirect quotes from Nietzsche, his impact is
more clearly visible in specific themes of Homeric scholarship. The best example is the
role played by the Homeric gods in the context of the "immorality" of Homeric people.

2. Homeric polytheism and the question of living

Nietzsche belongs to the few thinkers of his time who take the Homeric gods
seriously.[18] His interest in them can be explained by the role they play in his critique
of monotheism, which he describes as a major threat to humanity. In other words, the
archaic (e.g. Homeric) world with its several gods but without Christian morality was,
in Nietzsche's view, a necessary precondition for the opposition between polytheism
and monotheism. According to Nietzsche, the plurality of gods gives the Archaic
people, especially those whose actions might be contrary to existing moral norms,
several coexisting possibilities for justifying their actions as a "higher" ideal:

> *The greatest advantage of polytheism.*—That the individual may set his *own* ideal
> and derive from it his own law, joys and rights—this might have been held as the
> most outrageous of all human errors and as idolatry as such; in fact, the few who
> have dared this have always needed an apology for themselves, one that usually
> sounded like this: "Not me! Not me! But a god through me!" The wonderful art
> and virtue to create gods—polytheism—was the manner in which this drive
> could be discharged, purified, perfected, ennobled: because originally it was a
> base and unprepossessing drive, related to stubbornness, disobedience and envy.
> To be *hostile* against this drive towards an ideal of one's own: that used to be
> the law of every morality. There was only one norm: *"man"*—and every people
> believed in *possessing* this one and last norm. But above and outside oneself, in a
> faraway supra-world, one was permitted in viewing a *multiplicity of norms*: one
> god was not the denial and heresy of another god! Here individuals were initially
> permitted, here the rights of individuals were initially honored. The invention of
> gods, heroes and super-humans of all kinds [...] was the invaluable preliminary to
> justifying the egoism and arrogance of the individual: the liberty, which once one
> granted to a god in relation to the other gods, one eventually also permitted to
> oneself in relation to laws, morals and neighbors. (GS 143; KSA 3, 490)[19]

Because one ideal alone did not exist in Archaic Greek culture, no universal moral
order existed either, "no eternal horizons and perspectives" (Ibid.), which, according

to Nietzsche, later manifested themselves in Plato's demiurge (the absolute god). In his evaluation of Greek faith, Nietzsche emphasizes the importance of the creative element. Whereas Christianity operates with once-created common ideals and values and knows of no free space for the creation of individual values, a pre-Platonic Greek had the possibility of creating a god as an image of the autonomous individual for himself, a chance to shape his actions after his personal ideals and therefore preserve the diversity of life.[20]

Nietzsche's method of examining the peculiarity of the Homeric gods within the framework of the opposition between the Greek and Christian faiths found its echo in Walter Friedrich Otto, a prominent scholar of Greek religion and mythology who belonged to the scientific committee of the Nietzsche-Archive in Weimar for 12 years and participated in the preparation of Nietzsche's *Philologica*-Edition. Otto's famous *Dionysos* (1933)[21] and his earlier works *Die Götter Griechenlands* (1929) and *Der Geist der Antike und die christliche Welt* (1923) each contain themes and theses which concur with Nietzsche's theory. Indeed, there are passages in the latter book that reveal a surprising affinity to Nietzsche's thoughts on the Homeric gods:

> Whoever reads the Homeric poems without a dogmatic bias [...] must be constantly surprised by their piety. Everything here is placed under a superhuman aspect. Never is there a report on something notable, whatever it may be, without the comment that a god had provided or given it. But there is indeed no higher meaning behind all of these providences, especially no moral meaning. They appear thousands of times without ulterior motives, like the good and evil, which humans cause one another when they love or hate each other. So it is a natural piety which the Homeric human conceives in the face of being, very different from the piety of so called revealed religion. [...] His faith in the gods is the religious interpretation of reality. [...] The abstract logic that took up the battle against this form of polytheism at an early stage, and in the end was victorious, could not have started if polytheism's living forces [Erlebniskraft] had not already declined. (Otto 1923, 21ff.)

Nietzsche's influence is clearly visible not only in Otto's method (e.g. his characterization of a "living" Greek polytheism in confrontation with a monotheism that hinders those living forces), but also in the overall tone of his book, where he addresses the immorality of the Homeric gods, the naturalness of the Homeric human's faith, and the necessity of an abstract logic for metaphysical questions as a sort of weapon against polytheism.

Otto's 1929 book is significantly less critical of Christianity than Nietzsche.[22] Nevertheless one can find many of the early ideas here as well[23]—especially when Otto, in the context of a "divine proximity" to humans, writes about a "natural" and quite "living" image of the gods in Homer:

> [T]he Homeric poems are so full of divine proximity and presence, unlike those of any other nation or time. In their world the divine is not placed over natural events as a sovereign power: it reveals itself in the forms of the natural, as its essence and being. (Otto 1929, 8)[24]

In the context of Otto's praise, the emphasis on the liveliness of the Homeric gods again reminds us of Nietzsche's judgment of polytheism within his critique of monotheism,[25] in which the "noble distance" of the gods to humans resembles the "pathos of distance":

> Indeed the Greek god does not reveal a law that is above nature as an absolute quantity. It is not a divine will which scares nature. [...] Their grand view requires honor and worship, but they retain a noble distance. (Otto 1929, 317)

Otto was, however, not the only one who recognized Nietzsche's stance towards the Homeric gods in the context of moral questions. Whereas Otto primarily adopts Nietzsche's opposition of polytheism and monotheism in his own thoughts, Nietzsche's thesis of Homer's "immorality" (in contrast to Platonic morality) becomes the main focus of later scholars. This aspect of Nietzsche's influence on Homeric studies is mainly connected to the highly interesting and important polemic on "Homeric morality."

3. Nietzsche and the study of "Homeric morality"

Nietzsche's critique of the Christian God is related to the fight against contemporary morality, i.e. the "shadow" of God.[26] This battle, waged in part with genealogical weapons, rests on the premise of an unbridgeable abyss[27] between the pre-Platonic and post-Platonic worldviews.[28] The "immorality" of the Archaic Greeks before Socrates and Plato—as a sort of counterpoint to the Platonic ethical ideal and a symbol for a pre-moral state of Greek culture—plays a major role here.

Nietzsche draws a clear connection between the immorality of the pre-Platonic Greeks and their aristocratism. That connection revolves around those Greeks, which belong to a society in which the "noble" or "well-natured" play the central role. This connection between Nietzsche's treatment of moral conceptions and his analysis of the Greek social structure, as it is for instance depicted in Homer, becomes quite clear when in the *Genealogy of Morals* he examines the origin of important Greek terms, ἀγαθός ("good," "virtuous," "noble"), κακός ("bad," "base," "ignoble") und ἐσθλός ("good," "noble," "courageous"):

> They call themselves the "truthful ones" for example: above all the Greek nobility, whose mouthpiece is the Megarian poet Theognis. The distinct term here for ἐσθλός by its root meaning someone who *is*, who has reality, who is actual, who is true; then, with a subjective twist, the true as the truthful: in this phase of its notion-transformation it becomes the catchphrase and keyword of the nobility and passes over into the meaning of "noble," for distinguishing from the *fraudulent* common man, as Theognis takes and portrays him,—until, finally, the term, after the decline of the nobility, remained to designate the noblesse of the soul and becomes so to say ripe and sweet. In the terms κακός as well as δειλός (the plebs in contrast to ἀγαθός) cowardice is emphasized: This might be a hint at the direction in which to find the etymological origin of the manifold interpretable ἀγαθός. (GM I, 5; KSA 5, 262f.)

Although only Theognis is mentioned here explicitly, it is clear that Nietzsche's thesis extends to earlier authors as well, especially to Homer, since the Greek nobility is at the heart of the *Iliad* and the *Odyssey*. Nietzsche therefore maintains that terms like ἀγαθός and κακός in Homer point towards a social standing, whereas their moral meaning derived from the original designation of the actions of the respective social groups.[29] In other words, he sees the contradistinction of "noble/common" as a precursor to the contradistinction "good/evil" and as a construction (or interpretation) of the ruling Greek class, which judged everything from their own perspective.[30]

Nietzsche's statements on the immorality of the Homeric humans follow closely on his early thesis that the Greeks view their personal traits as direct effects of the gods: "The Greek is envious and does not perceive this trait as a flaw, but as the effect of a benevolent god: what a divide between his ethical judgment and ours!" (GS; KSA 1, 787). The Greeks in Homer do not judge their success and failure morally. When they make a mistake, for example, they typically blame some god—most of the time not defined (or perhaps designated as Zeus)—as the cause of the mischief:

> "[F]olly," "ignorance," a little "disturbance in the head," this much was also *allowed* by the Greeks of strongest and bravest times for themselves, as reasons for many terrible and disastrous things:—folly, *not* sin! Do you understand this? ... But even this disturbance in the head was a problem—"well, how is it even possible? Where did it derive from, in heads, like *we* have them, we humans of noble descent, of fortune, of well-becoming [Wohlgeratenheit], of the best society, of noblesse, of virtue?"—this is what the noble Greek asked himself for hundreds of years in the face of all the incomprehensible atrocities and crimes with which his kind had tarnished themselves. "A *god* must have had bewitched [betören] him," he finally said to himself shaking his head ... This way out is *typical* for the Greeks ... In such a way the gods served humans to justify even bad things to the extent that they served as the origin of evil—back then they did not accept the punishment but, as it is noble, the guilt ... (GM II 23; KSA 5, 334f.)

It is thus clear why one's own guilt, according to Nietzsche, did not play an important role for the Homeric people.[31] One may think of Odysseus, who does not view the unfortunate voyage home that brings death to all of his comrades as his own fault, but rather speaks of the gods as the cause of this evil.[32] A good example for the "irresponsibility" of the Homeric humans is the famous scene from the *Iliad* (IX, 17ff.) where Agamemnon, shocked and downcast by the latest failures of the Achaeans, fails to express his own guilt at the repercussions of his earlier commands, but emphasizes Zeus' guilt and portrays himself as a puppet of the gods:

> Zeus, Cronus' son, has entangled me in heavy guilt!
> The harsh one, who promised me graciously,
> To go home as a devourer of high-walled Troy.
> But now he reveals his cruel deceit and ingloriously
> Lets me return to Argos, after many of my people died for me.

Book 17 of the *Iliad* (469ff.), where Alcimedon is amazed by the unreasonableness of Automedon, also revolves around the gods as a source of human failure and the possible dependence of human action on divine will: "Which of the gods, Automedon, was it, who laid the futile intent in your soul and stole your good consciousness?" Instead of having a feeling of one's own guilt before a god (as per Christianity), the pre-Socratic Greeks see the Olympic gods as a means "to keep away the 'bad conscience'" (GM II, 23; KSA 5, 333). According to Nietzsche, this procedure belongs to a "noble means [...] of using the fiction of the gods" (Ibid.), rather than to the "self-torment" (GM II, 22; KSA 5, 332) and the cruelty of the bad conscience directed at oneself. Nietzsche views the Greek gods as "a reflection of noble and self-aggrandizing humans, in whom the *animal* in man felt deified and did *not* tear itself apart, did *not* rage against itself!" (GM II, 23; KSA 5, 333). So the gods are the reason why the Greeks should not punish themselves for their own drives.

Nietzsche's ideas found reception primarily in Anglophone Homeric studies, though the first impulse came from outside the field. In 1934 the anthropologist Ruth Benedict published her book *Patterns of Culture*, in which she connects her comparison of Pueblo Indians with other North American cultures to Nietzsche's "Dionysian/Apollonian"[33] opposition:

> The basic contrast between the Pueblos and the other cultures of North America is the contrast that is named and described by Nietzsche in his studies of Greek tragedy. [...] The Dionysian [...] seeks to attain in his most valuable moments escape from the boundaries imposed upon him by his five senses, to break through into another order of experience. The desire of the Dionysian, in personal experience or in ritual, is to press through it towards a certain psychological state, to achieve excess. [...] The Apollonian distrusts all this, and has often little idea of the nature of such experiences. [...] He keeps the middle of the road, stays within the known map, does not meddle with disruptive psychological states. [...] The South-West Pueblos are Apollonian. (Benedict 1968, 56f.)[34]

Benedict's attempt to find an adequate scheme for an intercultural analysis is continued in a later work devoted to Japanese culture *The Chrysanthemum and the Sword* (1946). This time the opposition of "shame culture" and "guilt culture" is crucial:

> A society that inculcates absolute standards of morality and relies on men developing a conscience is a guilt culture by detention; but a man in such a society may [...] suffer in addition. [...] In a society where shame is a major sanction, people are chagrined about acts which we expect people to feel guilty about. [...] Where shame is a major sanction, a man does not experience relief when he makes his fault public even to a confessor. [...] True shame cultures rely on external sanctions for good behavior, not, as true guilt cultures do, on an internalized conviction of sin. (Benedict 1946, 22f.)

Benedict's thesis, which still resonates within anthropology, reminds us of Nietzsche's description of the noble Greeks who feel no guilt before the gods. This parallel has become an important point in the discussion on Greek morality, where Benedict's contradistinction was at first adopted unquestioned and later criticized heavily.[35] Five years later, Benedict's arguments found their way into Classical Philology. In his *The Greeks and the Irrational* (1951) Eric Robertson Dodds makes the same opposition between the "shame culture" and the "guilt culture" the foundation of his analysis of Homer's epics. Dodds, who receptively read several of Nietzsche's writings in his younger years,[36] turns his attention to one of the passages in Homer's *Iliad* (XIX, 86ff.), in which Agamemnon points out Zeus' guilt in place of his own:

> "Not I," he declared, "not I was the cause of this act, but Zeus and my portion and the Erinys who walks in darkness: they it was who in the assembly put wild ἄτη in my understanding, on that day when I arbitrarily took Achilles' prize from him. So what could I do? The divine will always have its way. (Dodds 1951, 3)[37]

According to Dodds, Agamemnon's reference to ἄτη[38] is not incidental and indicates an important tendency: the Homeric human, whose feelings belong to "shame culture," projects his shame onto an external authority (Dodds 1951, 17). This thought again runs parallel to Nietzsche's description of the noble Greeks. And like Nietzsche, Dodds contours his historical claim about "shame culture" along the lines of the Archaic period of Greek culture.[39]

Further traces of Nietzsche's theses can be found in Arthur Adkins 1960 book *Merit and Responsibility*, in which he treats the development of Greek morality from Archaic times until Plato and Aristotle. Postulating an insurmountable divide between our worldviews and those of the Greeks in reference to morality (Adkins 1960, 2 f.),[40] Adkins illustrates his idea of an unavoidable "deficit in terms" in the description of the Archaic-Greek moral system with the same examples as Nietzsche did. The third chapter of his book *Homer: Mistake and Moral Error* is devoted to the analysis of ἀγαθός, κακός and αἰδώς ("shame")[41] and the description of these terms resembles the one in the *Genealogy of Morals*. Observing a Homeric case (*Odyssey* XV, 324),[42] he comments on the role of ἀγαθός and κακός as follows:

> Here evidently *agathoi* and *cherees* characterize high and low social position respectively. This usage [...] forms part of one world-view. *Agathos* commends the most admired type of man; and he is the man who possesses the skills and qualities of the warrior-chieftain in war and [...] in peace, together with the social advantages which such a chieftain possessed. (Adkins 1960, 32)

Although Adkins never mentions Nietzsche by name, one can at least infer an indirect connection. Many of his key points, e.g. his postulated Archaic "ethics of performance," where deeds rather than intentions are considered paramount (and such criteria as justice play no important role[43]), directly follow the approaches of his teacher, namely, E. R. Dodds.[44]

Just like Dodds, Adkins' book also had a great influence on Classical Philology generally—and particularly on Homer studies as its most important subfield.[45] One of his most serious opponents—and one who helped to certify Nietzsche's influence on the discipline—was Sir Hugh Lloyd-Jones. In his book *The Justice of Zeus* (1971) Lloyd-Jones depicts an archaic value-system whose cornerstone is divine control over justice (δίκη), especially by Zeus:

> Like men the gods also have their king, whose attributes are based on those of human rulers. [...] Being father of gods and men, he rules over men also. [...]

He defends the established order (dikē) by punishing mortals whose injustices
disturb it, and at the same time by sternly repressing any attempt of men to rise
above the humble place where they belong. (Lloyd-Jones 1971, 27)

Lloyd-Jones supposes a continuity and homogeneity of the Greek value-system from
Homer until the Classical period. His thesis that the sole measure for human action
can be reduced to the will of Zeus, however, is foreign to Adkins as well as Nietzsche.

Nietzsche's approaches were, some decades after, taken into account by Bernard
Williams, who dealt with the problems of Archaic-Greek morality, too. In his 1993
book *Shame and Necessity*, crucial aspects of Nietzsche's critique of morality are
adopted.[46] Although Williams does not emphasize the great divide between Archaic
Greek culture and Platonic-Christian paradigm (unlike Adkins, he does not underline
the problem of a "deficit in terms"[47]), and though he endeavors to demonstrate the
similarity between our concepts and those of the Greeks, he nevertheless realizes that
we must clearly distinguish between our traditional *ways* of thinking and the Greek
way:

Cultural anthropologists [...] understand and describe another form of human
life. The kind of work I have mentioned helps us to understand the Greeks by
first making them seem strange [...] We cannot live with the ancient Greeks
or to any substantial degree imagine ourselves doing so. Much of their life is
hidden from us, and just because of that, it is important for us to keep a sense
of their otherness, a sense which the methods of cultural anthropology helps us
to sustain. This study does not use such methods. [...] But I do not want to deny
the otherness of the Greek world. I shall not be saying that Greeks of the fifth
century B.C. were [...] really almost as much like Victorian English gentlemen [...]
(Williams 1993, 1f.)

Similar to Nietzsche, Williams tries to untie the Archaic/Greek opposition of shame
and guilt from the common contradistinction of "moral/not moral."[48] William's
distinction between ethics and morality is highly interesting in this case; at the same
time it is instructive for the examination of Nietzsche's conception of "aristocratic
morality,"[49] which Nietzsche already attributes to Homer in an embryonic form.[50]
According to Williams, morality encompasses "an entire array of ethical views," which
"is so close to us, that moral philosophy dedicates much time to examining the differences between these different views, instead of discussing the differences between
these views as a whole and completely opposite ones."[51] By distinguishing between
morality in a narrow sense (as a duty towards other humans in society) and ethics (as a
practical necessity connected to the aims of the individual), the seeming inconsistency
in Nietzsche's simultaneous critique of morality and praise of aristocratic values can
be resolved.

Although the conceptions of ethics and morality are used differently in Williams
and Nietzsche they can still be used to explain Nietzsche's distinction between morals
[Sitte] and morality—in connection with his idea of a trans-moral [übersittlich]
morality, which only a conscious individual can attain (GM II, 2; KSA 5, 294). Another
similarity between both thinkers is their "immoral" tendency, which manifests itself

in the manner in which they analyze certain Archaic-Greek terms and concepts. One can therefore conclude that traces of Nietzsche can be found at the beginning of the discussion on Homeric morality as well as in its climax, as represented by Williams' publication.

While Nietzsche's influence on Classical Philology has been recognized as a serious theme, the focus is mostly on his contribution to Greek tragedy and historiography. It would, however, be beneficial to consider Nietzsche's influence on the analysis of Homer's epics as well. The methodological (Unitarianism and the early period of Oral-Poetry-Research) as well as thematic examples (Homeric polytheism and "immorality") reveal that research in this direction promises to be fruitful. Although Nietzsche's ideas cannot be considered as a crucial element of the mainstream tradition in Homeric Studies (e.g. in "Oral Theory," Neoanalysis, Semiotic approaches, narratological studies etc.), they play a significant role in some of its parts. The most important aspects of Nietzsche's influence are connected with the successful expansion of Homeric Studies in the second half of the twentieth century due to interdisciplinary approaches, including elements of philosophy, sociology, archeology, and psychology. The overall development of this discipline, resulting in a broader spectrum of its subjects and methods, accords with Nietzsche's idea of a Classical Philology which transcends its own limitations.

Translated by Philip Roth

Notes

1   The first part appeared in the *Rheinische Museum für Philologie* (RhM) of 1870 (Vol. 25, 528–40), and the second part only in 1873 (RhM, Vol. 28, 211–49), i.e. after the publication of BT and after Nietzsche's dispute with Ritschl. Nietzsche also prepared a critical-philological edition of the "Certamen," which was published in 1871 with Teubner Verlag. For a detailed analysis of Nietzsche's dealings with the "Certamen", cf. Vogt 1962, 105ff. as well as J. Latacz's contribution in this volume.

2   The title *Homer and Classical Philology* only appears in the published version of the text.

3   Cf. Vogt 1962, 104: "Already Nietzsche's early philologica is characterized by traits, in which his later development is indicated in an embryonic state. One of the most important traits is the peculiarity of [his] relationship to the object of inquiry."

4   See the quote from Goethe's poem on Wolf and his successors: "Scharfsinnig habt Ihr, wie Ihr seid, / von aller Verehrung uns befreit, / und wir bekannten überfrei, / das Ilias nur ein Flickwerk sei. / Mög' unser Abfall niemand kränken; / denn Jugend weiß uns zu entzünden, / daß wir ihn lieber als Ganzes denken, / als Ganzes freudig ihn empfinden" Cf. HCP; KGW II/1, 250; see also Porter 2002, 68f.

5   "Immer zerreißet den Kranz des Homer und zählet die Väter / Des vollendeten ewigen Werks! / Hat es doch *eine* Mutter nur und die Züge der Mutter, / Deine unsterblichen Züge, Natur!" Cf. HCP; KGW II/1, 250; see Martin 1996, 109.

6   An indirect critique of Wolf's position can also be found in Schiller's letter to Goethe on April 27, 1798: "By the way, if one has read up on some of the passages, the thought of a rhapsodic stringing together and of a variety of origins seems

necessarily barbaric: because the splendid continuity and reciprocity of the whole is one of its most effectual beauties." Cf. NA XXIII, 82 and Schröter 1982, 45.

7   Cf. Poetics 1448b, 1451a and passim.

8   A very short and pointed description of the meaning of this reformulation is given in Acampora 2000, 554: Eventually Nietzsche's intention was the preparation to the question "What do the Greeks mean to us?"

9   On the apologetic character of Nietzsche's inaugural speech see Lachtermann 1992, 24f.

10   Compare Nietzsche's thesis that Classical Philology is "just as much a piece of history as a piece of natural science and a piece of aesthetics." See also Schröter 1982, 24.

11   See Hölscher 1965, 35f. and passim; cf. Lloyd-Jones 1976, 1. For a complete list of Nietzsche's philological students as well as those philologists among his correspondents and those who worked at the Weimar Nietzsche-Archive, see Cancik 1999, 237ff.

12   Cf. Schröter 1982, 43.

13   Cf. Schröter, 1982, 43f. Nietzsche's Basel lecture as well as the question of Homer's personality as its main interest are mentioned on p. 15 of Schadewaldt's book.

14   Cf. Nietzsche's letter to Rohde, July 16, 1872; KSB 4, 23: "If only I would not keep hearing these weak assertions about the Homeric world as a youthful one, as the spring of a people, etc.! In *this* sense, in which it is mentioned, it is false. That a tremendous, wild contest, from a dark crudity and cruelty, precedes it, that Homer stands as the victor at the end of this long grim period, is one of my most certain convictions. The Greeks are much older than one thinks. One can speak of spring as long as one sets winter before spring: but this world of purity and beauty did not drop from the sky."

15   See e.g. the use of Nietzsche's conception of the "character" of Homer (with direct reference to Nietzsche's Basel lecture) in Shein 1984, 14.

16   Arend's methodological reference to Nietzsche was however criticized by Milman Parry: "Having nothing better, Arend outlines a philosophic and almost mystic theory, to which he seems to have been inspired (cf. p. 2, n. 3) by Nietzsche's oracular utterances about Homer dancing in chains." Parry 1936, 358.

17   There certainly are earlier important predecessors to "oral theory," like Herder (with his theses on Homer as a popular poet, on the oral character of his epics as well as on their structure) or Hermann. Whereas Nietzsche's influence on Arend is obvious, his ideas were either criticized in the works of important representatives of "oral theory" or—which is much more often the case—simply disregarded.

18   Cf. Lloyd-Jones 1971, 10.

19   Cf. NF 1881, 12[186]; KSA 9, 608: "The individual was 'immoral' for a long time—so it hid oneself consequently, e.g. the genius (like Homer) behind the name of a hero. Or a god was made responsible."

20   Cf. Nietzsche's confrontation of Plato with Homer in GM III 25; KSA 5, 402f.: "Plato *vs.* Homer: that is the whole, the real antagonism—there the 'beyond one' [Jenseitiger] of best will, the great denier of life, here his involuntary deifying one, the *golden* nature." Here Homer represents the diversity of life in contrast to Plato, who stands for a "dead" singularity.

21   On Nietzsche's influence on the book see Cancik 1986.

22   Otto's first book generated serious discussion, which earned him the name of "Nietzsche redivivus." Later Otto critically revised his text and abandoned the idea of

publishing it in a new edition. Cf. the bibliographic index in Otto 1962, 383. See also Cancik 1986, 105 and Wessels 2003, 197.

23   There are, however, also important differences. For example, Otto no longer speaks of an "immorality" of the Greek gods, but of a relatively low rank of morality. Cf. Otto 1929, 3: "[O]ne should not call them immoral, but they are perhaps too natural and naturally cheerful [naturfroh], as that they may attribute the highest value to morality."

24   See also Otto 1929, 7: "Now one should remember that nothing happens in Homer without that the god who is responsible for it. But in this unheard of proximity of the divine everything still happens in a natural way." On the naturalness of Homeric "religious perception" see Ibid., 19ff. Cf. Nietzsche on the proximity of the Homeric gods to humans in NF 1885, 40[35]; KSA 11, 646: "The general untruthfulness of humanity about itself, morally interpreting what they do and want, would be despicable, if it would not also be something very amusing: it would only need spectators—that is how interesting the play is! Not by gods, as Epicurus thought of them! But Homeric gods: so far and near to humans and watching them, perhaps like Galiani with his cats and monkeys:—namely, a bit related to the humans, but of a higher kind!"

25   Nietzsche's and Otto's defenses of polytheism are described by some scholars as "neopaganism." Cf. Kutzner 1986 and Wessels 2003, 185ff.

26   Cf. GS 108; KSA 3, 467: "*New battles.*—After Buddha was dead his shadow was still shown for hundreds of years in a cave,—an enormous and frightening shadow. God is dead: but the way humans are, there might still be caves for thousands of years in which his shadow will be shown.—And we—we even have to defeat his shadow." Cf. NF 1886/87, 5[71]; KSA 12, 213: "at the bottom of it only the moral god has been defeated."

27   See NF 1883/84, 24[1]; KSA 10, 643: "That it is so difficult to come close to the Greeks that one even feels distant from them whenever one has observed them: this is the clause and the personal sigh with which I as a connoisseur of human nature want to begin my observation of the Greeks. One can live in a contradictory belief to theirs for a while / and we learn that our disconcertment is more educating than a sense of familiarity."

28   For Nietzsche's critique of Plato as an anti-Greek see NF 1888, 14[94]; KSA 13, 272: "Plato, the man of the good—but he detached the instincts *from* the polis, from competition, from military courage, from art and beauty, from the mysteries, from the belief in tradition and grandfathers [...] He is deeply compassionate in everything *anti*-Hellenic ... And: "The *forgery* of everything real through morality [...]. And for all of this *Plato* is to blame! He *remains* the greatest mishap of Europe!" To Overbeck, January 9, 1887; KSB 8, 9.

29   Nietzsche's theses on the role of the gods in Homer as well as the original social meanings of the terms "good" and "bad" correspond to those, which the Classicist Leopold Schmidt postulates in his book "Die Ethik der alten Griechen." Berlin 1882. It is also known that Nietzsche had a copy of the book in his personal library and read it attentively. See hereto Brusotti 1992, 123f. and Orsucci 1996, 250ff. The importance of Schmidt's book as a source for Nietzsche (especially for his elaborations in the *Genealogy of Morals*) is certainly great, but must not be overestimated. Nietzsche's thoughts on immorality in connection to the early Greeks are in very close relation to the themes of his earlier thoughts, as e.g. the agonistic, Archaic cruelty, the foreignness of the Greeks, and the connection between morals [Sittlichkeit] and morality [Moral].

30   Cf. GM I, 2; KSA 5, 259: "To me it is first of all obvious that the actual cause of the
      term 'good' is searched for at the wrong place in this theory: The verdict 'good' does
      not stem from those, upon whom 'goodness' is bestowed! It were rather 'the good
      ones' themselves, which means the noble, powerful, superior and high-minded, who
      perceived and assessed themselves and their actions as good, i.e. of the first rank in
      contradistinction to all the lower, lowly-minded common and vulgar."

31   Ibid., with reference to *Odyssey* I, 32–4: Zeus, the highest of the Olympic deities
      laments to the other participants in the gathering that the gods are too often called
      the source of evil by humanity.

32   In Od.ix.37–8 Odysseus says that the entire course of his voyage home (to which
      the loss of his companions naturally belongs) was orchestrated by Zeus: "[...] take
      [vernimm] now my sad voyage home, / which the thunderer Zeus has allotted to me
      from the Troic shore."

33   On the influence of Nietzsche on Benedict see also Mead 1959, 206–10.

34   Although Benedict emphasizes minor differences between the way of life of the
      Greeks and that of American Indians, she nevertheless finds the application
      of the pattern quite possible: "Not all of Nietzsche's discussions of the contrast
      between Apollonian and Dionysian applies to the contrast between the Pueblos
      and the surrounding peoples. [...] It is with no thought of equating the civilization
      of Greece with that of aboriginal America that I use, in describing the cultural
      configurations of the latter, terms borrowed from the culture of Greece. I use them
      mainly because they are categories that bring clearly to the fore the major qualities
      that differentiate Pueblo culture from those of other American Indians, not because
      all the attitudes that are found in Greece are found also in aboriginal America."
      Benedict 1968, 57.

35   For a well-argued critique on this confrontation within Classical Philology see
      Cairns 1993, 14ff.

36   Cf. Dodds 1977, 19f. Against this background one can assume that Nietzsche's
      contrasting of the irrationality of the early Greeks with the rationality of the Greeks
      since Plato became an important reason for Dodds' book.

37   Dodds adds many more examples from the *Iliad* (I, 412; VI, 234; IX, 376; XII, 254f.
      etc.) and the *Odyssey* (XII, 371f.; XXIII, 11ff.) while analyzing the *ate*-concept within
      the context of the guilt of the Homeric humans.

38   The word can literally be translated as "insanity." Even though the case of
      Agamemnon (as well as other cases) is not about realizing his own insanity (and
      certainly not about an illness!), but about the intervention of the punishing gods,
      who blur the minds of the humans. Cf. Nietzsche's "disturbance in the head" in GM
      II, 23.

39   See the chapter on "From Shame-Culture to Guilt-Culture" in Dodds 1951, 28ff.
      Unlike in Nietzsche the opposition between Homer and Plato plays no major role in
      Dodds. Nevertheless we can assume that he draws the borderline of "shame culture"
      at the same place where Nietzsche places the beginning of the reign of Socratism
      in Greek culture, e.g. Dodds speaks of Sophocles as "the last great exponent of the
      archaic world-view." Dodds 1951, 49; cf. Nietzsche on Euripides' "Socratism," the
      next of the great Greek poets, in BT 12.

40   Cf. also Adkins 1975. On the influence of Nietzsche's idea of the foreignness of the
      Greek on Adkins see Zhavoronkov 2012.

41   Cf. also Adkins 1960a, 23ff., where he mentions the problem of the difficulty and
      even impossibility of an adequate translation of several Homeric terms.

42 Odysseus, cloaked as a beggar, speaks to Eumaios of the difference between the noble ones and those who serve them.

43 Although acting people in Homer believe in gods as a trans-human authority, which is to judge the rightness of human action, the Olympian deities show no interest in punishing wrongdoers.

44 Cf. Louden 1996, 14n. 18. On the parallels between Nietzsche and Dodds see the above.

45 From 1960 until the mid-1980s an intense discussion took place, in which—next to Adkins and Lloyd-Jones—Anthony A. Long and Michael Gagarin also participated. The "second wave" of the fierce discussion (end of the 1980s until the mid-1990s) began with the publication of Bernard Williams' and Douglas L. Cairn's works, in which many of the early terms and approaches were revalued critically.

46 On Nietzsche's influence on Williams see Clark 2001.

47 Williams often directs harsh criticism against certain of Adkins' theses, e.g. against his assertion that the Archaic Greeks were primarily concerned with their own private success—often at the expense of others: see Williams 1993, 81ff.

48 See Williams 1993, 91f.: "If we ask exactly how great a difference lies between the Greeks and ourselves in this respect, we run into a problem that I mentioned in the first chapter, of distinguishing what we think from what we think that we think. One thing that a marked contrast between shame and guilt may express is the idea that it is important to distinguish between 'moral' and 'nonmoral' qualities. Shame is itself neutral to that distinction [...]."

49 See BGE 262; KSA 5, 214ff. Cf. BGE 260; KSA 5, 209: "The noble kinds of men feel *themselves* as value-commanding, it is not necessary for them to be endorsed, they judge 'whichever is harmful to me, is harmful in itself', they know themselves as that which first lends honor to things, they are *value-creating*." See also Solms-Laubach 2007, 117ff.

50 That Nietzsche does not see a fully developed aristocratic morality with Homer, the most important early Greek author, becomes evident e.g. by the mentioned "invention" of Greek heroes in GS 143, which was an "invaluable preliminary practice for the justification of the egoism and arrogance of the individual." Furthermore especially the "irresponsibility" of the Greeks is clear evidence for strength of morals [Sittlichkeit], which was typical in the pre-modern period.

51 Cf. Williams 1985, 174. On ethics in Williams and his critique of morality see Clark 2001, esp. 113: "Williams's case against morality [...] depends [...] on being able to make it plausible that the moral interpretation of ethical experience (and in particular the idea of moral obligation as an all-things-considered conclusion) conflates and hides from view a distinction we ought to accept: between obligations, on the one hand, and conclusions of practical necessity, on the other. What is principally hidden from view by the idea of moral obligation is the fact that obligations are rooted outside of us, in other people's expectations and the conditions of ethical life, whereas conclusions of unconditional practical necessity are rooted in one's own identity."

Works cited

Acampora, Christa Davis (2001): "Nietzsche's Problem of Homer." In *Nietzscheforschung*. Vol. 5/6, 553–74.

Adkins, Arthur W. H. (1960): *Merit and Responsibility: A Study in Greek Values*. Oxford (Clarendon Press).

—(1960a): "'Honour' and 'Punishment' in the Homeric Poems." In *Bulletin of the Institute of Classical Studies*. Vol. 7, 23–32.

Arend, Walter (1933): *Die typischen Scenen bei Homer*. Berlin (Weidmannsche Buchhandlung).

Benedict, Ruth (1946): *The Chrysanthemum and the Sword: Patterns of Japanese Culture*. Boston (Houghton Mifflin Company).

—(1968): *Patterns of Culture*. London (Routledge).

Brusotti, Marco (1992): "Die 'Selbstverkleinerung des Menschen' in der Moderne. Studien zu Nietzsches *Zur Genealogie der Moral*." In *Nietzsche-Studien*. Vol. 21, 81–136.

Cairns, Douglas L. (1993): *Aidōs: The Psychology and Ethics of Honour and Shame in Ancient Greek Literature*. Oxford (Clarendon Press).

Cancik, Hubert (1986): "Dionysos 1933: W. F. Otto, ein Religionswissenschaftler und Theologe am Ende der Weimarer Republik." In Richard Faber and Renate Schlesier (eds): *Die Restauration der Götter: Antike Religion und Neo-Paganismus*. Würzburg (Königshausen & Neumann), 105–23.

Cancik, Hubert and Hildegard Cancik-Lindemaier (1999): *Philolog und Kultfigur: Friedrich Nietzsche und seine Antike in Deutschland*. Stuttgart and Weimar (J. B. Metzler).

Clark, Maudemarie (2001): "On the Rejection of Morality: Bernard Williams's Debt to Nietzsche." In Richard Schacht (ed.): *Nietzsche's Postmoralism: Essays on Nietzsche's Prelude to Philosophy's Future*. Cambridge (Cambridge University Press), 100–22.

Dodds, Eric Robertson (1951): *The Greeks and the Irrational*. Berkeley and Los Angeles (University of California Press).

—(1977): *Missing Persons: An Autobiography*. Oxford (Clarendon Press).

Gerhardt, Volker (2004): "'Schuld', 'schlechtes Gewissen', und Verwandtes (II, 4–7)." In Ottfried Höffe (ed.): *Friedrich Nietzsche: Zur Genealogie der Moral*. Berlin (Akademie Verlag), 81–95.

Hölscher, Uvo (1965): "Karl Reinhardt." In his *Die Chance des Unbehagens: Drei Essais zur Situation der klassischen Studien*. Göttingen (Vandenhoeck & Ruprecht), 31–52.

Kutzner, Heinrich (1986): "Friedrich Nietzsches Antichristentum und Neuheidentum. Zu ihrer psychohistorischen Dimension." In Richard Faber and Renate Schlesier (eds): *Die Restauration der Götter: Antike Religion und Neo-Paganismus*. Würzburg (Königshausen & Neumann), 88–104.

Lloyd-Jones, Hugh (1971): *The Justice of Zeus*. Berkeley and Los Angeles (University of California Press).

—(1976): "Nietzsche and the Study of the Ancient World." In James C. O'Flaherty, Timothy F. Sellner, and Robert Helm (eds): *Studies in Nietzsche and the Classical Tradition*. Chapel Hill (The University of North Carolina Press), 1–15.

—(1982): "Nietzsche." In *Blood for the Ghosts: Classical Influences in the Nineteenth and Twentieth Centuries*. Baltimore (Duckworth), 165–81.

Louden, Robert B. (1996): "Introduction." In Robert B. Louden and Paul Schollmeier (eds): *The Greeks and Us: Essays in Honor of Arthur W. H. Adkins.* Chicago (University of Chicago Press), 1–16.

Martin, Nicholas (1996): *Nietzsche and Schiller: Untimely Aesthetics.* Oxford (Clarendon Press).

Mead, Margaret (1959): "Patters of Culture: 1922–34." In Margaret Mead (ed.): *An Anthropologist at Work: Ruth Benedict.* Boston (Houghton Mifflin Company), 201–12.

Müller, Enrico (2005): *Die Griechen im Denken Nietzsches.* Berlin and New York (Walter de Gruyter).

Orsucci, Andrea (1996): *Orient, Okzident: Nietzsches Versuch Einer Loslösung Vom Europäischen Weltbild.* Berlin and New York (Walter de Gruyter).

—(2000): "Homer." In Henning Ottmann (ed.): *Nietzsche-Handbuch.* Stuttgart and Weimar (J. B. Metzler), 366.

Otto, Walter F. (1923): *Der Geist der Antike und die christliche Welt.* Bonn (F. Cohen).

—(1929): *Die Götter Griechenlands: Das Bild des Göttlichen im Spiegel des griechischen Geistes.* Bonn (F. Cohen).

—(1933): *Dionysos. Mythos und Kultus.* Frankfurt am Main (V. Klostermann).

—(1962): *Das Wort der Antike.* Stuttgart (E. Klett).

Parry, Milman (1936): "On Typical Scenes in Homer." In *Classical Philology.* Vol. 31, 357–60.

Porter, James I. (2002): *Nietzsche and the Philology of the Future.* Stanford (Stanford University Press).

Schadewaldt, Wolfgang (1944): *Von Homers Welt und Werk: Aufsätze und Auslegungen zur homerischen Frage.* Stuttgart (Koehler & Amelang).

Schmidt, Leopold (1882): *Die Ethik der alten Griechen.* 2 vols. Berlin (W. Hertz).

Schröter, Hartmut (1982): *Historische Theorie und geschichtliches Handeln: Zur Wissenschaftskritik Nietzsches.* Mittenwald (Mäander Kunstverlag).

Shein, Seth L. (1984): *The Mortal Hero: An Introduction to Homer's Iliad.* Berkeley and Los Angeles (University of California Press).

Solms-Laubach, Franz Graf zu (2007): *Nietzsche and Early German and Austrian Sociology.* Berlin and New York (Walter de Gruyter).

Vogt, Ernst (1962): "Nietzsche und der Wettkampf Homers." In *Antike und Abendland.* Vol. 11, 103–13.

Wessels, Antje (2003): *Ursprungszauber: Zur Rezeption von Hermann Useners Lehre von der religiösen Begriffsbildung.* Berlin (Walter de Gruyter).

Williams, Bernard (1985): *Ethics and the Limits of Philosophy.* London (Fontana Press).

—(1993): *Shame and Necessity.* Berkeley and Los Angeles (University of California Press).

Zhavoronkov, Alexey (2012): "Nietzsches Idee der Fremdheit des Griechischen und ihre Rezeption in der klassischen Philologie." In Renate Reschke and Marco Brusotti (eds): *'Einige werden posthum geboren': Friedrich Nietzsches Wirkungen.* Berlin (Walter de Gruyter), 615–24.

Part Four

Literature, Language, Culture

8

The History of Literature as an Issue: Nietzsche's Attempt to Represent Antiquity

Carlotta Santini

1. Introduction

The confrontation with Greek antiquity is always mediated by the instruments and structures provided by Classical Philology. This holds true of the lectures held by Nietzsche as professor of Greek language and literature at Basel University from 1869–79. Yet though Nietzsche utilizes the forms, categories, and methods of philological science, he never ceases to be a reflective and creative interpreter. The lectures on the *Geschichte der griechischen Literatur*[1] (1874–6; hereafter GgL) are perhaps the best example of the way Nietzsche worked as a scholar. In these lectures he meant to offer his students an exhaustive description of ancient literature and its connections with Greek society. His lectures are implicitly inspired by the historical models proposed by August Boeckh, by Jacob Burckhardt,[2] and (through him) by Leopold von Ranke's idea of "Darstellung," even though the concrete sources used in the preparation of the course are simple and useful textbooks. But, in order to achieve his aim, he also reflects on the methods and structures of his own philological practice.

In this chapter, I aim to show how Nietzsche attempts to teach a history of Greek literature and at the same time to offer a meta-level reflection on the practice of reading Greek literature itself. As a point of departure, I will make reference to two excellent (but insufficiently noticed in the Anglophone world) articles: "Vom 'Sprachkunstwerk' zu 'Leseliteratur'" by Barbara von Reibnitz (1994) and "'Jetzt zieht mich das Allgemein-Menschliche an.' Ein Streifzug durch Nietzsches Aufzeichnungen zu einer 'Geschichte der litterarischen Studien'" by Federico Gerratana (1994). Apart from these two scholars, as far I am aware, nobody has worked on these particular lectures and has recognized the centrality of the question about 'Literaturgeschichte' in Nietzsche's critical approach to Classical Philology. My own work here will broaden the topic, and synthesize some main questions, in particular those that Nietzsche had to face in his attempt to write a history of ancient literature.

2. The history of literature as an issue

It appears evident in many notes of the *Nachlass* of 1867–8 that Nietzsche had doubts about the validity of the practice of the history of literature. In those notes he declared his intention to begin a study on the tradition of history of literature from ancient to contemporary times.[3] He was especially interested in the motives and methods through which academics stabilize and normalize "the" history of literature. Before reflecting on Greek literature itself, Nietzsche feels the need to make a meta-reflection on the limits and methods of this historical treatment of literary heritage. Not coincidentally, Nietzsche is interested both in modern contemporary authors (the most important philologists of his time, like Gottfried Bernhardy, Theodor Bergk, Karl Otfried Müller) and in ancient ones, for whom the demand for a historical-systematic categorization of literature first arose. This discussion, despite its fragmentary nature, can be roughly reconstructed as it allows the recognition of the main directions of Nietzsche's analysis.

Following the tracks of this reflection in the *Nachlass*, we see how Nietzsche sought out the first historical instantiation of the *need* of a history of literature. There must have been a transition from a stage, he argues, when literature was unhistorical or when the attitude towards the development of literature was unconscious, to a phase of historical consciousness about that development. Until this time, Greek literature simply happened—it was an *Ereignis* (so von Reibnitz 1994, 48); only thereafter did it start to reflect on its own development and attempt to define it, thereby fixing it in history (NF 1867/68, 56[1]; KGW I/4, 361).

To more fully understand Nietzsche's claim, an argument from the second *Untimely Meditation* will help. In this text *Historie*, which is meant as consciousness of the historical past and also of the past as historical knowledge, critically divides itself from an "unhistorical" past, which is defined by its unawareness of itself as a past. But this "beginning" that we seek to elucidate is in reality fictitious, a subjective selection of a point dividing the immense extension of the past into history and pre-history. Nietzsche reveals this arbitrariness in the consideration of the past in both contexts: the historical one and the historical-literary one. Even if we could track down a more or less precise historical period for the birth of literary history as a conscious reflection on ancient populations and their cultural heritage, there remains the fact that this demand must have existed psychologically prior to its formal outward expression. The need must have expressed itself in a historic-literary mythology prior to a scientific or a conscious and codified discipline (BAW 5, 212).

A related issue concerns what exactly this primitive attitude towards the historical consideration of literature consisted in: was it conceived as a sort of aesthetic judgment?—or maybe an ethical judgment? In the case of ancient scholars and literates it seems that the first form of historical-literary consideration was related to two contrary purposes: encomium or condemnation, both of which are related to the internal dynamics of Greek society (political and value judgments on the contents of the work). But the main character of each history of literature always brings attention to what is truly "historical," that is, that each work has value insofar as it has a place in the natural historical-literary development. Without consideration of its intrinsic aesthetic value as literature, each work is remembered only because it has been handed down, and it is handed down only because it has a determined role in history. The earliest histories of literature appear, indeed, to be very little interested in the beauty of literature: "Expecting from philologists the most lively pleasure in the Antiquity is like expecting from scientists the most lively feeling for nature and from anatomists the finest sensibility for human beautiful" (BAW 5, 270). Each work is considered important with respect to its persistence, in no way differentiating historical value from the aesthetic. On the contrary, for the modern awareness, art has value independent of any historical consideration: aesthetic value supersedes historical contingency.

But certainly some value judgment is necessarily required of a historian of literature. Literary history remains, in spite of its objective detachment, "a work of art" (NF 1867/68, 61[2]; KGW I/4, 533), in the double sense of an artificial production and of a manifestation of human creativity. Throughout all his academic and editorial activity in the philological field, Nietzsche was always interested as much in the history of literature as in the interpretation of those tendencies and methods that antiquity has given to it (NF 1867/68, 58[58]; KGW I/4, 498–9). And he always searched for a psychological, social or cultural motive within the origins of these tendencies. This is maybe one of the most original aspects of Nietzsche's approach to the study of antiquity. The ancient historical-literary tradition is thus as much interesting in its forms as in its matter, because it reveals so well the structures of thought of the ancients. Accordingly, Nietzsche was not only interested in having certain knowledge about antiquity, but also in observing the mistakes and falsifications, the deviated paths that typically accompany literary history. Those phenomena related to textual traditions are at the core of his interest. Cataloguing methods, such as pinacography, or the methods for the organization of the literary heritage, such as doxographical practices, could have given rise to unintentional manipulations of the tradition, which has been reorganized according to ideological presuppositions. We have evidence that these manipulations were not always unintentional: pseudoepigraphy, editorial falsifications, distortions of ideas or facts, the practical interests of authors and editors, the hostility between currents of thought, and the deeply masked mistakes caused by ignorance or malice, were common phenomena in antiquity, and the good historian of literature should be conscious of them.

The first target for the philologist seems to be the reconstitution of a text corrupted by these factors over times. These intentional or unintentional manipulations should be expunged, because they are only missteps in history. On the contrary, Nietzsche simultaneously intertwines the study of the corrupted conditions of a text and the reconstitution of that text. The reconstitution of a text tells us of the time in which it was conceived; but its corruption and all its incongruities tell us both what has then happened and how the future generations have interpreted the text in light of what happened. The history of the corruption of a text has also an inestimable historical value for the historian of literature. This tendency to recover the false tradition too is evident in Nietzsche's own authorial activity, for example in the thematic foci of his philological works.[4] When, in the "incipit" of his first published article, *Zur Geschichte der Theognideischen Spruchsammlung* (1867), he discusses the presence of repetitions and the opportunity or inopportunity various redactors had to exclude them from a critical edition, he argues:

> Each reader of Theognis cannot fail to see, that many sentences [...] appear twice in the collection. On a closer view he finds that most of these repetitions were expunged from the text by later editors. Maybe they were right, because we learn nothing new through repetition. But maybe they were wrong, because sometimes we learn just due to them. It would well be possible that we may find there useful cues to clarify Theognis' text tradition. (KGW II/1, 3)

The pseudo-epigraphical tendencies, transcriptional mistakes, and fragmentary transmission of the text of Theognis reveal, according to Nietzsche, many elements of the cultural atmosphere through which these texts have passed.[5] Each epoch has given its interpretation of the literary heritage of his past, and each of them has approached the Ancients with a certain lack of understanding (NF 1867/68, 52[31]; KGW I/4, 223–5). Value judgments, aesthetic tendencies, the personal tastes of redactors, varying professional standards of scholars, and every other possible element of distortion plays a decisive role in handing down ancient literature over time.

Due to the complexity of that fully contextualized historical-literary tradition, Nietzsche despairs of the possibility that strictly scientific method could approach it. If the aim of a scientific method is to reach the highest possible degree of objectivity, then that method

> must arouse repulsion from all natural-scientists, not to mention mathematicians, because it always operates with several connected possibilities. Subjectivity prevails. Lots of unconscious powers have raged against the text. Conscious powers should re-complement it. (NF 1867/68, 58[40]; KGW I/4, 476)

When Nietzsche analyzes the uses and disadvantages of the practice of literary history for the sake of pedagogy in his *Encyklopädie der klassischen Philologie* (hereafter EkP), he becomes very skeptical indeed:

> Concerning the History of Literature. It is time, given the prevailing opinions, to concede the precarious, too. Most mistakes secretly prevail due to the trust in the tradition: A history of literature is the sum of examples for ethical, aesthetic, social, and political maxims, and therefore highly subjective! (EkP; KGW II/3, 405)

What Nietzsche criticizes here is not the richness of perspectives (aesthetic, social, political) within the history of literature, but rather the lack of attention paid to them, which has resulted in the fragmentation of those points of view among modern scholars. Literary historians typically consider these points of view separately, in part because of the difficulty of accounting for their intersections and discontinuities. According to Nietzsche, this is the reason why philology traditionally prefers to make simplifications and to provide fixed schematic classifications of the ancient literary tradition. This practice as such may not be entirely unjustified, as simplification is necessary for every science; however, it is misleading for such a varied and dynamic phenomenon as the ancient literary tradition.

Considering the protean quality of the materials, each attempt at systematization risks illegitimacy. Strictly speaking, the systematic character of science should have a very narrow field. "Except for a vague and brief sketch and nomenclature of authors, history of literature is originally superfluous" (EkP; KGW II/3, 405). Were it strictly scientific, literary history would be reduced to a list of authors and books; but even so there would be difficulties since linking authors and their works is perhaps one of the philologist's most difficult tasks.[6] Taking a strictly scientific attitude, limiting oneself to pure confirmable fact—these are not only limitations indicative of a certain superficiality; a purely "scientific" attitude in philosophy is simply impossible to maintain.

For Nietzsche, a different approach is necessary. "Historical facts have something petrifying, like the Medusa, which can disappear only for the eyes of a poet. Out of the stone-blocks of the historical facts we must first carve a statue" (NF 1867/68, 56[3]; KGW I/4, 364). To teach and understand the literature of antiquity, Nietzsche experimented with a more elastic and thereby more effective form of knowledge. Nietzsche advocated a mutable form of inquiry, which entailed an increasingly closer approach to the totality of the ancient world, one revisable in light of further engagement with sources and later interpretations. "To each real philologist a serious task. Originality of his intuition [Anschauung]! Endless correction through new observations, comparing! Gradual widening of knowledge through growing confidence of perception and judgment!" (NF 1867/68, 56[3]; KGW I/4, 364).

Nietzsche's idea of a continuous approaching to truth is in fact the most fundamental and proper attitude of philology, according to the definition of August Boeckh in his *Encyklopädie* (Boeckh 1877). The result of this process of approximation is what Nietzsche calls "historisches Verständnis" (historical understanding) (EkP; KGW II/3, 344–5). In this concept, strictly related to the problem of "historische Objektivität" (historical objectiveness), Nietzsche's debt towards Leopold von Ranke's idea of history appears evident. According to Ranke, we cannot blindly trust in the success of our methods to obtain a final knowledge of the historical past. His conception of "historische Darstellung" (historical representation) introduces indeed a "weaker concept" of history and historiography, in comparison to the positivistic theories of his contemporaries. Ranke's approaching to history is a continuous, never-exhausted attempt, made by a historical epoch (for example the present time) to get near to another epoch in the past. This approach can also never be considered as finished, but must always be recognized as relative since it depends on a limited point of view, while each epoch results from manifold instances, which remain immanent to this epoch. Herein, however, lies the infinite richness of the experience of historical thought.

What Nietzsche really means in using Ranke's expression is that a complete comprehension of antiquity is not merely the total sum of single observations of its manifold aspects of antiquity, even though that should be indeed a necessary condition. Further necessary is an intuition (Anschauung), which is simultaneously the result and the guide of the historian's work and can at the same time make meaningful the massive accumulation of facts. This intuition is deduced by the integral, non-fragmented, knowledge of the ancient world and it is then set as a guide of this process, which must lead to this knowledge itself.

> Historical understanding is nothing else than the comprehension of particular
> facts under philosophical premises. The height of these premises determines
> the value of the historical understanding. Because a fact is something endless,
> something completely reproducible. There are also only grades of the historical
> understanding. One reaches for history and only finds in it a collection of
> exemplars for one's knowledge. The more the man thinks autonomously, the more
> will he be able to recognize himself in history. (EkP; KGW II/3, 344–5)

This main idea that guides the philologist in his study of antiquity and which he
deduces from the ancient world itself is that of the classical spirit of antiquity, of
its exemplariness, and of its character as "ewigmustergültig [eternally valid as an
exemplar]" (HkP; KGW II/1, 250). "The philosophical premise of Classical Philology
is the classicism of Antiquity. We want to understand its highest events and to grow
up on their model. Living-into is the task!" (EkP; KGW II/3, 345). The concept of the
classical that Nietzsche utilizes is first of all related to a formal characteristic that is
the model of the stylistic composition of the Greek literary works. As antiquity came
to us through texts, the philologist creates his concept of the classical on the basis of
the formal aspects of those texts. But the classical rises to an ethical value, too. As it
is really impossible to separate the ancient literary tradition from its world, from its
society, its politics, and its religious sense, the idea of the classical does not remain
only a formal characteristic, but also a spiritual and ethical one. Ultimately, it holds
the highest manifestation of the Greek life and spirit.

The writer of a history of literature must be guided by his conviction of the classical
character of antiquity. The comparison which the philologist makes between antiquity
and modernity for pedagogical reasons is also based on this conviction. Nietzsche
indeed defines making comparisons, seeing similarities, and confronting differences
as one of the most appropriate activities of the philologist:

> All that we see and that we are, stimulates to compare; the philologist therefore
> must have a contemplative mind. He should educate himself by this comparison.
> In this way he does not yet become Greek: but he trains himself with the highest
> educational materials. He will no more be upset by the storms of the present. The
> comparison with Antiquity first of all relies on the capacity to recognize in the
> most common and obvious facts their potential explanatory value: this is the true
> characteristic of a philosopher! For this reason we should begin with the philo-
> sophical investigation of Antiquity. (EkP; KGW II/3, 372)

The philologist takes the ability to make comparisons from his particular borderline
position between two worlds: the ancient and the modern. As he remains always at
the same time outside but familiar to these two worlds, he is the intermediary between
them. This definition bears some similarity to the later definition of "untimeliness"
given in the second *Untimely Meditation* (HL; KSA 1, 247), but it is perhaps more
radical. The philologist cannot simply learn from antiquity and he cannot reproduce
the same conditions of the ancient world in the modern one. He remains always
an indeterminate figure, a stranger to both these worlds. The philologist as modern
man and master of the moderns wields his judgment on antiquity for the advantage

of the moderns, of the teaching that the moderns take from antiquity. There is no guarantee about the exactitude of his teaching, but the philologist should be able to see as much the few similarities between Ancients and Moderns, as the many differences. Because of the impossibility of an exact knowledge of antiquity, the ability to see and to understand the differences is the most important profit we can derive from it. The balance between similarities and differences with the Ancients stimulates in the Moderns the comparison and the desire of emulation, which is the spark of each education.

This reflection on Nietzsche's part about the meaning of the differences is an essential element, too, in his critique of Comparativism as a scientific method in the study of antiquity. Comparativism, whose important results in linguistics Nietzsche accepted with enthusiasm (NF 1867/68, 58[52]; KGW I/4, 495), risked leading to uncertain results if applied as a method for the study of antiquity. The Greek case is so unique that for Nietzsche it does not allow recourse to general concepts that are to apply across all civilizations, or to parallels with other realities for explaining its phenomena. In particular, Nietzsche recognizes in cults, in political and social structures, and consequently (as we will see later) in literary productions, areas where the artistic spirit of the Greeks gains a strong national specificity—so strong as to become almost local or regional, which can be explained only by recourse to internal elements of this unique social and political sphere, and not by generalized external realities. What seems to Nietzsche decisive in the critique of the comparative method is now again the question about the adequacy and the legitimacy of such an approach. The question is no longer what is the best instrument to understand antiquity, but what can modern man learn from the study of antiquity?

What benefit can modern man obtain from comparing very different ancient societies, such as the Egyptian, the Hebraic, the Chinese if not a questionable satisfaction of his intellectual curiosity? Among all ancient societies, only the Greek and the Latin (and to a certain extent also the Hebraic) can yield really interesting results for the modern, in Nietzsche's opinion. These cultures are indeed useful for the education of modern man. Modern Western civilization can claim traditionally to be historically and culturally related only with these societies. Our civilization does not recognize itself in the history, literature, tradition or mythology of China, or Japan. On the contrary, the Greek and Latin literature and culture and the Hebraic tradition are at the base of our modern culture, beginning with religion, and encompassing philosophy and politics. According to Nietzsche, finding similarities between ancient oriental societies and our modern society is not relevant for the education of modern man. We are interested in the Greeks and the Latins, because they are, to some extent, similar and comparable to us: "because we speak only for ourselves about classicism, for our modern world, and not with regard to Indians, Babylonians, Egyptians" (EkP; KGW II/3, 390).[7]

3. Initial conceptions of the history of literature

We now proceed to examine how Nietzsche put these reflections into practice, when towards the middle of the 1870s he covers the history of Greek literature. In his written introduction (the "Vorbegriffe"), Nietzsche begins with a meticulous and rather pitiless terminological and conceptual analysis intended to destabilize the usual presumptions in the field. The "incipit" of his longest course, titled *Geschichte der griechischen Literatur*, reads as follows:

> The word literature is doubtful and it involves a prejudice. Similar to the ancient mistake of grammar of starting from the letters and not from the phoneme, is the ancient mistake of history of literature, too: it thinks first of all of the writing tradition of a people, and not of their artful oral practices, i.e. it starts with a period in which the originally oral artwork is only enjoyed by a reader. (GgL; KGW II/5, 7)

Nietzsche proceeds with a reflective critique of the title of his own lectures themselves, contesting the legitimacy of even speaking about Greek "literature." The prejudice consists in attributing to Greece a phenomenon similar to that found in our modern culture. Just the term "literature," as Nietzsche demonstrates in an etymological "adnotatio" (N.B. in Latin rather than Greek), presupposes something written.[8] Greek culture, on the contrary, trusted mainly in oral expression, recitation, and performance, but never in reading. Proof of this fact is the abundance of technical words that identify the different forms of reciting (GgL; KGW II/5, 22–9), like λέγειν, καταλέγειν (if recited), ᾄδειν (if sung), παίζειν (with accompaniment of dance), μέλος, παρακαταλογή (recitation of tragedy).

> Now, in the case of the main and most important part of Greek literature we should refrain from thinking about reading and writing. Not that writing was missing—but it was only an instrument of the poet, who went in front of his public only speaking and singing. It makes an extraordinary difference, whether e.g. a drama was made for readers or rather for hearers and spectators, and whether all artists of language, like in earlier Greece, actually think of hearers and spectators only; just like the reception of the artwork is also very different in reading or in listening. (GgL; KGW II/5, 7)

To define the literary phenomenon in Greece, and especially in archaic and classical Greece, Nietzsche utilizes the expression "Kunstwerk der Sprache" (artwork of language) instead of "Literatur," since it already and misleadingly implies a "Leseliteratur" (reading literature). This preferred expression should give back the sense of a cultural phenomenon alive and changing, related to the living language of a people that cannot be made static and fixed within a system of classification without being distorted. But in fact even the expression "Kunstwerk der Sprache" is nothing other than a periphrasis for a word that in fact does not exist. Nietzsche often neglects it and falls back upon the execrated word "literature."[9] In any case, this popular misunderstanding of the basic oral structure of Greek culture is only enabled by the application of an anachronistic structure of thought towards the Greek world, what he called in 1867 the true "Philosopheme" (NF 1867/68, 52[30–1]; KGW I/4, 221–3).[10] Throughout the preface Nietzsche continues to show these incongruities and anachronisms, evidencing a critical tendency especially through terminological analyses.

That is clearly the case with his lectures on "Die Griechischen Lyriker" (hereafter GL).[11] Here Nietzsche tries to explicate the practice of recitation in Greece. To differentiate it from modern practices of Shakespearean theater or of French tragedy, Nietzsche utilizes two different German words: "Vortrag" and "Vorstellung" (GL; KGW II/2, 107). "Vorstellung" should represent the modern example of a reciting based on a fixed written text, in front of which the audience situates itself in a way similar to that typical of a straightforward reading. The concept of "Vortrag" as applied by Nietzsche to an ancient Greek context should instead be understood as an integral part of the artwork. Without it, the work itself cannot reach its aim in front of its public—its "Hörer" and "Zuschauer" (hearers and spectators).

The use of the word "Vortrag" by Nietzsche is obviously arbitrary and anachronistic. But he uses it only to investigate whether this ancient concrete distinction can be translated into modern terminology, and also into modern experience. In order to explain this contrast better, which is essential to understanding the essence of the Greek "Kunstwerk der Sprache," Nietzsche should have instead returned to the Greek concept, as he will do on other occasions. He utilizes also the distinction of Dionysius Thrax between *apotelestic* artistic genres and *practical* genres (GL; KGW II/2, 107), which was drawn on by Rudolf Westphal in his *Metrik* (Westphal-Rossbach 1867, 3–4). According to this bipartition, the "Kunstwerk der Sprache" should stand out from arts like painting and sculpture, because they differ in purpose, namely, to produce a final, materialized result. It needs instead a secondary level of expression, namely, being re-produced, which means it must necessarily be recited in front of an audience. Also, if painting and sculpture can be defined as apotelestic genres insofar as they obtain their aim only when the work is finished, then the arts of the productive genres instead need to fulfill their aim in being represented in front of an audience: they need a performance. In this sense we can understand Nietzsche's resumption of the romantic topos according to which an Aeschylean tragedy, if written and read, shows itself to be only a surrogate of the genuinely represented tragedy. A Shakespearean tragedy, by contrast, does not suffer to the same degree if, instead of being represented, it is read.

Another prejudice Nietzsche ascribes to modernity is its tendency to regard "Lesen und Schreiben" (reading and writing) as indispensable elements of culture itself. Herein lies another entirely modern distinction about the access to culture. The dyad "Lesen und Schreiben" presumes a type of "literary" society, in which it is possible to differentiate between who is "cultivated"—who can read and has access to the knowledge through written works—or "uncultivated," those to whom access to literature is precluded. Early Greek culture, on the contrary, was a type of "un-literary" society. As long as it remained so and it was resistant to the handing down of knowledge through written texts, the modern social distinction between the cultivated and uncultivated was meaningless.[12]

Nietzsche draws attention to this distinction between "literary" and "un-literary" in the third part of his lessons on "Geschichte der griechischen Literatur" (GgL; KGW II/5, 271), and utilizes it to problematize another notion already proven to be crucial in literary history: the concept of the classical. This third and final part of the lectures on Greek literature starts with a "Vorbemerkung" to the students. "The problem (presented a year ago) with which we will deal on the Thursdays of this winter, is the genesis of classical literature. Or, in the form of a question: how did the Greeks come to their classical literature" (GgL; KGW II/5, 273). This issue, Nietzsche believes, summarizes his entire work on the history of literature best. Here we have that mistrusted word "literature" combined with another term that seemingly has no place here: "classical." Although Nietzsche recognizes that at the base of literary history there is and must be the concept of the classical, he proceeds immediately to show how this concept is based on an illegitimate epistemological presumption (an epistemological illegitimacy that is compensated, as we saw earlier, by a higher pedagogical legitimacy).

An analysis of the Latin origin of the word "classical" is already present in a marginal note within the *Encyklopädie*, which reveals both its original social-political meaning and also its later, derivative axiological meaning.[13] "Classical" in the modern connotation is a judgment, specifically, a value judgment. In Nietzsche's opinion, the value of the pair of contraries *classic/non-classic* can be understood only if referred in the form of a chiasmus to the previously analyzed couple *literary/non-literary*: *classic* is to *non-literary* as *literary* is to *non-classic*. The concept of the classical implies that a value judgment is expressed about a range of historically transmitted works and, further, that among these there is a selected group, defined as "classical," which is exemplary by some formal standards of legitimacy. The word "classical" identifies a canon or model that can be imitated and is worthy of such imitation.

The concept of classical literature can shape itself only inside a literary culture, which itself is based on a heritage of written texts that are considered as classic (i.e. in this context "valid" and "worth teaching"). A literary culture like the Alexandrian Greeks (the first that founded an explicit canon of ancient texts) or the modern Germans bases its development on the fixation of a canon on which to shape its taste and to which to conform its cultural productions. To the first question in the previous quotation, then, Nietzsche implicitly adds another: can we today be creators of a literature that can be considered "classical" by future generations? The answer is negative: we moderns cannot be creators of a classical literature because we are sons of a literary epoch that based itself on what already is considered classical. A literature, to become classic, must base and develop itself on the ground of a non-literary culture, like the Greek culture.[14]

4. The attempt at a history of literature

The origin of the Greek masterpieces, defined today as "classics," has so many conditions that modernity can hardly imagine. All these conditions can never more be satisfied from our culture, which is completely dependent on ancient models and has lost its originality. Nietzsche tries however to reconstruct the panorama of the ancient "Kunstwerk der Sprache," insofar as it has left traces in the later written versions of what we call "Greek Literature." If the first problem in approaching a history of literature was to dismantle the concepts and the anachronistic classifications under which modernity wants to fit the Greeks, then Nietzsche now has to find a new way and indeed new words to describe their achievements. He needs, that is, to redefine the boundaries within which he can work. Nietzsche thus begins with a redefinition of the object of the history of literature. "I consider it as history of the use of language according to norms of art. It includes prose and poetry. Excluded is therefore non-artful usage like everyday communication, as well as real erudite or scientific writing" (GgL; KGW II/5, 8). This definition seems to be too essential and not so convincing. In reality there are two points of this definition, which are very important for Nietzsche's general interpretation of Greek literature.

First of all, the center of the definition: "the history of the use of language according to norms of art," or, in German, the "kunstmäßige Behandlung der Sprache." Nietzsche does not explain clearly what he means by the adjective "kunstmäßig." If we consult other occurrences of this term (GgL; KGW, II/5, 7), it appears evident that it is related to the typical expression of art in opposition to the common use of language in everyday life. The particular use of the old-fashioned "kunstmäßig," instead of the more obvious "künstlerisch," depends on a specific semantic exigency. According to the *Deutsches Wörterbuch* of the brothers Grimm (1854–61, Vol. 11, Article 2718), this adjective means precisely "according to the norms of the art," and it is opposed as the "artificiosum" to nature. Art is also understood as the capacity to produce an artwork according to the norms of a particular art. The definition concerns also only the formal aspects, the composition, the structure, which are the result of the "savoir faire" of the artist. Aesthetic pleasure is here excluded from the definition. On the contrary, the "art," and the norm become now the protagonists of this literature. The judgment about an artwork of the language cannot be also a judgment about the beauty, but rather about the success of its composition: "well done."

The second element I would like to point out in this definition is the undifferentiated inclusion of poetry and prose as forms of the artwork. The coexistence of these two forms in his history of literature was not as obvious as one might think, but had greater and stronger justifications than normally conceived. In the modern handbooks of Greek literature, both prose and poetry are usually included in lists of classical works, but their inclusion depends on historical exigency, to offer a complete panoramic of the ancient literature. There is indeed a particular distinction between what is considered pure art (poetry, epic, lyric, elegy, tragedy) and what, on the contrary, is considered only literature (the prose works of the historiographer, of the philosopher, the rhetorical speeches of lawyers and politicians) and becomes interesting only from a historical point of view. The formal distinction between these two categories is the use of meter: poetry is the designation for works which use meter, prose for the works that do not.

According to his definition of the artwork as the use of language according to specific norms of an art, Nietzsche insists ardently on the reappraisal of this completely modern caesura between prose genres and poetic genres. First of all, he highlights the fundamental difference between rhythm and meter. Even if meter is properly lacking in prose, this does not mean that prose lacks rhythm. Rhythm, and not meter, is in Nietzsche's opinion the very basis of each "Kunstwerk der Sprache".[15]

Meter is only one of the possible manifestations of rhythm. Even if poetry benefits from a direct translation of rhythm into the measure of the syllables (i.e. meter), prose works also show a measure of their internal time, as is evident in the case of rhetoric. In fact "poetry may well have the μέτρα, but the Prose has the *measure* [*das Metron*] in itself" (GgL; KGW II/5, 30–1). This lack of distinction between metrical composition and prose works in Greece is evident, for example, in the case of rhetoric, which is one of the most complex and structured arts of that time. A rhetorical speech has nothing to do with the spontaneity of the common language. On the contrary, it is formally deep, structured, and artificial; its rhythm can be calculated in each singular part of the speech. Another example given by Nietzsche is elegy. Even though elegy employs meter and can also be recognized as poetry formally, it was instead considered as a form of prose in Greece. The elegiac distich and the iambic were also meter, but were more used (for example in the dialogs of tragedy) to give the effect of prose.[16]

After having articulated the rough borders of the "kunstmässige Behandlung der Sprache," Nietzsche comes to define the fundamental issues that dominate its development: "[...] three main points of view: A the artworks of language themselves, B their effects and their audience, C their producers [the artists]" (GgL; KGW II/5, 30–1). Of these (A) and (B) are most important for our discussion, because Nietzsche seems to pay more attention to the cultural factors which produced this literature, more than to the personalities of the artists. The "Author" is the most notable absentee in his history of literature. When he treats the point (C) at the end of the third part of his lectures, Nietzsche will speak only about the external (social, economical, political) influences received from the artists, and not about personal intuitions or artistic differentiations. Studying the "Kunstwerk der Sprache" means studying the culture that produced it: the historical context, the occasion on which the artistic creation is presented, its effects, its intended audience, the materiality of its language in terms of dialect and style, in terms of its composition, and in its relations with other arts like dance, music, dramaturgy—all elements necessary for the creation of a phenomenon such as the "Kunstwerk der Sprache."

After the enumeration of the fundamental questions, Nietzsche chooses a method to follow in the historical representation of literature. While defining the structure of his lecture, Nietzsche consults and confronts several literary histories by some common scholars of his time. In some cases, his impressions are clearly negative, for instance, on the first book of Theodor Bergk's *Litteraturgeschichte* (Bergk 1872), which contains "nicht ein Fünkchen griechischen Feuers und griechischen Sinnes [not one single spark of the Greek fire and soul]" (NF 1875, 3[29]; KSA 8, 23). Another denigrating judgment is about the "schlechte Sudelei [terrible botch]" (EkP; KGW II/3, 406) of Rudolf Nicolai (Nicolai 1867). Nietzsche pays much attention to the *History of Literature* by Gottfried Bernhardy (Bernhardy 1836–45), due to its consideration of Greek literature in its socio-political contexts and for its attempt to reconstruct through those contexts the "Weltanschauung" of the Greek world. Nietzsche's lectures follow Bernhardy's *Literature* both in inspiration and execution in terms of the refinement and richness of its historical, linguistic, and cultural observations. But Bernhardy's history lacks the decisive structural element insofar as it only describes ancient poetry and ignores prose—something, as we saw, Nietzsche opposes in his own lectures.[17] The history of literature that Nietzsche references perhaps most often, though, is that by Karl Otfried Müller (Müller 1841). Despite the fact that Nietzsche blames it for a certain superficiality, it is, together with the handbook of Bergk, one of the few handbooks that Nietzsche explicitly and frequently mentions as a source.[18]

With respect to the composition and structure of these alternative histories, the most common criterion applied is that of a general chronological treatment of the whole of ancient literature. This is done in two ways: first, by making a general consideration of all ancient works indifferently and in chronological order (Bernhardy); or, second, by treating the individual literary genres framed within a chronological succession of historical-cultural "epochs" (Bergk). Nicolai attempted a hybrid approach, nearer to Nietzsche's, as a compromise between the autonomous treatment of the different literary genres and traditional chronology; but, per Nietzsche's judgment above, the results were in fact quite confused. So even if the contents of Nietzsche's history of literature lack in originality, he seems to claim a large autonomy for the compositional structure of his cycle of lectures:

> To structure all this, it would be possible to use the rubrics above [A, B, C] as titles for chapters and to discuss the associated phenomena from the beginning to the end of the literature within each chapter. Otherwise, to describe the artworks according to their historical succession. [...] Finally, third, one could treat the main literary genres isolated and each of them again according to the given points of view either chronologically-historically, or to average. I make the attempt for the first time, and I don't want to select the most difficult method for me. (GgL; KGW II/5, 8–9)

The principal method Nietzsche utilizes follows the beginning and development of the literary genres in Greece, applies fundamental questions to each (what is their occasion?—language?—audience?), and through them gradually reconstructs the panorama of ancient literary production. The choice to treat texts according to their literary genres is perhaps more problematic today than in Nietzsche's time, due to the delegitimizing of the concept of literary genre since at least Benedetto Croce.[19] Literary genres for Nietzsche are not merely pretexts to give an arbitrary classification to the literary heritage of Antiquity. They are instead the forms in which the creativity of Greeks spontaneously expressed itself. Literary genres are necessary forms of the Greek spirit on a par with social structures and religious beliefs.

Far from a consideration of art as pure entertainment and disinterested pleasure, Nietzsche considers the birth of the "Kunstwerk der Sprache" in Greece, in its multiple forms, as a necessary phenomenon related to a precise utility. He attributes this utility to its preeminent importance in the cult of gods, and an associated requirement in all other manifestations of the Greek world.[20] All kinds of art in Greece were occasional, episodic. The origin of each literary genre derives from this variety of occasions for which the art was necessary: the cult, the feast, the symposium, and the agon.[21] The differentiation between literary genres is thus from the start quite rigid and concerns a number of socio-cultural elements that the historian of literature cannot ignore in the analysis of a work of art. Above all, the language: the different Greek dialects testify to the origin of the different genres by the different Greek tribes and disclose their development and hegemonies. Beyond language, the meter differentiates the various poetical genres, and so, too, the tonality and the instrumentation of the musical accompaniment. The subject and topics, the composition, and indeed the performative occasion itself, were all determined by tradition. The rigid norms of the system of literary genres determine the forms in which each artwork exerted its influence on his public, by codifying a particular ethos and a corresponding effect on the public. That, for Nietzsche, is the correct point of view from which to interpret the whole Greek literature:

> Now, an extraordinary fear of all new education dominated in the earlier πόλις. For the polis measure and character were determined by rules and normative education: One was afraid that the loosening of this measure, caused by external teachers, could destroy the city. [...] This added to the feeling, that these poets and musicians could enravish and overcome and lead you to anything: enthusiasm and alarm. The cities therefore sought again and again to force these influences inside the limits of law. One accepted for example an innovation in the music, this was declared legal, but then stated even stronger: "now, no more!"—(GgL; KGW II/5, 298)

Every poetical composition was codified so as to produce a particular emotive effect, generating a certain type of feeling proper to the occasion: the joy of victory, the pain of death, the exaltation of a god, the euphoric drunkenness of the symposium. In response to each song the soul reacts to a different feeling according to the composite effect of tonality, meter, and musical rhythm.

But also in this case, we must advise caution in considering this correspondence between artworks and a particular influence on the affects from the point of view of the modern experience. To illustrate this correlation between poetical genres and action upon the affects, Nietzsche draws reference to a distinction proper to the ancients between the different types of characters (ἤθη). The idea that each literary genre corresponds to a specific character, to which it always stands in a causal relationship, is an ancient tradition that becomes a first theoretical systematization only with the musical theories of Damon.[22] According to this theory, each poetical Greek genre has its effect in different ways according to three fundamental typologies:

> The ancient Greek technicians divided the *cantica* [songs] according to their ἤθος [character] (how the sentiment was affected). There were three main ἤθη [characters]: the διασταλτικὸν [diastaltic], expression of μεγαλοπρέπεια [a great soul]; the συσταλτικὸν [systaltic], the contrary, the character of unmanly pains and of the low comic poetry. Third, the ἡσυχαστικὸν [character hesychastic]. (GL; KGW II/3, 15)[23]

To this rigid cage of genre rules a particular effect was always associated, and, accordingly, a given audience. The author addressed his audience according to his genre's structure and the audience reciprocated with the same efficacy since it was already prepared to receive the artwork in a particular way. In his lectures on literature, Nietzsche insists on the value of the audience for a correct evaluation of the artwork. It was the audience—those who were to be influenced through precise tonal, stylistic techniques—for whom the works were guided into their particular forms.

What happens, on the contrary, to this correspondence between the ethos of the audience and the ethos of the artwork in a literary culture, such as the modern culture? The author of a literary culture composes his works so that others can read them. In this case the audience is no more a particular audience (here and now at the moment of the recitation), but it becomes anyone who can read. This is a destabilizing factor, because the direct receiver of the artwork (the audience in the theater or in the public square) will be removed. The work hereby frees itself from the occasion which was its principal motive, and renounces the specific references to common experience between the public and the artist. The formal and compositional structure responsible for the calculation of the effects on the audience is dismantled, and the feelings and passions directly enter in the frame of the artwork in order to have a direct influence on its audience. This phenomenon is what Nietzsche criticized already in 1867 and considered a "Grundirrtum," an unforgivable misunderstanding of the character of art: when art, music, and poetry become the direct expression of feelings—the "Sprache des Gefühls" (NF 1867/68, 26[1] and 43[1]; KGW I/4, 32 and 127–8)—it loses its original role of controlling and ruling the feelings themselves. Here Nietzsche's decisive confrontation with modern literature shows itself once more.[24] Modern prose has lost its capacity of exerting an immediate effect on its audience and it must replace it with giving itself these affects directly as contents. The prose becomes intellectual in order to convince reason, passionate in order to move the passions, etc. If ancient prose ruled over the passions by arousing and assuaging them through rhythm, then modern prose becomes unseemly by altering the rhythm in order to produce the affect of the passion.

His diagnosis in the Basel lectures of this degeneration persisted in Nietzsche's reflections long enough to motivate his formulation of the "grand style" in *Menschliches, Allzumenschliches*: "Grand style originates when the beautiful carries off the victory over the monstrous" (HH 96; KSA 2, 596; translation from Hollingdale). The victory of beauty over the immense and the tremendous is the victory of rules and artificial action over the natural. The keys used by Nietzsche to rethink the modern relationship to literature are in my opinion essentially two: the discovery of the centrality of rhythm and memory in ancient civilization. Rhythm constitutes the framework of all ancient compositions (music, dance or literary work) from the most ancient lyrics to the latest orations (as an integral part of the "style" or "character" of the oration). Nietzsche recognizes in rhythm a primary value, because it is one of man's first forms of perception of the world and had a central role in the cult of the god (GS 84; KSA 3, 440). The capacity of effect of the "Kunstwerk der Sprache" was also formally involved in a triad of elements which were typical of the oral tradition: the norm of the specific genre, the rhythm at the base of its formal structure are responsible for the particular oral expression, and the memory which allowed the handing down of the tradition, and the persistence of its effects on the people of the Greek nation.

The correlation between rhythm, norm given by rhythm, and interiorization of the norm through memory is according to Nietzsche the essential feature of Greek experience. In fact, a single word sufficed for the Greeks to define this entire process:

"nomos," which means at the same time the norm of a musical structure, the law of the polis, and, as cultural outcome, the object of the oral tradition. This triad, rhythm/norm/memory, is not however unidirectional and does not designate necessarily a static configuration: it is not the formula of the tradition understood as immutability and unchanged reiteration of the past. On the contrary, we are facing an active formula that is able to modify a society and to modify itself. Greek society has indeed developed itself and has changed its forms through the implementation of this formula within a variety of artistic, social, and politic realizations, from the most ancient time to the Hellenistic and Roman epochs. If Nietzsche studied, at the very beginning, this formula in Greece, he was not, however, reluctant to extrapolate it as a function that could be applied to different contexts, for example to the context of modernity. If ancient Greek society made the whole development of this process possible, thanks to the essentially oral character of its culture, this does not mean that the same procedure cannot be applied to a literary culture too, such as modern culture. The interdependence between cultural norm and ethos, transformations of the character, is maybe one of Nietzsche's most interesting intuitions about the ancient Greek world.

5. Conclusion

If we consider the entire development of Nietzsche's reflection about the history of literature, we should certainly admit, at least from a formal and stylistic point of view, that we find ourselves confronted by a work in progress. His Basel lectures and his notebook entries alike cannot indeed aspire to be considered a completed scientific work. Nevertheless, this reflection, above all in the *Lectures on History of Greek Literature*, demonstrates a strong internal coherence, which allows us to speak of a general and original interpretation of the ancient Greek world by Nietzsche. The core of this interpretation is, in my opinion, the recognition of the fundamentally oral nature of ancient Greek civilization. Thanks to a careful analysis of the panorama of ancient literary production in the *Lectures on the History of Greek Literature*, Nietzsche tries to highlight all the elements that testify to the centrality of orality in Greek experience from the very beginning in ancient times. The emphasis given to these elements by Nietzsche seems to me firstly to be functional to a reconstruction of the different levels of ancient time communication, which, if they cannot be directly perceived by a modern scholar, can at least be reconstructed by means of their imagination.

However, Nietzsche is not only interested in artworks, even though they are the best expression of how the ancient oral structure of communication worked. His reflection is broader and includes all of ancient society, in its different epochs and constitutive elements. The entire effect of the linguistic work of art was indeed, according to Nietzsche, possible only within an oral culture, more specifically, a non-*literary* culture. What is particularly interesting at this point is how Nietzsche tries to offer a phenomenology of the mechanisms that are at the base of both those realities: on one hand the ancient oral tradition, on the other hand the literary traditions, such as the culture of Nietzsche's time, our contemporary culture, but also, for several aspects, the ancient culture too. The transition from the "Kunstwerk der

Sprache" to a literary culture, a definitive "Leseliteratur," occurred in Greece only after Aristotle, especially with the widening of Hellas in the Hellenistic kingdoms. It can be explained by the modification of the necessities and of the feeling of the public. The question whether the emergence of a "Leseliteratur" in Greece is a phenomenon of decadence or else a legitimately progressive development that is justified by the mutation of the necessities of Greek society remains very ambiguous and problematic indeed. In Nietzsche's opinion, the whole history of Greek civilization can be interpreted in the light of the conflict between orality and writing, between oral tradition and the progressive affirmation of the medium of writing, which is evident at all levels and in all epochs of ancient society.

The introduction and the establishment of writing in Greece cannot be considered, in Nietzsche's view, as a "revolution" or a "fracture." It is on the contrary a progressive and continuous process. That seems to me to be one of the most original elements of Nietzsche's interpretation. In fact, according to his reconstruction, this process cannot be said to be ever really concluded in Greek civilization, which shows until the latest epochs a strong mixture of both orality and writing. If we consider how this kind of study about orality in ancient Greece has been enormously successful in the later contributions of Eric Havelock and Walter James Ong (to quote only two of the most important names), it is impossible not to define Nietzsche as a pioneer. His intuitions are really very close, even in detail, to the mature reflection on orality through the twentieth century and the conceptual systematization of Eric Havelock. With Havelock in particular, Nietzsche share the awareness that Greek culture has conserved its oral character until the latest epochs. More radical than Havelock, Nietzsche is convinced that not only the earliest works (the Homeric epic and the ancient lyric), but the prose works and the written works of rhetoric and philosophy, cannot hide their fundamentally oral structure in the weaving of their texts. However, it is difficult if not impossible to demonstrate a direct influence of these theories on these later scholars. Nietzsche's Basel lectures remain indeed essentially unknown even today. We can however take into account these deep reflections about orality in Nietzsche's work at least as evidence of the existence of this discussion in the second half of the nineteenth century in Germany. In this sense, the analysis of the tradition of the studies on Homeric poems would be very important as it is frequently discussed in Nietzsche. In fact, this particular philological tradition, which has more ancient roots, constitutes the red thread running through the reflection on orality and the related question on memory through the eighteenth and nineteenth centuries and it comes to maturity in the twentieth century with the fundamental contributions of Milman Parry.

Notes

1   These lectures are divided into three parts, held without interruption during three semesters (WS 1874/75; SS 1875; WS 1875/76) and they constitute hereby the most important and most complete example of Nietzsche's didactical activity in Basel. The preparation for these lectures kept him busy more than any other and the variety of

consulted texts is impressive. All translations from this and other works are my own unless otherwise noted.

2   As we know, Nietzsche does not read the edition of Burckhardt's lectures on *Griechische Kulturgeschichte*, because it was published only posthumously, many years after the death of the philosopher. Nietzsche could not also attend these courses; however, he knew their contents thanks to notices reorganized in five red notebooks from his student Luis Kelterborn, who had attended these courses. Nietzsche could consult these notebooks from 1875.

3   Cf. NF 1867/68, 52[31; 66]; 56[1–8]; 57[27; 41–2; 58]; 58[58]; 61[2–3]; KGW I/4, 223–5; 276–7; 361–9; 394–6; 404–5; 498–9; 532–7.

4   If we go through the titles of Nietzsche's philological activity we find indeed a work on the artificial fixation of the Διαδοκαί (successions) of the pre-Platonic philosophers, many texts on Theognis and in particular *Zur Geschichte der Theognideischen Spruchsammlung* (1867), a work on the πίνακες (catalogues) of the works of Aristotle's works, and many works on Diogenes Laertius and on the Suda lexicon. In particular these last works are important to show that meta-level of Nietzsche's considerations on the history of literature. Diogenes Laertius' *Lives and Opinions of Eminent Philosophers* and the Suda lexicon are indeed not only ancient works but also historical and critical-literary works and they give Nietzsche as much information on the literary tradition as on the methods and the tendencies of the ancient historical-literary tradition.

5   In his article *Zur Geschichte der Theognideischen Spruchsammlung* (KGW II/1, 1–58) Nietzsche tries to reconstruct the history of the text-tradition of Theognides' anthology. He demonstrates how it is the result of later compiling, which has turned an elegiac author active in symposiac circles into an uplifting reading for the education of youth. Theognis' anthology would also be an arbitrary collation, maybe originally with parodistic intention. Through successive compiling, disassembling, and removal of the materials which were not conforming to the expectations, the anthology was finally attributed to the gnomological genre, even though any concrete proof in this sense does not exist (cf. also Jensen 2008).

6   Under the factors that must be considered in the study of ancient tradition, under the falsifying pseudepigraphical tendencies, Nietzsche always puts the question of the homonymous, of the patronymics, of the false attributions and, not least, what he calls "Die Methode des Titels [The method of the title]" (NF 1867/68, 57[27]; KGW, I/4, 394), namely the main base where the tradition attributes titles, names, to the ancient works.

7   We can find the same reflection about the comparative methods in linguistics in the *Enzyklopädie* in the part "Über Sprachvergleichung und klassische Philologie" (EkP; KGW II/3, 390) and in the later work *Über die Zukunft unserer Bildungsanstalten* (FEI; KSA 1, 704).

8   "Literature appears once in Tacitus [...] and it corresponds to 'Alphabet.' Elsewhere it is the art of reading and writing, the translation of Grammatik" (GgL; KGW II/5, 9).

9   The same difficulty in defining oral experience is described by Walter J. Ong (Ong 1982, 12–14). He gives a list of the many attempts by scholars to give a name to this tradition (above all, the definition "oral literature") and he shows the same skepticism about the legitimacy of these definitions, which he compares with the attempt to define an automobile as a horse without wheels.

10 In particular in NF 1867/68, 52[31]; KGW I/4, 223–5 the term "Philosophema" is

reinforced by the expressive paragon with the dominant religions ("Herrschenden Religionen") or ethics.

11 Lectures on *Die Griechischen Lyriker* (SS 1869, SS 1871, SS 1874, WS 1874/75, WS 1878/79). Nietzsche utilizes these lessons in WS 1874/75, to integrate §7 *Die Hauptformen der lyrischen Kunstwerke* into his lessons on *Geschichte der griechischen Literatur*.

12 To explain this point Nietzsche uses a paradox. According to him in GgL; II/5, 195, 308, Socrates did not write because he had never learnt to. The paradox of an illiterate Socrates is quickly explained from Nietzsche itself. He doesn't argue that Socrates could not write and read, because these basic abilities were common in Greece at his time. Nietzsche means that Socrates was not able to write according to the stylistic norms required of a writer of his time, namely the rhetorical norms. Socrates did not need to be "cultivated" in the ancient sense (i.e. having a rhetorical education) to be a philosopher, because his teaching was eminently oral. On the contrary, if he had wanted to write, like his student Plato, he would have become a cultivated writer. Socrates was uncultivated in the sense that he was illiterate, i.e. he had no literary education. This difference was not yet exclusive at his time, but it becomes more and more central in the Hellenistic world.

13 "'Classical' is a political concept transformed to others conditions. [...] But 'classicus' in the sense of 'the first class' goes back to Cato [...]. Since the Renaissance the Roman writers from Cicero to August were called 'classical,' and only in a broader sense all Greek and Roman writers. 'Classical Antiquity' occupies the first place among all antiquities. Here lies an aesthetic judgment" (EkP; KGW II/3, 341).

14 In those lectures Nietzsche seems to be decidedly skeptical regarding the possibility of achieving culture, in the highest sense, in the modern age. On the contrary, even in 1872, in the lectures *Über die Zukunft unserer Bildungsanstalten*, he seeks a conciliation between the literary and the unliterary level, to achieve a concrete pedagogical project, a project of which we have isolated elements in the *Encyklopädie* too. But the chronology of these works (the third part of the GgL is of 1875/76) indicates an evolution of this reflection towards an increasingly marked skepticism.

15 For a more exhaustive treatment of the question of rhythm in earlier Nietzsche works and in the Basel lectures, see Günther 2008.

16 For these discussion about the groundlessness of the modern distinction between poetry and prose and the other types of formal categorization of the ancient literary genres, cf.: GgL; KGW II/5, 27–32, §4, *Prosa und Poesie [und ihre Hauptgattungen] in ihrem Unterschiede* and the article on Simonide's "Lamentation of Danae" (KGW II/1, 59).

17 Bernhardy actually had intended to dedicate a third book of his *Literature* to ancient prose, but this last book was never published.

18 See for Bergk, GgL; KGW II/5, 28, 33, 103, 152, 180, 281–2, and for Otfried Müller, GgL; KGW II/5, 75, 132.

19 Benedetto Croce considers the categories of the literary genres as epiphenomena of the artworks. They have been fixed by scholars with the intention of simplifying the various panoramas of the ancient works and to make of them a more comfortable object of studies (Croce 1900, 41). Croce is on the contrary convinced of the unity of the phenomenon of the artistic inspiration, even thought in the impressive variety of the forms in which it concretizes itself. The literary genres are only arbitrary

catalogings in which the artist suffers an unjustified constriction to his talent (Croce 1920, 44; 1935, 22).

20 Nietzsche persists in this theory in the published works too. See above all §84 "Vom Ursprunge der Poesie," in *Die fröhliche Wissenschaft* (GS 84; KSA 3, 440).

21 The epic genre was originally recited in public competitions related to the main festivity. Tragedy and Comedy were related to public occasions and competitions, and to the holy feasts too. The elegy was on the contrary more strictly reserved for the private sphere of the symposium. The hymn has as many particular genres as the various occasions of its use: encomiastic, mournful, triumphant, etc.

22 Damon was a Greek musicologist of the fifth century BC. We know his work, the oration *Areopagitic*, only through fragments and other testimonies. His famous theory of the ἤθη (characters) was then used by Plato in his *Republic* to explain music as a force, capable of dominating the human soul.

23 The music of the tragedy (τραγικὸς τρόπος) has an ἦθος διασταλτικὸν, because it should show high contents, the comedy has a character συσταλτικὸν, because of its lower language level.

24 When Nietzsche confronts modern literature, the repeatedly referenced exemplar is Richard Wagner, who considers music the language of passion. Wagner, even if he is a musician and not a writer, is the apotheosis of the modern literary society, incapable of immediacy unless it is the immediacy of the affect. He is the novelist/musician, the musician, who has introduced writing even in music. "Wagner has no real trust in music: he introduces related emotions for giving the impression of the character of greatness. He tunes himself with others, he offers stirring drinks to his audience, to make them believe that the music has made them drunk" (NF 1878, 30[73]; KSA 8, 535). We can also find a lot of references for this particular criticism of Wagner in all of Nietzsche's works. To give only a brief list of the most important quotations: BGE; 91 KSA 5, 90; CW; KSA 6, 16; HH; KSA 2, 698, 436–7. In this critique of Wagner's *Sprache des Gefühls* Nietzsche follows, as we know, Eduard von Hanslick (1865).

Works cited

Bergk, Theodor (1872): *Griechische Literaturgeschichte*. Berlin (Weidmann). Vol. 1.

Bernhardy, Gottfried (1836–45): *Grundriß der griechischen Litteratur mit einem vergleichenden Überblick der römischen*. Halle (Eduard Anton).

Boeckh, August (1877): *Encyklopädie und Methodologie der philologischen Wissenschaften*. Bratuscheck (ed.). Leipzig (Teubner).

Croce, Benedetto (1900): *Estetica come scienza dell'espressione e linguistica generale*. Bari (Laterza).

—(1920): "Breviario di estetica." In his *Nuovi saggi di estetica*. Bari (Laterza).

—(1935): "Aesthetica in nuce." In his *Ultimi saggi di estetica*. Bari (Laterza).

Gerratana, Federico (1994): "'Jetzt zieht mich das Allgemein-Menschliche an.' Ein Streifzug durch Nietzsches Aufzeichnungen zu einer 'Geschichte der literarischen Studien.'" In Tilman Borsche, Federico Gerratana, and Aldo Venturelli (eds): *"Centauren-Geburten." Wissenschaft, Kunst und Philosophie beim jungen Nietzsche*. Berlin and New York (Walter de Gruyter), 326–50.

Grimm, Jakob and Wilhelm Grimm (1854–61): *Deutsches Wörterbuch*. Leipzig (Hirzel).

Günther, Friederike Felicitas (2008): *Rhythmus beim frühen Nietzsche*. Berlin (Walter de Gruyter).

Havelock, Eric A. (1963): *Preface to Plato*. Oxford (Basil Blackwell).

—(1982): *The Literate Revolution in Greece and its Cultural Consequences*. Princeton (Princeton University Press).

—(1986): *The Muse Learns to Write: Reflections on Orality and Literacy from Antiquity to the Present*. New Haven (Yale University Press).

Hollingdale, R. G. (ed. and trans.) (1986): *Human all-too-Human*. Cambridge (Cambridge University Press).

Jensen, Anthony (2008): "Anti-Politicality and Agon in Nietzsche's Philology." In Herman Siemens (ed.): *Nietzsche, Power and Politics*. Berlin (Walter de Gruyter), 281–307.

Müller, Karl Otfried (1841): *Geschichte der griechischen Literatur bis auf das Zeitalter Alexander's*. Breslau (Josef Max und Komp).

Nicolai, Rudolf (1867): *Geschichte der gesamten griechischen Literatur: ein Versuch*. Magdeburg (Heinrichshofen).

Ong, Walter J. (1982): *Orality and Literacy*. London and New York (Methuen).

von Hanslick, Eduard (1865): *Vom Musikalisch-Schönen. Ein Beitrag zur Revision der Aesthetik der Tonkunst*. Leipzig (R. Wiegel).

von Reibnitz, Barbara (1994): "Vom 'Sprachkunstwerk' zu 'Leselitteratur.' Nietzsches Blick auf die griechische Literaturgeschichte als Gegenentwurf zur aristotelischen Poetik." In Tilman Borsche, Federico Gerratana, and Aldo Venturelli (eds): *"Centauren-Geburten." Wissenschaft, Kunst und Philosophie beim jungen Nietzsche*. Berlin and New York (Walter de Gruyter), 47–66.

Westphal, Rudolf and August Rossbach (1867): *Metrik der Griechen im Vereine mit den übrigen musischen Künsten*. Leipzig (Teubner). Vol. 1.

9

Greek Audience: Performance and Effect of the Different Literary Genres in Nietzsche's *Philologica*[1]

Vivetta Vivarelli

1. Audience in Greek poetry

As early as 1864, in one of his first important philological studies on the Megarian poet Theognis, 20-year-old Nietzsche paid special attention to the social context in which a poem arose and was situated (KGW I/3, 464–5). Concerning the reception of Theognis in antiquity,[2] Nietzsche pointed out that the elegies were destined for convivial gatherings of aristocrats and only in this context were they interpreted correctly, for they were not considered to have an ethical meaning. The middle classes subsequently approached them with different values and a different mentality, finding ethical principles where once everything had been viewed from an aristocratic stand-point. The context, therefore, the "horizon of expectation," reflects on the work itself and its meaning. The lectures on Greek lyric poetry, which Nietzsche was to give some years later,[3] began with a warning: to approach Greek lyrics, it was necessary to abandon the modern perpective of a "reading public." No Greek poetry, even that of the classical period, had a reader, but only a listener who was, moreover, also a spectator. Poetry, as *praktikon*, was linked to musical diction (KGW II/2, 107 and 375). Nietzsche alludes here to an ancient classification regarding the triad of arts which needed "representation," that is, which had to be presented to the spectator or listener through the activity of a singer, actor, or rhapsode: music, orchestikos, and poetry.[4] The Greeks knew poetry only through song. Text and music arose together, created by the same artist, as would happen later with the troubadors and the Minnesänger. The audience were therefore listeners of a sung text. The attention to the recipient is the corollary that directly results from the importance that Nietzsche attributes to the "Vortrag," the performance, and therefore, to its effect, the "Wirkung."[5] It is not by chance that in this context (KGW II/2, 109) Nietzsche, speaking of Terpander, mentions Westphal's *History of Music*, which claims that "the origin of music is as ancient as poetry given that everywhere the earliest poetry was sung" (Westphal and Hermann 1864, 2).[6]

Nietzsche shared an interest in the bards and the active role of the audience with his older colleague from Basel, Jacob Burckhardt, whose weekly lectures on the study of history he attended in 1870 and whose *Griechische Culturgeschichte* he read in 1875. In the second chapter (on the "Greeks and their Mythology"), Burckhardt points out the interaction between the bards and their audience:

> The Greek audience consisted mostly of city dwellers with, undeniably, extraordinary gifts for the understanding and elaboration of what they heard, as well as with the will and the capacity to devote themselves to it continuously; such an audience gave an ideal reception to the art of the bards, without whom the dissemination of the legenda which now became universally known in Greece would have been unthinkable. (Burckhardt [1898] 1999, 24)

In the chapter on the agonal age, Burckhardt quotes the description by the poet of the Homeric hymn to Apollo of the splendid society of the Ionians as they appeared at the festivals of Delos (Burckhardt [1898] 1999, 162).

In a note from the summer of 1875, Nietzsche opposed those philologists who "torment themselves over the question of whether Homer really wrote" as they did not understand that "Greek art harboured a long and intimate animosity towards writing and did not want to be read" (NF 1875, 5[114]; KSA 8, 70). Nietzsche in this passage implicitly refers to a text by Joachim Adam Hartung, an author whom he cites more than once in his work on Simonides, as well as in his lessons on Greek poetry. In his introduction, Hartung highlighted the difference between a people accustomed to reading and one used to listening, considering that poetry chronologically precedes prose:

> What we call reading, for the ancients was listening. [...] Prose is not fit for reading out loud, let alone for reciting or declaiming. But the listener [...] demands *orationem numeris modisque clausam*, that is to say, verse not prose. (Hartung 1856, V–VI)[7]

Hartung, then, goes back to the origins of poetry, prayers, magic formulas, and oaths, suggesting a very important aspect of "Wirkung" to Nietzsche, that is, the enchantment of rhythm, its compelling quality:

> these magic formulas are meant to have a binding force, even a compelling power over gods and spirits. But to have this binding force, they must themselves have a formally binding formula and their magic power is in their rhythm, metrics and rhyme. (Hartung 1856, VI)

The influence on the gods that can be had through magic formulas, prayers, and exorcisms is equivalent to the power of enchantment over someone listening to the rhythmic cadence of poetry.

The audience and the type of society for which the Homeric poems were created were also a crucial point of the Homeric issue for Nietzsche. According to Nietzsche, Wolf was the first to acknowledge the importance of an audience: no public would have been able to listen to and understand or grasp at one and the same time the whole of Homer's work during a performance. In his lecture notes on the *History of Greek*

Literature (KGW II/5, 279, 294, 298), Nietzsche outlined the contentious problem of how Homer's work was transmitted by referring to a fundamental passage of Wolf's *Prolegomena to Homer* (1795):

> it is scarcely credible, and no authority attests, that a number of singers were ever brought together for several days or weeks to pour out such lengthy poems to the listener [...] but no nation was so ingenious as to make it possible for someone to appear at such a public show without spectators or for the length of a performance to exceed 15,000 verses. Similarly, if Homer lacked readers, then I certainly do not understand what in the world could have impelled him to plan and think out poems which were so long and were strung together with an unbroken connection of parts. (Wolf [1795] 1985, 115f.)

Nietzsche was fascinated by a striking image that Wolf used, which pointed out the problem of the absence of readers: The *Iliad* and the *Odyssey* seemed to Wolf to be

> an enormous ship, constructed somewhere inland in the first beginnings of navigation: its maker would have had no access to winches and wooden rollers to push it forward, and therefore no access to the sea itself in which he could make some trial of his skill. (Wolf [1795] 1985, 116)

In the same lectures Nietzsche also explained the birth of literacy and a reading public as poetry went beyond the boundaries of a closed community (KGW II/5, 296–302). To start from artworks for which there was no written word but which were conceived for a performance means assigning an important role to the recipient, their mentality, and the religious and social context to which they belonged. It also means dealing with the fluid and elusive cultural and social realities of Greek life and endorsing a philological tradition which does not rely on textual criticism alone (the "Textgeschichte"), but which incorporates extra-textual elements as well; this approach fits with Nietzsche's growing interest in historical-cultural, antiquarian, anthropological, and ethnological studies.

2. The public in the different literary genres

Attention to those watching or listening is a crucial element in the first paragraph of *The History of Greek Literature* (the lectures held between 1874/75 and 1878/79), entitled "Vorbegriffe" (preliminary concepts). Here Nietzsche proposes right at the start abandoning any reference to written literature in favor of an ancient tradition in which all "the artists of word" are thinking only of "listeners and spectators" while conceiving their works (cf. von Reibnitz 1994). He then considers the history of Greek literature from three different perspectives: the second of these specifically concerns works of art seen in relation to their "effect on the public." In the third paragraph, entitled "Verbindung der sprachlichen Kunstwerke mit anderen Künsten" (affinities between language artworks and other arts), Nietzsche highlights the connections between song, mimic dancing, and oratory: a sort of "Schauspielerkunst" is expected from the orator.[8] Hence it was no coincidence that Demosthenes had studied and trained with great actors: his eloquence was compared to "corybantic enthusiasm" (KGW II/5, 27). In this series of lectures Nietzsche begins his discussion by focusing on the recipients of artwork before going on to reflect on the different genres as well. The third paragraph is entitled "das ursprüngl. [sic] Publikum jeder Gattung" (the Originary Public of Each Genre) and begins with the following words:

> every Greek genre has its own public, this is very important. This does not mean that every Greek work of art has later found its admirers: one could say that the public is there and it is just for this public one finds the work of art that suits it best. Without his audience Homer would not have been possible, like Sophocles without the Athenian citizens. (KGW II/5, 289)

Referring to Goethe, who was a friend of Wolf, Nietzsche then makes a distinction between the arts of the rhapsode and those of the mime, "the first with his circle of peaceful listeners, the second with his restless and impatient public" (KGW II/5, 289). According to Nietzsche, the birth of epos and drama can be traced back to the radically different demands of their respective audiences. Nietzsche refers to an essay that Goethe enclosed in a letter to Schiller on December 23, 1797, in which Goethe focuses on the different groups of people surrounding the two types of artists who consequently have different purposes:

> [the rhapsode's] exposition will aim to calm his listeners in order to have them listen gladly and at length [...]. The mime on the other hand [...] wants the sufferings of his soul and body to be perceived, his hardships shared, and that through him one may forget about oneself [...]. Spectators and listeners must remain in a continuous tension of the senses, must not reach reflection, must follow things passionately, their imagination must be silenced. (Goethe [1797a] 2006, 127f.)

3. The audience in Greek tragedy: From text to stage

A reflection on the role of the recipient of artwork is essential when dealing with ancient tragedy, the performative art *par exellence*. In Aristophanes' *Frogs*, Aeschylus and Euripides argue about the effects their tragedies are having on the public: Aeschylus proudly states that his *Seven against Thebes* and *Persians* inspired Athenians to fight and win, whereas he rebukes Euripides for quelling their warlike virtues (see KGW II/5, 326). In his *Poetics* (6, 1449b 24–8), Aristotle stresses the importance of the effects of tragic drama on its audience. Pity and fear are the tragic emotions and precisely the responses that a good drama should arouse in an audience.[9] But Nietzsche could not share Aristotle's view of tragedy because the latter did not value scenic *opsis*, sight, theatrical performance or music (Aristotle, *Poet.* 1450b16–20; 1453b7–8; cf. NF 1869/70, 3[66]; KSA 7, 78). An even more severe critique is to be found in *The Birth of Tragedy* (§14) regarding a famous passage in Plato's *Gorgias*, in which Socrates says that the aim of drama should be to procure pleasure and gratification in the spectators (Plato, *Gorg.*, 502b–c).[10] For Nietzsche, Socrates is essentially unable to look into the Dionysian abysses (§14). Nietzsche insists on the close connection between music, words, performance, and viewing on stage, on ritual celebrations of which the Athenian public is an integral part. For this reason, he frequently stresses the profound difference between Greek and Shakespearean theater.

As early as the early 1870s, in his lecture notes on Sophocles' *Oedipus Rex* (SS 1870 and 1871), an entire paragraph (§3) was entitled *Publikum der Tragödie*. Nietzsche, agreeing with Wagner, considers tragedy an eminently popular art, not court theater. In this passage he deals with the mass participation and ample number of 20,000 spectators, whose moods had an enormous influence on the subsequent development of theater: "The mood of the listener was solemn: it was a cult. Originally everybody took part in the performance [...] everything worked together to favor meditation" (KGW II/3, 18). The behavior of the Athenian audience was completely different from that of French classic tragedy and the Shakespearean public (KGW II/3, 18–19).[11] In the preceding paragraph, on the subject of the dithyramb, Nietzsche stresses the "popular poetry of the the masses [Volkspoesie der Masse]" during the "fascinating and demonic" Dionysia, in which "all the rapture of feelings erupted," and the fact that at that time cantica were distinguished from each other according to the way they affected the spectator's *ethos*, character or temperament (KGW II/3, 14–15).[12]

In the 1872/74 additions to Aeschylus' *Coefore's Prolegomena* (SS 1869/70; WS 1877/78), Nietzsche mentions the fact that since we have no evidence regarding the performance of the *Oresteia*, we must guess how it was enacted ("ein mühsames Errathen der Dinge" is required). Referring to Aeschylus' "artistic style," he highlights some affects, for instance the musical, or the sinister ("unheimlich") affect, but, above all, he cites the

> sculpture-like element, which was created by the spectators' distance from the stage: limited movement. The perspective element. Masks. Severe hieratic symmetry. Stage set. Stichomythia. Phidias style is anticipated. How can the longevity of the sculpture-like element be explained?" (KGW II/2, 35f.)[13]

In these remarks on "Wirkung," what is striking is the insistence on the coupling of tragedy and sculpture; and of the musical and visual ("anschaulich") elements. Nietzsche finds various models for this nexus, both in classic-romantic literature and in the work of an archeologist such as Joseph Anselm Feuerbach.[14] The notion of a potential interaction between the arts linked to their effects on audience is also found in Nietzsche's lecture notes on lyric poetry among his considerations regarding *iporchemi*: like Plutarch (*Quaestiones Conviviales*, 748a; *Symp.* IX, 15), Nietzsche defines dance as "mute poetry" and poetry as "spoken dance": "the arts of dance and poetry [...] create a sculpture-like representation through words and gestures, united in the genre of iporchemi" (KGW II/2, 144). But when he was writing his lecture notes on *The History of Greek Literature*, Nietzsche was no longer interested in an "aesthetic public" and in the ideal community of Wagnerian art recipients.[15] Even if his primary interest concerns the relations between a certain kind of society and a certain type of art, in his last series of lectures the audience is no longer idealized as it was in his Wagnerian phase. In paragraph 8 ("On the Public of Greek Poets, Orators and Writers"), Nietzsche's conception of the Greek audience changes, and he wonders whether they possessed the capacity to actually comprehend and therefore judge artworks and artists. Here his analysis becomes more articulated and complex. The vision of an idealized public makes room for a sort of disjunction ("Ungereimtheit") between Greek artworks and their aesthetic judgments. This critique does not spare the judgments of philosophers or of the artists themselves. Even Aristophanes' judgments on Euripides (exalted in the *Birth of Tragedy*) are considered "pedantic and finicky." The taste of the public is essentially immature,[16] it does not measure up to the artwork; and, even more importantly, what is really appreciated by most of the public is already a decadent art, since only decadent poets are able to satisfy the tastes of the audience and to understand what they want. But Nietzsche highly doubts that the majority of the spectators in the great age of tragedy could really comprehend a choral ode by Aeschylus, which he called "convoluted, mysterious and darkly foreboding." Nietzsche declares himself convinced that for this public "den stimmungsvollen Eindruck," the atmosphere and the impression of this choral ode, illustrated with music and orchestics rather than the spoken word, was what mattered (KGW II/5, 328).

4. The audience in the history of German classical scholarship of the nineteenth century

For Nietzsche, ritual circumstances such as religious festivals or agonal competitions were crucial moments in the history of Greek culture, from which the pleasure of the spoken works of art ("sprachliches Kunstwerk") derived (KGW II/5, 8). This initial moment had already been the focus not only of the Romantics, but also of historians of antiquity such as Hans Christian Genelli. In his rarely cited piece, *Das Theater zu Athen* (1818), Genelli describes the role of a poet capable of channeling and guiding the disordered energies of the participants into listening attentively by using satyrs and Sileni as masks to distribute roles. Through the use of epic narration and artistic unity in solemn religious celebrations, the poet succeeded in concentrating the assembly on listening alone ("das bloße Zuhören"—Genelli 1818, 10). When he describes the satyrs and Sileni as jumping creatures characterized in joy as in pain by unbridled passion in their expression, tone of voice, and gestures, it is as if Genelli implicitly and symbolically correlated the subjection of these savage creatures to the subjection of the public by the artist. Genelli's text on theater was mentioned in *Der vaticanische Apollo* by Joseph Anselm Feuerbach. This book, published in 1833 and borrowed by Nietzsche in 1869, is characterized by a broad vision of classical antiquity that emphasizes aesthetic pleasure, while the different arts are often viewed within a network of reciprocal relationships (as in Wagner's total artwork). Feuerbach's book was unusual, halfway between a piece of writing on archeology and aesthetics, and a treatise on the visual arts, in which the author tried to find a link between sculpture and Greek tragedy. For this reason, Wagner must have been particularly impressed by it. *The Vatican Apollo* was reviewed by Welcker in the journal he founded, the *Rheinisches Museum*.[17] The chapters of this book, which must have been embarrassing to Welcker, were precisely what attracted the heretical gaze of Nietzsche. Welcker, who nonetheless wrote a good review, stressed that Chapters 13 and 14 do not clarify the relationship between figurative art and poetry (Müller 1848, 631).

Nietzsche quoted an extended portion of this work in his lecture on *Greek Music Drama* (GMD; KSA 1, 518f.). The long quotation ends with the sentence: "If in fact poetry is the most intimate and basic element of the drama, it is however true that it meets together with sculpture." In the next step, Feuerbach stopped to analyze "the natural sculpture of dramatic poetry" and likened the playwright to a sculptor; in particular he compared the Minerva of Phidias to the *Electra* of Aeschylus and Sophocles (Feuerbach [1833] 1855, 283; 285). The same remarks can be read in a fragment of Nietzsche: "That simple Aeschylean sculpture must have represented the first step towards Phidias [...]."[18] In this passage, Nietzsche also reconnected with Feuerbach to explain the "sculpture-like representation" of Wagner's *Tristan*, where the actors maintain a Winckelmann-like "calm grandeur." The same theme resurfaces in §21 in the *Birth of Tragedy*. According to Anselm Feuerbach, the audience of a tragedy is composed essentially of spectators, linked together by the gaze that is directed at the object of the performance. He speaks of "Beschauer," "schaulustiges Volk," "Genuss der Betrachtenden," equating the theatrical spectator with one who religiously contemplates a statue. The relevance of Anselm Feuerbach's text was recognized by Charles Andler, who judged it to be one of the sources of the *Birth of Tragedy* (Andler 1921, 229ff.).[19] As pointed out by Andler, for Feuerbach, "the Apollo of Belvedere is the same Apollo as that of Aeschylus, Aeschylean thought crystallized into marble" (Andler 1921, 233). On the other hand, the spectators of antiquity observed the actors as if they were marble statues on the stage, and saw themselves aesthetically transfigured. Andler noted that August Wilhelm Schlegel also saw a similarity between the art of poetry and the art of Greek sculpture, comparing Greek tragedy to sculptures on stage (he compared tragic figures to statues in motion) (Schlegel 1809, 58; 69). This similarity can also be found in the letter from Goethe to Schiller of April 8, 1797,[20] in which Goethe stated that in theater one can create great effects by learning from the plastic arts; for example some scenes of Aristophanes seemed to be bas-reliefs (cf. Goethe [1797b] 2006).

Nietzsche shared with Feuerbach the idea of the spectator who becomes a work of art, as described in *The Vatican Apollo*: "But what does the chorus mean for the tragedy? The same thing as the person who contemplated the statue was for the statue, the spectator–sculpture that is accepted into a work of art as an integral part of itself" (Feuerbach [1833] 1855, 298). From this perspective, one can understand more fully Nietzsche's references to the man who, under the spell of Dionysus, becomes a work of art, and also to the "aesthetic spectator" described in the final chapters of *The Birth of Tragedy*. According to Feuerbach, Greek statues, like poetry, for the modern man are shorn of the thousands of threads which tied them to religion and the political and social life of the Greeks (Feuerbach [1833] 1855, 272).

> We know the whole of Greek poetry only in relation to the letters of the alphabet; and so we can get an idea of its effect in the same way as if we were to observe a statue by looking only at its "drawn profile." [...] [P]oetry owed much of its effect to musical diction, singing or reciting accompanied by the cithara or by the sound

of the flute; therefore to the contribution of an art that, with magical powers, dominates the sentiments, inflames them [...] giving wings and impetus to the imagination. (Feuerbach [1833] 1855, 274)

Nietzsche reiterated the same arguments with very similar images when he stated that Aeschylus and Sophocles were known only as "authors of a written text, as librettists" and that music should be to poetry what color and shading are to a drawing (GMD; KSA 1, 517 and 528). From Feuerbach, he deduces how ancient performances were conducted with the use of superhuman-sized puppets and the custom within the audience of ridiculing any wrong accents (GMD; KSA 1, 520). As Nietzsche pointed out in *Greek Music Drama*, the Athenian festival performance probably would appear today a strange and barbaric spectacle; but the audience, like the actor, was fully involved in the sacredness of the performance. The soul of the Athenian who watched the tragedy incorporated part of the Dionysian element from which it arose. In Nietzsche's view, the Athenian audience of ancient musical drama is always in the foreground and, with a clearly polemical tone, is repeatedly contrasted against the weary and distracted modern viewers.

In his lectures on the history of Greek literature, Nietzsche used the same metaphor that we found in the conference on *Greek Music Drama*: "today it is as if a musician does not write an opera to perform music but to read the music-score" (KGW II/5, 280). Only beginning with Isocrates do authors write for a reader, however, as Nietzsche expounds with an eloquent image, it is for a "sublimated" reader capable of rebuilding and hearing the sound of the speech (KGW II/5, 280).[21]

The need to broaden the perspective of an artwork, including its public and its socio-historical context rather than limiting the issue to grammatical, linguistic and "internal" aspects, had already emerged during the so-called "Eumenidenstreit," a controversy following the publication of Aeschylus' *Eumenides* (1833) by Boeckh's pupil Karl Otfried Müller and his attack on Gottfried Hermann's method (the same year as Feuerbach's *Vatican Apollo*). Müller believed one must first bring the Athenian tragedy to the stage in order "to extract from what we read today the image of what the Athenians saw" (Müller 1833, I, IV).[22] Müller referred to Aeschylus' relationship with his audience, especially when Orestes, at the behest of Athena, goes before the Athenian people's court. "[T]he poet evidently considered it important to be able to view the Aereopagus in the drama and the Athenians as spectators united as one, whom Athena addresses in her 'Stiftungsrede' (founding Aeropagus)" (Müller 1833, 107). Wilamowitz recognized Müller's pioneering role in the reconstruction of an ancient world into which modern interpreters can try to immerse themselves, when in his *Introduction to Greek Tragedy* he explains his own method of investigation. According to Wilamowitz, a philologist must have something of the true artist, "who gives life to the dead word through the blood of his heart" (Wilamowitz 1907, 257). In so doing, he guides the modern reader to relive the same conditions and state of mind that the Athenians brought to the Theater of Dionysus when they went to see a drama. And so, through classical scholarship, the modern reader recovers the pleasure of the ancient listener. While recognizing the great merits of Hermann, Wilamowitz nonetheless feared that if we limit ourselves to textual analysis and the "forma loquendi" of the ancient author, a whole universe simply becomes words on paper (a "paper-horizon") (Candio 2008, 59).[23] It is therefore necessary in tragedy, as Müller suggests, to widen the horizon of the interpreter by moving from the text to the stage. If one reads those lines of Nietzsche's most famous opponent, one cannot miss the coincidence of intent and basic thrust of argument. It is not by chance that the Nietzsche-research discovered almost identical metaphors in their writings, such as those of blood for the ghosts[24] and the desert of science.[25] The "Streit" had evidently left its mark on both. Both wanted to resurrect a distant and buried past through a kind of Homeric necromancy or νέκυια before the journey in the underworld.[26] For Nietzsche, educated in the critical method of Ritschl, the primary resources for a philologist were the skills of intuition, conjecture, "divinatio," and "supposition" ("errathen") based on experience (Benne 2005, 84); for Wilamowitz, on the other hand, what mattered was a comprehensive vision of antiquity combined with the interpretive talents of the individual.[27]

According to Pöschl, Nietzsche was divided between the great legacy of classicism, which he had experienced at Pforta (grecophilia, linked to the contemplation of a "live" antiquity) and a philology which had both adopted the longing for the Greece of Weimar classicism and at the same time enervated it from an excess of erudition (Pöschl 1979, 41ff.). Wilamowitz seemed stubbornly intent on preserving both aspects; on the one hand, the erudition and the scholarly merits of the great philological school that preceded him, and on the other, the vitality of the ancient world, which was to be resurrected as an all-encompassing vision.

The public played a crucial role in Nietzsche's reconstruction of this complex picture of antiquity. Friedrich Schlegel had already viewed Greek artworks as a collective process rather than individual product. In addition, most of the great German writers of the second half of the eighteenth century (when aesthetics appeared in Germany)—writers like Winckelmann, Lessing, and Herder—explored the effects, whether calming or energetic, which emanated from a work of art. A debate developed concerning tragedy in German literature, which was also related to the creation of a German national theater (Silk and Stern 1981, 1ff.). The long hermeneutic dispute continued among the philologists of the time thanks to Jacob Bernays, who, like Nietzsche, was Ritschl's student. His short revolutionary treatise, *Grundzüge der verlorenen Abhandlung des Aristoteles über Wirkung der Tragödie* (Breslau 1857), which at one time made him famous, was used several times by Nietzsche, who borrowed it from the university library in Basel in 1869 and 1871. Bernays' essay begins with the interpretation of one of the most celebrated and controversial passages in the *Poetics* of Aristotle, "tragic catharsis," which is reached through pity and fear (1449b 24–8). Bernays interpreted this term as a simile which derived from medicine from a sentence in the eighth book of *Politics*. In this passage, Aristotle spoke of the benefits of music, adding that he would explain the meaning of catharsis when speaking about poetry; he likened catharsis to a "medical cure." "[T]he enthusiasts have experimented, so to speak, on a medical cure and a catharsis." Through music, everyone can attain catharsis and pleasant relief (Aristotle, *Pol.* 1341b32–1342a27). Bernays pointed out that in the same passage in the *Politics* Aristotle referred to a "double audience" in the theater, a free and cultured one, and also a lower class, composed of artisans, day laborers, and the like, who had different types of needs and for whom shows and music were meant to provide amusement, in keeping with their nature. Bernays also linked catharsis to orgiastic and Dionysian cults, and believed that this was essentially a physiological outlet ("Entladung"), which provided a state of arousal, and an "emptying" of the humors which would restore the body's balance (somewhat like the purgamentum of the Romans). More specifically, he felt it related to the treatment of the anxiety of those who cannot "transform" or repress what causes this condition, and the subconsequent sense of relief (Bernays [1857] 1970, 12). Previously, catharsis was generally interpreted, especially by Lessing, as purification (Läuterung) in a moral sense (Lessing [1767–9] 1958, 308). Bernays instead ironically observed that Aristotle was far from considering that the Greek theater was an institution in competition with the church (Bernays [1857] 1970, 8). Even Goethe did not share Lessing's conception of catharsis which was based on the "transformation of passions into virtuous dispositions".[28] In his opinion neither music nor art in general can have any influence on morals, and tragedies, like novels, are not able to "calm the soul," but rather tend to disturb and excite. Goethe also denied that tragedy deals with the effect this has on audiences. He proposed, therefore, relating the experience of catharsis to the tragic characters themselves, rather than the audience (cf. Goethe [1826] 2006, 340–3). This point is contested by Bernays as Aristotle, in the passage already mentioned in the *Politics* (1341b32),[29] writes that this word means an event that occurs in the soul of the listener and spectator. In his letter to Richard Wagner, in which he defended Nietzsche from Wilamowitz's attack, Rohde wrote that Bernays' interpretation of catharsis seemed the only plausible one. Nietzsche (who mentioned Bernays at NF 1869/70 3[38]; KSA 7, 142) used the term Entladung several times. In §22 of the *Birth of Tragedy*, Nietzsche spoke of "a pathological discharge," or "the purging of emotions" which "philologists do not know whether to place among medical or moral phenomena" (BT 22; KSA 1, 142).[30]

Yorck von Wartenburg then expanded on Bernays' theses in his 1866 dissertation *Catharsis of Aristotle and Sophocles' Oedipus at Colonus*, which Nietzsche borrowed in May 1870. In this text, which provided Nietzsche with several insights relating to the cult of Dionysus, Wartenburg recognized that the riddle of catharsis was solved by the brilliant ("geistreichen") Bernays, who gave the pathological interpretation of the "profound and calming effect of tragic catharsis" (Wartenburg 1866, 24).

5. Conclusions

Nietzsche's focus on musical performance or recitation is related to his ongoing interest in the origins of language and its gestural, theatrical, and symbolic dimensions. The essence of language, which for Nietzsche is the same as rhetoric, lies in its "Wirkung," which is the effect it produces. In his university lectures on Latin grammar, Nietzsche compared language to a system of mimic signs, to a pantomime. He considered language "as a product of instinct" and as "teleology without a conscience" (KGW II/2, 186).[31] Federico Gerratana ascribed Nietzsche's interests in the origin of language and the link between voice and gestures to the stimuli of the pre-Schopenhauer Wagner (in his writings of the late 1840s and early 1850s) (Gerratana 1994, 343). Nietzsche's main interest during that period was the system of relations and the dynamical interchange between the individual and the community. This probably dates back to Wagner's attention to the role of tragedy within the community of spectators. Nietzsche's insistence on the sculpture-like performances of antiquity, e.g. in fragment 25 [1], refers to the communion between the Athenians and the actors on stage, which Nietzsche compared to Wagner's ideal community. In this sense, the *Birth of Tragedy* also recuperates Schlegel's image of the chorus as an "idealized spectator," an image that he had initially seemed to reject (NF 1872/73; KSA 7, 566).

In Nietzsche's last university lectures, and especially as he moved increasingly away from the Wagnerian perspective, he viewed the Greek audience as being less compact, more complex and heterogeneous; in particular it was no longer able to appreciate the work of art while nonetheless it continued to feel its effects. While at the start Nietzsche undoubtedly followed Wagner's ideas, his attention to the ancient beholder of a work of art began to disengage from immediate aims, especially when he developed ethnological and anthropological interests.

Nietzsche's insistence on the role of the listeners and spectators in the Basel lectures is also, in contrast to his previous notes and records from his military period (from autumn 1867 to spring 1868), gathered under the Humboldtian title *Encyclopädie*. In these notes, Nietzsche did not seem to be particularly interested in the audience, but already had a need to immerse himself in the life of the ancient world ("hineinleben"). In his notes, Nietzsche mentioned the "Letter to a Young Philologist" by the classical historian B. G. Niebuhr: "Niebuhr, Brief an einen jungen Philol[ogen]. Leip[zig], 1839. Its main idea is the living vision [lebendige Anschauung] of antiquity" (KGW I/5, 198).

Nietzsche refers to page 133 of Niebuhr's book, in which, among other things, the historian viewed antiquity as an immense "Ruinenstadt," where one needs to know how to manage without a map. Furthermore, in his notes from his military period, Nietzsche devoted an entry ("Philologie im Bunde mit den schönen Wissenschaften") to the links between philology and literature in Germany in the mid-eighteenth century, mentioning the pioneering influence of Lessing, who freed philology from the dust of books and scholarship, like Winckelmann had.

On the other side, Wilamowitz in his *History of Classical Scholarship* stated that Lessing, Herder, and Goethe could not, stricktly speaking, be included in this history (Wilamowitz 1959, 47). Wilamowitz also rejected Jakob Burckhardt's theories.[32] Nietzsche's philological models were thus more diverse and less conventional than those of Wilamowitz and were primarily eminently creative minds, such as the poet-philologists, the Italian humanists, Leopardi,[33] as well as Goethe himself. For Nietzsche, German classicism represented an important model not only for the importance attributed to the influence of a work of art in antiquity, but also for its educational and formative aims. Pöschl, who underlined how important the pedagogic aspect was for Nietzsche, attributed Nietzsche's "practical" attitude to Humboldt who, like him, also wrote an *Encyclopedia of Classical Studies*. He asserted that precisely this normative element in Nietzsche foreshadowed the attention to practical implications, the "Anwendung" in Gadamer's hermeneutics (Pöschl 1979, 143).

When considering the different periods in which Nietzsche wrote his lecture notes, one can easily see not so much a change in focus on certain issues, which remained constant, but rather how he interpreted them. In the last series of lectures, such as the history of Greek literature, Nietzsche analyzed the aesthetic sense and the social composition of the Athenian public and noted that if emulation had produced a refinement of the artists this was not the case for the public (KGW II/5, 322ff.). This reflects the already strong anthropological and ethnological orientation of his studies, so that the topics relating to feasts and collective rituals are transferred from the sphere of the religious to the profane, as can be seen in his lectures on *The Greek Cult of Gods*, which he delivered in Basel in 1875. The heterogeneity of Nietzsche's sources and his uninhibited use of such studies, in which he recognized and used the most innovative aspects, characterize his approach and his original insights into early antiquity. Through his wide interestes as a classical scholar he raised issues that would engage interpreters and be widely investigated only in the following century.[34]

To conclude, Nietzsche holds a consistent point of view towards the performance and public with respect to how each genre is addressed. In his remarks on the nature and rhetorical features of language we find the same interest in the function of the listener and spectator. The numerous references to the artistic and creative dimension of the language, to the transformation of a nerve stimulus into sound images (KSA 1, 572) and to the language of gestures ("Geberdensprache") as universally intellegible symbols, suggest a consistent attitude towards emotion or empathy excited through the senses of sight and hearing. Nietzsche's interests in linguistics intertwine with his understanding of ancient rhetoric as a conscious application and development of the unconscious power of language to discover and to select "that, which works and has an effect" ("was wirkt und Effekt macht") (KGW II/4, 425–8). Nietzsche emphasizes that for Cicero (*De Oratore* III, 14), the audience beholds with astonishment the speaker who produces in his language a sort of rhythm and harmony (KGW II/4, 435). On the other hand, ancient literature, like ancient rhetoric, was an echo of speech and wanted to entice or captivate ("bestechen") the ears. Visual, auditory, and rhythmic elements characterize Nietzsche's own philosophical style, which displays the same captivating quality and power of persuasion of ancient rhetoric: Nietzsche would like to teach his own reader how to listen well, enabling him to hear every nuance and resonance of the text, and thus transforming his modern reader somehow into the ancient listener with his keen sense of hearing (KGW II/5, 280).

Translated by Henry Albert and Laura Fatuzzo

Notes

1   I wish to thank Ann Desjardins for her observations while reading this paper.
2   On Nietzsche's *Dissertatio de Theognide Megarensi* (the "valedictorian paper," i.e. graduation thesis for Pforta students) and on his article published thereafter in *Rheinisches Museum für Philologie* (1867, Vol. 12, 161–200) see A. K. Jensen. According to Jensen, Nietzsche "focused on the reception of the poet who portrayed

the culture clash between the Doric aristocratic culture and the rising merchant class" (Jensen 2008, 320).

3   These lectures were given from the summer semester of 1869 to the winter one in 1878/79 (the notes on the 1878/79 semester are not written by Nietzsche).

4   Nietzsche found the division into apotelestic and practical arts in the first pages of a book on Greek metrics that he owned and mentions in his letters. Cf. Rossbach and Westphal 1867, 3f.

5   Note that *Die Wirkung der Tragoedie* was the title of the third section of Nietzsche's school essay of 1864 (*primum Oedipodis regis carmen choricum*) (KGW I/3, 334).

6   Cf. KGW II/2, 109. Nietzsche quotes this work as a source at page 173 as well, mentioning the fact that this author was the first to recognize the importance of Plutarch's *De musica* (see Westphal and Hermann 1864, VIII).

7   For this author cf. Orsucci 1996, 78. On poetry older than prose and the link between prose and writing, see KGW II/5, 28.

8   The sophist Gorgias of Leontini likens poetry and rhetoric in the name of their psychagogic and sentimental effects.

9   Even Socrates, in Plato's *Ion*, describes the mysterious power of the muses moving poets, rhapsodes, and their listeners like a magnet (533d). Ion, the rhapsode, describes the various emotions of his listeners: "for I look down upon them from the stage, and I see them crying, and look askance, and be appalled, according to what I am reciting" (Plato, *Ion* 535e). Similar considerations on the effects of poetry on the public are to be found in *Gorgias*.

10 Cf. Nietzsche's introduction to the study of the Platonic dialogues: "Plato must admit that the aim of tragedy is pleasure and therefore calls it a popular oratory" (KGW II/4, 118).

11 On the peculiarities of ancient Greek compared to the Shakespearean public, cf. NF 1869, 1[76]; KSA 7, 34. See also KGW II/5, 82.

12 It is one of the themes found in Aristoxenus' musical theory and recovered in Plutarch's *De musica*.

13 Cf. NF 21[2]; KSA 7, 253.

14 Joseph Anselm Feuerbach was the brother of the philosopher and father of the painter. I discuss him more thoroughly below.

15 In Wagner's "Gesamtkunstwerk" (the utopian project of a rebirth of the ancient greek drama) the ideal community and the audience played a crucial role as part of the religious mystical ritual of the dramatic performance.

16 Wallace quotes some passages from Plato's *Laws* about musical virtuosity, which the philosopher condemned as the main reason for the corruption of the public's taste. Wallace 1997, 97ff.

17 See Welcker 1835, 630–4. See also the review of Müller, "Der vaticanische Apollo von Anselm Feuerbach" in Müller 1848, 487–95.

18 See fragment 25[1] (NF 1872/73; KSA 7, 568), which was supposed to become an addition to the *Birth of Tragedy*.

19 On Feuerbach's *Vatican Apollo* as the source of *The Birth of Tragedy* see also Brobjer 2005, 291.

20 Nietzsche references this letter at NF 1872, 25 [1]; KSA 7, 569.

21 Babich suggests an interesting thesis: *The Birth of Tragedy* refers to the contemporary reader as well, who through the ancient writings has to put himself in the perspective of the listener: "read not with our eyes, but with our ears: the texts of the past offer a *readable repository of sound* in the written word." (Babich 2006, 46).

22 On Müller's essay cf. Candio 2008, 61ff. In her book, Candio focuses on the theme of "sich versenken" and on Müller's influence on Wilamowitz and his method. As she points out, Wilamowitz's later studies on Aeschylus abandoned his previous global hermeneutics of the ancient text (in a way different than Nietzsche), moving towards "Textgeschichte."

23 Wilamowitz's thoughts on the duties ("*Die wahren Aufgaben*") of philology can be found in the first edition of his comment to Euripides' *Heracles* (cf. Wilamowitz-Moellendorff 1889).

24 See Silk and Stern 1981, 102.

25 Aphorism 31 of *Assorted Opinions and Maxims* is entitled "desert of science," the desolated region symbolizing the "tiring journeys" of the scientific man. This landscape resembles closely the arid and dusty one of philological erudition, which Wilamowitz, in his second attack against Rhode, declared himself to prefer to Nietzsche's initiatory paths. See Benne 2005, 163.

26 *Blood for the Ghosts* is also the title of a collection of essays by Hugh Lloyd-Jones 1983.

27 Medda, in his foreword to Candio, finds hints of Hermann's textual philology in the conception of "sich versenken," as well as in Boeckh's historical research (Candio 2008, III).

28 Lessing, in his *Hamburg Dramaturgy*, translated *katharsis* with purification ["Reinigung"]. Cf. Lessing [1767–9] 1958, 308.

29 Cf. Paduano's note concerning the "medical reading" of catharsis in Aristotle 1998, 74.

30 Gödde 2003, 206ff. suggests a parallel influence of Bernays on Nietzsche and Freud. Bernays was Freud's wife's uncle.

31 Language is for Nietzsche a "complete organism" and "a product of instinct, as with bees—the anthills, etc." (KGW II/2, 186). For his teleological view of instinct and for the simile of the bees, Nietzsche has probably in mind the "Kunsttriebe" of Lichtenberg, i.e. the unconscious artistic sense of bees building their hives. See e.g. "das Bienenartige im Menschen" (Wastebook L 955 and 956) in Lichtenberg 1991, 533.

32 Among philologists, Burckhardt's *Cultural History of Greece* was mostly either ignored or criticized. Wilamowitz doesn't even mention him in his *History of Philology* (1959). Elsewhere, he writes, for example, "I should here be taken for a coward were I not to speak out against the Griechische Kulturgeschichte of Jacob Burckhardt [...] [This book] does not exist for science [...]. It can say nothing worth hearing about either Greek religion or the Greek state, since it ignores what the past fifty years of science has achieved in terms of documents, facts, methods, and perspectives" (Wilamowitz-Moellendorff 1899, 6–7).

33 It is interesting to observe that the volume of the *Rheinisches Museum*, which contained Welcker's review of Feuerbach's *Vatican Apollo* (dritter Jahrgang 1835), opened with a study dedicated to Leopardi.

34 For a more extensive discussion and a bibliography on these matters, see, above all, Gentili 1995; see also Wallace 1997.

Works cited

Andler, Charles (1921): *Nietzsche, sa vie et sa pensée* (1920–31). Paris (Éditions Bossard). Vol. 2 (*La jeunesse de Nietzsche*).

Aristotle (1998): *Poetica. Traduzione e introduzione di Guido Paduano.* Bari (Laterza).

Babich, Babette (2006): "The Birth of Tragedy: Lyric Poetry and the Music of Words." In her *Words in Blood, Like Flowers: Philosophy and Poetry, Music and Eros in Hölderlin, Nietzsche and Heidegger.* New York (State University of New York).

Benne, Christian (2005): *Nietzsche und die historisch-kritische Philologie.* Berlin and New York (Walter de Gruyter).

Bernays, Jacob ([1857] 1970): *Grundzüge der verlorenen Abhandlung des Aristoteles über Wirkung der Tragödie.* Hildesheim (G. Olms).

Brobjer, Thomas H. (2005): "Sources of and Influences on Nietzsche's *The Birth of Tragedy.*" In *Nietzsche-Studien.* Vol. 34, 278–99.

Burckhardt, Jacob ([1898] 1999): *The Greeks and Greek Civilisation.* Oswin Murray (ed.), Sheila Stern (trans.). London (HarperCollins Fontana).

Candio, Antonella (2008): *"Ein lebendiges Ganzes." La filologia come scienza e storia nelle Coefore di Ulrich von Wilamowitz-Moellendorff.* Amsterdam (Hakkert).

Feuerbach, Anselm ([1833] 1855): *Der vatikanische Apollo. Eine Reihe archäologisch-ästhetischer Betrachtungen.* Stuttgart and Augsburg (Cotta).

Genelli, Hans Christian (1818): *Das Theater zu Athen: hinsichtlich auf Architectur, Scenerie und Darstellungskunst überhaupt.* Berlin and Leipzig (Nauck).

Gentili, Bruno (1995): *Poesia e pubblico nella Grecia antica. Da Omero al V secolo.* Bari (Laterza).

Gerratana, Federico (1994): "'Jetzt zieht mich das Allgemein-Menschliche an': Ein Streifzug durch Nietzsches Aufzeichnungen zu einer 'Geschichte der litterarischen Studien.'" In Tilman Borsche, Federico Gerratana, and Aldo Venturelli (eds): *Centauren-Geburten. Wissenschaft, Kunst und Philosophie beim jungen Nietzsche.* Berlin and New York (Walter de Gruyter), 326–50.

Gödde, Günter (2003): "Die antike Therapeutik als gemeinsamer Bezugspunkt für Nietzsche und Freud." In *Nietzsche-Studien.* Vol. 32, 206–25.

Goethe, Johann Wolfgang von ([1797a] 2006): "Über epische und dramatische Dichtung." In Karl Richter (ed.): *Sämtliche Werke,* Munich (Hanser). Vol. 4/2, 126–8.

—([1797b] 2006): "Briefwechsel zwischen Schiller und Goethe in den Jahren 1794 bis 1805." In Karl Richter (ed.): *Sämtliche Werke,* Munich (Hanser), 2006. Vol. 8/1, 325–6.

—([1826] 2006): "Nachlese zu Aristoteles' Poetik." In Karl Richter (ed.): *Sämtliche Werke,* Munich (Hanser). Vol. 13/1, 340–3.

Hartung, Johann Adam (1856): *Die griechischen Lyriker.* Leipzig (Engelmann). Vol. 5.

Jensen, Anthony K. (2008): "Anti-Politicality and Agon in Nietzsche's Philology." In Herman W. Siemens and Vasti Roodt (eds): *Nietzsche, Power and Politics.* Berlin and New York (Walter de Gruyter), 319–45.

Lessing, Gotthold Ephraim ([1767–9] 1958): *Hamburgische Dramaturgie.* Otto Mann (ed.). Stuttgart (Kröner).

Lichtenberg, Georg Christoph (1991): *Sudelbücher.* Wolfgang Promies (ed.). Munich (Hanser).

Lloyd-Jones, Hugh (1982): *Blood for the Ghosts: Classical Influences in the 19th and 20th Centuries.* London (Johns Hopkins University Press).

Lowell, Edmunds and Robert W. Wallace (eds): *Poet, Public, and Performance in Ancient Greece*. London (Johns Hopkins University Press).

Müller, Karl Otfried (1833): *Aischylos Eumeniden*. Göttingen (Dieterische Verlags-Buchhandlung).

—(1848): "Der vaticanische Apollo von Anselm Feuerbach." In Karl Otfried Müller: *Kleine deutsche Schriften über Religion, Kunst, Sprache und Literatur, Leben und Geschichte des Alterthums*. Breslau (Max und Komp). Vol. 2, 487–95.

Niebuhr, Barthold Georg (1839): *Brief an einem jungen Philologen*. Leipzig (Vogel).

Orsucci, Andrea (1996): *Orient-Okzident, Nietzsches Versuch einer Loslösung vom europäischen Weltbild*. Berlin and New York (Walter de Gruyter).

Pöschl, Viktor (1979): "Nietzsche und die klassische Philologie." In Hellmut Flashar, et al. (eds): *Philologie und Hermeneutik im 19. Jahrhundert*. Göttingen (Vandenhoeck & Ruprecht), 141–55.

Rossbach, August and Rudolf Westphal (1867): *Metrik der Griechen im Vereine mit den übrigen musischen Künsten*. Leipzig (Teubner). Vol. 1.

Schlegel, August Wilhelm (1809): *Ueber dramatische Kunst und Literatur. Vorlesungen*. Heidelberg (Mohr & Zimmer). Vol. 1.

Silk, Michael S. and Joseph P. Stern (1981): *Nietzsche on Tragedy*. Cambridge (Cambridge University Press).

von Reibnitz, Barbara (1994): "Vom 'Sprachkunstwerk' zur 'Leselitteratur'" In Tilman Borsche, et al. (eds): *Centauren-Geburten. Wissenschaft, Kunst und Philosophie beim jungen Nietzsche*. Berlin and New York (Walter de Gruyter), 47–66.

Wallace, Robert W. (1997): "Poet, Public and 'Theatrocracy': Audience Performance in Classical Athens." In Robert Wallace and Lowell Edmunds (eds): *Poet, Public, and Performance in Ancient Greece*. Baltimore (Johns Hopkins Press), 97–111.

Welcker, Friedrich Gottlob (1835): "Der vaticanische Apollo von A. Feuerbach." In *Rheinisches Museum für Philologie*. Vol. 3, 630–4.

Westphal, Rudolf and Georg Hermann (1864): *Geschichte der alten und mittelalterlichen Musik*. Breslau (Leuckart).

Wilamowitz-Moellendorff, U. von (1889): *Euripides Herakles, erklärt von U. von Wilamowitz-Moellendorff*. Berlin (Weidmann).

—(1899) (ed. and trans.): *Griechische Tragödien Band 2, Aischylos: Agamemnon, Das Opfer am Grabe, & Die Versöhnung*. Berlin (Wiedmannsche Buchhandlung).

—(1907): *Einleitung in die griechische Tragödie*. Berlin (Weidmannsche Buchhandlung).

—(1959): *Geschichte der Philologie*. 4th edn. Günther Klaffenbach (ed.). Leipzig (Teubner).

Wolf, Friedrich August ([1795] 1985): *Prolegomena to Homer*, 3rd edn. Anthony Grafton, et al. (eds) Princeton (Princeton University Press).

Yorck v. Wartenburg, Paul (1866): *Die Katharsis des Aristoteles und der Oedipus Coloneus des Sophokles*. Berlin (Hertz).

10

The Ancient Quarrel between Philosophy and Poetry in Nietzsche's Early Writings

Matthew Meyer

1. Introduction

In *Republic* X, Plato has Socrates speak of an ancient quarrel between philosophy and poetry (*Rep.* 607b).[1] Although some have questioned whether there was any such quarrel prior to this pronouncement (Most 2011, 1–20), Plato's writings generated a skepticism about poetry on both epistemic and ethical grounds and initiated a long-standing conversation about the compatibility of philosophy and poetry.[2] In this paper, I argue that Nietzsche's first work, *The Birth of Tragedy out of the Spirit of Music*, can be read through the lens of and as a contribution to this quarrel. This is because the work is structured around an original antithesis between the world of poetry and the death of this poetic world at the hands of Socratic philosophy; this antithesis is then overcome through a union of the philosophy of Kant and Schopenhauer with the music of Bach, Beethoven, and Wagner (BT 19; KSA 1, 127ff.). The figure that symbolizes the reconciliation of this philosophy and poetry is the music-making Socrates (BT 15; KSA 1, 102), and therefore this figure provides the key to understanding the structure and argument of *The Birth of Tragedy* as a whole.

The antithesis and ultimate resolution of the quarrel between philosophy and poetry in *The Birth of Tragedy* depends on a specific understanding of the quarrel that Nietzsche shares with Plato. Specifically, Nietzsche follows Plato in understanding the quarrel as a clash between two activities rooted in two distinct worldviews. Whereas a pessimistic understanding of life and the world provided the framework for both Homeric epic and Attic tragedy, it was Socrates' coupling of philosophical activity with an optimistic worldview that brought a corresponding end to poetry and the poetic worldview. Nevertheless, Nietzsche believes that it is possible for philosophy to align itself with a pessimistic worldview and therewith a framework for the flourishing of tragedy in particular and poetry more generally, and this is what Nietzsche saw in the German philosophy of his day and why he thought German philosophy was preparing the ground for the rebirth of tragedy in the operas of Richard Wagner.

After explicating the way in which this understanding of the ancient quarrel structures the whole of *The Birth of Tragedy*, I conclude with some observations on how Nietzsche, soon after the publication of his first work, revised his account of the tragic worldview in "Philosophy in the Tragic Age of the Greeks." Rather than casting the poetic Greeks as pre-philosophical, as he implicitly does in *The Birth of Tragedy*, Nietzsche begins to argue that pre-Socratic philosophy in general and the philosophy of Heraclitus in particular gave expression to a tragic worldview that, in turn, provided the conditions for the flourishing of tragedy. In my conclusion, I suggest that this development has important consequences for assessing Nietzsche's relationship to Plato, his contribution to the ancient quarrel between philosophy and poetry, and his value as a scholar of antiquity.

2. The birth of tragedy in *The Birth of Tragedy*

It is sometimes believed that the central idea of *The Birth of Tragedy* is the Apollonian–Dionysian duality found at the beginning of the work.[3] Although this antithesis is crucial for understanding the opening sections of the work, this duality falls away once the figure of Socrates is introduced in section ten. This is because Socrates does not represent an emphasis on the Apollonian at the expense of the Dionysian,[4] but rather new forces of rationalism and optimism that are, according to Nietzsche, hostile to art (BT 12; KSA 1, 83).[5] Because of this, the text as a whole should be understood through a different dynamic. Specifically, it should be understood in terms of the relationship between pessimism and optimism, poetry and philosophy. In the first ten sections, Nietzsche argues that Greek poetry emerged as a response to a pessimistic understanding of the world, expressed in the wisdom of Silenus. In sections ten through fifteen, Nietzsche details how tragedy died at the hands of Socratic optimism and a corresponding rejection of Silenus' pessimism. In the final sections, Nietzsche explains how philosophy has again revealed the truth of pessimism and thereby established the conditions for a rebirth of genuine tragedy.[6]

Nevertheless, the Apollonian–Dionysian duality is crucial for understanding Nietzsche's account of Greek poetry in general and the genesis of tragedy in particular. To begin, Nietzsche links these two deities to two types of art, the Apollonian art of images and sculpture and the Dionysian art of non-imagistic music. He then associates these two deities with two psychological phenomena: dreaming and intoxication. In dreams, glorious "superhuman beings" appear in the imagination of the dreamer (BT 1; KSA 1, 26), and art forms like sculpture are related to dreaming in that the sculptor attempts to reproduce the dream image in her work. In intoxication, human subjectivity and the boundaries that separate individuals are destroyed, creating a sea of mystical oneness. Here, "the union between man and man" is not only reaffirmed, "but nature which has become alienated, hostile, or subjugated, celebrates once more her reconciliation with her lost son" (BT 1; KSA 1, 29). An art form like music is related to intoxication because it both emerges from and causes the destruction of boundaries that separate the individual "I" from others and from nature.

Although Nietzsche does not present the art world of the Greeks as emerging from or related to a certain philosophical understanding of the world, he does attempt to articulate his Apollonian-Dionysian aesthetics in terms of a metaphysical distinction, taken from Arthur Schopenhauer, between an apparent world of individuation and a metaphysical reality of a unified, but contradictory, will beyond the "principium individuationis" (BT 1; KSA 1, 28). This allows Nietzsche, on the one hand, to argue that the so-called reality of everyday life has a dream-like status that can be shaped and so transfigured by the vision of a poet like Homer and, on the other hand, to argue that music can break through the apparent world of individuation and provide a direct copy of the will, which, for Schopenhauer, is the thing-in-itself (BT 16; KSA 1, 104).

Although Nietzsche's explanation of Greek art is infused with philosophical ideas, he implicitly casts the art world of the Greeks as relatively bereft of philosophical reflection. Nevertheless, Nietzsche does find in the poetry of these pre-Socratic Greeks a larger vision of the world and the human condition. Specifically, Nietzsche attributes to the mythical figure of Silenus a pessimistic understanding of existence or what can also be called a Dionysian worldview.[7]

In order to distinguish the wisdom of Silenus and the Greeks' response to it from optimism, it is important to identify two features of Silenic wisdom and, in turn, two corresponding types of pessimism. This can be done by looking at Silenus' response to King Midas' question as to what is best for humans. Here, Nietzsche writes:

> Oh, wretched ephemeral race, children of chance and misery, why do you compel me to tell you what it would be most expedient for you not to hear? What is best of all is utterly beyond your reach: not to be born, not to be, to be nothing. But the second best for you is—to die soon. (BT 3; KSA 1, 35)

Based on this passage, one can say that there is a *factual* and an *evaluative* component to Silenic pessimism.[8] The *factual* claim is an assertion about the human condition: it is wretched, ephemeral, and subject to chance and misery. The *evaluative* claim is a response to this fact. Because life is filled with meaningless suffering, non-existence is preferable to existence.

In a move that prefigures his mature philosophy,[9] Nietzsche contends that the poetic Greeks accepted the factual pessimism of Silenus but rejected the evaluative component of his wisdom. That is, they "knew and felt the terror and horror of existence" (BT 3; KSA 1, 35), but they nevertheless transfigured this suffering by creating their pantheon of gods. The effect, according to Nietzsche, was that these Greeks came to believe that "to die soon [was] worst of all for them, the next worst—to die at all" (BT 3; KSA 1, 36). For Nietzsche, it was Greek poetry that enabled them to reverse the evaluative portion of Silenic wisdom. In the language of Nietzsche's 1886 preface to the work, these artistic Greeks represent a "pessimism of *strength*" (BT Attempt 1; KSA 1, 12). They were pessimists because they acknowledged the truth of factual pessimism. However, they represent a pessimism of strength because they reversed the evaluative claim of Silenus, such that even a suffering-filled life is seen as the greatest good and death as a terrible loss.

Nietzsche dedicates chapters three through nine to explaining how the various forms of poetry—epic, lyric, and tragic—engendered a life-affirming response to the factual component of Silenic wisdom. Specifically, Nietzsche devotes sections three and four to explaining the way in which Homeric epic performed this function. For Nietzsche, Homeric epic is a form of Apollonian art. This is because it emerges from the imagination of the poet, where the poet's task is to communicate these dream sequences in verse. Like sculpture, such poetry is not a Dionysian *art form* because it is not inspired by the rapturous and intoxicating power of music. Nevertheless, Nietzsche takes pains to argue that this Apollonian poetry is intimately associated with Dionysian or Silenic *wisdom*. According to Nietzsche, the art world of Homer emerged from a confrontation with factual pessimism, where the bleakness of existence drove the poet to produce a comforting veil that he cast over existence for the benefit of the Greek world. In short, Homer invented the pantheon of the gods to protect the Greeks from the horrors of existence such that the life of man appeared justified precisely because the gods lived it, which, according to Nietzsche, is "the only satisfactory theodicy" (BT 3; KSA 1, 36).

Some have taken this dynamic between Dionysian wisdom and Apollonian poetry to be Nietzsche's primary statement on how art justifies life. The idea is that the truth is ugly, and poetic lies are needed to protect us from the ugly truth.[10] Although this is a correct reading of these sections, it does not represent the full extent of Nietzsche's understanding of how art can respond to the factual pessimism of Silenus. This is because sections five through nine delve into the Dionysian arts of music, dance, lyric poetry, and the genre of tragedy, which is a combination of the Apollonian and the Dionysian. In the Dionysian arts, the ugly and disharmonic aspects of existence, such as suffering and death, are directly confronted, transfigured, and affirmed.

That the relationship between Apollo and Dionysus detailed in sections three and four is only part of the story is evidenced by the fact that Nietzsche begins section five by identifying Archilochus as the figurehead of a new sort of poetry different from that of the Homeric (BT 5; KSA 1, 42). What distinguishes the two types of poetry, for Nietzsche, is that the creation of lyric poetry begins with a *musical mood* (BT 5; KSA 1, 43). That is, it begins not with a series of images generated from a confrontation with an all-too-bleak reality, but in a psychological state in which a poet like Archilochus loses his everyday identity and instead identifies with the "primal unity, its pain and contradiction" (BT 5; KSA 1, 43f.).

Although his description of lyric poetry depends on an appearance–reality distinction taken from Schopenhauer, it should be noted that Nietzsche has modified Schopenhauer's metaphysics in a subtle way (Decher 1984). This is because suffering occurs not only at the level of individuation, but also at the metaphysical level of the unified one. For Nietzsche, the Ur-Eine is conflicted with itself (BT 5; KSA 1, 43f.). Thus, when the lyric poet, qua Dionysian artist, identifies with the "primal unity," the lyric poet is also identifying with the pain and suffering that lies at the heart of the world. This stands in sharp contrast to the epic poet who turns away from the suffering of existence to create a veil of beauty that he casts over the ugly truth and contemplates with insatiable delight.

As Nietzsche points out at the beginning of section five, the purpose of discussing both epic and lyric poetry is to progress towards the ultimate goal of explaining the way in which tragedy reconciles the Apollonian–Dionysian duality announced at the beginning of the text. This Nietzsche does in sections seven through nine, and he argues for their reconciliation on two related levels. The first is at the level of the psychology of the tragic poet. Specifically, the musical mood that allows the poet to merge with and expresses the primal pain and contradiction of the world can also generate symbolic dream images. Here, "Apollo appears and touches [the lyric poet] with the laurel" (BT 5; KSA 1, 44), such that the poet, now enchanted by Dionysian music, becomes conscious of a world of Apollonian images and symbols. According to Nietzsche, the highest development of this symbolic dream world can be found in tragedy and the dithyramb (BT 5; KSA 1, 42). In the dithyramb, the chorus and the chorus leader imagine themselves transformed, acting as if they "had actually entered into another body, another character" (BT 8; KSA 1, 61). This ecstatic experience marks the beginning of drama, symbolized by the donning of the mask, and the drama develops into a fully formed tragedy when the chorus, now transformed into a chorus of satyrs, sees an image of the god (BT 8; KSA 1, 61). This, according to Nietzsche, is the Apollonian complement of the ecstatic state of the Dionysian chorus. Here, the drama is completed when this Apollonian dream image is represented by an actor who stands amidst the Dionysian chorus. It is here that Dionysus and Apollo are reconciled, such that the Apollonian world of the stage emerges from the Dionysian womb of the musically inspired chorus.

The other union of the Dionysian and Apollonian that tragedy achieves can be located in the effects that the genre is said to produce. Specifically, Nietzsche singles out tragedy as the greatest of the life-affirming arts precisely because it achieves a twofold affirmation of existence. On the one hand, tragedy offers an Apollonian justification of existence. Much like Homeric epic, tragedy presents the spectator with a beautiful dream image in the tragic hero, an idealized form of humanity. Here, existence is justified because man himself is elevated to the status of a god (BT 16; KSA 1, 108). On the other hand, and this is where Dionysian art directly confronts Dionysian wisdom, tragedy revels in the destruction of the individual and so provides the chorus and the spectators with a face-to-face confrontation with suffering and death. Specifically, tragic art reveals and appeals to the "joy involved in the annihilation of the individual," where "the hero, the highest manifestation of the will, is negated for our pleasure, because he is only phenomenon, and because the eternal life of the will is not affected by this annihilation" (BT 16; KSA 1, 108).

The element of the tragic performance that allows us to experience the joys of the annihilation of the individual is, according to Nietzsche, the music and dance of the chorus. In particular, Nietzsche points to musical dissonance, a phenomenon, like the tragic myth itself, which reveals that humans actually want, and so affirm, suffering (BT 24; KSA 1, 152). The phenomenon of musical dissonance, Nietzsche tells us, is the key to understanding a central claim of the work: "for it is only as an *aesthetic phenomenon* that existence and the world are eternally *justified*" (BT 5; KSA 1, 47). This is because in both musical dissonance and the tragic myth, one does not affirm a world covered over with the beautiful lies of Apollo, but rather one affirms suffering and death as part of an eternal game that "the will in the eternal amplitude of its pleasure plays with itself" (BT 24; KSA 1, 152). Thus, it is through tragedy that we take delight in the "playful construction and destruction of the individual world" just as a child—here Nietzsche is explicitly borrowing an image from Heraclitus—takes delight in building "sand hills only to overthrow them again" (BT 24; KSA 1, 153).

3. The death of tragedy in *The Birth of Tragedy*

Near the end of section ten, Nietzsche begins his account of the death of tragedy. Although Euripides is the figure he initially holds responsible for this event (BT 10; KSA 1, 74), Nietzsche eventually claims that behind Euripides was a "newborn daemon, called Socrates" (BT 12; KSA 1, 83).[11] Socrates is neither Dionysian nor Apollonian and so does not represent an "imbalance" in the Dionysian–Apollonian relationship in favor of the Apollonian.[12] Instead, he represents a completely new force, one that is alien and even hostile to the Apollonian and Dionysian forces that generated the art world of ancient Greece, and Nietzsche claims that this Socratic force animated the work of Euripides and ultimately led to the "suicide" of tragedy in ancient Greece.

So what is this mysterious force that Socrates represents? One might think that it is philosophy and the related drive to truth. Although Nietzsche does attribute this drive to Socrates and sees in Socrates the theoretical man *par excellence* (BT 15; KSA 1, 98), this is not all that Socrates represents in the work, and it is not the force that results in the death of tragedy. Instead, the death of tragedy can be attributed to Socratic optimism and the exalted role that reason and knowledge play in contributing to the optimist's quest for happiness or "eudaimonia." Thus, when Nietzsche claims that "we may recognize in Socrates the opponent of Dionysus" (BT 12; KSA 1, 88), we should understand this as an opposition between Socratic optimism and Dionysian wisdom (and so the factual pessimism of Silenus).

Whereas factual pessimism asserts the impossibility of happiness or "eudaimonia," optimism holds that it is possible for at least some to attain this end. According to the optimist, the so-called "eternal wound of existence" can be healed (BT 18; KSA 1, 115) and the primordial pain and contradiction of the world can be overcome (BT 5; KSA 1, 43f.). The reason why Nietzsche thinks that optimism is hostile to poetry is because poetry functions as a response to factual pessimism. On this view, human beings suffer necessarily, and there is no cure for this situation. Thus, the question is how to redeem, justify, and affirm what some might call a fallen world, and the answer that Nietzsche provides, both in *The Birth of Tragedy* and in his later works, is the trans-figuring powers of the tragedies and comedies associated with Dionysus. In denying the disjointed nature of the world, the optimist no longer sees the need to engage in the justificatory or affirmative project that the artist, on Nietzsche's view, undertakes.[13] Because happiness is a genuine possibility, the purpose of life is to become happy by minimizing or even eliminating suffering, and this, according to Nietzsche, is what lies at the heart of the Socratic project. Although philosophers following Socrates disagreed on the nature of the good life and the means to achieve it, there was never-theless agreement among post-Socratic philosophers that "eudaimonia" is the goal of human life and therefore a central component of the philosophical project.[14] It is for this reason that Nietzsche sees in the optimism of Socrates "the one turning point and vortex of so-called world history" (BT 15; KSA 1, 100).

Although Nietzsche believes that genuine art withers and dies once factual pessimism is rejected, this does not mean that *all* art, as *we* understand it, withers and dies. In Nietzsche's view, art takes on a different, bastardized function within an optimistic framework. Specifically, art must contribute to, or at least not inhibit, the quest for happiness, and if the optimistic quest for happiness is bound up with virtue, rationality, and knowledge, then art must play some role in making people more virtuous, rational, and knowledgeable. Nietzsche argues that, historically, art came to be seen as an especially effective tool for training people who cannot understand philosophy. Mockingly, Nietzsche identifies Aesop's fables as the new paradigm for artistic creation, and he points to the Platonic dialogue and the novel that grew from the dialogue as more advanced forms of the Aesopian fable (BT 14; KSA 1, 93). According to Nietzsche, "the Platonic dialogue was, as it were, the barge on which the shipwrecked ancient poetry saved herself with all her children" (BT 14; KSA 1, 93). However, the art that was rescued had to cling to the "trunk of dialectic" and ultimately become, as it does in the Platonic dialogue, subservient to the demands of philosophy.

Although philosophy increased in popularity once it attached itself to Socratic optimism, it is nevertheless optimism, and not philosophy itself, that "killed" tragedy. While it is easy to find in the Platonic Socrates the optimism of which Nietzsche speaks, it is more difficult to find Socratic optimism in Euripides' plays. This is especially true if being an optimistic playwright means producing plays in which the tensions of the story eventually resolve themselves in a happy and morally edifying ending. So construed, one problem with Nietzsche's argument is that Aristotle sees in Euripides the most tragic of poets (*Poet.* 1453a27–30). Not only is the climax of *Medea* particularly gruesome, where a mother murders her own children to avenge her disloyal husband; one cannot overlook the horrific conclusion to the *Bacchae*, where a mother realizes that she is carrying the head of her son whom she has, in a fit of Bacchic madness, just dismembered.

Given such endings, the association between Euripides and Socratic optimism seems tenuous at best. However, Nietzsche defends his point by claiming that although Euripidean tragedy did have some horrific endings in its infancy, its true nature soon revealed itself as it grew into New Attic Comedy (BT 11; KSA 1, 76). So, on this view, even if it can be argued that Euripides is the most tragic of poets in the sense that his tragedies leave us with a foreboding sense of cruelty and human misery,[15] they nevertheless provide a framework for a genre known for its happy, optimistic, and superficial endings. For Nietzsche, New Attic Comedy epitomized a superficial *semblance* of Greek cheerfulness, one born not from a confrontation with suffering and death, but rather from an attempt to deny the powerful role they play in human existence (BT 11; KSA 1, 78).

To develop the connection between Euripides and Socrates even further, it is necessary to specify the kind of optimism Nietzsche finds in Euripides' work. Here, it is necessary to note that Socratic optimism couples the promise of happiness with rationality and the quest for knowledge. The idea is that reason and knowledge are either a means to or constitutive of happiness (or both). With this in hand, one can say that Nietzsche's Euripides was an optimist because he sought to educate the public with his plays. Similar to Nietzsche's assessment of the Aesopian fable, the idea is that Euripides saw theater as a tool for enlightening the masses. Thus, art is valuable because it spreads knowledge and so, on the optimist's picture, happiness. According to Nietzsche, Euripides achieved this effect by bringing the spectator onto the stage, as it was through his plays that people learned "how to observe, debate, and draw conclusions according to the rule of art with the cleverest sophistries" (BT 11; KSA 1, 77). Thus, Nietzsche writes: "If the entire populace now philosophized, managed land and goods, and conducted lawsuits with unheard-of circumspection, [Euripides] deserved the credit, for this was the result of the wisdom he had inculcated in the people" (BT 11; KSA 1, 77).

As a result of his desire to educate the larger populace through his plays, Euripides adopted what Nietzsche calls "*aesthetic Socratism*," which states that, "to be beautiful everything must be intelligible" (BT 12; KSA 1, 85). If the spectators are going to learn anything from the theater, they must understand what is being presented, and therefore Euripides took to adding a prologue and expelling anything in tragedy that left an ugly trail of mystery and unintelligibility. Furthermore, if Euripides was going to make everything intelligible, he himself had to produce his plays as a thinker and not as a musically inspired poet (BT 12; KSA 1, 87). Thus, Euripides appeared as the first "sober" poet among a bunch of "drunks" like Aeschylus. In this way, the demand for intelligibility led him to adopt and follow the related Socratic demand that "to be good everything must be conscious." For these reasons, Nietzsche claims, "we may consider Euripides as the poet of aesthetic Socratism" (BT 12; KSA 1, 87).

Although these elements link Euripidean drama to Socratic optimism, the real blow that Euripides landed in "killing" tragedy was his attempt to divorce tragedy from its musical origin. Indeed, this goes to the heart of Nietzsche's attempt to link Euripides to Socrates, and it is a point that has been largely overlooked by those critical of Nietzsche's damnatio of Euripides.[16] Specifically, the charge that Nietzsche levels against Socrates and Euripides is that they are both *amusical* and therefore un-Dionysian and so un-Greek. According to Nietzsche, Euripidean tragedy was an effort "to separate this original and all-powerful Dionysian element from tragedy, and to reconstruct tragedy purely on the basis of an un-Dionysian art, morality, and worldview" (BT 12; KSA 1, 82). In terms of artistic production, Euripides effectively abandoned the musical mood essential to the production of lyric, dithyrambic, and tragic poetry, and because he abandoned Dionysus (the music), he also failed to generate the dream world of Apollonian images. Thus, he was forced to piece together his characters from everyday experience, and so he could not help but bring the spectator onto the tragic stage.

In terms of the performance itself, Euripides both altered the music and reduced the significance of the chorus (BT 14; KSA 1, 95). He altered the music because he adopted what Nietzsche sees as a degenerative form of music in the *New Attic Dithyramb*. Rather than going beyond everyday reality and providing an immediate copy of the will itself, this new kind of music imitated the phenomenal world governed by the "principium individuationis" (BT 17; KSA 1, 111f.). Here again, this neglect of Dionysian music results in the inability to create the mythical world that is central to the tragic experience. Similarly, Euripides undermined the significance of the chorus because he made it functionally equivalent to another actor. In so doing, he destroyed "the essence of tragedy, which can be interpreted only as a manifestation and projection into images of Dionysian states" (BT 14; KSA 1, 95). Thus, on Nietzsche's view, the tragedies that Euripides created were completely different from those of his predecessors, and in this sense, he can be seen as having led tragedy to its suicidal death (BT 11; KSA 1, 75).

This, then, is how Nietzsche argues that Socratic optimism led to the destruction of the genuine art that flourished prior to Socrates. On the one hand, Socratic optimism eliminated the need that Nietzsche thinks genuine art fulfills. On the other hand, Socratic optimism was hostile to the kind of art that responded to the aforementioned need. This is because the glories of the Greek art world were created by liberating the non-rational elements of the human psyche, namely the will (Dionysus) and the imagination (Apollo), from the tyranny of reason (Socrates). Since the followers of Socratic optimism were encouraged to become perfectly rational, Socratic optimism undermined genuine artistic creativity and condemned the enjoyment of artistic works that appealed to non-rational desires and emotions. Thus, if art was going to survive, it would have to transform itself into something that could contribute to making people more ethical, knowledgeable, rational, and ultimately happy. According to Nietzsche, this did not transform genuine art, but eventually killed it. That is, this process of transformation killed genuine tragedy because it became an art that was not, in Nietzsche's view, *really* art. Nevertheless, there is hope for a rebirth of genuine tragedy, but if this is going to happen, there must be a rebirth of a tragic worldview and so a corresponding death of Socratic optimism, and this, Nietzsche believes, can come about through the advancement of a philosophy that is willing to see the world as it truly is.

4. Philosophy and the rebirth of tragedy in *The Birth of Tragedy*

The figure that helps unlock the structure of *The Birth of Tragedy* is the music-playing or artistic Socrates. This is because the artistic Socrates combines the philosophical drive for truth with a love of and need for an art that redeems, justifies, and affirms the tragic worldview that philosophical and scientific inquiry reveals. According to the young Nietzsche, the world has never seen such a figure because the Western intellectual tradition has been defined by an unresolved opposition between the artistic achievements of ancient Greece and the philosophical project that Socrates initiated. It is only now, according to Nietzsche, that this opposition can be resolved. This is because recent developments in German philosophy are preparing the way for a rebirth of tragedy via German music. This, then, is the topic of the final ten sections of *The Birth of Tragedy*, where the initial opposition between the poetic culture described in the first ten sections and the philosophical culture described in sections ten through fifteen is overcome. As one can see, the structure and the argument of the work do smell "offensively Hegelian" (EH Books BT: 1; KSA 6, 310).

The key to understanding how this reconciliation might work is to see the way in which the Socratic project contains within it concealed tensions that begin to reveal themselves as the Socratic project advances. As Nietzsche tells us, the Socratic project is rooted in "the unshakeable faith that thought, using the thread of causality, can penetrate the deepest abysses of being, and that thought is capable not only of knowing being but even of *correcting* it" (BT 15; KSA 1, 99). There are two claims here, and they can be linked to the two ways in which the Socratic project is, according to Nietzsche, destroying itself. On the one hand, the Socratic project depends on the belief that reality is intelligible. On the other hand, the Socratic project holds that the knowledge we can attain will correct existence, thereby functioning as a "panacea" for human suffering (BT 15; KSA 1, 100).

There is, however, a tension within the Socratic project because these beliefs are coupled with an unrelenting drive for truth. The drive for truth is a problem for Socratic optimism because this drive, on Nietzsche's view, ultimately reveals the falsity of Socratic optimism. Thus, the Socratic quest for truth culminates in the destruction of the optimism that transformed the quest for truth into a widespread, world-historical force. According to Nietzsche, the two truth-loving philosophers who have revealed the falsity of Socratic optimism are Kant and Schopenhauer. On the one hand, Kant has shown that the knowable world is only a phenomenal world and that we have no access to the world as it is in itself. On the other hand, Schopenhauer provides a wisdom that transcends the limitations of the sciences and "seeks to grasp, with sympathetic feelings of love, the eternal suffering as its own" (BT 18; KSA 1, 118). In other words, Schopenhauer has shown that suffering is an ineluctable feature of human existence. Thus, his philosophy has put an end to any hope that knowledge can cure the eternal wound of existence. Indeed, Schopenhauer's philosophy proves just the opposite: knowledge is not a cure for human suffering, but reveals its ineluctability, and the knowledge of this fact can itself be a cause of suffering. In this sense, the paradigmatic philosopher is not Socrates, but Oedipus, and what Oedipus' quest reveals is the truth of factual pessimism (BT 9; KSA 1, 65f.).

As one can see, these two means of putting an end to Socratic optimism can conflict with each other. Whereas Kant seems to be the individual responsible for using "the paraphernalia of science itself, to point out the limits and the relativity of knowledge generally" (BT 18; KSA 1, 118), Schopenhauer's work depends on certain insights that go beyond the limits that Kant's philosophy establishes. Although this is a tension that runs throughout Nietzsche's mature philosophy, it is nevertheless the case that each of these positions points to the end of Socratic optimism. At the same time, these forces have emerged from the Socratic drive for truth, and what they have done is meet the Socratic demand to make a wisdom that was once mythological into something that is explicit and conceptual. In other words, what Kant and Schopenhauer have revealed is "Dionysian wisdom now comprised in concepts" (BT 19; KSA 1, 128).

So what we see from Nietzsche's analysis is an attempt to read the history of philosophy as a slow unfolding of a Socratic elenchus applied to Socrates' own belief set. Quite simply, the love of truth is incompatible, first, with the belief that truth is accessible to human minds and, second, with the belief that truth and knowledge are panaceas for human suffering. To be a genuine lover of truth is to be one who acknowledges that the truth might not be accessible to our understanding or that it might even be hostile to the happiness-project essential to Socratic optimism. It is here, then, that optimism speeds towards its "shipwreck," where those committed to the optimistic project "see to their horror how logic coils up at these boundaries and finally bites its own tail" (BT 15; KSA 1, 101). In this situation, Nietzsche proclaims that "a new form of insight breaks through," a "*tragic insight*, which, merely to be endured, needs art as a protection and remedy" (BT 15; KSA 1, 101).

Given this twofold attack on optimism, Nietzsche's claim that the philosophical quest for truth will naturally result in a turn to art can be understood in two ways. On the one hand, the turn to art can be understood as completing the epistemic project that philosophy initiates. This is because the young Nietzsche attributes to music the ability to go beyond mere phenomena and the related principle of individuation by providing an immediate copy of the will and so the thing in itself (BT 16; KSA 1, 104f.). However, Nietzsche's call for a turn to art in light of the self-destruction of Socratic optimism seems to have more to do with meeting an existential need than an epistemic one. That is, we need art, and in particular music, to endure or even affirm the tragic insight that philosophy reveals. This, of course, recalls the very dynamic that Nietzsche attributes to the Greeks' confrontation with Silenic wisdom in section three, and it is one that Nietzsche repeats in section seven:

> With this chorus the profound Hellene, uniquely susceptible to the tenderest and deepest suffering, comforts himself, having looked boldly right into the terrible destructiveness of so-called world history as well as the cruelty of nature, and in danger of longing for a Buddhistic negation of the will. Art saves him, and through art—life. (BT 7; KSA 1, 56)

In *The Birth of Tragedy*, Nietzsche does not identify any one person who embodies the ideal of the musical or artistic Socrates. Instead, he sees the fulfillment of this ideal in the convergence or "oneness" of German philosophy with German music. Just as he sees the gradual self-destruction of Socratic optimism in the philosophies of Kant and Schopenhauer, he sees, as an independent force, "the *gradual awakening of the Dionysian spirit*" in German music "from Bach to Beethoven, from Beethoven to Wagner" (BT 19; KSA 1, 127). Because he argues at length that tragedy is primarily a musical phenomenon, Nietzsche's turn to German music as the proper means of affirming life in response to the truths of German philosophy can be understood as a turn to tragedy and, more specifically, a "*rebirth of tragedy*" (BT 19; KSA 1, 129). Just as Schopenhauer stands at the culmination of these developments in philosophy, Wagner stands at the end of these developments in German music. Specifically, Nietzsche sees in Wagner's operas a rebirth of Aeschylean-style tragedy that is nevertheless distinctively German. What this indicates, however, is that the music-playing Socrates is really a combination of Schopenhauer and Wagner, neither one embodying this ideal on their own. Thus, Nietzsche's argument leaves open the possibility for a single individual to fulfill this ideal, and I think this is precisely what Nietzsche tries to do in his post-1876 works.[17]

5. The tragic worldview in "Philosophy in the Tragic Age of the Greeks"

Although Nietzsche remains committed to the basic framework of *The Birth of Tragedy* throughout his career (TI Ancients 5; KSA 6, 160 and NF 1883, 16[11]; KSA 10, 510), his thinking on these matters does undergo some evolution, and although I cannot provide a detailed account of this evolution here, I do want to say something about how his thinking about the tragic Greeks changes in a small but significant way just after the publication of his first work. In *The Birth of Tragedy*, Nietzsche largely depicts the tragic age of the Greeks as pre-philosophical. Nevertheless, Nietzsche does not entirely overlook the philosophy during the tragic age in the work. As noted above, Nietzsche refers to Heraclitus in the penultimate section of the work as he explains how tragedy can justify existence as an aesthetic phenomenon (BT 24; KSA 1, 153).

The reference to Heraclitus is subtle, but it provides a link to the unpublished essay, "Philosophy in the Tragic Age of the Greeks," which Nietzsche composed as a companion piece to *The Birth of Tragedy* (to von Gersdorff, March 2, 1873; KSB 4, 132). In terms of understanding the argument of *The Birth of Tragedy*, "Philosophy in the Tragic Age of the Greeks" is valuable because it develops a tragic worldview that is both philosophical and decisively anti-metaphysical. Based on his exposition of Anaximander's philosophy, Nietzsche can now be said to see metaphysics itself as complicit in the life-denying attitude that Schopenhauer propounds. That is, it is the existence of a second, metaphysical world that is used to condemn the world of becoming as something that ought not to be. Thus, if the evaluative pessimism of Schopenhauer is to be overcome, then Schopenhauer's metaphysical understanding of reality and so the metaphysics that run throughout *The Birth of Tragedy* must also be rejected. This is precisely what Nietzsche's Heraclitus does. According to Nietzsche, Heraclitus does not distinguish a metaphysical from a physical world, and this move is related to a "second, far bolder negation: he altogether denied being" (PTAG 5; KSA 1, 822f.). As the philosopher of becoming, Nietzsche's Heraclitus conceives of reality as simply *Wirken*, such that "everything which coexists in space and time has but a relative existence, that each thing exists through and for another like it, which is to say through and for an equally relative one" (PTAG 5; KSA 1, 824).

In terms of *The Birth of Tragedy*, Nietzsche's portrayal of Heraclitus not only provides an account of the philosophy that flourished during the tragic age of the Greeks, it also shifts the divide that Nietzsche locates in ancient Greek culture from the tension between the pessimism of the pre-Socratic Greeks and the optimism of Socrates to the gulf between the anti-metaphysical philosophy of Heraclitus and the metaphysical philosophy of Parmenides. This is because Nietzsche not only sees in Parmenides a response to Heraclitus' philosophy, but he also characterizes Parmenides' discovery of the doctrine of being as a moment that "divides pre-Socratic thinking into two halves" and "un-Greek as no other in the two centuries of the Tragic Age" (PTAG 9; KSA 1, 836). Moreover, because Nietzsche also sees in Parmenides' a priori argumentation a break with the empiricism of predecessors like Heraclitus, the division that Nietzsche finds in antiquity can also be articulated in terms of the epistemological debate between empiricism and rationalism. Taken together, what we see Nietzsche doing is coupling together the optimism of Socrates with the rationalism and metaphysics of Parmenides and opposing these to the factual pessimism of Greek poetry and a Heraclitean theory of becoming that best describes the empirical world. In the next section, I suggest that one can find a similar constellation in Plato's writings. The only difference is that Plato defends Socratic optimism and a rationalist metaphysics against a poetic worldview that he links not only to a rather grim portrayal of the human condition, but also to a Heraclitean theory of becoming that derives from an empiricist epistemology.

6. Plato and the poetic worldview

Although my remarks on Plato can only be cursory, I think enough can be said here to make the case that Nietzsche understands antiquity in a way that prefigures recent scholarship on Plato's understanding of the ancient quarrel between philosophy and poetry. Specifically, recent scholars such as Stephen Halliwell have argued that Plato links the poetry of ancient Greece to a way of life situated within a larger worldview. As evidence for the claim that Plato sees in tragedy a larger vision of life, Halliwell points to a passage from Plato's *Laws*, where the lawgivers of a well-governed city will not allow tragic actors into their community because the lawgivers themselves are tragedians and their "tragedy is the finest and best" in that their city has been "constructed as a representation of the finest and best life" (*Laws* 817b; Halliwell 1996, 338). Halliwell also refers to a passage from the *Philebus* where we are told that "in lamentations as well as in tragedies and comedies, not on stage but also in all of life's tragedies and comedies, pleasures are mixed with pains, and so it is on infinitely other occasions" (*Phil.* 50b; Halliwell 1996, 337). Based on these and other passages, Halliwell contends that Plato views tragedy (and comedy) "as the vehicle of a highly distinctive sense of life—so much so, indeed, that it becomes equally possible to regard tragedy as an interpretation of life, and life itself as a quasi-aesthetic phenomenon possessing the kinds of properties which are exhibited in their most concentrated form in theatrical works" (Ibid.).

Halliwell also claims that one can find in Plato not only an understanding of a tragic (and comic) way of life, but also a worldview that corresponds to this way of life. Indeed, it is in moving from the genre of tragedy to a general sense of life and the world that Plato can characterize Homer as "the first teacher and leader of all these fine tragedians" (*Rep.* 595b). That is, Homer is the leader of tragedians not because he composed tragedies for the dramatic stage, but because his poetry expresses a tragic vision of life and the world. This is a point that becomes evident in Plato's critique of Homeric poetry in *Republic* II and III. According to Halliwell, Plato sees in Homeric poetry a worldview that includes gods who are the cause of evil, humans who experience death as a great loss, and social orders that ensure a disjunction between justice and human happiness. In short, Plato understands the tragic worldview as "a mentality which finds the structure of the world—governed by divine powers capable of ruthless destructiveness, and limited by the inevitability of death—to be fundamentally hostile to human needs and values, and irreconcilable with a positive moral significance" (Halliwell 1996, 340).

Although these are Halliwell's words, this description of Plato's understanding of Homer's tragic worldview certainly resonates with the understanding of the world that Nietzsche places in the mouth of Silenus. What is also striking about Plato's engagement with Homeric poetry—and this is a point that Halliwell does not make—is that there are reasons for thinking that Plato, like Nietzsche, links this tragic worldview to Heraclitean becoming. Intimations of this can be found in the *Republic* itself. This is because Plato refers to certain lovers of sights and sounds who would never miss a Dionysian festival (*Rep.* 475d) and yet deny the existence of "beauty itself" (*Rep.* 476c). In denying the existence of beauty itself and so Plato's Forms, the lovers of sights and sounds believe in the existence of a sensible world only, which is described as a world in which things both are and are not (*Rep.* 478d). Although there is much controversy surrounding the meaning of what it is for something both to be and not be, it has been argued that just as the world of things that *are* is a world of *being*, the world in which things both are and are not is the realm of Heraclitean becoming (Bolton 1975, 77). If this is right, then the lovers of sights and sounds who would never miss a Dionysian festival believe that the sensible world is the only world and that the sensible world is a world of Heraclitean becoming.

The connections between poetry, the sensible world, and Heraclitean becoming are further developed in and substantiated by a passage from the *Theaetetus*. This is because Plato has Socrates link the ontology of pre-Socratic figures like Protagoras and Heraclitus to the claim that knowledge is perception (*Tht.* 151e). This nexus of views can be linked to the lovers of sights and sounds from the *Republic* not only because reality is said to be known through the senses, but also because the Heraclitean and Protagorean positions are bound together by their denial of things that exist and are what they are in virtue of themselves. For Plato's Heraclitus and Protagoras,

> the things of which we naturally say that they "are," are in a process of coming to be, as the result of movement and change and blending with one another. We are wrong when we say they "are," since nothing even is, but everything is coming to be. (*Tht.* 152d–e)

On this view, the sensible world is a realm of becoming, and the realm of becoming is a realm of dynamic entities that exist and are what they are only in relation to other dynamic entities. In the language of the *Republic*, we can say that the things of the sensible world *are*, because they exist, but also *are not*, because they exist only in relation to something that they are not.

In terms of the ancient quarrel between philosophy and poetry, the most important passage in the *Theaetetus* comes just after the Protagorean and Heraclitean theory of relative being or becoming is introduced. Specifically, Plato has Socrates put forth the surprising claim that this understanding of the world can be traced back to Homer:

> And as regards this point of view, let us take it as a fact that all the wise men of the past, with the exception of Parmenides, stand together. Let us take it that we find on this side Protagoras and Heraclitus and Empedocles; and also the masters of

the two kinds of poetry, Epicharmus in comedy and Homer in tragedy. For when Homer talked about "Ocean, begetter of gods, and Tethys their mother," he made all things the offspring of flux and motion. (*Tht.* 152e)

Although it is unlikely that Plato saw Homer as having a worked-out philosophical theory of becoming, Plato does claim that such a view is implicit in Homeric poetry. If this is right, one can say that, for both Plato and Nietzsche, there is a tragic worldview that Homeric poetry expresses and Heraclitus provides the most explicit philosophical formulation of this worldview.

At this point, a chorus of objections may arise concerning the legitimacy of this interpretation of Heraclitus and the potential relationship between his philosophy and the poetry of Homer. My point, however, is not to prove the accuracy of Nietzsche's or even Plato's interpretation of Heraclitus, but simply to show that Nietzsche's attempt to link Heraclitus' philosophy to the world of poetry is something that can also be found in Plato. Because Nietzsche also follows Plato in singling out Parmenides as the lone philosopher who stands firm against Homer's army of flux theorists (cf. PTAG 9; KSA 1, 836), one can make the further claim that Nietzsche's understanding of pre-Socratic philosophy largely parallels that of Plato.

7. Nietzsche's value as a scholar of the ancient quarrel between philosophy and poetry

If my brief sketch of Plato's critique of poetry is right, then Nietzsche's value as a scholar of antiquity can be assessed on two levels. First, he encourages us to see the intimate connection between Plato's critique of certain philosophical views and the critique of poetry executed in a work like the *Republic*. Just as Nietzsche sees the death of tragedy in terms of the introduction of a worldview foreign to the worldview embedded within tragedy, Plato's philosophy is designed to overthrow poetry by attacking the philosophical positions that it depends upon and conveys. Second, Nietzsche presents us with a vision of antiquity that establishes a sharp cultural divide between figures like Homer, Heraclitus, Aeschylus, and Aristophanes, on the one hand, and figures like Parmenides, Socrates, Euripides, Plato, and Aristotle, on the other hand. Although some will object to dividing antiquity in this way, it does offer an interesting alternative to those who understand antiquity as having undergone a smooth process of development from the mythos of Homer to the logos of Aristotle.[18] Moreover, Nietzsche's understanding of antiquity is supported by the fact that Plato tends to see his own work as a radical break from the philosophy and poetry of his predecessors. Thus, one can say that the legitimacy of Nietzsche's reading of antiquity stands or falls with the accuracy of the vision of antiquity that Plato subtly articulates throughout his dialogues and the position that Plato assigns to himself within the culture.

Despite this broad agreement between Nietzsche and Plato, it should nevertheless be clear that these two thinkers take different sides in the ancient quarrel between philosophy and poetry, and that *The Birth of Tragedy* is Nietzsche's initial attempt to revive this ancient quarrel with his attack on Socratic optimism and his related call for a rebirth of tragedy. It should also be clear that Nietzsche, like Plato, construes the ancient quarrel in terms of competing worldviews, and so one could argue that much of Nietzsche's later philosophy is a contribution to this quarrel insofar as it is designed to replace a metaphysical understanding of the world with an anti-metaphysical, tragic vision of existence. One interesting upshot of construing the ancient quarrel between philosophy and poetry in this way is that the quarrel ultimately turns on a set of philosophical questions. Just as Plato's rejection of poetry as the highest activity of human existence is bound up with his rejection of a tragic vision of existence and a worldview that he links to the philosophy of Heraclitus, Nietzsche's attempt to re-establish the superiority of poetry goes hand in hand with his eventual attempt to revive a certain worldview that he finds in the philosophy of Heraclitus. Thus, for both Plato and Nietzsche, the question as to whether philosophical contemplation or poetic production is the highest activity of this life ultimately turns on questions such as whether the real world is the sensible world and whether the sensible world can be reduced to a set of dynamic relations such that nothing exists in and for itself. Because these are questions that fall under the province of philosophy as we understand it, it turns out that only the philosopher can resolve the ancient quarrel between philosophy and poetry as Plato and Nietzsche construe it.

Notes

1. All translations and references to Plato's works are from *Plato: The Complete Works*, J. M. Cooper (ed.), Indianapolis: Hackett Publishing Co., 1997. Translations of Nietzsche's works are: *The Birth of Tragedy out of the Spirit of Music*, trans. W. Kaufmann. New York: Vintage Books, 1967; *On the Genealogy of Morals and Ecce Homo*, trans. W. Kaufmann, New York: Random House, 1989; *Human, All Too Human I and II*, R. J. Hollingdale (trans.), Cambridge: Cambridge University Press, 1996; *Philosophy in the Tragic Age of the Greeks*, M. Cowan (trans.). Washington, DC: Gateway, 1962.

2. See Barfield 2011 for the most recent account of this long-standing quarrel.

3. For an example of this approach to the text, see Magnus and Higgins 1996, 21ff.

4. Magnus and Higgins 1996, 23 claim that, in Nietzsche's eyes, "Socrates was responsible for directing Western culture towards an imbalanced, exaggerated reliance on the Apollonian point of view."

5. See von Reibnitz 1992, 316 on this point.

6. For an alternative reading that attempts to divide the text into two parts, see Burnham and Jesinghausen 2010, 10f.

7. Speaking of a tragic worldview here is evidenced by the fact that Nietzsche titled one of the preliminary essays to *The Birth of Tragedy*, "Die dionysische Weltanschauung" or "The Dionysian Worldview" (KSA 1, 551ff.).

8. A similar distinction between descriptive and evaluative forms of pessimism has been made by Soll 1988, 113f. and Came 2004, 41.

9. For a similar reading, see Came 2004, 39.

10 See Reginster 2006, 248 for such a reading.

11 See Henrichs 1986, 371 for remarks on this controversial claim.

12 See Douglas Burnham's contribution to this volume for the relation between the Socratic and Apollonian.

13 However, this is not to say that Socratic optimism did function as a certain sort of artistic justification, albeit a self-deceived one. That is, the hope for a suffering-free existence is what justified existence in the face of occurrent suffering; this is a sort of artistic justification of existence because this hope is founded on an illusion and so a form of art. According to Nietzsche, Socrates instinctively generated this illusion and thereby prevented the logical-critical urge from turning against his own conviction that nothing was more valuable than the truth (BT 13; KSA 1, 90ff.).

14 This is what Vlastos 1991, 203ff. has called the "eudaemonist axiom" that runs throughout post-Socratic philosophy.

15 This, of course, is contestable because a number of Euripides' plays did have happy endings, most notably *Iphigeneia in Tauris*. For analysis of such plays, see Burnett 1971.

16 See Henrichs 1986 for a critical assessment of Nietzsche's treatment of Euripides that nevertheless overlooks Nietzsche's claim that Euripides' primarily failing was his neglect of the chorus and so the musical elements of tragedy and the production of tragedy.

17 I have developed this theme in Meyer 2004.

18 See Buxton 1999, 1–25 on the prevalence of this understanding of antiquity and reflections on some problems with it.

Works cited

Barfield, Raymond (2011): *The Ancient Quarrel between Philosophy and Poetry*. Cambridge (Cambridge University Press).

Bolton, Robert (1975): "Plato's Distinction between Being and Becoming." In *Review of Metaphysics*. Vol. 34, 66–95.

Burnett, Anne Pippin (1971): *Catastrophe Survived: Euripides' Plays of Mixed Reversal*. Oxford (Clarendon Press).

Burnham, Douglas and Martin Jesinghausen (2010): *Nietzsche's* The Birth of Tragedy: *A Reader's Guide*. New York (Continuum).

Buxton, Richard (1999): "Introduction." In Richard Buxton (ed.): *From Myth to Reason? Studies in the Development of Greek Thought*. Oxford (Oxford University Press), 1–24.

Came, Daniel (2004): "Nietzsche's Attempt at a Self-Criticism: Art and Morality in *The Birth of Tragedy*." In *Nietzsche Studien*. Vol. 33, 37–67.

Decher, Friedhelm (1984): "Nietzsches Metaphysik in der 'Geburt der Tragoedie' im Verhältnis zur Philosophie Schopenhauers." In *Nietzsche Studien*. Vol. 13, 110–25.

Halliwell, Stephen (1996): "Plato's Repudiation of the Tragic." In Michael Silk (ed.): *Tragedy and the Tragic*. Oxford (Clarendon Press), 332–49.

Henrichs, Albert (1986): "The Last of the Detractors: Friedrich Nietzsche's Condemnation of Euripides." In *Greek, Roman, and Byzantine Studies*. Vol. 27 (4), 369–97.

Magnus, Bernd and Kathleen Higgins (1996): "Nietzsche's Works and their Themes." In Magnus and Higgins (eds): *The Cambridge Companion to Nietzsche*. Cambridge (Cambridge University Press), 21–70.

Meyer, Matthew (2004): "*Human, All Too Human* and the Socrates Who Plays Music." In *International Studies in Philosophy*. Vol. 36 (3), 171–82.

Most, Glenn (2011): "What Ancient Quarrel between Philosophy and Poetry?" In Pierre Destrée and Fritz-Gregor Herrmann (eds): *Plato and the Poets*. Boston (Brill), 1–20.

Reginster, Bernard (2006): *The Affirmation of Life: Nietzsche on Overcoming Nihilism.* Cambridge, MA (Harvard University Press).

Soll, Ivan (1988): "Pessimism and the Tragic View of Life: Reconsiderations of Nietzsche's *Birth of Tragedy*." In Robert C. Salomon and Kathleen M. Higgins (eds): *Reading Nietzsche*. New York and Oxford (Oxford University Press), 104–31.

Vlastos, Gregory (1991): *Socrates: Ironist and Moral Philosopher.* Ithaca, NY (Cornell University Press).

Von Reibnitz, Barbara (1992): *Ein Kommentar zu Friedrich Nietzsche,* Die Geburt der Tragödie aus dem Geiste der Musik: *Kap. 1–12.* Stuttgart (Metzler).

Part Five

Philosophy, Science, Religion

11

Nietzsche's Genealogy of Early Greek Philosophy

Helmut Heit

"So much depends on the development of Greek culture, since our occidental world as a whole received its impetus from them."

NF 1875, 6[11]; KSA 8, 101

Nietzsche's engagement with early Greek philosophy is instructive not only to those with a genuine interest in Nietzsche, but also due to the significance of this epoch in our cultural historiography and self-understanding. Whoever develops an interest in the history and evolution of Western philosophy might be tempted to study early Greek thought, since the so-called pre-Socratics are often considered as the foundational "first philosophers." However, as Nietzsche stated in his unpublished essay on "Philosophy in the Tragic Age of Greece" (1873): "Greek philosophy seems to begin with an absurd notion, with the proposition that *water* is the primal origin and the womb of all things: Is it really necessary to stand silent and become serious here?" (PTG 3; KSA 1, 813).[1] Given that we take almost any positive statement of these thinkers to be outdated and wrong, it might appear as an unjustified prejudice in favor of Greek culture. Despite the fact that Phil-Hellenism has been challenged by several objections, enthusiasm for early Greek achievements remains widespread. Paradigmatically, the most recent comprehensive English edition of early Greek philosophers states in its first sentences:

> The Presocratics introduced a new kind of wisdom to the world. They appeared suddenly in the sixth century BC as sages who wanted to explain, not just this or that fact or custom or institution, but everything at once. They began as students of nature, who took nature as an independent realm to be understood in terms of its own capacities. In their time of mythical and magical thinking even the very concept of nature was stunningly new and unprecedented. They gave birth to two important disciplines that have characterized Western thought ever since: philosophy and science. (Graham 2010: I, 1)

According to these claims, the beginning of philosophy can be located historically and geographically in ancient Greece at about 600 BC. The origin of philosophy is taken to be unprecedented and spontaneous. In addition to these empirical claims on originality, the systematic content of this emergence is seen in a new kind of wisdom, namely in the first approach to universal explanation, a new concept of nature, and the rise of philosophy and science simultaneously. Despite these claims, neatly captured in Wilhelm Nestle's handy teleological phrase *Vom Mythos zum Logos* (Nestle 1940) and continuously repeated one way or the other in almost every history of Western philosophy, the exact content, scope, and explanation of the supposed early Greek achievements still remains a subject of dispute.[2] This paper argues that Nietzsche's engagement with early Greek philosophy provides a significant contribution to this ongoing issue. First I shall introduce basic sources indicating an early Greek beginning of philosophy and science, especially Aristotle and Diogenes Laertius, as well as some historical treatises prevalent in Nietzsche's time like those of Hegel, Ueberweg, and Zeller. The second step is devoted to a reconstruction of Nietzsche's alternative genealogy of early Greek philosophy. Third, I try to evaluate his interpretation by distinguishing typical and timely elements of his account from untimely and original ones.

1. From myth to reason: The traditional answer

The standard account of the first historical and systematic beginnings of philosophy is neatly laid out in the first book of Aristotle's *Metaphysics*, our oldest exposition on early Greek philosophy. From this source derives the widely shared view to honor Thales of Miletus with the title of a first philosopher, because he supposedly introduced the idea of *archē*, understood as material principle underlying all things:

> That of which all things consist, from which they first come and into which on their destruction they are ultimately resolved, of which the essence persists although modified by its affections—this, they say, is an element and principle [στοιχεῖον καὶ ταύτην ἀρχήν] of existing things. [...] Thales, the founder of this school of philosophy, says the permanent entity is water. (Aristotle, *Met.* 983b)

Thales is considered as the first philosopher here, because he recognized one of the four prime causes Aristotle distinguishes, and because he made a universal but non-religious statement on the nature of everything. Aristotle provided the standard genealogical explanation for the emergence of this new mode of thought, too. The first sentence of *Metaphysics* states the anthropological assumption "[a]ll men naturally desire [ὀρέγονται φύσει] knowledge" (Aristotle, *Met.* 980a), and continues with an argument that the most privileged and most desired form of wisdom consists in universal knowledge for its own sake. A few pages later he famously adds: "It is through wonder [θαυμάζειν] that men now begin and originally began to philosophize" and "speculation of this kind began with a view to recreation and pastime [ῥᾳστώνην καὶ διαγωγὴν], at a time when practically all the necessities of life were already supplied" (Aristotle, *Met.* 982b). The origin of philosophy therefore results from three elements: natural desire or striving, wonder or puzzlement, and a state of good conditions or leisure-time. It is therefore explained by a combination of natural potentials, human curiosity, and applicable conditions, which allow these potentialities to become actualities. Within such a framework the origin of philosophy is not really in need of further explanation, because it naturally emerges as soon as conditions apply.

Despite this foundation of philosophy in human nature, Aristotle and most of his followers insist on a particularly and exclusively Greek achievement. Diogenes Laertius dedicates the first passages of his collection of anecdotes and philosophical positions to defend decisively Greek origins while refusing claims on philosophy or philosophy-like modes of thought in other, "barbaric" cultures. "These authors forget that the achievements which they attribute to the barbarians belong to the Greeks, with whom not merely philosophy but the human race itself began" (Diogenes Laertius, *Lives* I, 2).[3] Like Graham centuries later, these ancient authors saw their early predecessors as the original, autonomous, and sudden creators of a new mode of thought, which aspires to capture and explain nature as such for the first time in the history of mankind. Most nineteenth-century scholars held this view, too. And despite Graham's argument for a new edition of pre-Socratic texts, on the grounds that "a few things have happened in the scholarly world" since Hermann Diels and Walter Kranz's seminal work (Graham 2010, I, xiii), one should not neglect certain continuities in this regard. To see how Nietzsche's account of early Greek philosophy relates and differs from his contemporary approaches, let us consider some of the comparable sources he consulted.

Arguably the most influential history of philosophy in the nineteenth century was Hegel's lectures, held nine times between 1805/06 in Jena and his death in 1831 in Berlin, and published in 1833–6 by Karl Ludwig Michelet. After an extended argument that no history of philosophy could be written without a concept of philosophy, Hegel claims philosophy proper was only developed by the Greeks: "With Thales we, properly speaking, first begin the history of Philosophy" (Hegel 1892, 171). The Greek thinkers did not invent philosophy out of the blue but transformed and improved everything they adopted from preceding and neighboring cultures by means of an *interpretatio graeca*. Thales might have used Babylonian observational data to foretell a solar eclipse (DK 11A5), and Egyptian wisdom to calculate the heights of the pyramids (DK 11A1), but:

> The proposition of Thales that water is the Absolute, or as the Ancients say, the principle, is the beginning of Philosophy, because with it the consciousness is arrived at that essence, truth, that which is alone in and for itself, are one. (Hegel 1892, 178)

Note that the conception of universal unity is not stated, invented, or proposed, but consciously recognized, i.e. discovered. Hegel also emphasizes the significant difference of this metaphysical insight to the world of perception. It represents a "departure from what is in our sensuous perception" (Hegel 1892, 178), of practical knowledge, and of Homeric myth, namely the "wild, endlessly varied imagination of Homer is set at rest by the proposition that existence is water" (Hegel 1892, 179). The source of Thales' assumption is neither perception nor tradition; its results are counter-intuitive and counter-empirical. According to Hegel, however, it captures true nature nonetheless, because philosophy as introduced by the ancient Greeks is an ideal usage of reason. Reason is the prime feature of human beings as distinguished from other animals, the rise of philosophy in ancient Greece is an essential step in the rise of mankind to its full capacities. Like Aristotle or Diogenes, Hegel sees the origin of philosophy as a realization of human nature and as such as the beginning of the human race itself. Its rise depended on conditions like economic leisure, freedom from religious indoctrination by a caste of priests, cultural contacts, and other cultural achievements. But its underlying dynamic is none of these arbitrary conditions but the natural development of reason: "the history of philosophy is a progression impelled by an inherent necessity, and one that is implicitly rational [...] Contingency must vanish on the appearance of philosophy" (Hegel 1892, 36f.). From Thales onwards, Hegel sees a continuous development of philosophical principles following his concept of dialectical logic.

After Hegel's death it soon became popular to reject his apotheosis of reason in history as an unconvincing deification of concepts. In Nietzsche's words: "By the way, everything would be quite nice, if only it wasn't so absurd to talk of 'world-history': assuming there would be a world-purpose, we could not possibly know it, since we are earthly fleas and not world-rulers" (NF 1873, 29[74]; KSA 7, 662).[4] Despite such criticism, Hegel's basic Aristotelian assumption of a continuous and progressive development of philosophy from its Ionian beginnings underlies many alternative accounts as well. Historians continuously reconstruct early Greek philosophy as a process from earlier mythology via humble Ionian beginnings through the contrast between Heraclitean and Parmenidean doctrines, the refinements in Anaxagoras and the atomists up until its culmination in the classic works of Plato and Aristotle. Friedrich Ueberweg explicitly states that Hegel (only) "hyperbolized in an unacceptable manner the otherwise justified basic concept of a step-by-step development, which can be found in the course of events in general and in particular in the succession of philosophical systems" (Ueberweg 1868, 10).[5] Eduard Zeller, in probably the most important work on Greek philosophy for Nietzsche, defends a similar attitude: a reconstruction like that of Hegel is "misled principally as well as practically, and the only thing justified about it is the general conviction regarding the inner lawfulness of historical evolution" (Zeller 1869, 11). To value Nietzsche's originality it is worthwhile to emphasize the peculiarities of this anti-Hegelian historicism. Scholars like Ueberweg or Zeller reject the broader philosophical background of Hegel's account, but they deny neither the inner lawfulness of historical evolution, nor the idea that the first Greek philosophers made decisive progress in the history of human reason.

> The Greeks were the first to achieve such freedom of thought, not to turn to religious tradition but to the things themselves to uncover the truth about the nature of things; only with them were strict scientific procedures and reasoning solely according to its own rules possible. This formal character alone suffices to separate Greek philosophy completely from the systems and attempts of the oriental's [...] who stands un-free in nature and can therefore neither reach valid explanations of phenomena out of their natural causes nor the freedom of a civil society or a pure human education [Bildung], while the Greeks are able to see a

lawful order in nature and to aspire to a free and beautiful morality in human life. (Zeller 1869, 105f.)

These lines repeat essential features of the Aristotelian-Hegelian model of continuous and general progress in early Greek thought. Its basic features are a naturalistic metaphysics and the aspiration to an accurate, free, and morally valid rational worldview. Its origin is explained by a combination of anthropology with a certain concept of rationality and certain favorable external conditions. Nietzsche's value as a scholar of antiquity derives in part from the question-marks he adds to this standard account.

2. The tragic age of Greece: Nietzsche on early Greek philosophy

Nietzsche mainly dealt with the early Greek philosophers during his early years in Basel with a peak between 1869 and 1873, when he composed his university lectures on the "Pre-Platonic Philosophers" (1869/70?, 1872, and 1876),[6] and in his unfinished and unpublished essay on "Philosophy in the Tragic Age of Greece" (1873). While PPP, being private notes for an introductory lecture-course, covers detailed source-criticisms and scholarly debates, PTG exhibits a free essayistic style and was meant for publication. PPP—as expected for a general introduction—is closer to the standard account than PTG, but both sources overlap and respectively illuminate one another despite their differences. A third source to reconstruct Nietzsche's view on early Greek thought is the treatise "Διαδοχαί of the Pre-Platonic Philosophers." He dictated the text to Gersdorff most likely in 1874 and may have used it for his lecture on the topic in 1876 (KGW II/5, 613–23). This study on the successors, i.e. early historians of Greek philosophy, belongs to the field of doxographic studies. With the prominent exceptions of Empedocles and Heraclitus, Nietzsche only seldom refers to pre-Platonic philosophers in later publications, e.g. in HH 261. It is also interesting to note that the young Nietzsche does not discuss those thinkers who are designated by the label "sophists" (Brobjer 2008, 58). However, his engagement with the first philosophers of the occidental tradition sustainably influenced his critical engagement with this tradition.

To present-day readers the title of his lectures seems to be particularly significant, but one should not overestimate its philosophical weight for Nietzsche. To speak of pre-Platonic instead of pre-Socratic philosophy is relevant in terms of historical classifications, but neither Nietzsche nor his contemporaries are consistent in that regard. Hegel has no general label for these thinkers, Zeller speaks of "pre-Socratic" philosophy, Ueberweg dubs them "pre-Sophistic" (and in later editions "pre-attic"). The terminology was more flexible before Diels and Kranz published their seminal collection *Die Fragmente der Vorsokratiker*. Other scholars wish to avoid the "not yet" implication of "pre-" and prefer the less charged notion of Early Greek Philosophy. Nietzsche did not restrict himself to the usage of pre-Platonic and simultaneously used phrases like "tragic," "earlier," "archaic," or even "pre-Socratic" (PTG 9; KSA

1, 836). His first announcement of the lectures in autumn 1869 advertised a course on "History of the Older Greek Philosophy [Geschichte der älteren griechischen Philosophie]" (KGW II/4, 209).

Nietzsche commanded profound knowledge of early Greek philosophy, which he reconstructed from a multitude of sources. The lack of a standard edition such as that of Diels and Kranz (DK 1903) was only partly ameliorated by earlier collections of fragments. A valuable source was Diogenes Laertius, whom Nietzsche had studied repeatedly in detail. As Jonathan Barnes points out in his contribution to this volume, about half of Nietzsche's published philological works are devoted to Diogenes Laertius and his sources (KGW II/1, 75–245). These studies were particularly decisive for his understanding of Greek philosophy from a doxo-biographic perspective (Müller 2005, 103–17). In addition to Zeller, Ueberweg, and—particularly in regard of Democritus—Friedrich Albert Lange's *Geschichte des Materialismus*, Nietzsche read other histories of philosophy like Christoph Meiners' *Geschichte des Ursprungs, Fortgangs und Verfalls der Wissenschaften in Griechenland und Rom* (Lemgo 1781), Karl Prantl's *Übersicht der griechisch-römischen Philosophie* (Stuttgart 1854), and Jacob Bernays' study on the Heraclitean letter (Berlin 1869). But his main focus is on ancient sources. In the "Encyclopedia of Classical Philology" he advises his students:

> The fragments must be studied in original: in Mullach fragm. philos. (poor esp. Democritus), the personal-notes in Laert. Diogenes. Numerous historical writings are lost. Valuable compendium with excerpts of sources Ritter a. Preller. Comprehensive account from Zeller, now 3 ed.— (EkP 18; KGW II/3, 407)[7]

Despite this philological focus *ad fontes*, Nietzsche is well aware of the selective limits of our sources. What we have and what we do not have results in almost every case from earlier prejudices and value judgments of generations of scholars and scribes. Our sources illuminate and simultaneously obscure our view; the lack of reliable information about the early Greek philosophers is particularly unfortunate and misleading. "It is a true misfortune that we have so little left from these original philosophers, and we involuntarily measure them too modestly, where from Plato onward voluminous literary legacies lie before us" (PPP 1; KGW II/4, 214). The dominant and "classic" role of Plato and Aristotle derives to a significant degree from "the sheer accident that they never lacked connoisseurs and copyists" (PTG 2; KSA 1, 810). Nietzsche not only advises against naïve trust in our limited sources but suggests a reverse order between classic and early Greek philosophy. "Very likely the most impressive part of Greek thought and its verbal expression is lost to us, a fate not to be wondered at" (PTG 2; KSA 1, 811) if one keeps the poor taste and the mean and petty character of most people in mind, copyists included.

It has been argued that Nietzsche is reading himself into the sparse ancient sources (Borsche 1985, 81) and that his concept of early Greek philosophy is to a certain degree only a human, all-too-human model and invention (Rehn 1992, 41). Is his interpretation of the pre-Platonics, as much as his account of Greek thought in general, not ultimately untrue, but decisively *Nietzsches Antike* (per the title of Cancik 1995)?

This is obviously the case and—as Nietzsche was particularly well aware—inevitably so. Our sparse sources are not only thick palimpsests of earlier value judgments; the preserved texts also speak only to certain ears. And

> when I carefully listened to the general sound of the older Greek philosophers, I meant to perceive tones which I was used to hear from Greek art, namely tragedy. How much this was due to the Greeks but how much only due to my ears (the ears of a very art-loving man)—this I cannot say with certainty even today. (NF 1878, 30[52]; KSA 8, 530)

Nietzsche's account is construction, of course, but this fact alone does not separate him from any other historiography. It seems fair to speak of Hegel's antiquity, or Zeller's, or—for that matter—Aristotle's or Diogenes'. To value Nietzsche's contribution to the field, a comparison of his specific results and interpretations to alternative readings is advisable, insofar as it highlights the typical and timely as well as the idiosyncratic and original features of his interpretation.

3. Nietzsche's genealogy of early Greek philosophy: Timely and untimely

Nietzsche's engagement with the pre-Platonic philosophers to certain degrees exemplifies the standard views of nineteenth-century scholarship. The selection of relevant figures is more or less traditional. In PTG Nietzsche reconstructs Thales (§3), Anaximander (§4), Heraclitus (§§5–8), Parmenides (§§9–13), and Anaxagoras (§§14–19). The fact that he does not deliver the announced treatment "from Thales till Socrates" (PTG 1; KSA 1, 808) is due to the fragmentary status of the text. PPP covers a broader spectrum including pre-Ionian and post-Anaxagorean thinkers like Democritus and Socrates. Nietzsche's proud claim to have developed a "beautiful table of categories, main guy [Hauptkerl], precursor and follower" (to Rohde, June 11, 1872; KSB 4, 10) is only partly justified, since other historians made similar distinctions between central and less central figures within philosophical schools. It is almost common sense to treat Anaximander as the "main guy" of Ionian philosophy, preceded by Thales and followed by Anaximenes. But Nietzsche rejects the idea, prevalent in Hegel or—later—in Diels (Heit 2011b), that early Greek philosophy was an enterprise organized in schools. This, he argues, is an anachronistic prejudice introduced by Alexandrian *diadochai*: "Philosophical schools did not exist at that time" (PPP 7; KGW II/4, 240; cf. KGW II/4, 613). Nietzsche also uses the established tools to determine biographical dates and chronological order. In questionable cases he usually takes against the Hegelian side. While Hegel and Zeller for example take Heraclitus' philosophy of becoming as a response to the Eleatic school of being, Nietzsche sides with Ueberweg and assumes that Parmenides responds to Heraclitus. His decision against Zeller to place the Pythagorean philosophy and mathematics a century after Pythagoras in Plato's time (PPP 16; cf. to Rohde, June 11, 1872; KSB 4, 10) seems confirmed by most modern scholars (cf. Heit 2011a, 54f.).

Nietzsche shares the widely acknowledged view that the Greeks were original. With respect to the "strange question" of Thales' supposed Phoenician descent, the solution he suggests coincides with the majority of his contemporaries: "He is a Phoenician only in the sense that his family may be traced back to Cadmus" (PPP 6; KGW II/4, 231). Nietzsche also uncovers this issue as a consequence of "oriental tendencies of later scholars," namely, the Alexandrians: "Greek philosophy is said to have not originated in Greece" (PPP 6; KGW II/4, 231). Very similar to Hegel or Zeller, he argues that intercultural exchange must have been natural to the Ionian tradesmen and colonialists. They were not isolated, but embedded in various cultural interactions; but philosophy is a completely original Greek achievement nonetheless.

> Nothing would be sillier than to claim an autochthonous development for the Greeks. On the contrary, they invariably absorbed other living cultures. The very reason they got so far is that they knew how to pick up the spear and throw it onward from the point where others had left it. (PTG 1; KSA 1, 806)

Therefore, as Nietzsche clarifies in accordance with the majority of his time, the general context of Greek culture provides no support for the unjustified conclusion "that philosophy was thus merely imported into Greece rather than having grown and developed there in a soil natural and native to it" (PTG 1; KSA 1, 806). Philosophy is a particularly Greek development and it is constitutive for the course of Western culture. However, despite his insistence on their foundational role, Nietzsche's interest in the pre-Platonic philosophers does not derive from a self-affirming search for humble beginnings, which set the basis for glorious, distinguished, and continuous progress. His view on early Greek philosophy and on Western culture respectively differs in some significant ways from many nineteenth- (and twentieth-)century thinkers.

A first and obvious feature of Nietzsche's original perspective is his focus on *early* Greek culture. He reverses the standard order between archaic and classic Greek philosophy. Most scholars agree with Aristotle's dictum that the earlier philosophers "are like untrained soldiers in a battle, who rush about and often strike good blows, but without science" (Aristotle, *Met.* 985a), and that "the earliest philosophy speaks falteringly, as it were, on all subjects; being new and in its infancy" (Aristotle, *Met.* 993a). In consequence, most appreciate Plato's and Aristotle's philosophy as the highest, "classic" culmination of earlier approaches. Nietzsche, on the other hand, tends to think of them as late, actually too late expressions of decline. The Greeks "knew precisely how to begin at the proper time [...] in the midst of good fortune, at the peak of good fortune, the peak of mature manhood, as a pursuit springing from the ardent joyousness of courageous and victorious maturity". But they knew not when to stop, and by "the fact that they were unable to stop in time, they considerably diminished their merit" (PTG 1; KSA 1, 805). The later Greek philosophers were lacking an important feature: "from Plato on there is something essentially amiss with philosophers when one compares them to that 'republic of creative minds' ['Genialen-Republik'] from Thales to Socrates." Namely, Nietzsche sees these later thinkers as "philosophic mixed types, and the former as pure types" (PTG 2; KSA 1, 810). This judgment matches his general enthusiasm for the early, archaic, the tragic age of Greece. But is also expresses a different heuristics.

Not only the subject but also his approach is original. Nietzsche is driven by the ambition to find alternative modes of living and thinking. In PPP 1 he states: "*We desire to ask, What do we learn from the history of their philosophy on behalf of the Greeks? Not, What do we learn on behalf of philosophy*" (KGW II/4, 211). In that regard the first lesson to take is that "the Greeks produced *archetypal philosophers* [*Philosophentypen*]" (PPP 1; KGW II/4, 212), "the *typical philosopher-heads* [*die typischen Philosophenköpfe*]" (PTG 1; KSA 1, 807). The emergence and sustainability of philosophers among them is a remarkable fact itself, because—unlike the Aristotelian tradition—it seems far from natural to Nietzsche to philosophize.

> I am going to tell the story—simplified—of certain philosophers. I am going to emphasize only that point of each of their systems which constitutes a slice of personality and hence belongs to that incontrovertible, non-debatable evidence, which is the task of history to preserve. (PTG 1st Preface; KSA 1, 801)

He even explicitly rehabilitates the long-out-fashioned genre of anecdotes, which was excessively used by Diogenes Laertius.

> The only thing of interest in a refuted system is the personal element. It alone is what is forever irrefutable. It is possible to present the image of a man in three anecdotes; I shall try to emphasize three anecdotes in each system and abandon the rest. (PTG 2nd Preface; KSA 1, 803)

Actually, I was not able to detect these three anecdotes in any of the following chapters, but the emphasis is clear. In direct contrast to Hegel, who stated that "personality and character do not enter to any large degree" into the content and matter of the historiography of philosophy (Hegel 1892, 1), Nietzsche draws our attention to the individual person.[8] The focus on "what we must *ever love and honor* and what no subsequent enlightenment can take away: the great human being" (PTG 1st Preface; KSA 1, 802) received mixed reactions. Christof Rapp acknowledges Nietzsche's account as an idiosyncratic and ignorable obsession with biographical, i.e. non-philosophical, concerns and—like Hegel—explicitly ignores such questions (Rapp 2007, 11). Heinrich Niehues-Pröbsting, on the other hand, sympathizes with Nietzsche's reservations about "common doxographic historiography of philosophy" and the "boring" "multi-volumed and thick-bodied handbooks on the history of philosophy, of which the nineteenth century produced so many" (Niehues-Pröbsting 2004, 148f.). He also sympathizes with his focus on exemplars of personality and on historically real and therefore possible kinds of living and looking at the human scene (PTG 1st Preface; KSA 1, 801). But he complains that Nietzsche does not fully translate his program into action (Niehues-Pröbsting 2004, 152f.). This is a justified objection, but the incompleteness derives from the fact that the lecture-course on pre-Platonic philosophy was meant to introduce students, and that the essay on the philosophers of the tragic age of Greece remained fragmentary. What Nietzsche—due to his focus on unique personality—succeeds in showing, however, is the fact that early Greek thought does not represent a rational evolution of doctrines but rather a "multitude of largely conceptually unrelated voices" (Müller 2005, 4). Nietzsche's PTG aspires to present a polyphony of individual original perspectives. "It is meant to be a beginning, by means of a comparative approach, towards the recovery and re-creation of certain characters [jene Naturen], so that the polyphony of Greek nature at long last may resound once more" (PTG 2nd Preface; KSA 1, 803). One of those grand voices is Thales of Miletus.

We may now turn back to the initial question whether one should take Thales seriously as the originator of philosophy. "Yes," Nietzsche answers,

> and for three reasons. First, because it tells us something about the primal origin of all things; second, because it does so in language devoid of image or fable, and finally, because contained in it, if only embryonically, is the thought, "all things are one." (PTG 10; KSA 1, 813)

Like Zeller, et al., Nietzsche constructs an emergence of philosophy as a new and distinct mode of thought out of preceding mythical poetry and practical knowledge. While the first reason also applies to religious cosmogonies, Thales' naturalistic language indicates a completely different enterprise that lifts him to the status of science. Actually, Nietzsche relates the water-principle to later scientific developments and not only informs his audience that the theory of transformative water reappeared twice in the history of natural science, i.e. in Paracelsus and in Lavoisier. He also invites us to "recall the Kant-Laplace hypothesis concerning a gaseous precondition of the universe" as support for the Ionian idea that the universe emerged out of less solid aggregate conditions (PPP 6; KGW II/4, 236f.). Such considerations, widespread in PPP but not in PTG, prove Nietzsche's early and continuous interest in natural sciences and contemporary scientific findings.[9] The profane naturalism, however, is something Thales has in common with his supposedly only practically and empirically minded contemporary and preceding cultures, namely Babylonian science. "Had he said, water turns into earth, we should have but a scientific hypothesis, a wrong one but hard to disprove. But he went beyond scientific considerations" (PTG 3; KSA 1, 813). What separates the Ionian from the observational empiricism and practical knowledge of Babylonian science is his jump beyond contemporary knowledge and common sense.

> The sparse and un-ordered observations of an empirical nature which he made regarding the occurrence and the transformations of water (more specifically, of moisture) would have allowed, much less made available, no such outrageous generalization [ungeheuerliche Verallgemeinerung]. What drove him to it was a metaphysical conviction which had its origins in a mystic intuition. We meet it in every philosophy, together with the ever-renewed attempts at a more suitable expression, this proposition that "all things are one." (PTG 3; KSA, 1, 813)

So Nietzsche agrees with the standard view: "Thales is the first philosopher" (PPP 2; KGW II/4, 218), but he gives a different meaning to this title. Thales is not the first representative of proper usage of human rationality, who was "able to see a lawful order in nature and to aspire to a free and beautiful morality in human life" (Zeller 1869, 106). His water-assumption does not represent "the first really rational attempts to describe the nature of the world" (Kirk, et. al. 1983, 75), but expresses an "outrageous generalization" and a statement of faith dealing "high-handedly with all empiricism" (PTG 3; KSA 1, 813). According to Nietzsche's interpretation, the tradition of metaphysical hypotheses inaugurated by the Ionian *physikoi* hardly appears like the work of "students of nature, who took nature as an independent realm to be understood in terms of its own capacities" (Graham 2010: I, 1). It is, as he pointedly writes in a notepad, "the artistic impulse in the chrysalis of philosophy" (NF 1872/73, 21[20]; KSA 7, 529). Thales introduced a new perspective on the world, a perspective informed by other sources and directed by other needs and values than preceding ones, but a perspective nonetheless.[10] However, the philosophic impulse to clarify and unify the observational world of chaos and becoming, namely its logical purification by Parmenides, served as a point of departure for Western philosophy. Even the very late Nietzsche relates the continuously prevalent idea of a unified being, which underlies an only apparent worldly change and variety, to these early Greek deifications of human thought:

> In fact, nothing has so far had a more naïve persuasion than the error of Being, as it was formulated, for example, by the Eleatic: every word, every sentence we speak is in favor of it! – Opponents of the Eleatics also still subject to the seduction of their concept of being [Seins-Begriff]: Democritus, among others, when he invented his *atom* ... The 'reason' in the language: oh what a deceitful old vixen! I'm afraid we are not getting rid of God because we still believe in grammar ... (TI Reason 5; KSA 6, 78)

4. Epilogue: Philosophy as an artwork built on sand

In his preface to *Daybreak* Nietzsche poses the question, "why is it that all philosophical architects from Plato onwards build in vain; that everything threatens to collapse or already lies in ruins, which they themselves honestly and seriously took for aere perennius" (D Preface 3; KSA 3, 13). The answer is not that they failed to provide the proper philosophical foundations and "groundwork," but that they were misled by moral needs and aspirations. Nikolaos Loukidelis (2007) proved that Nietzsche consulted a passage from Heinrich Romundt's *Grundlegung zur Reform der Philosophie* when he drafted this passage. However, Romundt's text differs in a significant way:

> The systems of philosophy from Thales up to the latest time were buildings of doctrines [Lehrgebäude], but they were not science. The human mind's drive and desire to build was stronger than the pursuit of knowledge and science in the philosophers. The thinkers resembled inventors rather than discoverers. (Romundt 1885, 8f.)

While Romundt dates the beginning of systematic ambitions in philosophy back to Thales, Nietzsche applies it to Plato and his followers, distinguishing early from classic Greek philosophy. In the *Birth of Tragedy*, it was neither Thales nor Plato, but "Socrates, the prototype of the theoretical optimist, who [...] attaches the force of a universal medicine to knowledge and cognition in his faith in the discoverability of the nature of things" (BT 15; KSA 1, 100). Nietzsche seems to be slightly unclear about the precise historical beginning of this specific mode of thought and clear-cut demarcation between early grand polyphonic voices and later dogmatic mixed types. However, his suspicion against the new mode of thought essentially stays the same. Theoretical optimism introduced in ancient Greece did not uncover the nature of things as such, because that is beyond human grasp. Philosophy from its Greek beginning onwards is an artwork build on sand. But it introduced a forceful belief and the value of intellectual honesty, which generated a succession of schools and attempts, until the philosophical enterprise itself, "spurred by its powerful illusion, speeds irresistibly towards its limits where its optimism, concealed in the essence of logic, suffers shipwreck" (BT 15; KSA 1, 101). At that stage, Nietzsche sees the alternative as being between drowning or building new ships (GS 289; KSA 3, 529f.).

The lasting value of Nietzsche's engagement with early Greek philosophers derives from the fundamental change of perspective on the nature of their achievements. Unlike the traditional (and Eurocentric) euphoria about a world-historical break-through from myth to reason, Nietzsche invites a perception of the Greek miracle as an essential variation in our human activities of world-making. He allows us to perceive the pre-Platonic philosophers as creative thinkers, who introduce new images of the world and new modes of life, but who neither discover the objectively given essence of nature nor introduce the one and only proper way of living. They polyphonically and pluralistically represent opportunities of thinking and living, and role models for philosophers. They do so by artful play, experimentation, and unreasonably optimistic trust in reason. According to Nietzsche, the polyphonous philosophers in the tragic age of Greece set an impetus, but they did not fall for the dogmatic petrifications of later occidental philosophy.

Notes

1   For PTG I used the translation of Marianne Cowan (1962), and for PPP the translation of Greg Whitlock (2001). All other translations of German sources, namely those of Nietzsche's unpublished notes as well as of German secondary literature are my own, unless stated otherwise.

2   I gave a detailed analysis of this set of claims, its development from ancient sources and Hegel to contemporary studies on the history of Western philosophy, its modes of justification, and its probable anachronism and Eurocentrism in (Heit 2007). Inspiration to this work was due to my philosophical teacher, who also introduced me to Nietzsche, Joachim Müller-Warden. See (Müller-Warden 1998, 2003).

3   On the demarcation from the barbarians in Diogenes Laertius, his predecessors and later authors, see (Heit 2005).

4   There is no direct evidence that Nietzsche read Hegel's *History of Philosophy*. The 1873 notes 79[72–4] contain quotations from his *Philosophy of History*; he also owned his *Encyclopedia of the Philosophical Sciences* for some time (Campioni, et al. 2003, 281).

5   Nietzsche bought the three volumes of Ueberweg's *Grundriß der Geschichte der Philosophie* in 1867 or 1868 in the context of his Democritus-studies and consulted them repeatedly.

6   In his translation and edition of these lecture-notes Greg Whitlock comes to
     the conclusion that Nietzsche probably delivered the lectures in the winter
     semester 1869/70, but the lecture-notes we have now were most likely compiled
     in 1872 (Whitlock 2001, XXIIf.). His introduction emphasizes their value for
     understanding Nietzsche's further philosophical development. Their significance
     for our understanding of Greek culture was also noted occasionally since their
     first publication, e.g. by Lloyd-Jones: "The lecture notes published in the Musarion
     edition of Nietzsche's work in 1920 are highly interesting to students of the origins
     of philosophy" (1976, 7).

7   The two collections of fragments and testimonies he suggests are: Friedrich
     Wilhelm August Mullach (1860): *Fragmenta philosophorum graecorum. Collegit,
     recensuit, vertit annotationibus et prolegomenis illustravit indicibus* Paris (Didot);
     and: Heinrich Ritter and Ludwig Preller (1869): *Historia philosophiae graecae et
     romanae ex fontium locis contexta. Locos collegerunt, disposuerunt, notis auxerunt
     H. Ritter et L. Preller. Editio quarta.* Gotha (Perthes). For convenience I provide the
     DK-references of his quotations.

8   In his introduction to the study of Platonic dialogues Nietzsche also takes Plato's
     philosophy as main testimony for Plato as a man (KGW II/4, 148); and he
     later continuously applies a heuristics of reading philosophical systems as "the
     self-confession of its originator and a form of unintentional and unrecorded
     memoir" (BGE 6; KSA 5, 19); cf. Heit 2013.

9   The lecture on Heraclitus for example provides the only evidence that Nietzsche not
     only borrowed Hermann von Helmholtz from the Basel library, but actually read it,
     and quotes his paper on the interdependency of natural force to illustrate Heraclitus'
     idea that nothing is beyond change and even the most stable things must finally
     transform and perish (PPP 10; KGW II/4, 270).

10   Lawrence Hatab, one of the few Nietzsche-scholars who also devoted a book-length
     study to the ancient origin of philosophy, comes to similar conclusions: "To sum
     up, we have found the following characteristics of philosophy contained in its first
     historical moments: The search for a unified explanation; an emphasis upon profane
     experience as opposed to sacred imagery; the active role of the unaided conscious
     mind, free of sacred interruptions; and a distinction between appearance and reality.
     In general we can say that Thales discovers what has come to be called an objective
     view of the world, a view which screens out the affective, existential, and sacred
     aspects of the world. But we cannot equate objectivity with 'truth'. It is, rather, a *new*
     criterion which *disengages* itself from the context of myth. When Anaxagoras, for
     example, proclaimed that the sun is not a god but an incandescent stone, he was not
     unveiling the real 'sun' but rather a different way of understanding the sun" (Hatab
     1990, 163f.).

Works cited

Aristotle (*Met.*) (1933): "Metaphysics." In Hugh Tredennick (trans.): *Aristotle in 23
Volumes.* Cambridge, MA (Harvard University Press). Vol. 17.
Borsche, Tilman (1985): "Nietzsches Erfindung der Vorsokratiker." In Josef Simon (ed.):
Nietzsche und die philosophische Tradition. Würzburg (Königshausen & Neumann),
62–87.

Brobjer, Thomas H. (2008): *Nietzsche's Philosophical Context: An Intellectual Biography*. Urbana (University of Illinois Press).

Campioni, Giuliano, Paolo D'Iorio, Maria Cristina Fornari, Francesco Fronterotta and Andrea Orsucci (2003): *Nietzsches persönliche Bibliothek*. Berlin and New York (Walter de Gruyter).

Cancik, Hubert (1995): *Nietzsches Antike. Vorlesung*. Stuttgart and Weimar (Metzler).

Cowan, Marianne (1962): *Philosophy in the Tragic Age of the Greeks: Friedrich Nietzsche*. With an Introduction by Marianne Cowan (trans.). Washington (Regnery).

Diels, Hermann (DK) (1951): *Die Fragmente der Vorsokratiker*. Greek and German. Walter Kranz (ed.). Zürich (Weidmann).

Diogenes Laertius (*Lives*) (1925): "Lives of Eminent Philosophers." In Robert D. Hicks (trans.): *Lives of Eminent Philosophers*. Cambridge, MA (Harvard University Press).

Graham, Daniel W. (2010): *The Texts of Early Greek Philosophy: The Complete Fragments and Selected Testimonies of the Major Presocratics*. Cambridge (Cambridge University Press).

Hatab, Lawrence J. (1990): *Myth and Philosophy: A Contest of Truths*. La Salle (Open Court).

Hegel, Georg W. F. (1892): "Lectures on the History of Philosophy II: Greek Philosophy to Plato." In E. S. Haldane and Frances S. Simon (trans.): *Hegel's Lectures on the History of Philosophy*. London (Routledge & Kegan Paul).

Heit, Helmut (2005): "Western Identity, Barbarians, and the Inheritance of Greek Universalism." In *The European Legacy: Toward New Paradigms*. Vol. 10 (7), 725–39.

—(2007): *Der Ursprungsmythos der Vernunft. Zur philosophiehistorischen Genealogie des griechischen Wunders*. Würzburg (Königshausen & Neumann).

—(2011a): *Grundwissen Philosophie: Frühgriechische Philosophie*. Stuttgart (Reclam).

—(2011b): "Diels (H.) Frühgriechische Philosophie. Vorlesungsmitschrift aus dem Wintersemester 1897/98. Stuttgart 2010." In *The Classical Review*. Vol. 61 (1), 320–1.

—(2013): "Lesen und Erraten. Philosophie als 'Selbstbekenntnis ihres Urhebers.'" Forthcoming in Marcus Born and Axel Pichler (eds): *Texturen des Denkens*. Berlin and Boston (Walter de Gruyter), 123–43.

Kirk, Geoffrey S., John E. Raven and Malcolm Schofield (1983): *The Presocratic Philosophers: A Critical History with a Selection of Texts*. Cambridge (Cambridge University Press).

Lloyd-Jones, Hugh (1976): "Nietzsche and the Study of the Ancient World." In James C. O'Flaherty, Timothy F. Sellner, and Robert M. Helm (eds): *Studies in Nietzsche and the Classical Tradition*. Chapel Hill (University of North Carolina Press), 1–15.

Loukidelis, Nikolaos (2007): "Nachweise aus Heinrich Romundt, 'Grundlegung zur Reform der Philosophie.'" In *Nietzsche-Studien*. Vol. 36, 403–5.

Müller, Enrico (2005): *Die Griechen im Denken Nietzsches*. Berlin and New York (Walter de Gruyter).

Müller-Warden, Joachim (1998): "Die aktuelle Entwicklung Europas, erörtert im Lichte der Philosophie Friedrich Nietzsches." In Volker Gerhardt and Renate Reschke (eds): *Nietzscheforschung*. Berlin (Akademie). Vol. 4, 119–46.

—(2003): "Nietzsches Frage nach der 'Herkunft der Werte'. Zur Ätiologie der okzidentalen Zivilisation." In *Ästhetik und Kommunikation*. Vol. 120, 103–10.

Nestle, Wilhelm (1940): *Vom Mythos zum Logos. Die Selbstentfaltung des griechischen Denkens von Homer bis auf die Sophistik und Sokrates*. Stuttgart (Kröner).

Niehues-Pröbsting, Heinrich (2004): *Die antike Philosophie. Schrift, Schule, Lebensform.* Frankfurt am Main (Fischer).

Rapp, Christof (2007): *Vorsokratiker.* Munich (Beck).

Rehn, Rudolf (1992): "Nietzsches Modell der Vorsokratik." In Rudolf Rehn and Daniel W. Conway (eds): *Nietzsche und die antike Philosophie.* Trier (WVT), 37–45.

Romundt, Heinrich (1885): *Grundlegung zur Reform der Philosophie. Vereinfachte und erweiterte Darstellung von Immanuel Kants Kritik der reinen Vernunft.* Berlin (Stricker).

Ueberweg, Friedrich (1868): *Grundriß der Geschichte der Philosophie von Thales bis auf die Gegenwart.—Erster Theil: Das Altertum. Dritte, berichtigte und ergänzte und mit einem Philosophen- und Litteratoren-Register versehene Auflage.* Berlin (Mittler).

Whitlock, Greg (2001): "Translator's Preface and Translator's Introduction." In his (trans. and ed.): *The Pre-Platonic Philosophers.* Urbana (University of Illinois Press), viii–xlvi.

Zeller, Eduard (1869): *Die Philosophie der Griechen in Ihrer geschichtlichen Entwicklung. Erster Theil. Allgemeine Einleitung. Vorsokratische Philosophie. Dritte Auflage.* Leipzig (Fues).

12

Nietzsche's Philology and the Science of Antiquity

Babette Babich

1. Nietzsche's science

Nietzsche established himself in his own field of ancient philology or classics with path-breaking discoveries that have in the interim (albeit without fanfare) come to be standard in his profession: specifically his contributions to prosody (see, for example, Babich 2005, 47–78). These discoveries grew out of his studies of meter and rhythm, especially quantitational or quantifying rhythm.[1] Nietzsche would go on to make still-broader claims for music and word in his work on the *Birth of Tragedy out of the Spirit of Music*; claims that continue to be more rather than less ignored.[2] To this extent and despite his contributions to his own field, as Hugh Lloyd-Jones and William Arrowsmith, each with differing degrees of rigor (and humor) have argued before me, along with Karl Reinhardt and Viktor Poschl, Nietzsche's name tends to remain absent from the registers of noteworthy voices in Classical Philology in the course of what is now more than a full century of fairly complete non-attention with exceptions now and then that bring Nietzsche into the fold, yet even such welcome expert authors tend to leave him an outsider and routinely fail to acknowledge even his mainstream contributions on prosody, still more commonly condemning his work on tragedy altogether.

In the context of the philosophy of science (including both mainstream and continental approaches), and following Thomas Kuhn's point in this regard, which followed the sociological scientific work of Ludwik Fleck (among others) and which recurs, more mischievously, in Paul Feyerabend's defense of the forgotten precisions of Robert Bellarmine contra the more well-known rhetorical devices of Galileo, I have argued that intellectual inattention—which effectively amounts to academic suppression— tends to be the rule for discoveries, perhaps especially for "path-breaking" discoveries. And to be sure, even the explicitly so-named "Nietzsche philology" passes over Nietzsche's classical philological discoveries in silence.[3] If in my own work on Nietzsche I have sought to emphasize this "suppression" rather more politically than most, it is relevant that similar arguments on scholarship, specifically with respect to science, may be found, in different ways and to different ends, in Feyerabend as already noted and in Bruno Latour among others.[4] What compounds matters in the present context is that academic, or scholarly, suppression is self-confirming; indeed: automatically so.

To take the specific case of what Nietzsche called "science," by which he meant not only physics and chemistry and physiology (as the term tends to be restricted to the natural sciences in English convention) but also his own discipline of Classical Philology (and to which we may add philosophy), mainstream scholarly resistance to reflection on his discoveries continues to be the rule. Note that I am not talking about the claims made by this Nietzsche scholar or that Nietzsche scholar, from Karl Löwith to Wolfgang Müller-Lauter, from Hans Vaihinger to Friedrich Kaulbach, from John Wilcox to Maudemarie Clark and so on. Rather, I am talking about the range of what Nietzsche himself wrote about with respect to his own scholarly field of classics. Part of the problem here is certainly the sheer difficulty of these studies (in metric and quantitational rhythm and so on) but no smaller part of the problem is that this esoteric complexity is compounded by the self-consciously reflexive radicality of Nietzsche's classically Kantian (his is not a neo-Kantianism) and hence overtly *critical* orientation to science in general and thereby his own discipline. This critical approach is already evident in his inaugural lecture on the Homer question.[5]

Adding to the complexity of his own research and the dissonance, as conventionally as today's scholars tend to read him, of his sheerly critical sensibility, there is also the fall-out of the same for today's scholars. This fall-out (this is where the self-confirming bit enters the dynamic) entails that "reading" Nietzsche tends not to be a part of the average classicist's formation today, no matter whether German or French or Italian or Anglophone and so on. Compounding this deficit, reading ancient Greek or studying classics as such, likewise tends not to be part of the formation of the average Nietzsche scholar in any tradition, no matter whether analytic or continental, no matter whether literary or philosophical. And finally, although this is arguably the most elusive further detail, one must also add the dimming of wide reading in general. Erudition has become a term of rebuke for scholars, even in what is called the "history of philosophy" today (especially in mainstream or analytic philosophy with its focus on a few hand-picked cases, done to death in the literature). This streamlined and often digitally mediated relationship to the tradition cannot but be a handicap when it comes to Nietzsche who, by all evidence, read so very much himself that the sub-discipline of Nietzsche source scholarship was seemingly founded to sift through it all.[6]

Nietzsche termed such a lack of background, a lack which he argued was already in evidence in his own day, a "lack of philology," by which he meant the constant "confusion of the *explanandum* with the text" as *explanans* (KSA 13, 15[82], 456; cf. 460).[7] This lack has only grown worse in the interim so that if it was possible for Francis MacDonald Cornford (1874–943), in a book written a dozen years after Nietzsche's death in a context distinguishing between "mystery religions" and the cults of the Olympian gods, to describe Nietzsche's *The Birth of Tragedy* as "a work of profound imaginative insight, which left the scholarship of a generation toiling in the rear" (Cornford 1912, 111n. 1), scholars today have trouble parsing Cornford's meaning (never mind its context). Indeed, those who bother to quote Cornford on Nietzsche at all, already a small minority, are inclined to bracket the context altogether or reduce it to a passing mention. This too is representative of the troubles faced with coming to terms with Nietzsche and Classical Philology. Thus in spite of Cornford's optimism we have yet to come to any consensus on the mystery religions themselves, as some of the debates around the Derveni papyrus cannot but make plain, as do indeed contemporary discussions of Dionysus.[8] The scholarly tension associated with Peter Kingsley's original work on Empedocles and his later (to some) more tendentious work also can be taken to illustrate part of this complex point.[9]

In the present context, the concern Cornford identifies as a concern with mystery religions and cults was Nietzsche's concern which he shared with his friend and colleague, Erwin Rohde.[10] The complexity of the previous reference to ancient mystery religions has hardly abated and in the context of philosophy today and at best when we are not striving for scientific sobriety and debunking things, we speak of a "way of life"—as Pierre Hadot has given this terminology a very Nietzschean tonality—a practice including, as Nietzsche also argued, a meditation on death, as Hadot likewise emphasizes via his own focus on Marcus Aurelius and Plotinus and to be sure and with respect to Lucian and others.[11]

In addition to Cornford's emphases on the difference between the Olympian deities and the cult and life of mystery traditions,[12] Nietzsche's own philological discoveries concerned word and music, especially quantificational rhythm,[13] including seemingly simple things like the pronunciation of ancient Greek itself,[14] as well as his work on iconically philological themes like the issue of Homer's reception,[15] all in addition to raising the still-relevant question of the origin of the tragic work of art which Nietzsche ranged as a part of sensible or phenomenological or what he called "aesthetic science" (BT 1; KSA 1, 25).[16] In addition, we may note that there is his study of the pre-Platonic thinkers. For Heidegger, as indeed for Eugen Fink, and to a lesser degree for the classicist and philosopher Hans-Georg Gadamer, this last emphasis would turn out to be indispensable.[17]

I began by noting my earlier essays where I argue that it will make all the difference that ancient Greek prosody may be grasped fairly literally *as music* for Nietzsche, a point explicitly emphasized in the subtitle of *The Birth of Tragedy—out of the Spirit of Music*.[18] In my most recent book, I take this further to argue that an understanding of Nietzsche's relationship to rhythm and meter can help us understand Nietzsche's own focus on Beethoven rather than (as continues very traditionally to be assumed) Wagner.[19] In addition, I have elsewhere also emphasized the importance of Lucian of Samosata in the old tradition of Menippean satire for Nietzsche as this emphasis, also relevant in the context of cult and religion, is manifest from *The Birth of Tragedy* to his *Thus Spoke Zarathustra* and beyond.[20]

What Nietzsche termed "monumental" history, i.e. classical archeological exploration, is an essential supplement to ancient philology as Nietzsche emphasizes in an early public lecture that was part of his initial appointment in Basel. There Nietzsche refers to the persistence of old prejudices. As we noted above, Thomas Kuhn calls this "normal" science, speaking as he does of "paradigms," corresponding in this case to the enduring paradigmatic phantasm of ancient Greece as iconic of the classical as such: that is to say the very whiteness of antiquity which Nietzsche in his early lecture contrasted with the polychromy of ancient statues and architecture, pointing out as he did that this same vibrant antiquity had been known since the previous century, without (and this was his point) making any dint of difference for the popular and academic image of ancient Greece.[21] In addition to highlighting the important influence of his teacher Otto Jahn for Nietzsche's thinking, we should also note that the durability of what I call the "Winckelmannian whiteness" of our vision of antiquity is so striking that the classicist art historian, Brunilde Ridgway could have pause in her scholarly discussion of this still-confounding problem.[22] I argue further in a more experimental or performative vein that Jahn's influence on Nietzsche may also be evident in his own proto-phenomenological practice, as Nietzsche might be seen to have had recourse to another archeological research methodology including experimental or performative re-enactment; here we may recall the attested image of a dancing, flute-playing Nietzsche conducting research, as we might put it, with his own body (see Babich 2013b; see, too, the conclusion of Babich 2011e). More soberly, this same point and the reference to the dance are already present in his first discussions of the ictus (1878–9) (see Babich 2013d, 207ff.).

Nietzsche posed the question of Homer's reception still more fundamentally in terms of an investigation into the nature of the scholarly discernment of style, articulated in terms of scholarly taste or judgment, in his public lectures in Basel (see Babich 2012). But precisely in this sense, we may read Nietzsche's bitter reaction at the end of his life in "What I Owe the Ancients" in his *Twilight of the Idols*, reflecting on pain and the orgiastic as a long-deferred response to Wilamowitz's characterization of his book on tragedy as overly prim or "repressed" with regard to the erotic in antiquity. This can be seen if we recall, for the sake of a phenomenological hermeneutics, Wilamowitz's epigraph which he drew, one younger man attacking another young man, from Aristophanes' fragments on the supposed fountain of youth in the comedy, *Age* [*Geras*].

᾿Οξωτὰ σιλφιωτὰ βαλβός τεύτλιον
ὑπότριμμα θρῖον ἐγκέφαλον ὀρίγανον
καταπυγοσύνη ταῦτ ἐστὶ πρὸς κρεας μέγα.[23]

With this quite overtly provocative epigraph—the translation of which turns on the scatologically nasty καταπυγοσύνη—and which might be rendered as "Condiments, vinegar, spicy seasonings, scallions, beets, highly refined sauces, leaves stuffed with brains, oregano—a catamite's delicacies beside a great hunk of meat"—Wilamowitz attacked Nietzsche's first book. The argument can be made that with this epigraph nearly everything involved on nearly every level in the German nineteenth-century profession of Classical Philology is in play (Babich 2002, 1f.). But here I only mean to note that—so far from the standard or received claim, common among Nietzsche scholars, that Nietzsche simply abandons the concerns of his first book—it is clear that with the very last section of his *Twilight of the Idols* ("What I Owe the Ancients," 5), Nietzsche seeks to rearticulate his original insights into tragic myth and indeed Dionysus. And to be sure he does this elsewhere, as I also argue, in his overall reprise of *The Birth of Tragedy* in *The Gay Science* (Babich 2006a, 97–114).

Referring to the same mystery cults and their challenge to the nineteenth-century conventions regarding Greek myth and religion (just as we noted Cornford's claim above), Nietzsche affirms here at the conclusion of *Twilight of the Idols* that both pain *and* pleasure are foregrounded in these mysteries. It was this convergence that Nietzsche had addressed from the first section of his first book, even including in later sections a reference to "the cynics," "which" same cynics, as Nietzsche argues (here again we note a reference to Lucian), had "invented" the so-called "Menippean satire" (TI Ancients, 2; KSA 6, 155). Nietzsche closes *The Birth of Tragedy* with an invocation of the flood disseminating these cults over the face of the earth and we can note that it is this point, linked indeed with satire, that he reprises at the end of *Twilight of the Idols*, just in advance of his reprinting of the aphoristic poem from his Zarathustra book: *The Hammer Speaks*. Here we read of the "psychology of the orgiastic as an overflowing feeling of life and power, within which even pain yet works as a stimulus," described as the "key to the concept of tragic feeling" (TI Ancients, 5; KSA 6, 160). Reviewing what Nietzsche called "the becoming-human of dissonance" in both music and tragedy (Babich 2013d), I argue on behalf of Nietzsche's claim that an understanding of this notion cannot but entail "going beyond fear and pity," thus beyond every residue of Aristotelianism: "to be oneself," i.e. to come to be in oneself "the eternal enjoyment of becoming" (Ibid.).

In connection with work on Nietzsche and science, I show that Nietzsche's *The Birth of Tragedy* is ineluctably concerned with both ancient philology qua science as well as the broader meaning of science as such.[24] Here it is relevant, as it is also Nietzsche's constant complaint that where all of his writings were so very many and so very Lucianic "fishhooks," that he as author himself failed to catch anything by them, owing less to the limitations of his rhetoric or style (Nietzsche regarded himself as a master in this respect) than to what he identified to be (this is also the point of Lucian's dialogue *The Fisherman*) the manifest lack of fish. If a lack of scholarly engagement is the rule, this cannot mean that it is not the task of scientific scholarship to endeavor to overcome this.[25]

2. What makes science science?

Nietzsche's reflective critical meditation on science considers science as science—that is: as such. His critical analysis of science finds its expression both in his first book, *The Birth of Tragedy*, as well as in his earlier reflections on style and taste in his inaugural lecture on Homer (and Classical Philology).

What are we doing, so Nietzsche asked, when we judge as scholars do? What is scholarly, scientific judgment? He argued that scholars and scientists tend to take their own intellectual sensibility, their taste, as the norm, exactly in the sense of David Hume's teasing reflection on taste and fashion and normative determination in Hume's little essay, *On the Standard of Taste* (see Babich 2012). To the extent that Nietzsche poses the question of mode or *style* in his own discipline of philology, he frames the question of science per se as a question concerning sense-directed or empirical science as such; that is, as an aesthetic question of taste in and for the sciences themselves.[26] In this context, Nietzsche raises the philosophical question of the foundations of science when he asks, in effect, what makes science to be science: "To what end, even worse: from whence—all science?" (BT Attempt, 1; KSA 1, 12).

Nietzsche's claim, borrowed in fair parts from both Schopenhauer and Feuerbach, is that both religion and science turn out to be pursued for the same value-charged reasons.[27] Thus both the Christian and the man of modern techno-science pursue a hoped-for advantage or benefit. The Christian believer seeks eternal salvation qua indemnification for living this life, on this earth, in this body, and subject to its frailties and transformations or illnesses and death. By the same token, and this faith is what Nietzsche will argue that the Greeks are lacking, the believer in science anticipates the practical uses of science as promising a direct transformation or salvation of this life, this earth, and above all this body, whereby the believer in science is confident in his expectation that science will (soon, very soon) conquer all bodily and earthly— meaning every human, all-too-human—limitation. If religion promises redemption in the life to come, science and technology promise the same benefits in this world, here and now or (more accurately and in keeping with its ongoing millenarian ideal) in the future. The direction of time, both Judeo-Christian time and modern, scientifico-historical time, is progressive and epochal: directed towards the future. Instead, as we know, Nietzsche's Zarathustra would reflect on the notion of loving not the life of the world to come (whether in the afterworld or in a "future-perfected" world of technoscience) but life as it is and above all, life as it was, exactly as it was, and without exception. The notion he offers us here of *amor fati* is of course his teaching of the eternal return, as an affirmation of life.

For Nietzsche, the scope of *aesthetics* as he defined it *as a science* corresponded to the *scientific* question of his own discipline of ancient or Classical Philology. In just this spirit, Nietzsche claimed himself to have been the first to "raise the question of science as a question," (BT Attempt, 2; KSA 1, 13) beginning with *The Birth of Tragedy*. But, as noted above, he certainly raises this question even before his first book inasmuch as the critical perspective Nietzsche urges, beginning with his inaugural lecture in Basel, is also the reason he is able to conclude that lecture with a conversion or reversed constitution of Seneca's dictum: philology is to become philosophically critical, which is also to say that philology has to be set on the path of a critical science.

For this reason I began by reviewing the modes of classical, literary, linguistic, and historical science for Nietzsche, in addition to the question of the critical science of style and aesthetics inasmuch as these "sciences" taken individually, and especially taken collectively, highlight the very question of science as a question for Nietzsche. Yet I also emphasized that the idea of conceiving science as a question, as Nietzsche does, beginning with his later written preface to *The Birth of Tragedy* where he thematizes science "as problematic, as questionable" (BT Attempt, 2; KSA 1, 13), i.e. as the quintessential problem of a book he simultaneously identifies as "questionable," could hardly be more alien to traditional philological or philosophical discourse, both then and now. And to be sure this is even more striking when the relevant philosophical discourse is the philosophy of science itself.[28]

For this reason, today's scholars are used to encountering Nietzsche as a "moral" thinker rather than as a specialist in ancient philosophy or classics (ancient philology) but not as a thinker with epistemological and philosophic concerns with science.[29] Yet by noting above that Nietzsche took his own project to be that of raising the precisely critical question of science *as a question*, it is also important to underscore that this means that he took his own concerns as *scientifically* motivated. Thus Nietzsche saw himself as offering both a meta-philological reflection on Classical Philology and a meta-scientific reflection on science per se. Nietzsche's overall question in this broad sense includes the critically philological and psychological (as Nietzsche uses the term) and even the physiological question: "What, indeed, does all science ultimately mean regarded as a *symptom* of life? To what end, still worse, from whence—all science? *What gives?*" (BT Attempt, 1; KSA 1, 12; my emphases).[30]

The style of questioning is immediately recognizable as Nietzsche's prototypically *genealogical* modality, a scholarly identification which corresponds to our tendency to read Nietzsche backwards, say, from Michel Foucault.[31] Attesting to this genealogical reading, however, we do well to keep Nietzsche's own explication as described in the preface to his own *On the Genealogy of Morals: A Polemic*, which must in turn be read as a necessary complement (or Derridean "supplement") to his earlier *Beyond Good and Evil: Prelude to a Philosophy of the Future*.[32] Once again, we ask, with Nietzsche, what is it that makes science science? What is the enabling condition of science, here philology? That is, again as we saw above: reviewing as we did classical philological research as encompassing the length and breadth of all academic scholarship; but above all, as this is the force of the question of science, as Nietzsche poses it in his later written preface to his first book: What makes science, once understood as such, necessary, still more exactly that is to say: *necessary for us*?

Nietzsche poses this question in the rigorously scientific and historical terms of his own era and his own scientific discipline by raising the question in historical terms with reference to the origins of science as such in antiquity, the very surprising question not of the difference between ancient and modern science but rather and given the sophistication of Greek science, asking *why* modern science, given this same sophistication, took *as long* as it took in order to become the dominant force in modern conceptual culture? (Cf. NF, 1869/70, 3[11]; KSA 7, 62).

His question is unprecedented and it is counter-intuitive just to the extent that we take the progressive or evolutionary character of knowledge for granted. Thus Nietzsche pursues the question of what he calls "The Origin of Knowledge," in a series of aphorisms in the third book of *The Gay Science*, challenging the notion of substance and substantial, substantive, identity—"that there are equal things, that there are things, substances, bodies" (GS 110; KSA 3, 469) and going on to ask how logic came into existence and noting its literally, necessarily literally "illogical origins," (GS 111; KSA 3, 472) and to challenge the notion of explanation and causation along with it: "Cause and effect: there is apparently no such duality—in truth a continuum stands before us from out of which we isolate a couple of items ..." (GS 112; KSA 3, 473). By posing, as Nietzsche does, the *question* of the genesis and development of modern scientific culture from the beginning through to the very end of his productive life,[33] Nietzsche inevitably challenges the modern convention regarding the logical and progressive development of science.

The mathematician and ancient historian, Lucio Russo, has also raised this same concern, albeit from a different perspective and for a modern sensibility in the history of science.[34] Russo argues against progress by pointing out, as does Nietzsche— although Russo, to be sure, does not refer to Nietzsche—that the Greeks were a good deal more advanced then we tend to think them to have been. For his own part, Russo remains within the narrow focus of today's historiology and he certainly does not share Nietzsche's complex reservations with regard to what he too names the Alexandrian achievement.[35] For his own part, Nietzsche emphasizes what he regards as Alexandrian "decadence" along with the continuity of the same with the legacies of both Aristotle and Plato, together with the more commonly cited denunciations of both Socrates and Euripides.[36]

As we have noted, Nietzsche writes ruefully in the *Antichrist* that it is quite as if all the effort of antiquity had been "in vain" (A 59; KSA 6, 247f.).[37] Like Russo, but also like Árpád Szabó and Charles Kahn (this is the point of departure for Kahn's indispensable study, *Anaximander and the Origins of Cosmology* [Kahn 1960]), Nietzsche makes this observation with reference to the philosophico-theoretical level of science concerned with the basis of science and mathematics (which last Nietzsche also refers to architecture, rather as Robert Hahn and others also emphasize).[38] To this I would also add the theoretical architectural reflections of Indra Kagis McEwen in her small *Socrates' Ancestor* (McEwen 1993). Important too, and in addition to the more mainstream and received discussions of mathematics in antiquity (Brumbaugh etc.), would be not only Friedrich Kittler's mathematical reflections (Nietzschean in more ways than one) in addition to Kittler's reflections on music in antiquity,[39] but also Jim Hankinson's study of cause, especially; although Hankinson certainly does not mention Nietzsche, he does feature two chapters matching Nietzsche's own thematic concerns with causality, including Stoic causality and skepticism.[40] Here we might add reflections on medicine and physiology, as Guy Métraux and others discuss this, and the present author has touched on related themes exploring the techniques of ancient bronze with reference to Pliny[41] and in the context of a review of the mechanical practical technology available in ancient Greece.[42]

It is in this broad context that I recommend that we *begin* to parse Nietzsche's observation in his *Antichrist* that "[...] all the scientific *methods* were already available" [alle wissenschaftlichen *Methoden* waren bereits da]" (A 59; KSA 6, 247). We need to begin such a reflection as it remains outstanding, just to repeat an observation Nietzsche had already made in his early notes.[43] For what is ultimately remarkable for Nietzsche is nothing other than the utter *lack* of consequentiality that this same scientific and mathematical methodology made for the Greeks themselves. Indeed the point for Nietzsche would be that in well-documented end-effect, the Greeks "made nothing" at all of the same precisely "scientific methods" they had perfected. And Nietzsche emphasized the same point with respect to method as such for the Greeks, arguing that this same "method" was already available, already developed to a certain perfection as he contended by speaking of the Alexandrian grammarians, but also more broadly as attested by an abundance of scientific methodologies, from the theoretical to the mathematical to the technological.[44]

What, as Nietzsche asks us to undertake this question, are we to make of this?

Why is it that modern science manages to take as long as it takes to become specifically *modern* science? In a longer paper I would seek to connect this question with
Heidegger's questioning concerning the difference that modern technology makes for
the purview of modern science, but for Nietzsche this question is perfectly, classically,
foundational and to that same extent this question is typical of Nietzsche's nineteenth
century.

What is required for modern science as we know it? Nietzsche's answer of course
(no mystery here given the context in which we find this question as he poses it in *The
Antichrist*) turns out to be religion of the modern Judeo-Christian kind. Nietzsche's
reply is not unique and it anticipates other contemporary theorists of the history
and philosophy of science, from Pierre Duhem to G. E. R. Lloyd and others. As Karl
Löwith points out, following Heidegger in his turn, this would be the point of the
"Anti-Christian repetition of Antiquity" (Löwith 1997, 111) as this calls for an antidote
to the Alexandrian, imagining as Nietzsche rather misguidedly imagined Wagner in
the last of his *Untimely Meditations*, as a kind of "Anti-Alexander" (WB 4; KSA 1,
447; see Löwith 1997, 111). Nietzsche for his own part would come to relinquish his
hopes for Wagner but this is not what matters here. Here the point is rather that what
Nietzsche finds necessary is not that one cuts through the complexity he describes as
the "Gordian knot of Greek culture" but, and much rather, "to retie it after it has been
loosened" (Ibid.).[45]

This recommendation is more recondite than most—in fact the very notion of
what Nietzsche named the "binding of the scientific drive" or impetus [Bändigung des
Wissenstriebes] became a watchword of much Nietzsche scholarship in the 1970s and
1980s. Yet that research project has not advanced, perhaps as a result of its association
with drives and the will to power. To my reading, what is at issue is more a matter of
Nietzsche's contention that religion, particularly in its monotheist modality, turns out
to be no enemy to science but much rather its indispensable prelude, even its ally, as
Nietzsche writes in *The Gay Science* (GS 300; KSA 3, 539) and as he argues to conclude
the third essay of his *On the Genealogy of Morals*.[46]

In the *Antichrist*, Nietzsche explains the complicated tension that is at stake in the
alliance of religion and science. Already alive to *"factual sensibility"* [*Thatsachen-Sinn*]
(A 59; KSA 6, 248), this same ancient Greek empirical sensibility ought to have
evolved into something like modern science. Indeed, Nietzsche reminds us that
this same sensibility corresponded not to some Archimedean flash of insight, and
was accordingly no bare moment in time but represented an "already centuries-old
tradition" (Ibid.), complete with a variety of technological, scientific schools and
traditions of the same. For Nietzsche as a historian, what requires attention here is
the seemingly incidental detail that the Greek natural scientific tradition was never
repressed by anything like an anti-empiricist movement, paralleling the politicized
story of the scientific revolution as we like to tell ourselves this story to simplify the
account of what it took to break the geocentric schema in favor of the heliocentric
account that was already known, of course, to the Greeks, in our typical story of,
for example, Galileo's suppression by the church.[47] Galileo's tale is one thing but for
Nietzsche even the supposed antagonism of the church cannot be invoked in the case
of antiquity because there was no church, simply enough: hence no clerical or religious

tradition to be antithetical to ancient Greek science. With no religion to play the anti-science role, Nietzsche's very historical question to philology asked why modern science *failed* to develop in antiquity?

We need to emphasize this question and the issues it involves as a question just because many classicists and historians of philosophy have already eliminated it by the best means available for not posing a question to begin with, by not asking the question in the first place. Thus we already know, as the literature attests, that there is a social reason: one notes the vulgar status of the technician or artist or technical craftsman in the judgment of noble youth in ancient Greece—and Nietzsche himself points to this, if not in the context of science, then in art, particularly sculpture where he reflects that in Pericles' day it was the heroic that mattered, a point Alastair MacIntyre likewise emphasizes with respect to the virtues in Athens, and not the star quality of the artist: to wit "no noble born youth, upon gazing upon the Zeus in Pisa, would have the desire to be himself a Phidias, or when he saw Hera in Argos to become a Polycleitus himself" (GSt Preface; KSA 1, 766).

Where Nietzsche is concerned to explicate the different understanding of the notion of the "arts" and of the artist in antiquity and our own (and indeed nineteenth-century) cult of art for its own sake and of the artist or "genius," his argument regarding the development of modern science is similarly distinguished. Other scholars do not make Nietzsche's distinctions and collapse his themes (this is what it means to cut the Gordian knot of Greek culture, a simplification we continue to pursue with a good conscience). Thus, one reads that in spite of their mathematical and technical prowess, the reason the Greeks failed to develop modern science was due to their denigration of the practical, due to their disdain for the empirical (here, just casually, we may think of the arguments concerning Aristotle's putative scholasticism). In other terms, classicists argue for Greek diffidence *vis-à-vis* science as deriving from a classically anti-banausic tendency, a diffidence which has made the reception of Kahn's scholarship as indeed of Russo and Hahn as conflicted or, better said, as restricted as it has been, although it is inaccurate and although it has been challenged at least since Nietzsche (see for example Couprie 2011). Yet this is the paradigm, this is the assumption that Nietzsche questions from his first book to his *Antichrist*. And a similarly nuanced question, similarly seeking to reweave the strands of Greek culture after the mindlessly scholarly unraveling of these same strands, forms the core of his theoretical reflections on the Greek musical work of art.[48]

The same convenient and simplistic anti-banausic assumptions, as applied to ancient science and technology, have also had the very consequent resultant of rendering the contemporary image of the Greeks as so many antique "mandarins": if not themselves horrified by technology then at least innocent of it. This supposed innocence is what makes studies like Russo's but also Kahn's and more recently Couprie and Hahn and others as dissonant as they have tended to be. What is remarkable, although it is this that testifies to an entrenched paradigm, is that any listing of the machine and theoretical technologies available in Greek and Roman worlds can be as striking as they continue to be, as evidenced in a handbook published fifty years ago, Aage Gerhardt Drachmann's *The Mechanical Technology of Greek and Roman Antiquity*,[49] and certainly even more dramatically so in the still-ongoing fascination with the discovery of the bronze Antikythera mechanism, in the year of Nietzsche's death in 1900, a mechanism that has taken more than a century in the interval to explore and to theorize, using all available modern technology for the purpose, and which, to be sure, we by no means fully understand. These extraordinary achievements remain ill-understood and—what is perhaps more telling—in the spirit of what Nietzsche called monumental history (that is: as explored with the means of experimental archeological research or the phantasms of popular television programs like those shown on the History Channel), such achievements are not understandable using current means. Said otherwise, we, with all our modern technology, cannot replicate these achievements. Furthermore and this makes it difficult to attempt Nietzsche's proposed plan to "reweave" the warp and woof of the fabric of Greek culture, reflection on these same achievements also remain the object of ongoing durable intellectual resistance, not only to Nietzsche but even to the vastly more conservative or mainstream Russo as well. Nevertheless and if anything, recent work in classics confirms Nietzsche's emphasis on the achievements of ancient Greek science in not only sheerly, purely theoretical detail but also consummately practical,[50] techno-logical sophistication. The above-mentioned example of the Antikythera mechanism, a complex of machined gears, popularly illuminates this point for us. Manifestly or patently a kind of "computer," perhaps used for cosmological calculations or as a calendar, the Antikythera mechanism serves us because it seems, for contemporary tastes, sufficiently modern-like, and is thus a modern-seeming illustration of the urgency but not less of the complexity of Nietzsche's questions.[51]

This example is most compelling—more so, I suspect, than what I have elsewhere argued as the similarly elusive and similarly technically problematic question of the production of ancient Greek bronze statues (both in terms of their lifelike precision and in their sheer abundance) (see again, Babich 2008), just because the mechanism itself seems as familiar as it seems: with its shape and all its gearing it is almost like finding Paley's watch, not "crossing a heath" as Paley put it or on the shores of an uninhabited island, but in the waters of the Adriatic.

And this set of assumptions, too, Nietzsche thematized in his theory of what counts as scientific knowledge. For, as Nietzsche observed, familiarity is essential to any claim of knowledge. Hence the goal of knowledge in general, as Nietzsche writes again and again in his published and unpublished works, is reductive: reducing the unknown to the known. Nietzsche's most important corollary is that in cases where we are *unable* to reduce the unknown to the known, we know—and can know—nothing.

Declaring in *The Gay Science* that "We simply lack any organ for knowledge" (GS 354; KSA 3, 593), Nietzsche proposes to reflect upon what we take as knowledge, a reflection which also entails a reflection on what knowledge would have to be, regarded from a rigorous perspective or taking a philosophical perspective on the question of knowledge (as of science) from antiquity to Kant. From this critical perspective on knowledge, once again, claims to knowledge, for Nietzsche, simply mean that something strange has been "reduced to something *familiar*" (GS 355; KSA 3, 593f.).

Nietzsche's claim can thus be restated in terms of the present theme: What does it mean that the Greeks could *already* possess every theoretical, mathematical, and technical prerequisite for the development of modern science, as they did in fact, while not going on from these prerequisites to develop these same preludes into modern science? For, as Nietzsche reminds us, Greek natural science was from the start (or *already*) articulated from the perspective of "the natural sciences, in association with mathematics and mechanics" (A 59; KSA 6, 247). Regarded from a modern scientific perspective, the Greeks *ought to have been* "on the best possible road" (Ibid.) to modern science. In this sense, the Greeks, prized as the inventors of science and mathematics and logic and philosophy and every other science, ought to have been on the high road of modern science—and yet they were not.

Nietzsche's point here is that something seems to be lacking and more importantly his claim points to a significant difference between Greek and modern science.

What were they missing? What else did they need?

By raising this question Nietzsche questions the developmental model of Western science as such. And to the same extent, the Greeks, source of so much that we regard as the heart of Western scientific culture, present a conundrum, a conundrum Nietzsche articulates in the spirit of his lifelong effort to raise the question of science to (and in and with) his own science of philology.

What is needed or required for the development of modern science? Will it be mathematics? No: the ancient Greeks had that.[52] Will it be theory? That's even harder to argue. Will it be technology? The mechanisms for which we have positive evidence, never mind the ones we do not know, suggest that this is also not the answer. Nietzsche's answer, which remains elusive for us no matter how it is expressed, is monotheistic religion, specifically the Judeo-Christian tradition as such.

The substantive point Nietzsche seeks to make here—*stylistically* distant as it is from the more current reflections on Greek scientific philosophy that can also be adduced in support of his assertions—is anything but obvious. And here, writing in his posthumously published *Antichrist*, although similar reflections appear throughout his work, it is significant that Nietzsche provides *even less* source material for his claims (though this can be had) than he had offered for his initially published discussion of the metric origin of tragedy out of the spirit of music in his book *The Birth of Tragedy*.[53] If, and indeed, to parse the latter, we have needed to turn to Nietzsche's unpublished early philological writings as I have argued along with many other scholars, beginning more generically with Pöschl and Bornmann, but also with Benn and Müller, Bosco and Günther, among others,[54] we cannot but expect that there will be even more need for a very specific articulation of Nietzsche's "philology" in the case of *The Antichrist*.

Thus we have noted Nietzsche's emphasis upon the indispensability of religion for the sake of science rather than as is commonly supposed as antagonist of modern science. In historical fact, as the medieval historian Lynn White has also argued (here echoing Duhem as noted above) but also as the historian of science Alistair Crombie has emphasized more neutrally and at almost equivalent length (that is to be counted in both cases in multi-volume studies), modern science turns out to be a quite religiously indebted, quite Judeo-Christian undertaking. Note here that to argue for science's religious "preludes," to use terminology already cited from *The Gay Science*, is hardly to argue that science is obviously or overtly or indeed or especially consciously "religious." Much rather, Nietzsche argues that science is not be regarded as the opponent of religion's ascetic ideal but as its most developed form, by which he means that science (and here he includes the whole breadth of scholarship and its institutional enterprises) requires the very same orientation to the world as does religion.

Thus Nietzsche claims that over the course of the

last centuries science has been promoted, partly because it was by means of science that one hoped to understand God's goodness and wisdom best [Newton] [...] partly because one believed in the absolute utility of knowledge, and especially in the most intimate association of morality, knowledge, and happiness [Voltaire] [...]; partly because one thought that in science one possessed and loved something unselfish, harmless, self-sufficient, and truly innocent, in which man's evil impulses had no part whatever [Spinoza] [...] (GS 37; KSA 3, 405f.)

Continuing the above-noted references to ancient science, there is a further tradition in the history of science importantly pioneered by Frances Yates and Betty Jo Teeter Dobbs, and more recently by Lawrence Principe, among others, who have explored the literary and experimental basis of what Nietzsche names the "preludes" of science (GS 300; KSA 3, 538) and our all-too-human, all-too-Alexandrine, we might say, taste for occult and secret powers, a taste that turns out to be less a hindrance or a prejudice than an indispensable cultivation not of the ideal or theoretical constructions of natural science but of exactly practical techniques.[55]

Above all Nietzsche makes the point that modern science seems to have elevated itself, contra religion, to the exact status of a religion. Hence he reprises the Christian attitude towards science as a kind of incidental and contingent occupation: "something second-class, not anything ultimate, unconditional, not an object of passion" (GS 123; KSA 3, 479). Science in antiquity was prized "as the means to virtue" (Ibid.). Hence Nietzsche's conclusion that with modern science "it is something new in history that science wants to be more than a mere means" (Ibid.) deserves further historical reflection.[56] Science becomes its own end but it is never pursued solely for this reason alone, and just as the Christian, as Nietzsche contends, seeks to be well-paid, so too we expect, just as Socrates first taught us to expect, that reason and science will "improve" life, and to this day we point to the advances of science and to the promise of further benefits: unimaginable riches.

For his own part, Nietzsche's argument could not be more specific as he contends that modern science would not exist if "the way had not been prepared by magicians, alchemists, astrologers, and witches whose promises and pretensions first had to create a thirst, a hunger, a taste for hidden and forbidden powers?" (GS 300; KSA 3, 538f.).[57]

If the concern for Nietzsche was ancient science in ancient Greece, as Nietzsche usually raises the question of the general origins of logic as such, as indeed of empirical science (and we note that he distinguishes these), etc., a number of additional questions follow. Here we turn to the next theme by recalling Nietzsche's own closing remarks on methods of science in antiquity, asking his readers (as he typically does) if he has been understood: "Does one comprehend this? Everything *essential* had been found in order to begin to go to work" [Alles *Wesentliche* war gefunden, um an die Arbeit gehn zu können] (A 59; KSA 6, 248). In this way, as we see below, Nietzsche's challenge to conventional assumptions in *The Antichrist* does not vary from his earliest concerns with the Socratic invention of reason in *The Birth of Tragedy* and what he originally named Alexandrian culture in his *Untimely Meditations*.

Again what is central is that what the Greeks lack is what we moderns have, whether from within the culture of faith or belief in the Judeo-Christian tradition or else, as by far the larger portion of contemporary culture, from Nietzsche's nineteenth-century to our own twenty-first-century tradition, as we know the latest avatar of this culture of faith to be belief in modern science and modern technology. What is certain today is that we do not doubt the latter and hope for nothing more than to enjoy its fruits.

3. Alexandrinian culture and Alexandrinian science

Nietzsche's "science of aesthetics," i.e., Nietzsche's study of tragedy concerns the parallel to be drawn between the "spirit of music" and "spirit of science," defining that latter spirit as "the faith that first came to light in the person of Socrates—the faith in the explicability of nature and in knowing as a panacea" (BT 17; KSA 1, 111).

This faith in the explicability of nature and in knowledge as panacea has not diminished and it is currently the only faith we have—or need. Nietzsche's critical philosophy of scientific reason draws out the logical consequences of this faith. Using "the paraphernalia of science itself," Nietzsche read Kant as outlining "the limits and the relativity of knowledge generally" and thereby and by means of these same limits or what Peter Strawson called the "bounds" of sense and sensibility, would ultimately "decisively" deny "the claims of science to universal validity and universal aims" (BT 18; KSA 1, 118). In this way, Nietzsche was able to argue that Kant's philosophic legacy signaled the logical destruction of "scientific Socratism's complacent delight in existence by establishing its boundaries" (BT 19; KSA 1, 128), whereby and by means of those same limits Kant had found a way to continue that same project.

Here Nietzsche articulates the "Socratic" culture of knowledge that he also names Alexandrian or "Alexandrine." To use the terminology of *The Genealogy of Morals*, "Alexandrine culture" is the slavish culmination of optimistic confidence as this continues to characterize scientific, especially techno-scientific culture. Key to this optimistic culture of knowledge is the ideal of science as the source of what Nietzsche earlier called "the delusion of limitless power" (BT 18; KSA 1, 117).[58]

The fantasy of limitless power through science describes modern culture on the millenarian basis of "the belief in the earthly happiness of all" (Ibid.). But as is typical for Nietzsche, he differs from the Frankfurt School theorists of the dialectic of enlightenment as he offers a genealogy of the modern technological and *consumerist* "demand for such an Alexandrine earthly happiness" (Ibid.). Here Nietzsche describes this demand as "the conjuring up of a Euripidean *deus ex machina*" (Ibid.). The reference to the machine is literal and, in the context of the book on tragedy, Nietzsche is speaking of the mechanical tricks of the divine as technical, theatrical inventions. The "mechanism" yields the idea of an "earthly consonance" (BT 17; KSA 1, 115) as this consonance comes to stand in place of the sheerly metaphysical comfort of past generations, whether in the "Nous" of Greek antiquity or the divine comforts of churchly and medieval Europe. The mechanical god becomes the god of the modern scientific, nineteenth-century (and twentieth- and twenty-first-century) world.[59]

We still regard technology as a mechanical—these days that would be an electronic or digital—replacement for the divine and its associations, a substitution Jean-Paul Sartre, following Heidegger, identifies as installing "the human being in God's place."[60] Nietzsche's point here and from the start is that science and technology is given an all-too-earthly, all-too-human expression as the "God of the machines and foundries" (Ibid.). To this extent we continue to believe in the divinity of the spirit that drives economic markets and we also believe in the spontaneous and universal benevolence of corporate invention. Even after the supposed death of god, as Nietzsche could well see in his nineteenth-century world, corporate and industrial invention remains the single deity everyone can believe in. Indeed, industry and scientific and technological know-how are gods we can believe in without believing in any god at all.

Thus it is significant that the consummately nineteenth-century image of Nietzsche's "God of the machines and foundries" [den Gott der Maschinen und Schmelztiegel] not only recurs after his first reference to it in the first of his *Untimely Meditations* but also culminates in the third essay of the *Genealogy of Morals*. Here Nietzsche echoes an analogical point regarding exploitation that Marx had expressed in 1844, the year of Nietzsche's birth, when Marx observed that in "the natural relationship of the sexes, man's relationship to nature is immediately his relationship to man, just as his relation to man is immediately his relation to nature" (Marx 1978, 83). Marx's argument was on behalf of humanism and naturalism, maintaining, in good dialectical fashion, what might yield "the *genuine* resolution of the conflict between man and nature and between man and man" (Ibid., 84).

The same ideal of overcoming may also be recognized in Nietzsche's reflections in *The Gay Science* where he repeats and refines his own earlier reflections contra idealizations of nature as so many expressions of the divine per se: "When will we complete our de-deification of nature? When may we begin to *naturalize* humanity in terms of a pure, newly discovered, newly redeemed nature?" (GS 109; KSA 3, 469). When we take Nietzsche's "naturalized" humanity for naturalism as we understand it today we tend to separate this notion from his critical reflections on scientific knowledge as a means for what he called the "humanization" of nature. Nietzsche meant this critically, writing as we have seen in his critique of causality that "It will do to consider science as an attempt to humanize things as faithfully as possible; as we describe things and their one-after-another, we learn how to describe ourselves more and more precisely" (GS 112; KSA 3, 473). In the process, and this point requires a return to Nietzsche's reading of Lucian as mentioned above (and Lucian's coordination of truth and falsity), whenever one valorizes truth at the expense of the lie, one ignores what a scientist familiar with what history has called the facts ignores at his or her peril, and that is the inevitable mixture of the two. It is tempting to simply cut through the tangled weave but the result is not the truth. As Nietzsche writes in *On Truth and Lie in an Extra-Moral Sense*, truth is beyond our sententious preoccupation with prevarication.

Nietzsche begins that essay just as Lucian begins his "True Story," recounting his visit to the moon and beyond, meeting Empedocles, tossed to the moon by the volcano, subsisting as a vegetarian can subsist on dew, by pointing to our all-too-human limits, to the limits of our senses, to the perspectival limits of our position in the universe, and to the limits of our species life and inevitable species death: we cannot help but lie. We are embroiled in lie to the extent that Nietzsche's question, as he later puts it, is "granted we want truth," but as he undertakes to ask "why not, much rather, the lie?" For we always lie, sometimes in conventional ways and as others do (this is the herd), sometimes just to ourselves (this is garden-variety convenience and self-pleasing).

The same Nietzsche who teaches the will to power underscores the very opposite of the avaricious and banausic disposition of the modern, scientific era in the third and summary book of his *On The Genealogy of Morals*, where he denounces the entirety of our modern "attitude toward nature, the way we violate her with machines and the heedless inventiveness of our technicians and engineers" (GM III, 9; KSA 5, 357). Nietzsche's argument presages both psychoanalysis and the new version of the same in the transhumanist enthusiasms of the digital as this includes both computer-driven, i.e. computational genomics, and the psychological phantom of today's network cyborgs. For Nietzsche, the mechanistic, engineer's disposition suffuses our scientific attitude towards ourselves: "we cheerfully vivisect our souls" (Ibid.)—and we ought here to think on the accelerating project of brain science, be it that of cognitive scientists in psychology or else in the different disciplines of the biological neurosciences (so that, on the level of the industrial mechanics of science, the numbers of animals needed for such research is always multiplied beyond our powers of imagining)[61]— whereby "in the wake of such" vivisection, both real and figurative, we proceed to "cure ourselves [...]we nutcrackers of the soul, ever questioning and questionable, as if life were nothing but cracking nuts" (Ibid.). Nietzsche invokes "*mechanical activity*" (GM III, 18; KSA 5, 382) as the preferred modern means of numbing sensibility, "this fact," he writes, "is called today, somewhat dishonestly, the 'blessings of work'" (Ibid.).

We work on ourselves and the self we create is the consuming self, consumed to be sure with its own creations.

For Nietzsche what is significant as he connects it with work—the critical theorist Günther Anders[62] and the political communications theorist Dallas Smythe spoke of it as home-work, whereby the work that we do as home-workers, in our own free time, is work on ourselves to produce ourselves in the corporate image of advertising and radio and television and today that would be network, be it by way of arbitrary plurality and garden-variety Google or Wikipedia and Gmail or blogs or YouTube or via social networking platforms like Twitter and Facebook and any latest thing still to come (all this is highly structured in advertising featured on the same networks and on television and radio)—functions on Nietzsche's analysis as a kind of narcotization. Today's psychologists call it "priming," Adorno, who inadvertently but quite directly helped to advance its efficacy in his work with Lazarsfeld on the Princeton Radio Project, described it with the term "ubiquity standard" and he went on with Max Horkheimer to name it "the culture industry," manufacturing culture itself and thus, as Anders and Smythe would also develop this point, manufacturing ourselves as consumers, home-workers, working on ourselves in this same commercially controlled, sometimes politically modulated direction. This industry, and the tactic of self-production and control, is effective, it "works" as Nietzsche observes, because "the chamber of human consciousness is *small*" (Ibid.).

In his first book, Nietzsche kept his metaphors in close contact with the world of the ancients. By the time he reached his later writings he had broadened his references, as Lucian also did, to include the modern myths of the Judeo-Christian world, as these myths themselves were in eclipse. Today's networked and mediatized world (internet, mobile phone, etc.) has transformed the ideal metaphoricity of Nietzsche's invocation of such a conjuring of godlike advantages out of the machine as such, and such a summoning forth would seem to be consummate, provided we leave (as we do leave) the question of "reality" to one side. I am, of course, speaking of the internet: the space/non-space of so much modern preoccupation, gaming life, second life, but also quite everyday communication, exchange—banking, purchases, plane tickets, movie and music downloads—and expression.[63]

Given what phenomenology has taught us about ourselves, the power of conscious intentionality is that we can (and we do) project ourselves very imaginatively, but that also means *really* in virtual transformations that we increasingly see as "real": these are our passions or at least what we take to be "ourselves," as first projected upon and then discovered in a screen that is nothing like the tragic "skene," a world-dream or net of fantasy and irreal space: all depth, like all tangibility, utterly unnecessary, no more than a perspective signifier. This Baudrilliardian unreal or hyperreal world is adumbrated in economic terms: advertisement and profit, disseminated as entertainment and the present allure of instant communication, with anyone, anywhere, on demand.

The Greeks, with their science, with their sense for facts and measurement, with their calculating skills and their engineering accomplishments in building and in large-scale metallurgy, all for the sake of what we call art but also for military and strategic ends, did not fail to emphasize that they dealt in every case with the contingent, changeable, merely apparent world. Thus the logical problem, which was not lost on Parmenides, requires monism or unity. But in a multifarious and mutable world, the condition of human action is plurality. As Hannah Arendt explicates, this entails an intrinsic difference one to another such "that we are all the same, that is human, in such a way that nobody is ever the same as anyone else who ever lived, lives, or will live" (Arendt 1998, 8). By contrast, as we have seen that Nietzsche emphasizes, "logic is bound to the condition: *assuming that identical cases exist*" (NF 1885, 40[13]; KSA 11, 633).[64] The presumption is untenable: it is never given, but always assumed *as if* it were given. Nietzsche's reflection here is the very specific (and many who go on about his naturalism persist in mistaking his point) insight, as he expresses it in an unpublished note labeled as a project or draft [Entwurf], concerned with articulating the depth to which "the 'will to truth' penetrates into things" together with nothing other than the "utter value of ignorance" (NF 1885, 43[1]; KSA 11, 699). For Nietzsche, as we have noted above, the importance of hermeneutics for his historical reflections, "the value of allusion [*Andeutungen*] and the measure to which not 'it is' but 'it means'" (Ibid.), entails what he calls

> the "will to truth" develops itself in the service of the "willing to power," precisely regarded, its real task is to help a certain kind of untruth to victory and permanence, to take a connected whole of falsifications as the basis for preserving a particular kind of living thing. (Ibid.)

To this extent, again like Lucian, Nietzsche's question, "what is truth" (NF 1886/87, 7[1]; KSA 12, 247) always turns out to articulate what he calls a "psychology of error" [Psychologie der Irrthums] (Ibid.), an error which lies in the attribution of a deliberate intention [Absicht], with or without (that would be destiny) a human subject: in the notion of goal: "the purpose for the sake of which there was doing, acting, living" (Ibid.). Precisely in a scientific modus, and here we may think of the psychological economies of Nietzsche's day, especially as we see these in Ernst Mach who traces similar considerations in his own work, Nietzsche reflects that the "phenomena of consciousness" might well simply represent "limit appearances," thereby constituting "the last members of a chain, but seeming to condition one another in their succession interior to a single plane of consciousness? This could be an illusion" (Ibid., 248).

To parse this illusion as error, Nietzsche underscores that "the 'essence' is *lacking*: The 'becoming,' 'phenomenal, is the only kind of being" [das "Wesen" *fehlt*: das "Werdende," "Phänomenale" ist die einzig Art Sein] (Ibid., 249). He repeats the point in the following section on the "value of truth and error" by emphasizing the importance of appearance beyond being for Plato, as Plato also spoke of a "world artist" in the *Timaeus*. Here Nietzsche's point is that this focus on the artist enabled Plato to contend that one could measure "the degree of reality" in accordance with value: "the more 'idea,' the more being" (Ibid., 253). Thus when Nietzsche here emphasizes the point, which the phenomenologist Heidegger will go on to take as emblematic for his own articulation of Nietzsche's thought, "To *imprint* upon becoming the character of being—that is the highest *will to power*" (NF 1886/87, 7[54]; KSA 12, 312), he emphasizes that what is at stake is a "*twofold falsification*, on the side of the senses and the spirit, for the sake of preserving a world of beings, enduring, of equal value, etc." (Ibid.).

Keen as he was to maintain the rigor of the Pre-Platonic thinkers on the matter of knowledge as such, especially in the physical realm of becoming and change (which both Plato and Aristotle concede), Nietzsche emphasized that the ancients resolved it only by metaphysical means: "Knowledge as such is impossible within becoming, ergo how is knowledge possible?" (Ibid., 313). To this extent, knowledge is only possible as "error about itself, as will to power, as will to deception" (Ibid.).

It is in this context that Nietzsche reflects "Against Positivism," attempting to take a stand "at the phenomena," qua facts and facts alone: "there are only facts." For Nietzsche, famously, "no, exactly facts are what there is not, merely interpretations. We cannot fix any fact 'in itself,' perhaps it is nonsense to wish to do so" (Ibid., 315). What is always at stake for Nietzsche is thus a reflection upon what determines what he calls our "psychological optic" (NF 1887, 9[106] (71); KSA 12, 395). And in this same context Nietzsche explains that "the opposite of this phenomenal world is not 'the true world,' but the formless, unformable world of the chaos of sensations—thus a different kind of phenomenal world, one not 'knowable by us" (Ibid.). This is the world of late nineteenth-century science, the same science that, with Mach, had already dissolved the atom into so many centers of force.

In this scientific world, reviewed with respect to the perspective of the scientific observer, everything turns upon the unknowability of the phenomenal world where what is knowable is what underlies or explains it. Philosophers, even analytic philosophers, still speak of metaphysics in this sense. Nietzsche and Heidegger always warned about the paradoxes of metaphysics in this same direction. There is, of course, a Nietzschean or perspectival perspective on quantum mechanics just as there is a connection with Schrödinger and Nietzsche's very ancient, Anaxagorean and Empedoclean and Heraclitean teaching of the eternal return of the same.[65] But to reweave all those strands and the many others that Nietzsche as the anti-Alexander also sought to disentangle for the precise sake of entanglement is a task for all philosophers of every stripe, as it is for both the human and the natural sciences today.

Notes

1   See further for a broader context, my discussion in Babich 2006b, especially chapter 3.

2   There are exceptions from Hugh Lloyd-Jones to Nicole Loraux among others. I discuss and cite several of these scholars in my most recent book, Babich 2013d, especially in chapters 8 and 9, reviewing both ancient Greek music and Nietzsche's phenomenological philology.

3   Part of this is the problem of peer review, which is inherently circular and just as inherently conservative, and which, when the reviewers are younger (as is increasingly the case) rather than older (as they once were), tends rather as Oscar Wilde once put it: "to straw the wheat and save the chaff." At the same time, and because of funding cuts, peer review as such is in dispute as part of the ongoing debate on open access but at issue are also deeper issues for sociology and anthropology and indeed politics of science concerning money, collusion, and general academic corruption.

4   See for an account (and further references), Babich 2003b, 97–107 as well as Babich 2010b, 343–91.

5   I offer an overview, with further references, in Babich 2012, 240–59.

6   See for a discussion the contributions to Borsche, Gerratana, and Venturelli 1994; and see, still more recently, Benne 2005.

7   I leave it as obvious here that in the case of Nietzsche a formation in analytic philosophy amounts to no formation at all, though I can make an exception for the old guard, including both Danto and Schacht, both of whom were experts in Hegel in addition the case of Danto, to art. See Babich 2011a, 37–71 as well as the second half of Babich 2003a, 63–103.

8   Thus one might compare Peter Kingsley's own publishing trajectory to see the challenges that seem to be at stake. See Kingsley 1995, as well as his 1999, and to be sure his 2003. For a discussion of the range of interpretive accounts from esoteric ritual to cosmology, see Funghi 1997, 25–38, in addition to Kahn 1997, 55–64 and Syder 1997, 129–49, as well as Burkert 1997, 167–74. The debates on Dionysus follow, of course, Pickard-Cambridge, Henrichs, and Bierl. Albert Henrichs' own overview exemplifies the abstemious presentism of today's scientifically classicist. See for a classic illustration his early review essay, Henrichs 1984, 205–40. For a recent philosophically focused example, among the other contributions in Renate Schlesier's book collection (including Henrich's own contribution), see Wildberg 2011, 205–32.

9   Richard Janko instructively highlights the recalcitrance of scholarly habits of
     inclusion (and exclusion) when he notes the silencing of alternate readings in the
     production of the designated definitive transcription of the Derveni papyrus: "By
     using a simple but bizarre expedient, P. and T. have contrived not to acknowledge
     that scholars other than themselves have toiled to reconstruct this text. They
     include no apparatus criticus!" Janko concludes that the authors "have chosen to
     benefit neither from the scholarship of the past decade nor from recent advances in
     reconstructing and reading carbonized papyri" (Janko 2006).

10   As an exception here that does not however engage Cornford or related scholars, see
     Cardew 2004, 458–73.

11   According to Pierre Hadot, Classical Philology suffers on the one hand from
     a positive draught of information, in that we are lacking most material while,
     conversely, "[...] mines of information, such as the works of Philo of Alexandria,
     Galen, Athenaeus, and Lucian or the commentaries on Plato and Aristotle written at
     the end of antiquity, have never been systematically made use of" (Hadot 1990, 489).
     The decided disadvantage of "fashions" or accepted trends of mention in scholarship,
     i.e. those we prefer to cite and those we prefer not to, is the death of scholarship.

12   The more conventional notion of the Olympian gods is the more esoteric point, to
     this day still little understood, foregrounded in the conclusion to Nietzsche's first
     book, The Birth of Tragedy.

13   See for further references, the final chapter on Nietzsche and Beethoven in Babich
     2013d and, again, Babich 2005, as well as and including still further references,
     Benne 2011, 189–212.

14   See on this, several chapters in Babich 2006b as well as Babich 2005.

15   I refer here again to a recent essay where I also feature a wide range of topical
     references (Babich 2012).

16   I discuss this in Babich 2011e, 291–311 as well as in Babich 2010b.

17   See for this connection, Babich 2011b, 57–88.

18   I have argued this elsewhere with respect to both the early and later Nietzsche. See,
     again, the final chapter in Babich 2013d, including further references to, among
     others, Günther and Benne as well as Walter Otto and Paul Maas, in addition to
     Hugh Lloyd-Jones, etc.

19   See, again, Babich 2013d, ch. 10.

20   Lucian is also crucial for Nietzsche in connection with his influence on French
     immoralists who were also important to Nietzsche, such as Voltaire and Fontenelle.
     In this same context, Nietzsche's remarks on Fontenelle and the idea of "Growth
     after Death" (GS 94; KSA 3, 449) is relevant beyond the French relation to Lucian's
     underworld shadows in the context of Norse mythology's ship of the dead, Naglfar,
     which is in the Sagas to be completed with the fingernails of the dead, and which
     will then ultimately take sail at the time of the twilight of the gods, Ragnarok.
     Indeed apart from Lucian, and this, as I emphasize, is well known: Nietzsche would
     not have had the term Übermensch—the post- or super- or overhuman. In keeping
     with the point of relative inattention noted above, I have sought input from Lucian
     experts today, from Heinrich Nieheus-Pröbsting to Heinz-Günther Nesselrath
     and Bracht Banham, all of whom duly confirm and, in the case of Banham, make
     this case in their own names, namely, that Nietzsche is not usually noted in this
     context. Patently, Peter Sloterdijk, who draws on Nieheus-Pröbsting, argues for a
     Nietzschean cynicism/kynicism. See for these and further references, Babich 2010a,
     70–93.

21 In Babich 2008, 127–89, I include a discussion of polychromy in antiquity, as this is already key to Nietzsche from the beginning of his time in Basel.

22 Ridgway 2004. Ridgway herself points (and she exemplifies to be sure) the difficulties the scholar faces when navigating the different kinds of standards for scholarship (for museum catalogues, for art history, for archeology and so on). The hermeneutic challenges remain considerable here and I point to some of these in the first section of Babich 2008 in my own exploration of ancient sculpture in the context of ancient materials and the technological manufacture and production of ancient statues, considered with respect to the extraordinary numbers, as ancient authors claim (particularly on Pliny's accounting but also elsewhere), of so-called iconic or portrait statues, as these are mentioned by Plato and others, posing the question of the public representation of space in antiquity, i.e. political relationships, and in this last context Nietzsche's notion of "Bildung" comes into crucial relief. See further Babich 2011d, 391–421, as well as my dictionary contribution: Babich 2009b, 325–8.

23 Aristophanes, *Age* 17. As cited in Wilamowitz-Möllendorff 2000, 1.

24 See most recently, including a good deal of further literature, Babich 2010b.

25 As the Canadian Thomist Bernard Lonergan was fond of emphasizing, nobody teaches if nobody learns. And like my teacher, Hans-Georg Gadamer, and like Nietzsche too following Hölderlin, so I would argue, the whole of philosophy (or there is no philosophy as Gadamer would gently suggest) is, like language: itself a conversation. And reciprocity, each interlocutor responding to each interlocutor, is the heart of conversation.

26 Thus I argue that with Kuhn and Fleck and even Feyerabend, we may justifiably speak of style, not as a metaphor, in the context of both Fleck's thought-styles and Kuhn's paradigms. See the first two sections of Babich 2010b.

27 Patently, both Max Weber and Martin Heidegger draw upon Nietzsche for their own reflections on religion and on science.

28 I address the conceptual dissonance of reading Nietzsche as a philosopher of science as well as the challenge that Nietzsche's philosophy of science brings to traditional conceptions of the philosophy of science in Babich 1994, especially ch. 2.

29 There are many who have raised epistemological concerns, especially Hans Vaihinger but also George Stack and John Wilcox and so on. See for references, Babich 1994. But in almost all cases interest in Nietzsche and epistemology or the philosophy of science is subordinated to mainstream epistemological concerns (changing to be sure as these concerns change over time) but refrains from taking Nietzsche's critique of these same epistemological convictions seriously. My own 1994 book takes this hermeneutic dissonance, by contrast, as its point of departure.

30 The original German is useful: " Ja, was bedeutet überhaupt, als Symptom des Lebens angesehn, alle Wissenschaft? Wozu, schlimmer noch, woher —alle Wissenschaft? Wie?"

31 I take up this theme in part in Babich 2009a, 19–41.

32 Nietzsche writes to Naumann in Leipzig that *On the Genealogy of Morals*, understood as what he there emphasizes as a "kleine Streitschrift" (this recurs in its subtitle), can be regarded as standing in "direktem Zuzammenhang mit dem voriges Jahrerschienenen 'Jenseits': schon dem *Titel* nach" (to Naumann, July 17, 1887; KSB 8, 111). And to be sure: the title constellation of the first part of *On the Genealogy of Morals* makes this clear: *"Good and Evil," "Good and Bad."* Volker Gerhardt cites this letter at the very beginning of his 1988 afterword to the little Reclam edition

of Nietzsche's *Jenseits von Gut und Böse: Vorspiel einer Philosophie der Zukunft*
and Sarah Kofman had already managed to underscore the importance of reading
Nietzsche's letters to his publisher in her two lecture courses on *Ecce homo*, see
especially Kofman 1992, 21ff. Indeed in his *Ecce Homo*, Nietzsche tells us that he
begins his "neinsagende, neintuende Hälfte" with *Beyond Good and Evil*. [Nachdem
der Jasagende Teil meiner Aufgabe gelöst war, kam die neinsagende, neintuende
Hälfte derselben an die Reihe] (EH Books, *Beyond Good and Evil* 1; KSA 6, 350).

33   See KSA 1, 804, 813; NF 1876/77, 23 [8]; KSA 8, 405, etc., in addition to the section
     of *The Antichrist* discussed here and beginning with the rueful musing "Die ganze
     Arbeit der antiken Welt *umsonst*" (AC 59; KSA 6, 247).

34   See here Russo 2004. Originally published in Italian as Russo 1996 and translated
     into German, with a nicely Nietzschean echo in the title, as Russo 2009. There
     is a long tradition on this theme going back to Nietzsche (and in Italian, see for
     example, Loria 1914), and Russo's point foregrounds the Alexandrian achievements
     of Hellenic Greece. I have been emphasizing here that Nietzsche underscores these
     achievements as they are interesting to modern scholars but also endeavors to take a
     step *behind* this same (all-too) modern appeal.

35   Quite to the contrary, to the extent that Russo's critics argue that Russo seems to
     attribute almost every level of mathematical and theoretical sophistication to them.

36   The history of science is often inevitably given a Comtean rather than Hegelian
     expression. See for an account of George Sarton, the long-time editor of *Isis* in this
     context, in Dear 2009, 89–93.

37   It is worth citing the full sentence here: "Die ganze Arbeit der antiken Welt *umsonst*:
     ich habe kein Wort dafür, das mein Gefühl etwas so Ungeheures ausdrückt." (A 59;
     KSA 6, 247).

38   See here Hahn 2001; and Couprie, Hahn, and Naddaf 2003.

39   See Kittler 2006a, 51–61 as well as Kittler 2009, and Kittler 2006b.

40   See Hankinson 1998. For Nietzsche and Hume on cause, see Babich 2013a, 397–431.

41   See, again, Babich 2008. An earlier and less developed English version appears as
     Babich 2007a, 1–30.

42   See here both Manfred Barthel's popular 1995 offering and Horst Bredekamp's at
     once stylistically (or conventionally) disenchantment-oriented as well as esoteric
     1992 account. And see too, as already noted, Russo 2004. And see too on Greek
     science in a broader sense, not only Szabó 1992, but also, again, Kahn 1960, in
     addition to Kraft 1971. In addition, see here, again, the joint work of Couprie, Hahn,
     and Naddaf 2003.

43   In fact, as Nietzsche glosses, developing this parallel still further, Plato and Socrates
     may be correlated with what he calls an antagonism to the natural sciences as such
     (NF 1872/73, 23[22]; KSA 7, 548), which he explains in terms of the scientific
     orientation of Epicurus and Pythagoras, especially together with Democritus as
     providing the foundation for the natural sciences. Cf. NF 1872/73, 23[40]; KSA 7,
     557.

44   Nietzsche's use of the term Alexandrinian, so in abundance in his first book, would
     merit a study all its own. Here it will have to suffice to cite his claim as we can
     perhaps use it to understand the sense of the new title that he eventually uses to
     replace the original subtitle of *The Birth of Tragedy*: "'Äufklärung' und alexandrinische
     Bildung ist es —besten Falls! —, was Philologen wollen. Nicht Hellenenthum"
     (NF 1875, 5[136]; KSA 8, 75; Cf. his revision, Ibid., 1[1], 121). Nicholas Martin
     expresses the distinction as one between a kind of bibliographical or source-scholarly

preoccupation and a creative mode in his discussion of Wolf and the traditional of "Alterthumswissenschaft" in Martin 1996, 130ff. But Martin, insightful as he is on Schiller, refers to traditional readings of the tradition of German classics in Nietzsche's day, which are as Nietzsche himself pointed out at the conclusion of his inaugural lecture on Homer, so many very classical Weimar silhouettes, lacking features and again, with reference to Alexander at the conclusion of "Homers Wettkampf."

45   It is in this sense that I hear Nietzsche's early reflection on the state of the lyric tradition, noting only Pindar as an exception in his *Vorlesung: Die griechische Lyrik*: "Wir stehen auf einem Trümmerfeld; spärliche Reste. Vollständiges außer Pindar fast gar nicht" (KGW II/2, 393).

46   I develop this further in Babich 1994, chapter 5, and still further in Babich 2011c, 305–38.

47   Although there are classical historians to this day who, rather whiggishly, continue to assume this, and many of these argue for scholastic readings of Aristotle (similarly ahistorically). But see Duhem 1969 for historical background and Feyerabend for a reading of Galileo and the church and the politics of the same but also and importantly of the empirical evidence that his telescopes could provide him (Feyerabend argues that Galileo's argument is not based as we tend to suppose on "science"), that cuts nicely to the chase. As Feyerabend argues, it is not exactly hermeneutically or scientifically rigorous to argue the history of science "sub specie aeternitatis," but we are inclined to attempt to wish to do. Feyerabend 1975, 106.

48   I say *nuanced* because Nietzsche himself hardly denies this anti-banausic insight in his "What is Noble," an emphasis recurring in his understanding of the Greek relationship to art as part of the ideal of perfecting one's own "statue," becoming as it were, a work of art. I note that this is complex and includes what counted for Nietzsche, on the cosmological level, as his artist's metaphysics. Thus Nietzsche continues: "Dieser vom Künstler Dionysos geformte Mensch verhält sich zur Natur, wie die Statue zum apollonischen Künstler." See here, again, with specific reference to the working of sculpture in Nietzsche's texts, Babich 2009b.

49   See, not with reference to Nietzsche, but generally on this topic, Drachmann 1963 in addition to Oleson 2008.

50   The practical and skeptical dimension in question led the Belgian philosopher René Berthelot to speak of Nietzsche as a pragmatist, comparing him to Pierce and James but not less, and this is most important for the context, to Poincaré. See Berthelot 1911.

51   See de Solla Price 1957, 60–7, and his 1964, 9–23; see in addition Drachmann 1963. Price himself offers a summary of his research in his 1974. For more recent discussions of the function of the mechanism, supported with MRI technology, see Freath, et al. 2006, 587–91. See here, again, Russo 2009, 375f.

52   Scholars from Otto Neugebauer to G. E. R. Lloyd to John Cleary and Árpád Szabó and to be sure many others have explored this.

53   We are—this is perhaps more than a convenient but an utterly critical parallel— only beginning to discover the literality of Nietzsche's titular claim with respect to tragedy. I explore this in Babich 2005 and develop this more broadly in Babich 2006b, chs. 3–5.

54   I detail these and other references in my essays cited above.

55   See for a recent, popular account of such scientific "preludes," as Nietzsche expresses these: Greenberg 2007, Moran 2005, as well as the collection of society proceedings by Debus 2004. See Principe 1998 for other references.

56   In this spirit, the historian of science, Peter Dear, characterizes "modern science" (which he notes is often described by today's scholars as "techno-science" to mark this modern practical or applied character) as a chimera or "hybrid" for reasons similar to those Nietzsche lists. In his 2008, Dear is more sober than Nietzsche, but he makes his point in his recent book with a certain energy, perhaps because he has repeatedly made the same point to (relatively) slim resonance in his several past books.

57   If Peter Dear, among other historians of science, can confirm Nietzsche's history of science (which Nietzsche calls a history of "errors") to affirm that the reasons for the pursuit of science in the past and the estimation of the object of science differed in antiquity and in scholastic times from the practical and applied aspect now thought inseparable from science, the historian William Eamon confirms Nietzsche's account of the alchemical and forbidden *"Preludes of Science"* in his book, *Science and the Secrets of Nature*. See Dear 2008 and Eamon 1996.

58   I connect this point with Heidegger's emphases in his *Introduction to Metaphysics* and his *Beiträge zur Philosophie* in Babich 2007b, 37–60.

59   Fritz Lang's Moloch Machine in his 1927 film, *Metropolis*, shows us how such a religious cult of the machine might work. The idea is an old one, but see, to begin with, White 1978 and Noble 1997 as well as Babich 2013c.

60   Sartre 1993, 972: "Mensch sein heißt danach streben, Gott zu sein oder, wenn man lieber will, grundlegend Begierde, Gott zu sein."

61   But see, just to start, Roberts 1980, as well as Ruesch 1978 and 1986.

62   Anders 1987. See for a further elaboration of Anders' insights on consumers' creating themselves as consumers via television, Smythe 1954, 143–56. And see too Ellul 1974, developing Edward Bernays' (1961) study of propaganda, initially published as Bernays 1923. See for further discussion and additional references, Babich 2013c.

63   See here, the first and last chapters of Babich 2013d, particularly the final chapter on what Nietzsche called the "becoming-human of dissonance."

64   The German here can be helpful, especially given Nietzsche's emphases: "Die Logik ist geknüpft an die Bedingung: *gesetzt, es giebt identische Fälle.*"

65   I include a range of relevant further references in Babich 1994 but see in particular Rüdiger Hermann Grimm's earlier thesis on Nietzsche, published as Grimm 1977; see in addition Stack 1983, which follows Grimm in considering quanta, or force points, as Nietzsche follows Boscovich. See, for discussions focusing on eternal recurrence in Nietzsche, Becker 1963, as well as more broadly, Harders 2007 and Small 2010. See, too, Stölzner 2012, 357–70, as well as Vaas 2012, 371–90. I discuss Nietzsche in relation to Schrödinger's analysis of memory and consciousness in Babich 2013e; and where Hans Seigfried offers a sustained reading of Nietzsche and complementarity, in Seigfried 1990, 619–30. Patrick A. Heelan mentions Nietzsche in passing in his 1998, 273–98.

Works cited

Anders, Günther (1987): *Die Antiquiertheit des Menschen. Vol. 1: Über die Seele im Zeitalter der zweiten industriellen Revolution.* Munich (Beck).

Arendt, Hannah (1998): *The Human Condition.* Chicago (University of Chicago Press).

Babich, Babette (1994): *Nietzsche's Philosophy of Science: Reflecting Science on the Ground of Art and Life*. Albany (State University of New York Press).

—(2002): "Editor's Commentary and Notes for Ulrich von Wilamowitz-Möllendorff, 'Future-Philology'." In *New Nietzsche Studies*. Vol. 4 (1/2), 1–32.

—(2003a): "On the Analytic–Continental Divide in Philosophy: Nietzsche's Lying Truth, Heidegger's Speaking Language, and Philosophy." In Carlos G. Prado (ed.): *A House Divided: Comparing Analytic and Continental Philosophy*. Amherst, NY (Humanity Books), 63–103.

—(2003b): "Paradigms and Thoughtstyles: Incommensurability and its Cold War Discontents from Kuhn's Harvard to Fleck's Unsung Lvov." In *Social Epistemology*. Vol. 17, 97–107.

—(2005): "The Science of Words or Philology: Music in *The Birth of Tragedy* and the Alchemy of Love in *The Gay Science*." In Tiziana Andina (ed.): *Revista di estetica*. Vol. 28, XLV. Turin (Rosenberg & Sellier), 47–78.

—(2006a): "Gay Science: Science and *Wissenschaft, Leidenschaft* and Music." In Keith Ansell-Pearson (ed.): *Companion to Nietzsche*. Cambridge (Blackwell), 97–114.

—(2006b): *Words in Blood, Like Flowers: Philosophy and Poetry, Music and Eros in Hölderlin, Nietzsche, and Heidegger*. Albany (State University of New York Press).

—(2007a): "Greek Bronze: Holding a Mirror to Life." In *Yearbook of the Irish Philosophical Society*. Vol. 7, 1–30.

—(2007b): "Heidegger's Will to Power." In *Journal of the British Society for Phenomenology*. Vol. 38 (1), 37–60.

—(2008): "Die Naturkunde der Griechischen Bronze im Spiegel des Lebens. Betrachtungen über Heideggers ästhetische Phänomenologie und Nietzsches agonale Politik." In Günter Figal (ed.), Harald Seubert and Babich (trans.): *Internationales Jahrbuch für Hermeneutik*. Tübingen (Mohr Siebeck), 127–89.

—(2009a): "'A Philosophical Shock': Foucault's Reading of Heidegger and Nietzsche." In Carlos G. Prado (ed.): *Foucault's Legacy*. London (Continuum), 19–41.

—(2009b): "Skulptur [Bildhauerkunst]." In Christian Niemeyer (ed.): *Nietzsche Lexikon*. Darmstadt (Wissenschaftliche Buchgesellschaft), 325–8.

—(2010a): "Le Zarathoustra de Nietzsche et le style parodique. A propos de l'*hyperanthropos* de Lucien et du surhomme de Nietzsche." In *Diogène. Revue Internationale des Sciences Humaines*. Vol. 232, 70–93.

—(2010b): "Towards a Critical Philosophy of Science: Continental Beginnings and Bugbears, Whigs and Waterbears." In *International Journal of the Philosophy of Science*. Vol. 24 (4), 343–91.

—(2011a): "An Impoverishment of Philosophy." In *Purlieu: Philosophy and the University*. Vol. 1, 37–71.

—(2011b): "Artisten Metaphysik und Welt-Spiel in Fink and Nietzsche." In Cathrin Nielsen and Hans Rainer Sepp (eds): *Welt denken. Annäherung an die Kosmologie Eugen Finks*. Freiburg im Breisgau (Alber), 57–88.

—(2011c): "Nietzsches Genealogie der Wissenschaft als Mythos: Religion, Moral und die Werte der Moderne." In Beatrix Vogel and Nikolaus Gerdes (eds): *Grenzen der Rationalität: Teilband 1: Kolloquien 2005–2009*. Munich (Allitera), 305–38.

—(2011d): "Zu Nietzsches Statuen: Skulptur und das Erhabene." In Beatrix Vogel and Nikolaus Gerdes (eds): *Grenzen der Rationalität: Teilband 2*. Munich (Allitera), 391–421.

—(2011e): "Zu Nietzsches Wissenschaftsphilosophie." In Helmut Heit, Günter Abel, and

Marco Brusotti (eds): *Nietzsches Wissenschaftsphilosophie. Aktualität, Rezeption und Hintergründe*. Berlin (Walter de Gruyter), 291–311.

—(2012): "On Nietzsche's Judgment of Style and Hume's Quixotic Taste: On the Science of Aesthetics and 'Playing' the Satyr." In *The Journal of Nietzsche Studies*. Vol. 43 (2), 240–59.

—(2013a): "Hume on Causality and Nietzsche on Cause and Error in Philosophy." In Babette Babich and Dimitri Ginev (eds): *The Multidimensionality of Hermeneutic Phenomenology*. Frankfurt am Main (Springer), 397–431.

—(2013b): "Nietzsche's Phenomenology: Musical Constitution and Performance Practice." In Élodie Boubil and Christine Daigle (eds): *Nietzsche and Phenomenology: Power, Life, Subjectivity*. Bloomington (Indiana University Press), 117–40.

—(2013c): "O, Superman! or Being Towards Transhumanism: Martin Heidegger, Günther Anders, and Media Aesthetics." In *Divinatio*. Vol. 36, 83–99.

—(2013d): *The Hallelujah Effect: Philosophical Reflections on Music, Performance Practice and Technology*. Surrey (Ashgate).

—(2013e): "Schrödinger and Nietzsche: Eternal Return and the Moment." In Christopher Key Chapple (ed.): *Festschrift for Antonio de Nicolas* (forthcoming).

Barthel, Manfred (1995): *Die Enkel des Archimedes. Eine etwas andere Kulturgeschichte*. Witten (Neuhaus).

Becker, Oskar (1963): "Nietzsches Beweis für sein Lehre von der ewigen Wiederkehr." In his *Dasein und Dawesen*. Pfullingen (Neske).

Benne, Christian (2005): *Nietzsche und die historisch-kritischen Philologie*. Berlin (Walter de Gruyter).

—(2011): "Von der Wissenschaft des Rhythmus zum Rhythmus der Wissenschaft." In Helmut Heit, Günter Abel, and Marco Brusotti (eds): *Nietzsches Wissenschaftsphilosophie. Aktualität, Rezeption und Hintergründe*. Berlin (Walter de Gruyter), 189–212.

Bernays, Edward (1923): *Crystallizing Public Opinion*. New York (Liveright).

Berthelot, René (1911): *Un romantisme utilitaire: étude sur le mouvement pragmatiste. 1, Le pragmatisme chez Nietzsche et chez Poincaré*. Paris (F. Alcan).

Bredekamp, Horst (1992): *Antikensehnsucht und Maschinenglauben. Die Geschichte der Kunstkammer und die Zukunft der Kunstgeschichte*. Berlin (Wagenbach).

Burkert, Walter (1997): "Star Wars or One Stable World: A Problem of Pre-Socratic Cosmogony (*PDervCol XXV*)." In André Laks and Glenn Most (eds): *Studies on the Derveni Papyrus*. Oxford (Oxford University Press), 167–74.

Cardew, Alan (2004): "The Dioscuri: Nietzsche and Rohde." In Paul Bishop (ed.): *Nietzsche and Antiquity: His Reaction and Response to the Classical Tradition*. Rochester (Camden), 458–73.

Cornford, Francis MacDonald (1912): *From Religion to Philosophy: A Study in the Origins of Western Speculation*. New York and London (Longmans, Green, and Co./Edward Arnold), 111.

Couprie, Dirk L. (2011): *Heaven and Earth in Ancient Greek Cosmology: From Thales to Heraclides Ponticus*. Frankfurt am Main (Springer).

Couprie, Dirk, Robert Hahn, and Gerard Naddaf (2003): *Anaximander in Context: New Studies in the Origins of Greek Philosophy*. Albany (State University of New York Press).

Dear, Peter (2008): *The Intelligibility of Nature: How Science Makes Sense of the World*. Chicago (University of Chicago Press).

—(2009): "The History of Science and the History of the Sciences: George Sarton, *Isis*, and the Two Cultures." In *Isis*. Vol. 100, 89–93.

Debus, Allen G. (2004): *Alchemy and Early Modern Chemistry: Papers from Ambix*. Huddersfield (Jeremy Mills).

Drachmann, Aage Gerhardt (1963): *The Mechanical Technology of Greek and Roman Antiquity*. Madison (University of Wisconsin Press).

Duhem, Pierre (1969): *To Save the Phenomena: An Essay on the Idea of Physical Theory from Plato to Galileo*. E. Dolan and C. Maschier (trans.). Chicago (University of Chicago Press).

Eamon, William (1996): *Science and the Secrets of Nature: Books of Secrets in Early Modern Culture*. Princeton (Princeton University Press).

Ellul, Jacques (1974): *Propaganda: The Formation of Men's Attitudes*. Konrad Kellen and Jean Lerner (trans.). New York (Knopf).

Feyerabend, Paul (1975): *Against Method*. London (Verso).

Freath, Tony, et al. (2006): "Decoding the Ancient Greek Astronomical Calculator Known as the Antikythera Mechanism." In *Nature*. Vol. 444, 587–91.

Funghi, Maria Serena (1997): "The Derveni Papyrus." In André Laks and Glenn Most (eds): *Studies on the Derveni Papyrus*. Oxford (Oxford University Press), 25–38.

Greenberg, Arthur (2007): *From Alchemy to Chemistry in Picture and Story*. Cambridge (Wiley).

Grimm, Rüdiger Hermann (1977): *Nietzsche's Theory of Knowledge*. Berlin (Walter de Gruyter).

Hadot, Pierre (1990): "Forms of Life and Forms of Discourse in Ancient Philosophy." In *Critical Inquiry*. Vol. 16 (3), 483–505.

Hahn, Robert (2001): *Anaximander and the Architects: The Contributions of Egyptian and Greek Architectural Technologies to the Origins of Greek Philosophy*. Albany (State University of New York Press).

Hankinson, R. J. (1998): *Cause and Explanation in Ancient Greek Thought*. Oxford (Oxford University Press).

Harders, Gerd (2007): *Der gerade Kreis – Nietzsche und die Geschichte der ewigen Wiederkehr. Eine wissensozialogische Untersuchung zu zyklischen Zeitvorstellungen*. Berlin (Duncker & Humblot).

Heelan, Patrick A. (1998): "The Scope of Hermeneutics in the Philosophy of Natural Science." In *Studies in the History and Philosophy of Science*. Vol. 29, 273–98.

Henrichs, Albert (1984): "Loss of Self, Suffering, Violence: The Modern View of Dionysus from Nietzsche to Girard." In *Harvard Studies in Classical Philology*. Vol. 88, 205–40.

Janko, Richard (2006): "Review of *The Derveni Papyrus*, edited by Theokritos Kouremenos, George M. Parássoglou, and Kyriakos Tsantsanoglou." In *Bryn Mawr Classical Review* (October 29). http://bmcr.brynmawr.edu/2006/2006-10-29.html

Kahn, Charles (1960): *Anaximander and the Origins of Greek Cosmology*. New York (Columbia University Press).

—(1997): "Was Euthyphro the Author of the Derveni Papyrus." In André Laks and Glenn Most (eds): *Studies on the Derveni Papyrus*. Oxford (Oxford University Press), 55–64.

Kingsley, Peter (1995): *Ancient Philosophy, Mystery, and Magic: Empedocles and Pythagorean Tradition*. Oxford (Clarendon Press).

—(1999): *In the Dark Places of Wisdom*. Inverness, CA (Golden Sufi Center).

—(2003): *Reality*. Inverness, CA (Golden Sufi Center).

Kittler, Friedrich (2006a): "Number and Numeral." In *Theory, Culture & Society*. Vol. 23 (7–8), 51–61.

—(2006b): *Musik und Mathematik. Vol. 1: Hellas, Part 1: Aphrodite.* Paderborn (Wilhelm Fink Verlag).

—(2009): *Musik und Mathematik. Vol. 1: Hellas, Part 2: Eros.* Paderborn (Wilhelm Fink Verlag).

Kofman, Sarah (1992): *Explosion I. De l'«Ecce Homo» de Nietzsche.* Paris (Galilee).

Kraft, Fritz (1971): *Geschichte der Naturwissenschaft I. Die Begründung einer Geschichte der Wissenschaft von der Natur durch die Griechen.* Freiburg im Breisgau (Rombach).

Loria, Gino (1914): *Le Scienze Estate nell'antica Grecia.* 5 vols. 2nd edn. Milan (Hoepli).

Löwith, Karl (1997): *Nietzsche's Philosophy of the Eternal Recurrence of the Same.* Harvey Lomax (trans.). Berkeley (University of California Press).

Martin, Nicholas (1996): *Nietzsche and Schiller: Untimely Aesthetics.* Oxford (Oxford University Press).

Marx, Karl (1978): "Economic and Philosophic Manuscripts of 1844." In Robert C. Tucker (ed.): *The Marx-Engels Reader.* 2nd edn. New York (Norton).

McEwen, Indra Kagis (1993): *Socrates' Ancestor: An Essay on Architectural Beginnings.* Cambridge, MA (MIT Press).

Moran, Bruce T. (2005): *Distilling Knowledge: Alchemy, Chemistry, and the Scientific Revolution.* Cambridge, MA (Harvard University Press).

Noble, David (1997): *The Religion of Technology: The Divinity of Man and the Spirit of Invention.* New York (Knopf).

Oleson, John Peter (2008): *The Oxford Handbook of Engineering and Technology in the Classical World.* New York (Oxford University Press).

Principe, Lawrence (1998): *The Aspiring Adept: Robert Boyle and his Alchemical Quest.* Princeton (Princeton University Press).

Ridgway, Brunilde Sismondo (2004): "Review of Vinzenz Brinkman and Raimund Wünsche (eds) (2004): *Bunte Götter. Die Farbigkeit antiker Skulptur. Eine Ausstellung der Staatlichen Antikensammlungen und Glyptothek München in Zusammenarbeit mit der Ny Carlsberg Glyptotek Kopenhagen und den Vatikanischen Museen, Rom.* Second Printing. Munich (Staatliche Antikensammlungen und Glyptothek)." In *Bryn Mawr Classical Review.* August 7, 2004. http://bmcr.brynmawr.edu/2004/2004-08-07.html.

Roberts, Catherine (1980): *Science, Animals, and Evolution: Reflections on Some Unrealized Potentials of Biology and Medicine.* Westport, CT (Greenwood).

Ruesch, Hans (1978): *Nackte Herrscherin. Entkleidung der medizinischen Wissenschaft.* Munich (Hirthammer).

—(1986): *Tausend Ärzte gegen Tierversuche.* Klosters (Civis).

Russo, Lucio (1996): *La Rivoluzione Dimenticata. Il Pensiero Scientifico Greco e la Scienza Moderna.* Milan (Feltrinelli).

—(2004): *The Forgotten Revolution: How Science Was Born in 300 BC and Why it Had to Be Reborn.* Silvio Levy (trans.). Berlin (Springer).

—(2009): *Die vergessene Revolution oder die Wiedergeburt des antiken Wissens.* Bärbel Deniger (trans.). Berlin (Springer).

Sartre, Jean Paul (1993): *Das Sein und das Nichts.* Justus Streller (trans.). Hamburg (Rowohlt Tb.).

Seigfried, Hans (1990): "Autonomy and Quantum Physics: Nietzsche, Heidegger, and Heisenberg." In *Philosophy of Science.* Vol. 57 (4), 619–30.

Small, Robin (2010): *Time and Becoming in Nietzsche's Thought.* London (Continuum).

Smythe, Dallas (1954): "Reality as Presented by Television." In *The Public Opinion Quarterly.* Vol. 18 (2), 143–56.

de Solla Price, Derek (1959): "An Ancient Greek Computer." In *The Scientific American*. Vol. 200 (6), 60–7.

—(1964): "Automata and the Origins of Mechanism and Mechanistic Philosophy." In *Technology and Culture*. Vol. 5 (1), 9–23.

—(1974): "Gears from the Greeks: The Antikythera Mechanism – A Calendar Computer from *ca.* 80 B.C." In *Transactions of the American Philosophical Society (New Series)*. Vol. 64 (7), 1–70.

Stack, George (1983): *Lange and Nietzsche*. Berlin (Walter de Gruyter).

Stölzner, Michael (2012): "Taking Eternal Recurrence Scientifically: A Comparative Study of Oskar Becker, Felix Hausdorff, and Abel Rey." In Helmut Heit, Günter Abel, and Marco Brusotti (eds): *Nietzsches Wissenschaftsphilosophie*. Berlin (Walter de Gruyter), 357–70.

Syder, David (1997): "Heraclitus in the Derveni Papyrus." In André Laks and Glenn Most (eds): *Studies on the Derveni Papyrus*. Oxford (Oxford University Press), 129–49.

Szabó, Árpád (1992): *Das geozentrische Weltbild*. Munich (dtv).

Tilman, Borsche, Federico Gerratana, and Aldo Venturelli (1994): *"Centauren-Geburten". Wissenschaft, Kunst, und Philosophie beim jungen Nietzsche*. Berlin (Walter de Gruyter).

Vaas, Rüdiger (2012): "'Ewig rollt das Rad des Seins': Der 'Ewige-Wiederkunft-Gedanke' und seine Aktualität in der modernen physikalischen Kosmologie." In Helmut Heit, Günter Abel, and Marco Brusotti (eds): *Nietzsches Wissenschaftsphilosophie*. 371–90.

White, Lynn (1978): *Medieval Religion and Technology*. Berkeley (University of California Press).

Wildberg, Christian (2011): "Dionysus in the Mirror of Philosophy." In Renate Schlesier (ed.): *A Different God?* Berlin (Walter de Gruyter), 205–32.

Wilamowitz-Möllendorff, Ulrich von (2000): "Future-Philology." Gertrude Postl, Babette Babich and Holger Schmid (trans.). In *New Nietzsche Studies*. Vol. 4 (1/2), 1–32.

13

The Religion of the "Older Greeks" in Nietzsche's "Notes to We Philologists"

Hubert Cancik and Hildegard Cancik-Lindemaier

1. The text: "Notes to We Philologists" (1875)

Religion as criterion: The theme of the "Notes"

In the never-completed fourth *Untimely Meditation*, the main objects of inquiry are the philologists and classical antiquity, as well as historical science and humanistic education. Modern philologists, so the *Meditation* claims, neither can nor want to understand antiquity; the notion of classical antiquity does not reveal the "real" Greeks; the business of philological-historical science produces no true education. To demonstrate these claims, Nietzsche construes a "pre-classical" antiquity and positions Greek religion in the center of his argument. For here, in the opposition between early Greek religion and Christian philologists, lies evident the latter's inability to understand antiquity, to appropriate it, to convey it. Other segments of Greek culture, such as Euclid's geometry, the medical theories of Hippocrates, the *Organon* of Aristotle, the musical theory of Aristoxenus, or the *Almagest* of Ptolemy, were each received in a less mangled and obfuscated way, and each progressed productively in the post-ancient Orient and Occident. But, per Nietzsche's diagnostics, no such meaningful diastasis between philology and antiquity could have been made. The presentation of the religion of "older antiquity" is, therefore, of great significance for the general argument of the "Notes." The theme is, basically, a comparative one, driven by a critical impulse that carries it far beyond the confined theme of this uncompleted *Meditation*.

Development and form of the "Notes"

Notebook [Heft] U II 8

In the red paper notebook given the Sigle U II 8 by the archivists of the "Nietzsche-Archiv" in Weimar, there are actually two "texts." The first, pages 239–108 according to the archival pagination, is written back to front (as was Nietzsche's wont) and is titled by Nietzsche: "Notes to We Philologists" (hereafter: WPh). That title specifies exactly the form and content of these notes. Nietzsche wrote the second text, pages 3–43, from front to back, after having turned the notebook around, probably after he finished the first text. Here, too, we are presented with a material and thematic unity. Nietzsche treats the older Greek philosophers from Thales to Socrates and the tension between the abstract sciences and living wisdom. This text features no header. But the "test title" Nietzsche inserted in the middle of the otherwise-blank fourth page can be accepted as a reasonably accurate description: "Science and Wisdom in Conflict as Depicted in the Older Greek Philosophers" (hereafter: WWK). The two investigations Nietzsche composed together in Notebook U II 8 (WPh and WWK) are not developed out of each other in terms of their textual genesis. They represent two independent plans, each of which can be traced back to the beginnings of Nietzsche's time at Basel and, in some of their motives, even further than that.

The "Notes to We Philologists" (U II 8, pp. 239–108) are developed out of technical philological introductions, programmatic writings, and Nietzsche's own commitment to the "Future of our Educational Institutions." The drafts, outlines, and notes to WWK (U II 8, pp. 3–43) lead to Nietzsche's first lecture at Basel on the pre-Platonic philosophers. It was announced for the winter semester 1869/70 and was to treat early Greek philosophy. WWK is thus another witness to Nietzsche's endeavor to constitute the period of the "older Greeks" as an autonomous and normative epoch as opposed to the Classical, the Athenian culture of the fifth century, and the Alexandrian-Roman culture. The expression "archaic" had not yet been discovered by Nietzsche.

The two note-aggregates are bound to each other through a historical-philosophical hypothesis. The Greek archaic period did not, according to Nietzsche, attain its completion in the classical. Greek culture on the whole was allegedly "not yet" ready and discovered; in the archaic period, there would be found still unknown "*possibilities of life*" (NF 1875, 6[48]; KSA 8, 115).[1] The true philology, i.e. Nietzsche's philology, will discover them and, through contact with this singularly creative period of Greece, become creative itself, and thus be educational in the highest sense: this is the genuine "Philology of the Future!" [Zukunftsphilologie!]

The two texts in U II 8 are thus on the whole not merely so-called "preparatory stages" of works which Nietzsche published later. Only certain themes were carried on further, only certain parts can be text-genetically demonstrated as having been developed and recycled in other publications. Neither this fourth proposed *Untimely Meditation* on "We Philologists" nor the tractate "Science and Wisdom in Conflict" were published by Nietzsche—nor were the tractate on "Philosophy in the Tragic Age of the Greeks" (1873) or the five public lectures on the "Future of our Educational Institutions" (1872), though these latter texts were in fact refined to the form of a print manuscript. A chronological survey of the manuscript evidence may clarify the genesis of WPh; for practical reasons, the letters A to E are used to label the different manuscript parts.

A　U II 8, pp. 239–108: Basel Notes until spring 1875; Nietzsche's handwriting (KSA 8, sources 2, 5).

B　Mp XIII 6b, pp. 1–22: Gersdorff version, Basel, March 1875; Carl von Gersdorff's handwriting (KSA 8, source 3).

C Mp XIII 6a, pp. 1–11: Basel composition; Basel (?), summer (?) 1875; Nietzsche's handwriting (KSA 8, source 7).

D M I 1: "The Plough," pp. 80–88: "On the Greeks"; September 1876; Peter Gast's handwriting (KSA 8, source 18).

E U II 5, pp. 113–14: Bex version (nrs. 1–6); "Bex from the 3. of October onward," 1876; Paul Rée's and Nietzsche's handwriting (KSA 8, source 19).

Further manuscripts for WPh (Mp XIII 6a and 6b; M I 1; U II 5)

The first indication that Nietzsche intended an *Untimely Meditation* on philology can be found in the summer of 1873: here "Classical Philology," "scholars," and "teachers" are the key words (NF 1873, 29[163]; KSA 7, 699; NF 1873, 30[38]; KSA 7, 744f.). More than a year after this first plan, immediately after the appearance of the third *Untimely Meditation*, Nietzsche apparently began his first concrete efforts on WPh in October 1874 (to Rohde, October 7, 1874; KSB 4, 263; to Wagner, c. October 10, 1874: KSB 4, 265). Entries on the new *Untimely Meditation* "Richard Wagner in Bayreuth" (NF 1874, 32[18]; KSA 7, 760)—the text that would eventually replace WPh in Nietzsche's plans—ran concurrently, as did plans for an *Untimely Meditation* on religion; this may also account for the emphasis on this theme in WPh. In November 1874, however, Nietzsche comes to understand that no further *Untimely Meditation* can be completed "this winter" (to Rohde, November 15, 1874; KSB 4, 275).

Nietzsche received new inspirations for WPh through his engagement with a philological-poet of his own tastes, Giacomo Leopardi (1798–837), and through Jakob Burckhardt's lecture on the culture of the Greeks. In notepad [Notizbuch] N I, there is a lecture plan dating from January,[2] which covers, among other things, Friedrich August Wolf's *Kleine Schriften*, Hermann Köchly's work on Gottfried Hermann, and Jacob Bernays' work on Joseph Justus Scaliger.[3] Each of these authors is treated in WPh. The similarly noted Basel colleague Jacob Achilles Mähly does not appear in WPh; his book on Angelus Politianus (Leipzig 1864), however, is already named in Nietzsche's "Encyclopedia of Classical Philology" (hereafter: EKP). Notably, French literature such as Montaigne is also included.[4] In February, Nietzsche hoped that WPh would be ready by Easter (to Rohde, February 28, 1875; KSB 5, 27). During his stay in Basel, Carl von Gersdorff was able to write a clean copy of the texts in U II 8, pp. 238/39–200 and design a title page that Nietzsche provided with a motto and a dedication (Mp XIII 6b). Nietzsche wrote about another 40 pages in Notebook U II 8 after his friend's departure (U II 8, pp. 198–c. 148).

In May 1875, Nietzsche received Louis Kelterborn's record of Burckhardt's lecture series on "Greek Culture" (448 quarto pages): this was a difficult test for Nietzsche's own "characterization" of the Greeks, which he intended to give in WPh and for which he had already been using Baumgartner's record of that same lecture (to Overbeck, May 30, 1875; KSB 5, 58; to Gersdorff, July 21, 1875; KSB 5, 87; see also pp. 266–7).

Composition of the new *Meditation*, "Richard Wagner in Bayreuth," began in spring 1875. It developed quickly—at the expense of WPh, which was still being planned for "summer 1875" (NF 1875, 4[3]; KSA 8, 39; see the traces in KSA 8, 128–30). Nevertheless, work on that new *Meditation* came to the foreground; and in

October 1875 it was declared "almost ready" (to Rohde, October 7, 1875; KSB 5, 119). The plan for an *Untimely Meditation* on the philologists was retained for a considerable time. Nietzsche took various approaches to continue the preparations. But these attempts already belong to a sort of dénouement. To this group belongs probably Mp XIII 6a (= C, dated summer 1875 or later?) and some pieces written down in Bex (= E, dated October 3 <1876>). Some further stages suggest Nietzsche's attempts to bring materials from WPh into the plans of his first major aphorism book.

Although "philology" as a theme appeared abandoned, the theme of "the Greeks" was not. Among the titles for a long row of planned *Untimely Meditations* found in notepad N II 1 (NF 1876, 16[8–12]; KSA 8, 288–90), words like "Greeks" and "Teacher" figure repeatedly (there is also one occurrence of "Cultural Philistine" [Bildungsphilister]); the word "Philologists," however, does not appear.

"On the Greeks" titles a chapter of the September 1876 collection of aphorisms titled "The Plough [Die Pflugschar]" (M I 1, pp. 80–88 = C: KSA 8, 314–31). Nietzsche evidently re-edited some texts on the subject of "Greeks" from U II 8 (A). Thus, for example, the judgment about Xenophon's Socrates stemming from some lines in A (p. 112,18f.: NF 1876, 5[193]; KSA 8, 95) and p. 112, 15ff.: NF 1876, 5[192]; KSA 8, 94f.) is bound to aphorism number 146 (NF 1876, 18[47]; KSA 8, 327); unlike some others from this chapter, this aphorism is not carried over into *Human all-too-Human*. Texts from chapter 4 ("Adumbrations on the Greeks"), and therewith parts of his presentation on early Greek religion, migrate from "The Plough" and the so-called "Sorrento Papers" into the print manuscript of *Human all-too-Human* (January 1878).

Preparations and sources

Nietzsche dealt with the religion of the Greeks in two lectures. In the summer semester of 1871, his EKP treated "The Religion and Mythology of the Ancients" and "The Study of Religious Antiquities" (EKP §§19 and 20; KGW II/3, 410–27). Here he reports on Max Müller's *Comparative Mythology*, employs the current advances in Indo-Germanic grammar to clarify the names of various gods, and classifies Christianity decisively within the history of ancient religions. The second lecture, "On the Religious Services of the Greeks [Der Gottesdienst der Griechen]" (winter semester 1875/76; KGW II/5, 355–520), concentrates on the "worship [Cultus] of the Greeks and Romans." The conspicuous and entirely un-classical title "Gottesdienst" may well owe itself to this noteworthy focus. Rather than mythology and the Dionysian-Apollonian "Theologoumena," here the main divisions are: "locations and topics of worship," "persons of worship," and "practices of worship."[5] These include images of gods and temples, sacred roads and offertory tables. The "adumbrations" about early Greek religion, which Nietzsche had planned for his fourth *Meditation*, were exceptionally well prepared and integrated into contemporary academic usage. In the "Notes," however, he avoids antiquarian details and the professional literature (which even then was massive). He hardly mentions dates, much less inscriptions, which carries the effect of narrowing his sources to high poetry like Homer, Pindar, Theognis, and the tragedians.[6]

On the other hand, Nietzsche avoids in his lectures the kinds of bitter, occasionally blasphemous criticism of Judaism, Christianity, and religion generally that he formulates in the "Notes": "The Jews the worst people" (WPh 5[166]; KSA 8, 88), "the utterly tremendous outrage [...] Christianity" (WPh 5[148]; KSA 8, 80), "God entirely superfluous" (WPh 5[166]; KSA 8, 88; cf. also 5[150]; KSA 8, 80f.). Why such formulations were not possible in his lectures at the University of Basel is obvious. Whether Nietzsche could have published them in an *Untimely Meditation* in 1875 is doubtful too. However, such phrases indicate how his later "Attempt at a Critique of Christianity" (NF 1888 19[8]; KSA 13, 545 and 22[14]; KSA 8,589), which still carries an academic title, could finally be named *Anti-Christ* and *A Curse on Christianity*.

The strongest impulse for Nietzsche's presentation of Greek religion came from Jacob Burckhardt's lecture series on *Greek Cultural History*.[7] In formulating his own "Notes" Nietzsche was able to rely on two available transcripts of these lectures, from Adolf Baumgartner and Louis Kelterborn respectively.[8] Burckhardt, too, oriented his sketch of Greek religion on the Homeric epics. In the gods, the poet reveals to the people "their own being," an "image of the entire world [Weltganzen]," and "a great ideal of their own enduring essence" (Burckhardt 1977, II, 36). The gods emerged from the vision of the whole people and have been designed by the artists as the "transfigured mirror of the nation" (Burckhardt 1977, II, 37). Burckhardt modernizes his sketch by means of cultural-critical remarks, like those against modern journal culture, and by comparison "with the God of the monotheistic religions" (Burckhardt 1977, II, 45). Greek religion knew "no sacred texts," had no systematic doctrine and made no internal moral demands upon the people—neither conversion nor asceticism (Burckhardt 1977, II, 197): it "taught nothing and thus offered nothing to be contradicted" (Burckhardt 1977, II, 125f.). Instead of a dogma, "worship" [Kultus] was richly developed. "The entire worship" was, Burckhardt claims, closely entwined "with enjoyment" (Burckhardt 1977, II, 197) and had "gradually taken into its service nearly all the joys of life" (Burckhardt 1977 II, 125). Nevertheless there were "no priestly orders and no priesthood": "above all, religion did not belong to the priests" (Burckhardt 1977 II, 127; cf. WPh 5[104]; KSA 8, 67). Each of Burckhardt's observations and evaluations of Greek religion here reappear in Nietzsche's "Notes to We Philologists." They belong for the most part to the tradition of European Phil-Hellenism, even with their critical tendencies with respect to Christianity. However, where the Basel historian argues with his own knowledge of the sources, independently and with magisterial restraint, the "Notes" of his young classicist colleague are at times sharply polemical and at others filled with joyful praise, an accusation and a yearning for confession: Ecce Philologus "I know them, I am one myself" (WPh 5[142]; KSA 8, 76).

2. The religion of the "**older** antiquity" (WPh 5[111]; KSA 8, 69)

"The older Greece" (WWK 6[11]; KSA 8, 101): On the constitution of an epoch

The religion Nietzsche seeks is intended to show the inability of modern philologists to understand antiquity or to act as educators. This religion, accordingly, cannot be that of the Greeks in the classical, Hellenistic, or imperial epoch.[9] Those Greeks are "dull" and "humane" (WPh 5[195]; KSA 8, 95), "degenerate" (WWK 6[11]; KSA 8, 101), "weak," "Romanized," and as such are in the end merely "allies" of Christianity and of the liberal, enlightened, bourgeoisie humanism of the present (WWK 6[14]; KSA 8, 103). Nietzsche instead seeks "the older Greeks" (WWK 6[11]; KSA 8, 101), "the **older** antiquity" (WPh 5[111]; KSA 8, 69), the "youthful times" (WPh 5[195]; KSA 8, 95), "the pure times of antiquity" (WPh 3[13]; KSA 8, 18). This was an antiquity that was never overcome by Christianity.[10] Nietzsche construes this pre-classical period as an epoch of its own; he names it "the *tragic age*" (WWK 6[18]; KSA 8, 105) since the first drama was performed around 530 BC. Here lived and worked the "pre-Platonic," "pre-Socratic" or "older" philosophers (WWK 6[5]; KSA 8, 98), those "tyrants of spirit [Tyrannen des Geistes]" (WPh 5[7]; KSA 8, 42). The Persian Wars ended this vital, creative, Dionysian phase of Greek history around 500 BC. Accordingly, Nietzsche fundamentally revalues the symbolic battles of the Occident at Marathon and Salamis: these wars and victories were a "national disaster" (WWK 6[27]; KSA 8, 108).[11] Nietzsche posits the year 776 BC as the beginning of the epoch, as that was the first time the Olympic games were celebrated (WWK 6[30]; KSA 8, 110).[12]

The first witness of the epoch is Homer. He is also the most important source for Nietzsche's presentation of early Greek religion. Homer "liberated" the Greeks from the raw, gloomy conditions of a still-older stage of culture (WPh 5[165]; KSA 8, 86).[13] The transformation of a wild, gloomy religion is indeed the great achievement. But from where, Nietzsche asks, did he get the strength for this rescue?[14] With Homer "Perfection [das Vollendete]" was there "at the beginning." It was thus not the result of development and progress. "But," Nietzsche asks, "is it really the beginning?" (GgL §5; KGW II/5, 36n. 2).[15]

From a different perspective, early antiquity seems a sort of late-ancient oriental fringe-culture [Randkultur], early Greek sculpture as a continuation of the late-Egyptian art, the Homeric epic as the late, written codification and perfection of a long oral tradition. The questions, which Nietzsche poses, should be tightened: What, really, in the cultural and religious history of Mediterranean civic culture is "the beginning"?

The fourth chapter of WPh: "Adumbrations on the Greeks"

1. Nietzsche wanted to sketch the religion of the "older antiquity," the old-Hellas, in the fourth chapter of his essay (WPh 5[111]; KSA 8, 69).[16] The sketch is part of the

"characteristics of the Greeks," thus worship, myth, and theology are put in connection with Greek culture: the history of religion is part of cultural history.[17] The sketch contains statements about religion generally, and, often only implicitly, a continuous critique of Christianity. The scope and theme of the fourth chapter can be determined by the following criteria:

a) The titles and plans that Nietzsche noted for this chapter ("4 . Adumbrations on the Greeks") in his various and divergent designs for the structure of this essay.[18]

b) The passages in manuscript A that Nietzsche designated with the numeral "4."

c) The passages that appear under numeral "4" in Gersdorff's clean copy (B): They treat the opposing-pair "the Greeks and the Philologists."

d) The following parts of A pp. 146–148, which Nietzsche did not order, can be attributed to the fourth chapter solely on the grounds of content—thus with considerable uncertainty:

> pp. 142–140: "Development" of Greek culture (WPh 5[146]; KSA 8, 77–79);
>
> p. 141: Catharsis – "a fundamental law of the Greek essence" (WPh 5[147]; KSA 8, 79);
>
> p. 136: Greek religion (WPh 5[150]; KSA 8, 80f.); behind which is inserted a plan for 18 lectures on Greek religion: p. 134 (WPh 5[152]; KSA 8, 81f.);
>
> pp. 132–130: The death of ancient culture (WPh 5[155]–5[158]; KSA 8, 83f.);
>
> pp. 110–108: Greek cultural history (WPh 5[195]–5[200]; KSA 8, 95f.).

The fourth chapter therefore has a relatively rigid theme; the classical-studies pieces in this part are relatively extensive.

2. Nietzsche's "adumbrations" claim that "genius" and "individuality" are the most important characteristics of Hellenism.[19] Greek religion, however, is just not a good indicator of these characteristics: Like art, it brings about a "temporary calming," acts as a palliative, as a "benumbing," thereby delaying work on a "genuine improvement" (5[162] and [163]; KSA 8, 85f.). Art, Nietzsche says, is "reactionary and resistant to the enlightenment"; religion should "entertain" the people and displace "adversity and boredom" (5[165]: KSA 8, 86f.). So religion offers no clear evidence for characteristics like "genius" and "individuality" and, conspicuously, neither does art. However, the example of religion allows Nietzsche to elucidate most easily the diastasis between modern philologists and the true, "older" antiquity (see above, p. 263). Despite the field's official admiration for Winckelmann, Greek art holds no use for Nietzsche's view of antiquity either in WPh or in other texts.[20]

"The gods who live at ease": "Homeric religion"

A sketch of Greek religion (A, p. 158, 16–22)

In several arrangements [Dispositionen] and short sketches Nietzsche tried to capture the theology, myth, worship, as well as the "layers" of Greek religion and their connections to the state, morality, and art.[21] One of these drafts (ms. p. 158) runs as follows:[22]

16	5[103]	Zu einem griechischen Polytheismus gehört viel Geist; es ist freilich sparsamer | mit dem Geist umgegangen, wenn man nur einen hat.|
	5[104]	Die Moral beruht nicht auf der Religion, sondern auf der πόλις.| Es gab nur Priester einzelner Götter, nicht Vertreter der ganzen Religion: also|
20		keinen Stand. Ebenfalls keine heilige Urkunde.
	5[105]	Die "leichtlebenden Götter" ist die höchste Verschönerung, die der Welt zu Theil| geworden ist; im Gefühl wie schwer es sich lebt.|

p. 158, 21–22 → N II 1 (16[8], 16[9]) p. 158, 22: cf. A, p. 239, 5

p. 158, 16–17: on the text a "4" is written
p. 158, 17: einen] einen <Gott> added KGW following GAK
p. 158, 18–20: on the text a "4" is written
p. 158, 21–22: on the text a "4" is written

The sketch begins and ends with Homeric theology, in between there are four fundamental characteristics of Greek religion: no monotheism, a morality hardly legitimized by religion, no priesthood, no inspired writing. Each of these points—polytheism, clergy, book-religion, a loose connection between religion and morality—are selected to emphasize the difference between the Hellenic and Judeo-Christian religions. Even if Judaism and Christianity are not named here, the comparative and critical tendency of the text is clear. German Romantic philologists like Friedrich Gottlieb Welcker (1784–1868), Friedrich Creuzer, and Jacob Grimm sought a Greek primordial monotheism that allegedly had existed as an original nature-religion, in the pre-Homeric period.[23] The so-called polytheism then appears as a deterioration: How far from the Greeks, Nietzsche asks, "how Christian" must one be, "to regard the Greeks, following Welcker, as the original monotheists" (WPh 5[114]; KSA 8, 70).[24] Nietzsche rightly insists, even if it is a cheap dig, on the independence of the so-called polytheism. Nietzsche underestimates the enormous intellectual strain required to think of Christology and the Trinity as a (moderate) monotheism. He did not regard the actual religious practices, in which the worship of the major gods and half-gods, local heroes, daemons, angels, souls, martyrs, prophets, saints, and good or harmful powers forms a wide continuum, which blurs the sharp boundaries of metaphysical-theological speculation.

Nietzsche considers the pre-Homeric epoch as a wild, gloomy, raw world out of which a poet "liberated" the people with his art. Homer's "gods who live at ease," he supposes, are not simply harmless illusions of a youthful little people, but the sign of a hard-won victory over inferior, but still effective "counter-currents" (WPh 5[165]; KSA 8, 86).[25] The religion of the older antiquity that Nietzsche wants to reconstruct is a Homeric "doctrine about the gods" [Götterlehre]. This includes the anthropomorphism of gods, but also their "envy": The gods make people "still more evil" and bring them down.[26] The gods are not "lords," their worshippers are not "servants [Knechte] like the Jews" (WPh 5[150]; KSA 8, 81).[27] "The god of the Greeks," Nietzsche writes, is "a beautiful dream-image" (WPh 3[53]; KSA 8, 29):[28]

that sounds anachronistic, like Epicurus' atomistic conception of the gods, and is one of the few examples of the "image-angling" language of BT to be found in WPh.[29] This probably unintentional self-reference draws attention to a negative consequence: Dionysos, the Dionysian, Satyrs, and Maenadisum are no longer permitted in this *Untimely Meditation*, barely two years after the appearance of the *Birth of Tragedy* (1872). And yet "Greek Pessimism," the anti-classical and anti-pedagogical turn against noble simplicity, the faith in truth and the false "transfiguration" of antiquity belong to the most meaningful "discoveries" of Nietzsche, the romantic enlightener. In WPh, knowledge shows itself to be less "image-angling and image-entangling [bilderwüthig und bilderwirrig]" (BT Attempt 3; KSA 1, 14), more sober, skeptical, and un-mythological.[30] The "dark sides of Greek culture" are assigned to the Pre-Homeric epoch: and thus, paradoxically, the same Homer who was once introduced as the key witness for the older, entirely different antiquity has become an enlightener and liberator.

"Homer liberated them" (A, p. 126)

Theology, as it was portrayed in the sketch cited above, is Homer's theology (Lamberton 1986). According to the ancient classification, it is "mythical theology" (Marcus Terentius Varro: *Antiquitates rerum divinarum*, frgs. 6–10)[31]—merely poetic, though of considerable influence. Nietzsche claims that Homer "liberates" the Hellenes from the darkness of the prehistoric. By his Pan-Hellenic epic he strengthened the cultural and religious cohesion of the very different Greek towns and tribes. Thus a political-military centralism is avoided in the older antiquity: "The great fact always remains the early Pan-Hellenic Homer" (WPh 5[146]; KSA 8, 78).[32]

The "pre-Homeric mind and manners [Gesinnung und Gesittung]" (WPh 5[155]; KSA 8, 83) influenced the history of Greek religion even after Homer overcame them. Mongols, Thracians, and Semites are the primordial peoples of the Greek soil (WPh 5[198]; KSA 8, 96): "everything is semitic" (KGW II/5, 380). Here, a "pre-existent Christianity" comes into being which will later destroy the Hellenic culture already weakened by "cross-currents" (Cancik and Cancik-Lindemaier 2008). Nietzsche writes (WPh 5[165]; KSA 8, 86 = A, p. 126):[33]

126, 1	Im griechischen Götterwesen und Cultus findet man alle Anzeichen eines rohen| und düstern uralten Zustandes, in dem die Griechen etwas sehr verschiedenes geworden| wären, wenn sie drin verharren mussten. <u>Homer</u> hat sie befreit, mit der eigen-| thümlichen Frivolität seiner Götter. Die Umbildung einer wilden düstern Religi-| on <u>zu einer homerischen</u> ist doch das <u>grösste Ereigniss</u>. Nun beachte man die| Gegenströmungen, das sich-offenbaren der alten Vorstellungen, das Ergreifen Ver-| wandter, Ausländischer. [De]
5	
	p. 126, 1–3: cf. to Rohde, July 16, 1872; KSB 4, 23 *p. 126, 3–5: cf. HH I, MA I 262; KSA 2, 218f.*
	p. 126 completely in Latin type and bright blue ink, here used for the last time. *p. 126, 7: De deleted without replacement by Nietzsche*

The Homeric religion and Greek religion as a whole contain "survivals [Überlebsel]" (WPh 5[155]; KSA 8, 83) of earlier stages of culture. As to content and terminology, Nietzsche here follows evolutionary theory.[34] The cult conserves the older conditions of "a pre-Homeric mentality and civilization." Typologically and historically, it is older than myth, which, like the deities themselves, is often pre- and un-Greek: "as even Aphrodite is Phoenician" (WPh 5[65]: KSA 8, 59).[35] Nietzsche insists, rightly and following the ancient tradition, on hybrid, impure beginnings. In another text for the fourth chapter, he writes: "Almost all Greek deities are accumulated, one layer over another, either grown together or roughly cemented" (WPh 5[113]; KSA 8, 70).[36]

The conglomeration of the gods corresponds to the stratifying, flooding, and sprinkling in the population of Greece. Here Nietzsche moves significantly away from the contemporary comparative linguistics and studies of religion, which sought the pure Indo-Germanic origin in pre-history.[37] Homer "liberated" the Greeks from this raw and gloomy "pre-history" (WPh 5[165]; KSA 8, 86f.):[38] He suppressed "fetishism," "fear of the dead" and "human sacrifice," and instead of these portrays serene "spectacles of worship," athletic contests, and the "frivolity" of the gods living at ease.[39] For this reason Nietzsche puts Homer at the beginning of an especially European history of freedom in his own book for Free Spirits (1878): "all the spiritual and human freedom which the Greeks achieved" proceeds from Homer and his Pan-Hellenic influence (HH I, 262; KSA 2, 218).[40] Homer was followed by Aeschylus and Aristophanes, the great artists of the renaissance, and Goethe (HH I 125; KSA 2, 121).[41] The progenitor of the older antiquity here becomes an autonomous artist who formed the gods in his own image, like the sculptor his clay and marble. Homer, Nietzsche supposes, must "have been deeply unreligious" (WPh 5[196]; KSA 8, 95).

3. "Critique of religion"

Hellenes/Jews—Christians

1. In Nietzsche's Adumbrations on Greek Religion three lines of argumentation interwine:

- the philhellenic tradition of the "gods of Greece" (Friedrich Schiller);
- the continuous, overt or tacit, "attempt at a critique of Christianity";[42]
- the general "Critique of Religion," which does not spare even the beautiful dream-figures of Hellas: "helplessness and needlessness of all Gods" (WPh 5[5]; KSA 8, 42 and 5[158]; KSA 8, 84).

Involving a "critique of Christianity" in a sketch of the older Greek religion is not anachronistic within the presuppositions of Nietzsche's construction of the older antiquity, according to which Christianity corresponds to "a pre-Greek condition of humanity: belief in magical operations in all and everything, bloody sacrifices, superstitious fear before a daemonic court, despair of themselves, ecstatic broodings and hallucinations [...]" (WPh 5[94]; KSA 8, 65):[43] The "pre-Homeric mind and manners" (WPh 5[155]; KSA 8, 83) is a continuous "counter-current" (5[165]; KSA 8, 86f.) within Greek religion as well. The older, gloomy epochs are revived in later ones: They are the soil out of which the Oriental, Phoenician, Jewish, and Christian worship could spread. The Christian and Greek religion therefore have, in Nietzsche's historical construction, partly the same basis: "A critique of the Greeks is equally a critique of Christianity, insofar as the foundation on the belief in spirits, on religious worship, on the enchantment of nature [Naturverzauberung] is the same for each" (WPh 5[156]; KSA 8, 83).[44]

In the three arrangements on worship and religion that Nietzsche already laid out in WPh 5[165] to [166] (KSA 8, 86–8), the gravitation of the Greek religion towards the Christian is significant. By the third collection of key-words, "On Religion," there remains only a critique of Christianity:

II Christian love, grounded on contempt. [...]
VII The greatest sin against human reason is historical Christianity.

The next point reveals the impulse that drives Nietzsche from a critique of Greek and Christian religion to a critique of religion as such:

VIII God entirely superfluous (WPh 5[166]: KSA 8, 88).[45]

2. Nietzsche imagined the "aboriginal people" on Greek soil as an ethnic mix [Völkergemisch]: accordingly, from the start there could have been no "pure" Greek religion. He envisions Mongols and Thracians: "The coast trimmed with a Semitic stripe" (WPh 5[198]; KSA 8, 96; cf. Cancik 1997, 55–75). A little later in his lecture on "The Religious Services of the Greeks" (1875/76), Nietzsche claims even more decisively: "The rule of the Semitic must have preceded the Hellenic" and "[...]: everything is Semitic" (KGW II/5, 377–83; citation: 377, 21f. and 380, 27f.).[46] Aphrodite is a Phoenician deity to him—the name, worship, and iconography confirm Nietzsche's assumption; even the polis, that collective of an autonomous and maximally self-sufficient community, "is a Phoenician invention" (WPh 5[65]; KSA 8, 59).[47] The accomplishments of the oriental high-culture, which hardly match the gloomy, raw, and wild aspects that Nietzsche assigned to his pre-Homeric epoch, were actually assimilated and improved by the Greeks. But the opposition to the Jews remained unbridgeable. The Greeks saw the gods "not as lords" over them, and saw "themselves not as servants, like the Jews" (WPh 5[150]; KSA 8, 81f.).[48] That much of Nietzsche's expression is right, since "Herr" (κύριος, δεσπότης—*kyrios, despotes*) and "Knecht," or "Sklave" (δοῦλος—*doulos*) is quite rare in the religious language of the Greeks.[49]

The third arrangement notes as its fourth point: "No religion of revenge and justice! the Jews the *worst* people" (WPh 5[166]; KSA 8, 88).[50] The series of these anti-Jewish statements begins in Nietzsche's early work; it combines the Phil-Hellenic with the anti-Semitic and finds its culmination in the "history of all de-naturalizing of natural values" which Nietzsche wrote in his "Curse on Christianity" (AC 24–6; KSA 6, 191–7, here 193).[51]

The Greek religion in the light of a radical enlightenment

1. The unfinished fourth *Untimely Meditation* destructs the assumptions of classical educational institutions and the unjustified self-assurance of the philologists, i.e.

the "classical philologists," as educators and scholars. The Christian-ness of our philology hinders it from understanding and communicating this "pagan" antiquity, especially its religion. Thus the *Meditation* on the educational system, the educator, and non-Christian antiquity leads to a critique of Christianity, of Greek religion, and finally of "all religion" generally (WPh 5[5]; KSA 8, 42).[52] This comprehensive, polemical, and consciously destructive tendency of the *Meditation*[53] bears consequences for the gods of Greece as well: they are superfluous, even deleterious, just like every religion. Greek religion had never been considered in this light, neither by their theological antagonists in antiquity and post-antiquity, nor by their philological admirers, who are hindered by their "mingling with Christianity" (WPh 5[39]; KSA 8, 51).[54]

2. Nietzsche's critique of religion stands in a long tradition. The hope of providence and the expectation of divine punishment in a world beyond were already contested in the ancient enlightenment.[55] The function of religion is to serve as a "benumbing," "tranquilizer," "palliative" or "narcotic."[56] It is used for "comfort" and "entertainment," for "consolation" and "stultification."[57] Religion is a useful tool for ruling: one needs it in order to tranquilize "the poor" and "the people," "the mobs and the reprobate" (cf. 5[18]; KSA 8, 44f.): "So should religion be there for the poor with its empty promises" (WPh 5[163]; KSA 8, 85f.; 5[165]; KSA 8, 86f.). But for the clever and the rich, "God" is "entirely superfluous" (WPh 5[166]; KSA 8, 88). They know that the "foundations" of all religions—even the Greek and the Christian—are based on "certain physical assumptions" (WPh 5[5]; KSA 8, 42) that have become "obsolete" (5[156]; 5[157]; 5[158]: KSA 8, 83–4.)

The praise of Homeric religion, of the liberation by the poets of Ionia, of the religion of the older antiquity, becomes crossed with the knowledge of the "death of the old culture" (WPh 5[157]; KSA 8, 83f.). Nietzsche is, like many in his time, convinced of the end of Christianity in modernity. The fall of the Greek religion, he thinks, could be considered as a pattern for that of Christianity (WPh 5[156]; KSA 8, 83 and 5[157]; KSA 8, 83f.). With the "disappearance of Christianity," however, antiquity itself grows less understandable. Since Christianity is, after all, "a piece of antiquity" (WPh 3[13]; KSA 8, 18).[58] "Antiquity will be cleared away along with Christianity" (WPh 5[148]; KSA 8, 79f.), Nietzsche claims—but is that a diagnosis or a wish? For if Greece and Christianity "disappear," then "the former foundations of our society and politics" crumble, too (WPh 5[148]; KSA 8, 79f.).

3. The reform of "Classical Education" (5[138]; KSA 8, 75), of the Gymnasium, and of Philology is nevertheless not relinquished in the unfinished fourth *Untimely*:[59] "One believes it's all over with philology—I believe it hasn't yet begun" (WPh 3[70]; KSA 8, 34). Nietzsche's "Adumbrations" on the older Greek religion serve this new beginning too. But, contrary to this reform, in the same text there stands a rabid will to progress, a radical enlightenment, and an abandoning of the "old culture," its religion, and history: "In its place must proceed the science of the *future*" (WPh 5[158]; KSA 8, 84).[60] For the Hellenic, for the religion of the older antiquity with its beautiful dream-figures, there is in this future but little room.

Translated by Anthony K. Jensen

Notes

1   [Translator's note: since there is yet no standard translation of Nietzsche's early notebooks, all translations of Nietzsche herein are my own.]

2   N I 4, p. 5 is not printed in the KGW, on the grounds that it is merely a "Gelegenheitsnotiz." These notes are meaningful, however, for a reconstruction of Nietzsche's way of working and his reading.

3   Joseph Justus Scaliger was, at least according to Nietzsche: "the most brilliant philologist of all time" (EKP § 2; KGW II/3, 355). Nietzsche refers to Jacob Bernays: Joseph Justus Scaliger, Berlin 1855; KGW has the date "1858."

4   From Christmas 1870, Nietzsche owned an edition "of the entire Montaigne (whom I regard so highly)" (to Franziska and Elisabeth Nietzsche, December 30, 1870; KSB 3, 172).

5   In a letter to Heinrich Romundt (September 9, 1875; KSB 5, 116) Nietzsche names another title: "I have begun a seven-year lecture cycle, from that I'm reading 'religious antiquities of the Greeks'. They are all new courses, which occupy me completely. Do not expect Untimely Meditations, that is my advice. But how I hate publishing!—In the meantime something is nearly ready, but not 'The Philologists'; but like I said, nothing for publication."

6   A few of the names of Nietzsche's sources must at least be mentioned: Karl Bötticher, Georg Curtius, Max Müller, Carl Otfried Müller, Heinrich Nissen, Ludwig Preller, Heinrich Roscher, Georg Friedrich Schoemann, Edward B. Tylor, Friedrich Gottlieb Welcker.

7   References are to Burckhardt 1977 (second volume, third part: "Religion and Cult II: The Greek and their Gods").

8   To Overbeck, May 30, 1875; KSB 5, 58: "The little Kelterborn sent me a handsomely bound book of 448 narrow Quarto pages. It's Burckhardt's Greek culture, and indeed has some advantages over Baumgartner's version [...]." Cf. to Gersdorff, July 21, 1875; KSB 5, 87. The references to Burckhardt's Cultural History are especially perceptible from WPh 5[60] (KSA 8, 58) up; cf. 3[12]; KSA 8, 17f.

9   On the constitution of an "archaic" epoch of Greek history, see Heuss 1946, 26–62; Ridgway 1977; Most 1989, 1–23; Faber 1990, 51–6; Cancik and Cancik-Lindemaier 1999, 54–63: "Friedrich Nietzsche: Das frühgriechische Modell."

10 See WPh 5[148]; KSA 8, 79f. Cf. further: WPh 3[4]; KSA 8, 14f.; 3[14]; KSA 8, 18. "Appraisal of the whole hellenic way of thinking" (WPh 3[15]; KSA 8, 18); WWK 6[6]; KSA 8, 98f.; 6[17]; KSA 8, 104).

11 Cf. WWK 6[13]; KSA 8, 102; 6[35]; KSA 8, 112; 6[38]; KSA 8, 112f. and WPh 5[95]; KSA 8, 60.

12 Cf. WPh 3[70]; KSA 8, 34: "The 6th–5th century are now to discover."

13 Cf. "Überlebsel" WPh 5[155]; KSA 8, 83; and WPh 5[118]; KSA 8, 71: "the Panhellenic Homer."

14 WPh 5[146] (KSA 8, 79): "Where did the Greeks have this freedom from? Apparently already from Homer; but wherefrom has he it?"

15 Here it is a matter of epic poetry and the beginning of Greek literature in general. Cf. WPh 5[1] (KSA 8, 41): "The Beginning at the beginning is always an illusion" Cf. Burkert 1985, 119–25 ("The spell of Homer").

16 WPh 3[74] (KSA 8, 35): "The contrast between the Hellenic and the Roman, and again between old-Hellenic and late-Hellenic." This point of view, i.e. the division of

the archaic from the classical and Hellenistic period of the Greek religious history, is clearly indicated by Nietzsche, but is not carried out further.

17 (WPh 5[4]; KSA 8, 41); the text is marked with the numeral "4" by Nietzsche. These and further marks are not documented in the KSA. Cf. WPh 5[41]; KSA 8, 52 = ms. p. 181, 1–5: "A Seminar about 'System of Culture'."

18 "Approximate plan" in 2[3] (= ms. p. 219); KSA 8, 11; cf. 5[59]; KSA 8, 57f., 5[36]; KSA 8, 50, and 5[70]; KSA 8, 60 offer a keyword list for the "adumbrations." The function of the "adumbrations" for the delegitimization of the philologists is formulated in the "plan" of 5[55] (= ms. p. 174); KSA 8, 55f.

19 WPh 5[136] (= ms. p. 146); KSA 8, 75; genius: 5[65]; KSA 8, 59; 5[70]; KSA 8, 60; 5[129]; KSA 8, 74; individuality: 5[70]; KSA 8, 60: "The individual raised to the highest power through the polis." On imagistic arts: 5[115]; KSA 8, 70 and 5[121]; KSA 8, 72.

20 On Winckelmann see WPh 5[46]; KSA 8, 53. Nietzsche names the Aeginetans (beginning of the fifth century BC) in 30[84]; KSA 8, 536 (summer 1878). Ancient art: cf. Cancik [1995] 2000, 3; 13f. as well as Cancik 1999, 3–33.

21 The sources from which Nietzsche drew are reported in KGW IV/4, especially the excerpts from Jacob Burckhardt; see above pp. 266–7.

22 In the left-hand column are the line numbers in Nietzsche's manuscript and the KGW-number of the passage; below the text are selected parallel texts and text-critical remarks in two (cursive) apparatus. The text says: "For a Greek polytheism much spirit is needed; it is admittedly more sparing in dealing with the spirit, if you have only one. Morality is not based on religion, but on the πόλις. There were only priests of individual gods, not representatives of the entire religion: thus no clergy class. Likewise no sacred document. The "gods who live at ease" ["leichtlebenden Götter"] is the highest beautification that has been given to the world; feeling, how hard it is to live."

23 Friedrich Gottlieb Welcker: *Griechische Götterlehre I–III*. Göttingen 1857 (1859–60; 1862–3). Nietzsche borrowed the work in April 1871 from the Basel University library; on February 18, 1875 he borrowed Welcker's *Kleine Schriften*, Vol. 4: *Zur griechischen Literatur III*. 1861. Cf. Henrichs 1986, 179–229.

24 In WPh 5[114]; KSA 8, 70. The numeral "4" is on top of the text.

25 Homer, *Iliad* VI, 138; Homer, *Odyssey* IV, 805. Cf. WPh 5[118]; KSA 8, 71; 5[150]; KSA 8, 80f.; cf. Rodenwaldt 1944; Wohlleben 1990, 5f. (On Nietzsche's concept of Homer see also Alexey Zhavaronkov's contribution to this volume.)

26 WPh 5[115]; KSA 8, 70 and 5[120]; KSA 8, 71. Cf. Homer, *Iliad* III, 365; VII, 478; Homer, *Odyssey* XX, 201; Aeschylus, *Persians* 362; Herodotus 1, 32; 7, 46.

27 Cf. pp. 266–7.

28 From chapter 4.

29 "In dreams, according to the conception of Lucretius, the glorious divine figures first appeared to the souls of men, in dreams the great shaper beheld the charming corporeal structure of superhuman beings" (BT 1; KSA 1, 26) [trans. Oskar Levy]. Cf. Reibnitz 1992, 68f. on this passage.

30 A few entries: WPh 3[4]; KSA 8, 14f.; 3[14]; KSA 8, 18; 3[17]; KSA 8, 19; 3[39]; KSA 8, 25; 3[52]; KSA 8, 28; 3[65]; KSA 8, 33; 5[12]; KSA 8, 43; 5[20] (KSA 8, 45): "To bring the unreason in human things to light." 5[146] (KSA 8, 78): "the lust for inebriation."

31 Edition of the fragments: Burkard Cardauns (ed.): *M. Terentius Varro. Antiquitates Rerum Divinarum*. Wiesbaden 1976.

32 Cf. 5[101]; KSA 8, 66; 5[118]; KSA 8, 71. The classical text for this point is Homer's "ship catalogue" in the second book of the *Iliad*.

33 "In the Greek deities and cults, one finds all the signs of a raw and gloomy age-old state, in which the Greeks would have become something very different if they had to remain. <u>Homer</u> had liberated them, with the peculiar frivolity of his gods. The transformation of a wild gloomy religion <u>to a Homeric one</u> is indeed <u>the greatest event</u>. Now watch the counter-currents, the emerging of the old imaginations, the grasping of related ones, of foreign ones [Verwandter, Ausländischer]."

34 For the concept of "survival"; see Edward Burnett Tylor: *Primitive Culture*. London 1871. Nietzsche borrowed the work in June 1873 from the Basel University library.

35 The text is overwritten with the numeral "4."

36 Cf. WPH 3[27]; KSA 8, 22.

37 WPh 5[198]; KSA 8, 96; cf. 2[5]; KSA 8, 12.

38 Bullet-point "1" of an arrangement on Greek religion in ten points.

39 WPh 5[118]; KSA 8, 71: "The Pan-Hellenic Homer has his pleasure with the levity of the gods."

40 Like the one referenced in the following, this text (HH I 125; KSA 2, 121) is developed out of WPh.

41 Cf. WPh 5[196]; KSA 8, 95. Notably, Empedocles' critique of religion is not mentioned.

42 Thus the draft of a title to the text that became the "Antichrist." This critique includes Judaism as an afterthought. Islam is mentioned only once in WPh (3[53]; KSA 8, 28f.): "The god Machoumet's"—"Vision of a dreadful fighter" in comparison to the Christian god of love and the gods of the Greek: "a beautiful dream-figure." Nietzsche's writing of the name—instead of Muhammad, Mohammed or, in European malapropism, Mahomet—is unexplained.

43 "Bloody sacrifice": Christianity denied animal sacrifice as part of its practice but retained its imagery; cf. *hostia* / host.

44 Cf. HH I 111; KSA 2, 112–16: "Origin of religious worship."

45 Cf. also WPh 5[5]; KSA 8, 42; Love: cf. U II b (summer 1876): 17[19]; KSA 8, 299.

46 Among other things, Nietzsche names here the seven planets, seven moon goddesses, and the seven gates of Thebes.

47 The text is marked with a "4"; cf. Herodot I, 105; 131. On Prometheus and Heracles, who "became pan-Hellenic," see 5[130]; KSA 8, 74.

48 The note is elaborated in HH I 114; KSA 2, 117f.: "The ungreek in Christianity." Remarkably, Nietzsche nevertheless designated his lecture as "God-service [Gottes-Dienst] of the Greeks."

49 An example: Sophocles *Oidipous Tyrannos* v. 410: Teiresias a δοῦλος (*doulos*) of Apollo.

50 Cf. also U II 5b (summer 1876), 17[20]; KSA 8, 299: "That the Jews are the worst people of the world [...]."

51 See Cancik [1995] 2000, 134–49; Cancik and Cancik-Lindemaier 1991, 21–46.

52 This passage is from A, p. 198, just after the beginning of the transcription; on the generalizing tendency cf. 5[157]; KSA 8, 83f.: "all culture."

53 WPh 5[30]; KSA 8, 48f.: "a community of men who [...] want to be called 'destroyer.'"

54 Cf. also 5[59]; KSA 8, 57: [Philologists] "intricate Christians"; 5[33]; KSA 8, 49f.: "The connection of humanism and religious rationalism [...]: the type of this philologist is G. Hermann." Cf. 5[107]; KSA 8, 67f.: "the humanistic" as instrument of the Christian mission.

55 WPh 5[20]; KSA 8, 45 and 5[24]; KSA 8, 46—ancient sources in Cancik-Lindemaier 2010, 61–83.

56 These are recurring topics: (a) WPh 5[163]; KSA 8, 85f. with "The Plough," nr. 113; KSA 8, 322; 5[165]; KSA 8, 86f. (b) 5[162]; KSA 8, 85. (c) 5[162]; KSA 8, 85. (d) 5[61]; KSA 8, 58; 5[162]; KSA 8, 85; 5[163]; KSA 8, 85f.

57 WPh 5[139]; KSA 8, 75 and 5[165]; KSA 8, 86f. 5[163]; KSA 8, 85f. and 5[188]; KSA 8, 94: "Christ stimulated stultification of men [...]."

58 Cf. WPh 5[15]; KSA 8, 43f.; 5[16]; KSA 8, 44.

59 The passage is from A, p. 222, thus at the beginning of the transcript; cf. 5[109]; KSA 8, 69.

60 Cf. 5[20]; KSA 8, 45; 5[88]; KSA 8, 64: "One should prefer scientific [concludings]."

Works cited

Burckhardt, Jakob (1977): *Griechische Culturgeschichte*. Munich (dtv).

Burkert, Walter (1985): *Greek Religion*. Cambridge, MA (Harvard University Press).

Cancik, Hubert ([1995] 2000): *Nietzsches Antike. Vorlesung*. 2nd edn. Stuttgart and Weimar (Metzler).

—(1997): "Mongols, Semites, and the Pure-Bred Greeks. Nietzsche's Handling of the Racial Doctrines of His Time." In Jacob Golomb (ed.): *Nietzsche and Jewish Culture*. London and New York (Routledge), 55–75.

—(1999a): "Otto Jahns Vorlesung 'Grundzüge der Archäologie' (Bonn, Sommer 1865) in den Mitschriften von Eduard Hiller und Friedrich Nietzsche." In Hubert Cancik and Hildegard Cancik-Lindemaier (eds): *Philolog und Kultfigur. Friedrich Nietzsche und seine Antike in Deutschland*. Stuttgart and Weimar (Metzler), 3–33.

—(1999b): "'Philologie als Beruf'. Zu Formengeschichte, Thema und Tradition der unvollenden Vierten Unzeitgemäßen Friedrich Nietzsches." In Hubert Cancik and Hildegard Cancik-Lindemaier (eds): *Philolog und Kultfigur. Friedrich Nietzsche und seine Antike in Deutschland*. Stuttgart and Weimar (Metzler), 69–84.

—(2011): "Die Pflugschar." In Christian Niemeyer (ed.): *Nietzsche Lexikon*, 2nd edn. Darmstadt (Wissenschaftliche Buchgesellschaft), 290f.

Cancik, Hubert and Hildegard Cancik-Lindemaier (1991): "Philhellénisme et antisémitisme en Allemagne. Le cas Nietzsche." In Dominique Bourel and Jacques Le Rider (eds): *De Sils-Maria à Jérusalem. Nietzsche et le judaïsme – Les intellectuels juifs et Nietzsche*. Paris (Cerf), 21–46.

—(1999): "Das Thema 'Religion und Kultur' bei Friedrich Nietzsche und Franz Overbeck." In Hubert Cancik and Hildegard Cancik-Lindemaier (eds): *Philolog und Kultfigur. Friedrich Nietzsche und seine Antike in Deutschland*. Stuttgart and Weimar (Metzler), 51–68.

—(2008): "The 'Pre-Existent-Form' (Präexistenz-Form) of Christianity. Philological Observations Concerning Nietzsche's Construction of the History of Ancient Religions." In Hubert Cancik: *Religionsgeschichten*. Hildegard Cancik-Lindemaier (ed.). Tübingen (Mohr – Siebeck), 168–90.

—(2011): "Wir Philologen (WPh)." In Christian Niemeyer (ed.): *Nietzsche Lexikon*, 2nd edn. Darmstadt (Wissenschaftliche Buchgesellschaft), 424f.

Cancik-Lindemaier, Hildegard (2010): "'Aus so großer Finsternis ein so helles Licht.' Die Religionskritik des Lukrez im Rahmen der antiken Aufklärung." In Richard Faber and Brunhilde Wehinger (eds): *Aufklärung in Geschichte und Gegenwart.* Würzburg (Königshausen und Neumann), 61–83.

Faber, Richard (1990): "Archaisch/Archaismus." In *Handbuch religionswissenschaftlicher Grundbegriffe.* Vol. 2, 51–6.

Henrichs, Albert (1986): "Welckers Götterlehre." In William M. Calder III et al. (eds): *Friedrich Gottlieb Welcker. Werk und Wirkung.* Hermes Einzelschriften 49. Stuttgart (Steiner), 179–229.

Heuss, Alfred (1946): "Die archaische Zeit Griechenlands als geschichtliche Epoche." In *Antike und Abendland.* Vol. 2, 26–62.

Lamberton, Robert (1986): *Homer the Theologian: Neoplatonist Allegorical Reading and the Growth of the Epic Tradition.* Berkeley (University of California Press).

Most, Glenn W. (1989): "Zur Archäologie der Archaik." In *Antike und Abendland.* Vol. 35, 1–23.

Reibnitz, Barbara von (1992): *Ein Kommentar zu Friedrich Nietzsche "Die Geburt der Tragödie aus dem Geiste der Musik" (Kapitel 1–12).* Stuttgart (Metzler).

Ridgway, Brunilde S. (1977): *The Archaic Style in Greek Sculpture.* Princeton (Princeton University Press).

Rodenwaldt, Gerhart (1944): *Theoi reia zōontes.* (Abhandlungen der Preußischen Akademie der Wissenschaften, Philosophisch-Historische Klasse; 1943, 13.) Berlin (Verlag der Akademie der Wissenschaften).

Wohlleben, Joachim (1990): *Die Sonne Homers. Zehn Kapitel deutscher Homer-Begeisterung von Winckelmann bis Schliemann.* Göttingen (Vandenhoeck & Ruprecht).

Index of Names

Index of Subjects

Lightning Source UK Ltd.
Milton Keynes UK
UKHW020259190419
341299UK00003B/24/P